Lives of the Signers to the Declaration of Independence

LIVES

OF

THE SIGNERS

OF THE

DECLARATION OF INDEPENDENCE.

BY REV CHARLES A GOODRICH.

HARTFORD.

R. G. H HUNTINGTON.

1841.

Southern District of New-York, ss

BE IT REMEMBERED, That on the twenty-fourth day of June, A D 1829, in the fifty third year of the Independence of the United States of America, Charles A Goodrich, of the said District, hath deposited in this office the title of a book, the right whereof he claims as author, in the words following, to wit :—" Lives of the Signers to the Declaration of Independence By the Rev Charles A Goodrich "

In conformity to the act of Congress of the United States, entitled, " an act for the encouragement of learning, by securing the copies of maps, charts, and books, to the authors and proprietors of such copies, during the time therein mentioned " And also to an act, entitled, " an act, supplementary to an act, entitled, an act for the encouragement of learning, by securing the copies of maps, charts, and books, to the authors and proprietors of such copies, during the times therein mentioned, and extending the benefits thereof to the arts of designing, engraving, and etching historical and other prints "

FRED J BETTS,
Clerk of the Southern District of New-York

PREFACE.

The author has had it in contemplation for several years, to present to the public a work of the following kind; but, until recently, he has not had leisure to complete his design. He was incited to the undertaking, by a belief that he might render an important service to his countrymen, especially to the rising generation, by giving them, in a volume of convenient size, some account of the distinguished band of patriots, who composed the congress of 1776, and to whose energy and wisdom the colonies, at that time, owed the declaration of their independent political existence.

No nation can dwell with more just satisfaction upon its annals, than the American people. The emigrants, who settled the country, were illustrious men, distinguished for their piety, wisdom, energy, and fortitude. Not less illustrious were their descendants, who served as the guides and counsellors of the colonies, or who fought their battles during the revolutionary struggle. No one who admits the intervention of a special providence in the affairs of nations, can hesitate to believe, that the statesmen and heroes of the revolution were raised up by the God of heaven, for the important and definite purpose of achieving the independence of America—of rescuing a people, whose ancestors had been eminently devoted to the duties of piety, from the thraldom under which they had groaned for years—and of presenting to the monarchical governments in the eastern hemisphere, the example of a government, founded upon principles of civil and religious liberty.

For the accomplishment of such a purpose, the statesmen and heroes of the revolution were eminently fitted. They were endowed with minds of distinguished power, and exhibited an example of political sagacity, and of high military prowess, which commanded the admiration of statesmen and heroes, throughout the world. Their patriotism was of a pure and exalted character; their zeal was commensurate with the noble objects which they had in view, and amid the toils, and privations, and sufferings, which they were called to endure, they exhibited a patience and fortitude, rarely equalled in the history of the world.

Of the revolutionary patriots, none present themselves with more interest to the rising generation, than those who composed the congress of 1776, and upon whom devolved the important political duty of severing the ties, which bound the colonies to the mother country. The lives of this illustrious band, we here present to our readers. Although the author regrets that his materials were not more abundant, he indulges the hope, that the subsequent pages will not be found devoid of interest. Even an unadorned recital of the virtues, which adorned the subjects of these memoirs; the piety of some—the patriotism and constancy and courage of them all—can scarcely fail of imparting a useful lesson to our readers. The obligations to cherish their memory, and to follow their example will be felt, nor can our readers fail to realize the debt of gratitude we owe in common, to that benignant providence, who fitted these men for the important work which was assigned them.

All the material facts, recorded in the following pages, the author has reason to believe are authentic, and entitled to credibility. Most of them are matters of public record. Some of the sketches will indeed be found to contain but few incidents; because, in respect to a portion of the signers, but few existed, and, in respect to others, the accurate knowledge of them has been irrevocably lost. The sources from which he has drawn the materials of the volume are too numerous to be particularly mentioned in this place, yet he would be doing injustice, not to express his special obligations to the authors of the following works: viz. Pitkin's Political and Civil History of the United States, North American Review, Walsh's Appeal, Marshall's Life

PREFACE.

of Washington, Botta's History of the Revolution, Allen's Biographical and Historical Dictionary, Biography of the Signers to the Declaration of Independence, Thatcher's Medical Biography, Austin's Life of Gerry, Tudor's Life of Otis, Witherspoon's Works, Select Eulogies, &c. &c.

While writing the following biographical notices of the signers to the declaration, the author has been struck with their *longevity*, as a body of men. They were fifty-six in number; and the average length of their lives was about sixty-five years. Four of the number attained to the age of ninety years, and upwards; fourteen exceeded eighty years; and twenty-three, or one in two and a half, reached three score years and ten. The longevity of the New-England delegation, was still more remarkable. Their number was fourteen, the average of whose lives was seventy-five years. Who will affirm that the unusual age to which the signers, as a body, attained, was not a reward bestowed upon them, for their fidelity to their country, and the trust which they in general reposed in the overruling providence of God. Who can doubt the kindness of that Providence to the American people, in thus prolonging the lives of these men, till the principles for which they had contended, through a long series of years, had been acknowledged, and a government had been founded upon them?

Of this venerable body, not a single one survives—They are now no more. "They are no more, as in 1776, bold and fearless advocates of independence. They are dead. But how little is there of the great and good which can die. To their country they yet live, and live for ever. They live, in all that perpetuates the remembrance of men on earth; in the recorded proofs of their own great actions, in the offspring of their intellect, in the deep engraved lines of public gratitude and in the respect and homage of mankind. They live in their example, and they live, emphatically, and will live, in the influence which their lives and efforts, their principles and opinions, now exercise, and will continue to exercise, on the affairs of men, not only in our own country, but throughout the civilized world."

"It remains to us to cherish their memory, and emulate their virtues, by perpetuating and extending the blessings which they have bequeathed. So long as we preserve our country, their fame cannot die, for it is reflected from the surface of every thing that is beautiful and valuable in our land. We cannot recur too often, nor dwell too long, upon the lives and characters of such men, for our own will take something of their form and impression from those on which they rest. If we inhale the moral atmosphere in which they moved, we must feel its purifying and invigorating influence. If we raise our thoughts to their elevation, our minds will be expanded and ennobled, in beholding the immeasurable distance beneath and around us. 'Can we breathe the pure mountain air, and not be refreshed; can we walk abroad amidst the beautiful and the grand of the works of creation, and feel no kindling of devotion?'

CONTENTS.

	Page.
Introduction,	7

MASSACHUSETTS DELEGATION.

John Hancock,	71
Samuel Adams,	81
John Adams,	92
Robert Treat Paine,	112
Elbridge Gerry,	120

NEW-HAMPSHIRE DELEGATION

Josiah Bartlett,	131
William Whipple,	139
Matthew Thornton,	143

RHODE ISLAND DELEGATION

Stephen Hopkins,	149
William Ellery,	153

CONNECTICUT DELEGATION.

Roger Sherman,	158
Samuel Huntington,	169
William Williams,	174
Oliver Wolcott,	179

NEW-YORK DELEGATION.

William Floyd,	183
Philip Livingston	186
Francis Lewis,	193
Lewis Morris,	197
Henry Misner, (See note, page 193)	

NEW-JERSEY DELEGATION

Richard Stockton,	204
John Witherspoon,	211
Francis Hopkinson,	222
John Hart,	225
Abraham Clark,	230

PENNSYLVANIA DELEGATION.

Robert Morris,	233
Benjamin Rush,	244

CONTENTS.

Benjamin Franklin,	251
John Morton,	282
George Clymer,	284
James Smith,	291
George Taylor,	296
James Wilson.	300
George Ross,	309

DELAWARE DELEGATION.

Cæsar Rodney,	313
George Read,	320
Thomas M'Kean,	323

MARYLAND DELEGATION.

Samuel Chase,	338
William Paca,	346
Thomas Stone,	351
Charles Carroll,	357

VIRGINIA DELEGATION

George Wythe,	364
Richard Henry Lee,	372
Thomas Jefferson,	380
Benjamin Harrison,	405
Thomas Nelson, jun.	410
Francis Lightfoot Lee,	416
Carter Braxton,	419

NORTH CAROLINA DELEGATION

William Hooper,	422
Joseph Hewes,	427
John Penn,	433

SOUTH CAROLINA DELEGATION

Edward Rutledge,	436
Thomas Heyward,	440
Thomas Lynch,	443
Arthur Middleton,	447

GEORGIA DELEGATION.

Button Gwinnett,	452
Lyman Hall,	455
George Walton,	458

SKETCH OF THE LIFE OF WASHINGTON   161

INTRODUCTION.

SUMMARY OF EVENTS WHICH LED TO THE DECLARATION OF INDEPENDENCE

The venerated emigrants who first planted America, and most of their distinguished successors who laid the foundation of our civil liberty, have found a resting place in the peaceful grave. But the virtues which adorned both these generations; their patience in days of suffering, the courage and patriotic zeal with which they asserted their rights; and the wisdom they displayed in laying the foundations of our government; will be held in lasting remembrance.

It has, indeed, been said, that the settlement of America, and the history of her revolution, are becoming "a trite theme." The remark is not founded in truth. Too well does the present generation appreciate the excellence of those men, who guided the destinies of our country in days of bitter trial; too well does it estimate the glorious events, which have exalted these United States to their present elevation, ever to be weary of the pages which shall record the virtues of the one, and the interesting character of the other.

The minuter portions of our history, and the humbler men who have acted a part therein, must, perhaps, pass into oblivion. But the more important transactions, and the more distinguished characters, instead of being lost to the remembrance and affections of posterity, will be the more regarded and admired the farther "we roll down the tide of time." Indeed, "an event of real magnitude in human history," as a recent literary journal has well observed, "is never seen, in all its grandeur and importance, till some time after its occurrence has elapsed. In proportion as the memory of small men, and small things, is lost, that of the truly great becomes more bright. The contemporary aspect of things is often confused and indistinct. The eye, which is placed too near the canvass, beholds, too distinctly, the separate touches of the pencil, and is perplexed with a cloud of seemingly discordant tints. It is only at a distance, that they melt into a harmonious, living picture."

Nor does it detract from the honour of the eminent personages, who were conspicuous in the transactions of our earlier history, that they foresaw not all the glorious consequences of their actions. Not one of our pilgrim fathers, it may be safely conjectured, had a distinct anticipation of the future progress of our country. Neither Smith, Newport, nor Gosnold, who led the emigrants of the south; nor Carver, Brewster, Bradford, or Standish, who conducted those of the north; looked forward to results like those which are witnessed by the present generation. But is the glory of their enterprise thereby diminished? By no means; it shines with an intenser light. They foresaw nothing with certainty, but hardships and sacrifices. These, they deliberately and manfully encountered. They went forward unassured, that even common prosperity would attend their enterprise They breasted themselves to every shock, as did the vessel which bore them, to the waves of the ocean.

Or, to take an example which has a more direct reference to the work before us, it may be fairly conjectured, that not a member of the illustrious assembly that declared the Independence of America, had any adequate conception of the great events which were disclosed in the next half century. But, will this detract from their merit in the estimation of posterity? again we say, it will enhance that merit. In the great national crisis of 1775, the minds of the leading men were wrought up to the highest pitch of fervour. They glowed with the loftiest enthusiasm. The future was, indeed, indistinct; but it was full of all that was momentous. What the particular consummation would be, they could not foresee. But conscious of their own magnanimous designs, and in a humble reliance on divine providence, they pledged to each other, their lives, their fortunes, and their sacred honour, either to die in the assertion of their unalienable rights, or to establish American liberty upon a solid foundation. The merit of these men, and of all who contributed to the happy condition of our republic, should be measured, by the grandeur of the actual consequences of their enterprise, although the precise extent of those consequences could not then have been foreseen.*

In a work, whose professed object is, to speak of men who lived and flourished in the days of our revolutionary struggle, we have little to do with the motives which induced the first settlers of our country to seek an asylum in what was then an unexplored wilderness. Nor is this the place to record the thousand sufferings which they endured, before the era of their landing; or their numberless sorrows and deprivations, while establishing themselves in the rude land of their adoption. The heroic and christian virtues of our fathers will occupy a conspicuous page in history, while the world shall stand.

Nor does it belong to our design, to enter minutely into the early history of the colonies, interesting as that history is. An outline, only, will be necessary, to understand the causes of that memorable event in the history of our country—*The Declaration of American Independence*—and to introduce to our more particular notice, the eminent men who proclaimed that independence to the world.

The year 1607 is the era of the first settlement of the English in America. During the interval between this date, and the year 1732, thirteen colonies were established; Virginia being the first, and Georgia the last. The others were Massachusetts, Connecticut, New-Hampshire, Rhode Island, New-York, New-Jersey, Pennsylvania, Delaware, Maryland, and the two Carolinas.

In the settlement of these colonies, three forms of government were established. These were severally denominated, charter, proprietary, and royal governments. This differ

* North American Review.

ence arose from the different circumstances which attended the settlement of different colonies, and the diversified views of the early emigrants The charter governments were confined to New-England. The proprietary governments were those of Maryland, Pennsylvania, the Carolinas, and the Jersies. The two former remained such, until the American revolution; the two latter became royal governments long before that period. In the charter governments, the people enjoyed the privileges and powers of self government; in the proprietary governments these privileges and powers were vested in the proprietor, but he was required to have the *advice* *assent*, and *approbation* of the greater part of the freemen, or their deputies; in the royal governments, the governor and council were appointed by the crown, and the people elected representatives to serve in the colonial legislatures.*

Under these respective forms of government, the colonists might have enjoyed peace, and a good share of liberty, had human nature been of a different character But all the colonies were soon more or less involved in troubles of various kinds, arising, in part, from the indefinite tenor of the charter and proprietary grants; but more than all, from the early jealousy which prevailed in the mother country with respect to the colonies, and the fixed determination of the crown to keep them in humble subjection to its authority.

The colonies, with the exception of Georgia, had all been established, and had attained to considerable strength, without even the slightest aid from the parent country. Whatever was expended in the acquisition of territory from the Indians, proceeded from the private resources of the European adventurers. Neither the crown, nor the parliament of England, made any compensation to the original masters of the soil; nor did they in any way contribute to those improvements which so soon bore testimony to the industry and intelligence of the planters. The settlement of the province of Massachusetts Bay alone cost 200,000*l.*;—an enormous sum at that period. Lord Baltimore expended 40,000*l.*, for

* Pitkin.

his contingent, in the establishment of his colony in Maryland. On that of Virginia, immense wealth was lavished; and we are told by Trumbull, that the first planters of Connecticut consumed great estates in purchasing lands from the Indians, and making their settlements in that province, in addition to large sums previously expended in the procuring of their patents, and of the rights of pre-emption.*

It is conceded by historians of every party, that from the earliest settlements in America, to the period of the revolution, the parent country, so far as her own unsettled state would permit, pursued towards those settlements a course of direct *oppression*. Without the enterprise to establish colonies herself, she was ready, in the very dawn of their existence, to claim them as her legitimate possessions, and to prescribe, in almost every minute particular, the policy they should pursue. Her jealousies, coeval with the foundation of the colonies, increased with every succeeding year; and led to a course of arbitrary exactions, and lordly oppressions, which resulted in the rupture of those ties that bound the colonies to the parent country.

No sooner did the colonies, emerging from the feebleness and poverty of their incipient state, begin to direct their attention to commerce and manufactures, than they were subjected by the parent country to many vexatious regulations, which seemed to indicate, that with regard to those subjects, they were expected to follow that line of policy, which she in her wisdom should mark out for them. At every indication of colonial prosperity, the complaints of the commercial and the manufacturing interests in Great Britain were loud and clamourous, and repeated demands were made upon the British government, to correct the growing evil, and to keep the colonies in due subjection. "The colonists," said the complainants, "are beginning to carry on trade:—they will soon be our formidable rivals: they are already setting up manufactures;—they will soon set up for independence.'

To the increase of this feverish excitement in the parent

* Walsh

country, the English writers of those days contributed not a little. As early as 1670, in a work, entitled, "Discourse on Trade," published by Sir Josiah Child, is the following language, which expresses the prevailing opinion of the day: "New England is the most prejudicial plantation to this kingdom"—"of all the American plantations, his majesty has none so apt for the building of shipping, as New-England, nor any comparably so qualified for the breeding of seamen, not only by reason of the natural industry of that people, but principally by reason of their cod and mackerel fisheries; and, in my poor opinion, there is nothing more prejudicial, and in prospect, more dangerous to any mother kingdom, than *the increase of shipping in her colonies, plantations, and provinces.*"

By another writer of still more influence and celebrity, Dr. Davenant, the idea of colonial *dependence*, at which Sir Josiah Child had hinted, was broadly asserted. "Colonies," he writes, "are a strength to their mother country, while they are under good *discipline;* while they are strictly made to observe the fundamental laws of the original country; and while they are kept dependant on it. But, otherwise, they are worse than members lopped from the body politic; being, indeed, like offensive arms wrested from a nation, to be turned against it, as occasion shall serve"

To the colonists, however, the subject presented itself in a very different light. They had spontaneously planted themselves on these shores, which were then desolate. They had asked no assistance from the government of Great Britain; nor had they drawn from her exchequer a single pound, during all the feebleness and imbecility of their infancy. And now, when they were beginning to emerge from a state of poverty and depression, which for years they had sustained without complaint, they very naturally supposed that they had a right to provide for their own interests.

It was not easy for them to see by what principle their removal to America should deprive them of the rights of Englishmen. It was difficult for them to comprehend the justice of restrictions so materially different from those at "home:"

or why they might not equally with their elder brethren in England, seek the best markets for their products, and, like them, manufacture such articles as were within their power, and essential to their comfort.

But the selfish politicians of England, and her still more selfish merchants and manufacturers, thought not so. A different doctrine was accordingly advanced, and a different policy pursued. Acts were, therefore, early passed, restricting the trade with the plantations, as well as with other parts of the world, to English-built ships, belonging to the subjects of England, or to her plantations. Not contented with thus confining the colonial *export* trade to the parent country, parliament, in 1663, limited the *import* trade in the same manner.

These acts, indeed, left free the trade and intercourse between the colonies. But even this privilege remained to them only a short period. In 1672, certain colonial products, transported from one colony to another, were subjected to duties. White sugars were to pay five shillings, and brown sugars one shilling and sixpence, per hundred; tobacco and indigo one penny, and cotton wool a half-penny, per pound.

The colonists deemed these acts highly injurious to their interest. They were deprived of the privilege of seeking the best market for their products, and of receiving, in exchange, the articles they wanted, without being charged the additional expense of a circuitous route through England. The acts themselves were considered by some as a violation of their charter rights; and in Massachusetts, they were, for a long time, totally disregarded.

The other colonies viewed them in the same light. Virginia presented a petition for their repeal; Rhode Island declared them unconstitutional, and contrary to their charter. The Carolinas, also, declared them not less grievous and illegal.

The disregard of these enactments on the part of the colonies—a disregard which sprung from a firm conviction of their illegal and oppressive character—occasioned loud and clamorous complaints in England. The revenue, it was urged would be injured; and the dependance of the colonies on the parent country would, in time, be totally destroyed. A stronger language was, therefore, held towards the colonies, and stronger measures adopted, to enforce the existing acts of navigation. The captains of his majesty's frigates were instructed to seize, and bring in, offenders who avoided making entries in England. The naval officers were required to give bonds for the faithful performance of their duties; the custom house officers in America were clothed with extraordinary powers; and the governors, for neglect of watchfulness on these points, were not only to be removed from office, and rendered incapable of the government of any colony, but also to forfeit one thousand pounds.

A similar sensibility prevailed, on the subject of *manufactures*. For many years after their settlement, the colonists were too much occupied in subduing their lands to engage in manufactures. When, at length, they turned their attention to them, the varieties were few, and of a coarse and imperfect texture. But even these were viewed with a jealous eye. In 1699, commenced a systematic course of restrictions on colonial manufactures, by an enactment of parliament, "that no wool, yarn, or woollen manufactures of their American plantations, should be shipped there, or even laden, in order to be transported thence to any place whatever."

Other acts followed, in subsequent years, having for their object the suppression of manufactures in America, and the continued *dependance* of the colonies on the parent country. In 1719, the house of commons declared, "that the erecting of manufactories in the colonies, tended to lessen their dependance upon Great Britain." In 1731, the board of trade reported to the house of commons, "that there are more trades carried on, and manufactures set up, in the provinces on the continent of America, to the northward of Virginia, prejudicial to the trade and manufactures of Great Britain, particularly in New-England, than in any other of the British colonies;" and hence they suggested, "whether it might not be expedient," in order to keep the colonies properly *dependant* upon the parent country, and to render her manufactures of *service to Great Britain*, "to give those colonies some encouragement."

From the London company of hatters loud complaints were made to parliament, and suitable restrictions demanded, upon the exportation of hats, which being manufactured in New-England, were exported to Spain, Portugal, and the British West India islands, to the serious injury of their trade. In consequence of these representations, the exportation of hats from the colonies to foreign countries, and from one plantation to another, was prohibited; and even restraints, to a certain extent, were imposed on their manufacture. In 1732 it was enacted, that hats should neither be shipped, nor even laden upon a horse, cart, or other carriage, with a view to transportation to any other colony, or to any place whatever. Nay, no hatter should employ more than *two* apprentices at once, nor make hats, unless he had served as an apprentice to the trade *seven* years; and, finally, that no *black* or *negro* should be allowed to work at the business at all.

The complaints and the claims of the manufacturers of *iron* were of an equally selfish character. The colonists might reduce the iron ore into pigs—they might convert it into bars—it might be furnished them duty free; but *they* must have the profit of manufacturing it, beyond this incipient stage. Similar success awaited the representations and petitions of the manufacturers of iron. In the year 1750, parliament allowed the importation of pig and bar iron from the colonies, into London, duty free, but prohibited the erection or continuance of any *mill*, or other *engine*, for *slitting* or *rolling* iron, or any *plating forge* to work with a tilt-hammer, or any furnace for making steel, in the colonies, under the penalty of two hundred pounds. Moreover, every such mill, engine, or plating forge, was declared a *common nuisance;* and the governors of the colonies, on the information of two witnesses, on oath, were directed to cause the same *to be abated* within thirty days, or, to forfeit the sum of five hundred pounds.

But if the colonist had just reason to complain on account

of the above restrictions and prohibitions,—as being extremely oppressive in themselves, and a plain violation of their rights;—some of them were equally misused with respect to their *charters*.

The charter governments, it has already been observed, were confined to the colonies of New-England. These charters had been granted by the crown in different years; and, under them, were exercised the powers of civil government.

Great difference of opinion early existed between the crown and the colonists, as to the nature, extent, and obligations of these instruments. By the *crown*, they were viewed as constituting petty corporations, similar to those established in England, which might be annulled or revoked at pleasure. To the *colonists*, on the other hand, they appeared as sacred and solemn compacts between themselves and the king, which could not be altered, either by the king or parliament, without a forfeiture on the part of the colonists. The only limitation to the legislative power conferred by these charters, was, that the laws made under their authority *should not be repugnant to those of England.*

Among the colonists, there prevailed no disposition to transcend the powers, or abuse the privileges, which had been granted them. They, indeed, regarded the charters as irrevocable, so long as they suitably acknowledged their own allegiance to the crown, and confined themselves to the rights with which they were invested. But, at length, the king seems to have repented of these extensive grants of political power; and measures were adopted again to attach the government of the charter colonies to the royal prerogative.

Accordingly, writs were issued against the several New-England colonies, at different times, requiring them to surrender these instruments into the royal hands. To this measure the strongest repugnance every where prevailed. It was like a surrender of life. It was a blow aimed at their dearest rights—an annihilation of that peace and liberty, which had been secured to them by the most solemn and inviolable compact.

INTRODUCTION. 17

With views and sentiments like these, the colonists supplicated the royal permission, " to remain as they were." They reminded his majesty of the sacred nature of their charters; they appealed to the laws which they had passed,—to the institutions they had founded,—to the regulations they had adopted,—in the spirit of which, there was not to be seen any departure from the powers with which they were invested. And they therefore humbly claimed the privilege of exercising these powers, with an assurance of their unalterable allegiance to the English crown.

In an address to his majesty, from the colony of Massachusetts, styled, " the humble supplication of the general court of the Massachusetts colony in New-England," the following language was adopted—language as honourable to the colonists, as the sentiments are tender and affecting. " Let our government live, our patent live, our magistrates live, our *laws* and *liberties* live, our *religious enjoyments* live, so shall we all yet have further cause to say from our hearts, let the *king live forever;*—and the blessings of those ready to perish shall come upon your majesty ; having delivered the poor that cried, and such as had none to help them."

The king, however, would listen to no arguments, and would admit of no appeal. A strong jealousy had taken possession of his breast, and had as firmly seated itself in the hearts of his ministry. The tree, planted by the colonists, fostered by their care, and watered by their tears, was taking too deep root, and spreading forth its branches too broadly. Its fall was determined upon, and too successfully was the axe applied.

The charters being in *effect* set aside ; those of Rhode Island and Connecticut being considered as surrendered, and that of Massachusetts having been violently wrested from her; the king, at that time James II., appointed Sir Edmund Andros governor-general of New-England. In December, 1686, he arrived in Boston, and published his commission.

The administration of Andros effected no inconsiderable change in the condition of New-England. For sixty years the people had lived happily, under constitutions and laws of their own adoption. Amidst the trials and sufferings which had fallen to their lot, while settling and subduing a wilderness, the privilege of self-government was one of their chief consolations. But now, deprived of this privilege, and subjected to the arbitrary laws, and cruel rapacity of Andros, a deep gloom spread over the whole territory of New-England.

"One of his first despotic acts," says a late interesting writer,* "was to place the press under censorship. Magistrates alone were permitted to solemnize marriages, and no marriages were allowed, until bonds, with sureties, were given to the governor, to be forfeited, if any lawful impediment should afterwards appear. No man could remove from the country without the consent of the governor.

"Fees of office, particularly in matters of probate, were exorbitant;—towns were not permitted to hold meetings but once a year, and then for the sole purpose of electing officers,—all former grants of lands were considered invalid, either because they were rendered void by the destruction of the charters under which they were made, or were destitute of the formality of a seal. The people were, therefore, obliged to take out new patents for their lands and houses, and to pay enormous patent fees, or suffer them to be granted to others, and they themselves ejected from their hard earned possessions.

"In addition to this, taxes were imposed at the will of the governor-general and a few of his council; nor had the poor New-Englanders even the privilege of complaining, and claiming the rights of Englishmen, without being liable to fine and imprisonment. These taxes the governor and council, by their act, assessed upon the several towns, and directed each town to appoint a commissioner, who, with the select men, was ordered to assess the same on the individual inhabitants. The citizens of the old town of Ipswich, at a meeting called for the purpose of carrying this act into effect, declared, that, "considering the said act doth infringe their liberty, as *free born English subjects* of his majesty, by interfering with the

* Pitkin.

statute laws of the land, by which it is enacted, that no taxes should be levied upon the subjects, without the consent of an assembly chosen by the freemen for assessing the same ; they do, therefore, vote, they are not willing to choose a commissioner for such an end, without such privilege ; and, moreover, consent not that the select men do proceed to lay any such rate, until it be appointed by a general assembly, concurring with the governor and council."

" The minister of the town, John Wise, together with John Appleton, John Andrews, Robert Kinsman, William Goodhue, and Thomas French, were active in procuring this patriotic resolution ; and for this, they were immediately brought before the governor and council at Boston ; and soon after tried before the star chamber judges, Dudley, Stoughton, Usher, and Randolph, and a packed jury. In his examination before the council, Mr. Wise, claiming the privilege of an English subject, was told by one of the judges, *he had no more privilege left him, than not to be sold for a slave.*'

" Wise was imprisoned by the governor general ; and the judges refused him the privilege of the writ of habeas corpus.

"On their trial, they defended themselves under magna charta, and the statutes, which solemnly secured to every British subject his property and estate. The judges, however, told them, ' they must not think the laws of England followed them to the ends of the earth, or wherever they went ;' and they were in a most arbitrary manner condemned.

" Mr. Wise was suspended from his ministerial functions, fined 50*l.*, and compelled to give a bond of 1000*l.* for his good behaviour, and the others were also subjected to fines, and obliged to give bonds of a similar nature."

Such is an outline of the despotic acts, during the odious administration of Andros. To these the people of New-England were obliged to submit, without the prospect of any alleviation of their condition.

Relief, however, was near at hand. At this important crisis in the affairs of the colonies, an event transpired which relieved them in a measure from the perplexities in which they were involved, and from the oppressions under which they groaned. The bigotted James II., by his acts of despotism, had become justly odious to all the subjects of his realm. So great was the excitement of public indignation, that the king was compelled to flee, in disgrace, from the kingdom; and his son-in-law, William, Prince of Orange, was invited to assume the crown.

The news of this event (1689) spread unusual joy throughout the colonies. In the height of their animation, the inhabitants of Boston seized Sir Edmund Andros, with fifty of his associates, and put them in close confinement, until he was ordered back to Great Britain. Connecticut and Rhode Island immediately resumed their charters, and re-established their former government. Massachusetts soon after obtained a new charter, which, however, failed to secure to the colony many rights, which they had enjoyed under the provisions of the former one; but which was finally accepted by a majority of the general court. Each of the colonies continued to exercise its government till the year 1775. In Rhode Island, the ancient charter is the only constitution at the present time; and in Connecticut, the charter was continued until the year 1818, when a new constitution was adopted by the people.

The grateful relief experienced by the colonies on the accession of William, was, however, of temporary continuance. Through other channels, trouble and distress were to be conveyed to them. From the above year (1689) to the peace of Paris 1763, the colonies, from New-Hampshire to Georgia, were engaged in almost unremitting hostilities with the aborigines on their borders. Their whole western frontier was a scene of havoc and desolation. During this long series of years, they were obliged to bear the "unworthy aspersion," as Dummer justly entitles it, of exciting these Indian wars; and of acquiring the dominion of the Indian territory by fraud, as well as by force.

To these trials were added others, which proceeded from the parent country. Disputes were frequently arising, as heretofore, between the crown and the colonies, respecting the powers conferred by the charters. Claims were set up, by the king and council, to the right of receiving and hearing appeals from the colonial courts, in private suits; and, at length, a serious and protracted controversy arose in those colonies, whose governors were appointed by royal authority, from a requisition of the king that a *fixed* and *permanent* salary should be provided for the representatives of the crown. This was a favourite project of the king, as it carried the show of authority on the part of the royal government, and of dependence on the part of the colonies; and it was an object of no less importance to the governors themselves, the most of whom were sent to America to repair fortunes which had been ruined by extravagance at home.

The disputes on this subject, in the province of Massachusetts, lasted thirty years. The assembly of that colony were ready to make grants for the support of their governors, from year to year, as they had been accustomed to do, under their charter government; but no menaces could induce them to establish a *permanent* salary. At length, satisfied that the house would never yield, the crown allowed their governors to ratify *temporary* grants.

Another grievance which the colonies suffered during this period, and of which they had reason loudly to complain, was the conduct of the parent country, in transporting to America those persons, who for their *crimes* had forfeited their liberty and lives in Great Britain. Various acts of parliament authorized this measure; and hence the country was becoming the asylum of the worst of felons. The conduct of the parent country, in thus sending the pestilential inmates of her prisons to the colonies, met with their strong and universal abhorrence; nor was this abhorrence lessened by the *reasons* assigned, beyond the waters, for the practice, *viz.* " that in many of his majesty's colonies and plantations, there was a great want of *servants*, who, by their labour and industry, might be the means of *improving*, and making the said colonies *more useful to his majesty !*"

"Very surprising," remarks an independent, and even eloquent writer of those times, "very surprising that thieves, burglars, pick-pockets, and cut-purses, and a horde of the most flagitious banditti upon earth, should be sent as *agreeable companions* to us! That the supreme legislature did intend a transportation to America as a punishment, I verily believe; but so great is the mistake, that confident I am, they are thereby on the contrary highly rewarded. For what can be more agreeable to a penurious wretch, driven through necessity to seek a livelihood by the breaking of houses and robbing upon the king's highway, than to be saved from the halter, redeemed from the stench of a gaol, and transported, without expense to himself, into a country, where, being unknown, no man can reproach him for his crimes; where labour is high, a little of which will maintain him; and where all his expenses will be moderate and low. There is scarce a thief in England that would not rather be transported than hanged."

"But the acts," continues the same writer, "are intended for the *better peopling* of the colonies. And will thieves and murderers conduce to that end? what advantage can we reap from a colony of unrestrainable renegadoes? will they exalt the glory of the crown? or rather will not the dignity of the most illustrious monarch in the world be sullied by a province of subjects so lawless, detestable, and ignorant? can agriculture be promoted, when the wild boar of the forest breaks down our hedges, and pulls up our vines? will trade flourish, or manufactures be encouraged, where property is made the spoil of such, who are too idle to work, and wicked enough to murder and steal?—How injurious does it seem to free one part of the dominions from the plagues of mankind, and cast them upon another! We want people, 'tis true; but not villains, ready at any time, encouraged by impunity, and habituated, upon the slightest occasion, to cut a man's throat for a small part of his property."

To this catalogue of grievances, not imaginary, but real; not transient, but long continued; not local, but mostly universal;—many others might be added, did our limits permit.

But under all these oppressions, amidst obstinate and various efforts of the crown, to extend the royal prerogative, and to keep the colonies in humble dependence, they retained, in general, a warm affection for the parent country. They regarded the sovereign as a father, and themselves as children. They acknowledged their obligations of obedience to him, in all things which were lawful, and consistent with their natural and unalienable rights; and they appealed to him in various disputes, which arose about colonial rights, limits, and jurisdiction.

It was a characteristic trait in the colonists to provide for their own defence. They had been taught to do this by the *neglect* of the parent country, from the very days of their infancy—even before the problem was solved, whether the country should longer continue the domain of pagan darkness, or the empire of cultivated mind. They might, indeed justly have claimed the assistance and protection of the land of their birth, but seldom did they urge their rights. On the contrary, their treasuries were often emptied, and the blood of their yeomanry shed, in furnishing assistance to the parent country. In her contests, and her wars, they engaged with all the enthusiasm of her native sons; and persevered with all the bravery of soldiers trained to the art of war.

The testimony to be adduced in support of these statements, is more ample than we have space to devote to it. "Whenever," said a conspicuous member of parliament, some years after the peace of 1763, "whenever Great Britain has declared war, the colonies have taken their part: They were engaged in King William's wars, and Queen Anne's wars, even in their infancy. They conquered Arcadia, in the last century, for us; and we then gave it up. Again, in Queen Anne's war, they conquered Nova Scotia, which from that time has belonged to Great Britain. They have been engaged in more than one expedition to Canada, ever foremost to partake of honour and danger with the mother country.

"Well, sir, what have we done for them? Have we conquered the country for them, from the Indians? Have we cleared it? Have we drained it? Have we made it habitable? What have we done for them? I believe precisely nothing at all, but just keeping *watch and ward over their trade, that they should receive nothing but from ourselves, at our own price.*

"I will not positively say, that we have spent nothing; though I don't recollect any such article upon our journals; I mean any national expense in setting them out as colonists. The royal military government of Nova Scotia cost, indeed, not a little sum; above 500,000*l.* for its plantations and its first years. Had your other colonies cost any thing similar, either in their outset or support, there would be something to say on that side, but instead of that, they have been left to themselves, for one hundred, or one hundred and fifty years, upon the fortune and capital of private adventurers, to encounter every difficulty and danger. What towns have we built for them? What forests have we cleared? What country have we conquered for them from the Indians? Name the officers—name the troops—the expeditions—their dates.—Where are they to be found? Not on the journals of this kingdom. They are no where to be found.

"In all the wars, which have been common to us and them, they have taken their full share. But in all their own dangers, in the difficulties belonging separately to their situation, in all the Indian wars, which did not immediately concern us, we left them to themselves, to struggle their way through. For the whim of a minister, you can bestow half a million to build a town, and to plant a royal colony of Nova Scotia; a greater sum than you have bestowed upon every other colony together.

"And, notwithstanding all these, which are the real facts, now that they have struggled through their difficulties, and begin to hold up their heads, and to shew an empire, which promises to be foremost in the world, we claim them, and theirs, as implicitly belonging to us, without any consideration of their own rights. We charge them with *ingratitude*, without the least regard to truth, just as if this kingdom had for a century and a half attended to no other subject; as if all our revenue, all our power, all our thought, had been bestowed upon them, and all our national debt had been con-

INTRODUCTION.

transacted in the Indian wars of America; totally forgetting the *subordination* in commerce and manufactures in which we have *bound* them, and for which, at least, we owe them help towards their protection.

"Look at the preamble of the act of navigation, and every other American act, and see if the *interest of this country is not the avowed object.* If they make a hat, or a piece of steel, an act of parliament calls it a *nuisance;* a tilting hammer, a steel furnace, must be *abated* in America, as a nuisance. Sir, I speak from facts. I call your books of statutes and journals to witness."

Of an equally high and honourable character, is the testimony of Pounal, one of the royal governors in America. "I profess," said he, in 1765, "an affection for the colonies, because, having lived amongst those people in a private as well as in a public character, I know them; I know that in their private, social relations, there is not a more friendly, and in their political ones, a *more zealously loyal* people, in all his majesty's dominions. When fairly and openly dealt with, there is not a people who have a truer sense of the necessary powers of government. They would sacrifice their dearest interests for the honour and prosperity of their mother country. I have a right to say this, because experience has given me a practical knowledge, and this impression of them.

"The duty of a colony is affection for the mother country. Here I may affirm, that in whatever form and temper this affection can lie in the human breast, in that form, by the deepest and most permanent affection, it ever did lie in the breast of the American people. They have no other idea of this country, than as their home; they have no other word by which to express it; and till of late, it has constantly been expressed by the name of home. That powerful affection, the love of our native country, which operates in every breast, operates in this people towards England, which they consider as their native country; nor is this a mere passive impression, a mere opinion in speculation—it has been wrought up in them to a vigilant and active zeal for the service of this country."

This affection for the parent country, and devotedness to her interests; this promptness to assist her, though unassisted by her themselves; this liberality in emptying their treasuries, and shedding their blood, were felt and cherished by the colonies, before, and for years after, the peace of 1763. They continued to be thus cherished, and thus manifested, until exactions and oppressions "left not a hook to hang a *doubt* on," that they must either passively submit to the arbitrary impositions of a jealous and rapacious parent, or rise in defence of those rights, which had been given to them by the God of nature, in common with his other children.

The peace of 1763, while it secured to Great Britain all the country east of the Mississippi, and annihilated the French power in America, restored peace to the colonies, and put an end to the calamities of a French and Indian war, by which they had been harrassed for nearly a century. The joy consequent upon an event so auspicious, was universal and sincere. But that joy was soon to be diminished by the agitation of the question, in England, as to the taxation of the colonies.

The project of laying internal taxes upon the American provinces, and drawing a *revenue* from them, had been suggested to the ministry, during the administrations of Sir Robert Walpole and Mr. Pitt. But to these wise and sagacious statesmen it appeared to be a measure of doubtful right, and of still more doubtful policy. " I will leave the *taxation* of the Americans," said Walpole, " for some of my successors, who may have more courage than I have, and are less friendly to commerce than I am."

After the termination of the French war, the consideration of the subject was renewed, and that moment seized as a favourable one, to commence the operation of the system. During the war, a heavy debt had been incurred by Great Britain, for the benefit and protection, as it was said, of the American colonies. It was, therefore, no more than an act of justice, that they should assist in the payment of that debt.

In the winter of 1764, Lord Grenville, who had recently been elevated to the premiership, announced to the agents of the colonies, then in England, his intention of drawing a revenue from them, and that, for this purpose, he should propose, in the ensuing session of parliament, a duty on *stamps*.

This intention of the minister being communicated to the colonies, the whole country immediately caught the alarm. Not only among private citizens, but also among public and corporate bodies, the same feeling of indignation prevailed; the same opinion of the injustice and unconstitutional character of the proposed measure was expressed, and the same disposition to resist it exhibited.

The house of representatives, in Massachusetts, in the following June, declared, " That the sole right of giving and granting the money of the people of that province, was vested in *them*, or their *representatives ;* and that the imposition of duties and taxes by the parliament of Great Britain, upon a people *not represented* in the house of commons, is absolutely irreconcilable with their *rights*. That no man can justly take the property of another, without his consent; upon which original principles, the power of making laws for levying taxes, one of the main pillars of the British constitution, is evidently founded."

Petitions, from several of the colonies, were immediately prepared, and forwarded to their agents in England, to be presented at the approaching meeting of parliament, when the contemplated measure was to be brought forward. The language of these petitions, though respectful, was in accordance with the spirit which pervaded the country. They acknowledged the right of parliament to regulate *trade*, but would not for a moment admit the existence of a right in the mother country, to impose duties for the purpose of a *revenue*. They did not claim this exemption as a *privilege ;* they founded it on a basis more honourable and solid; it was challenged as their indefeasible *right*

The above petitions reached England in season, and were offered to the acceptance and consideration of parliament: But no intreaties of the agents, could induce that body even to receive them; on the twofold ground, that the petitioners questioned the *right* of parliament to pass the contemplated bill ; and, moreover, it was an ancient standing rule of the house, "*that no petition should be received against a money bill.*" In the house of commons, the bill passed, by the large majority of 250 to 50. In the house of lords, the vote was nearly unanimous; and on the 22d of March, (1765,) it received the royal sanction.

By the act thus passed, duties were imposed not only on most of the written instruments used in judicial and commercial proceedings; but also upon those which were necessary in the ordinary transactions of the colonies. Deeds, indentures, pamphlets, newspapers, advertisements, almanacs, and even degrees conferred by seminaries of learning, were among the enumerated articles on which a tax was laid.

The discussions on the above bill, before its final passage, were unusually animated. The principle involved in it was felt to be important, both by its friends and opposers; and the measure was seen to be pregnant with consequences of the most serious nature. "It may be doubted," says an historian,[*] "whether, upon any other occasion, either in times past or present, there has been displayed more vigour or acuteness of intellect, more love of country, or of party spirit, or greater splendour of eloquence, than in these debates. Nor was the shock of opinion less violent without the walls of Westminster. All Europe, it may be said, and especially the commercial countries, were attentive to the decision of this important question."

The principal supporters of the bill were Lord Grenville and Charles Townshend. Unfortunately for the colonies, Mr. Pitt, their constant friend, was absent; being confined to his bed by sickness. The principal opposers, were Gen. Conway, Alderman Beckford, Col. Barre, Mr. Jackson, and Sir William Meredith. The two first of these opposed the measure on the ground that parliament had no *right* to tax the colonies; the others contended that it was not *expedient*.

In the conclusion of one of his speeches on the bill, Mr. Townshend exclaimed: "And now, will these Americans, *planted* by our care, *nourished* up by our indulgence, until they

---

[*] Botta.

are grown to a degree of strength and importance, and *protected by our arms*, will they grudge to contribute their mite to relieve us from the heavy burden we lie under?"

The honourable member had no sooner taken his seat, than Col. Barre rose, and replied: "They *planted* by your care. No, your *oppression* planted them in America. They fled from your tyranny, to a then uncultivated and inhospitable country, where they were exposed to almost all the hardships, to which human nature is liable, and among others, to the cruelties of a savage foe; the most subtle, and I will take upon me to say, the most formidable, of any people upon the face of God's earth; and yet actuated by principles of true English liberty, they met all hardships with pleasure, compared with those they suffered in their own country, from the hands of those who should have been their friends.

"They *nourished* by your indulgence! They grew by your *neglect* of them. As soon as you began to take care of them, that care was exercised in sending persons to rule them in one department and another, who were deputies of deputies to some members of this house, sent to prey upon them; men, whose behaviour, on many occasions, has caused the blood of those sons of liberty to recoil within them; men promoted to the highest seats of justice, some, to my knowledge, were glad by going to a foreign country, to escape being brought to a bar of justice in their own.

"They *protected* by your arms! They have nobly taken up arms in *your defence*; have exerted their valour, amidst their constant and laborious industry, for the defence of a country whose frontier was drenched in blood, while its interior parts yielded all its little savings to your emolument.

"And believe me, that same spirit of freedom which actuated that people at first, will accompany them still. But prudence forbids me to explain myself further.

"God knows, I do not, at this time, speak from party heat. However superior to me, in general knowledge and experience, the respectable body of this house may be, yet I claim to know more of America than most of you, having seen and been conversant in that country. The people, I believe, are as truly loyal as any subjects the king has; but a people jealous of their liberties, and who will vindicate them, if ever they should be violated—but the subject is too delicate—I will say no more."

For this unpremeditated appeal, pronounced with an energy and an eloquence fitted to the high occasion, the house was not prepared. For some minutes, the members remained motionless, as if petrified by surprise. But the opposition at length rallied. Their pride could not allow of retreat. The measure was again urged, the question was taken, and the bill adopted.

No act of the British government could have been more impolitic; and none ever excited, in the colonies, a more universal alarm. It gave birth to feelings, which could never be suppressed, and aroused those intestine commotions in America, which, after kindling a civil war, and involving all Europe in its calamities, terminated in the total disjunction from the British empire, of one of its fairest portions.

After the arrival of the news that the stamp act had been adopted in parliament, the first public body that met was the assembly of Virginia. Towards the close of the session, about the last of May, the following resolutions were introduced into the house of burgesses, by Patrick Henry; a lawyer, at that time a young man, but highly distinguished for the strength of his intellect, and the power of his eloquence.

"Resolved, that the first adventurers and settlers of this his majesty's colony and dominions of Virginia, brought with them, and transmitted to their posterity, and all others his majesty's subjects, since inhabiting in this his majesty's colony, all the privileges and immunities that have at any time been held, enjoyed, and possessed, by the people of Great Britain.

"Resolved, that by the two royal charters granted by King James I. the colonists aforesaid are declared entitled to all privileges of faithful, liege, and natural born subjects, to all intents and purposes, as if they had been abiding and born within the realms of England.

INTRODUCTION. 31

"Resolved, that his majesty's most liege people of this his most ancient colony, have enjoyed the right of being thus governed by their own authority, in the article of taxes and internal police, and that the same have never been forfeited, nor any other way yielded up, but have been constantly recognised by the king and people of Great Britain.

"Resolved, therefore, that the general assembly of this colony, together with his majesty, or his substitute, have, in their representative capacity, the only exclusive right and power to lay taxes and impositions upon the inhabitants of the colony; and that any attempt to vest such a power in any person or persons whatever, other than the general assembly aforesaid, is *illegal, unconstitutional*, and *unjust;* and has a manifest tendency to destroy British as well as American freedom."

The debate on these resolutions was animated, and even violent. Nothing like them had ever transpired in America. They evinced a settled purpose of resistance, and conveyed to the ministry of Great Britain a lesson, which had they read with unprejudiced minds, might have saved them the fruitless struggle of a seven years war. There were those, in the house of burgesses, who strongly opposed the resolutions; but the bold and powerful eloquence of Henry bore them down, and carried the resolutions through. In the heat of debate, he boldly *asserted*, that the king had acted the part of a *tyrant;* and alluding to the fate of other tyrants, he exclaimed, "Cæsar had his *Brutus*, Charles I. his *Cromwell*, and George III."—here pausing a moment, till the cry of "*treason, treason*," resounding from several parts of the house, had ended—he added—"may profit by their example; if this be treason, make the most of it."

The above resolutions had no sooner passed, than they found their way into the papers of the day, and were circulated widely and rapidly through the colonies. They were received with enthusiasm; and served to raise still higher the indignant feelings which pervaded the country.

Before these resolutions had reached Massachusetts, the house of representatives of that colony had declared the expediency of a congress, composed of commissioners from the several colonies, "to consult together on the present circumstances of the colonies;—the acts of parliament laying duties and taxes upon them; and to consider of a general and humble address to his majesty and the parliament for relief."

The measure thus proposed by Massachusetts, on being communicated to the several colonies, was received with cordial approbation by most of them; and on the 7th of October, 1765, commissioners from the colonies of Massachusetts, Rhode Island, Connecticut, New-York, New-Jersey, Pennsylvania, Delaware, Maryland, and South Carolina, met at New-York, on the important and responsible business assigned them.

This congress, the first that was ever held in America, published, as the result of their deliberation, a declaration of the rights and grievances of the colonists; and agreed upon a memorial to the house of lords, and a petition to the king and commons.

In their declaration, they acknowledged their allegiance to his majesty, and their willingness to render due honour to the rightful authority of parliament, but they claimed that *they* had *interests*, *rights*, and *liberties*, as the natural born subjects of his majesty, and that, as they could not be represented in parliament, that body had no right to impose taxes upon them without their consent. They declared the stamp act, and other acts of parliament, " to have a manifest tendency to subvert the rights and liberties of the colonists."

The address and petition, agreed to by this congress, were at this time signed by the commissioners from six colonies only. But their proceedings were warmly approved in every quarter of the country; and at a subsequent date, received the sanction of the assemblies, not only of South Carolina, Connecticut, and New-York, but of those colonies which had not been represented in the congress.

While the highest assemblies were thus bearing their official and solemn testimony against the oppressive and unconstitutional acts of the British parliament; the people, in every sec tion of the country, and especially in the principal towns, were manifesting their abhorrence of those measures, in a different, but not less decisive way.

On the morning of the 14th of August, two effigies were discovered hanging on the branch of an old elm, near the south entrance of Boston. One of these represented a *stamp office;* the other, a *jack boot*, out of which rose a horned head, which appeared to be looking round.

The singularity of this spectacle soon attracted the notice of great numbers; and before evening, the collection amounted to a multitude. The images were then taken down, placed upon a bier, and carried in procession with imposing solemnity. At a distance, in the rear, the multitude followed, shouting— "liberty and prosperity forever—no stamps!" Arriving in front of a house, owned by one Oliver, which was supposed to be a stamp office, they levelled it to the ground; and proceeding to his place of residence, they beheaded his effigy, and broke in the windows of his house. Oliver himself effected a timely escape; but his fences, the furniture of his house, and its dependencies, were destroyed. It was midnight before the multitude dispersed.

In the morning of the next day, the people re-assembled, and were proceeding to a repetition of their excesses; but upon hearing that Oliver had sent his resignation to England, they desisted, and repairing to the front of his house, they gave three cheers, and quietly returned to their homes.

A volume would scarcely suffice, to give a full recital of all the commotions which were excited by the stamp act, in the single province of Massachusetts. But these disorders were far from being confined to such circumscribed limits. A spirit of resistance pervaded the country. The very atmosphere seemed pregnant with revolt. Even sobriety was found off her guard, in the tumultuous crowd, and old age felt something of the impulses of younger days.

On the first day of November, the stamp act was to go into operation. As it drew near, the feelings of the colonists became more and more intense; less popular noise and clamour were, perhaps, to be heard; but a deep and settled hos tility to the act had taken possession of every breast. On the 5th of October, the ships which brought the stamps appeared in sight of Philadelphia, near Gloucester Point: The vessels in the harbour immediately hoisted their colours half mast high; the bells on the churches were muffled; and during the rest of the day were tolled, in token of a profound and general mourning.

On the 10th of September, the stamps, designed for Boston, arrived at that place. By order of the governor, they were conveyed to the castle, where they could be defended by the artillery, should occasion require. At length, the 1st of November arrived. The day in many places was ushered in with marks of funeral ceremony. Business was suspended, and shops and stores were closed. But at this time, not a single sheet of all the bales of stamps, which had been sent from England, could have been found in the colonies of New-England, of New-York, New-Jersey, Pennsylvania, Maryland, and the two Carolinas. They had either been committed to the flames, had been reshipped to England, or were safely guarded by the opposition, into whose hands they had fallen. A general suspension, or rather a total cessation, of all business, which required stamped paper, was the consequence. The printers of newspapers only, observes an historian, continued their occupation, alleging for excuse, that if *they* had done otherwise, the people would have given them such an admonition, as they little coveted. None would receive the gazettes coming from Canada, as they were printed on stamped paper. The courts of justice were shut; even marriages were no longer celebrated; and, in a word, an absolute stagnation in all the relations of social life was established.[*]

The mother country could not long remain in ignorance of the spirit which prevailed, and the disturbances which had been excited in the colonies, by the oppressive acts of parliament; and the stamp act in particular. The minds of all classes in that country were deeply affected; but as different interests swayed, different opinions were entertained and expressed.

The merchants, anticipating a loss on the credit given to the

---

[*] Botta.

Americans, were disposed to censure the extraordinary course of parliament. The manufacturers were not less loud in their complaint, since, as the orders for their wares were discontinued, ruin stared them in the face. A deep despondency pervaded the minds of some ; a lofty indignation took possession of others. By one class, the colonies were extravagantly extolled : by another, they were as pointedly condemned. By some, they were praised for their manly independence and bold decision ; by others, they were accused of ingratitude, turbulence, and rebellion.

Fortunately for the interests both of the colonies and of Great Britain, about this time, a change took place in the administration of England, by which several of the friends of America came into power. The Marquis of Rockingham, one of the wealthiest noblemen of the kingdom, and highly esteemed for the endowments of his mind, and the sincerity of his character, was appointed first lord of the treasury, in the room of Lord Grenville; Mr. Dowdeswell was made Chancellor of the Exchequer ; Lord Winchester took the place of the Duke of Bedford, as president of the council ; and the Seals were given to the young Duke of Grafton and General Conway, who so nobly defended the cause of the Americans, on the motion in parliament to tax them.

During the session of the parliament of 1766, the subject of the late disturbances in the colonies was brought forward, by the new administration, and the expediency of repealing the odious enactments was strongly urged. Petitions, from various quarters, were presented, to the same effect. Many of the merchants and manufacturers of the kingdom were deeply affected by the new regulations concerning America. An immense quantity of British manufactures were perishing in the warehouses ; while artisans and seamen were deprived of employment and support.

To the repeal of the stamp act, its original advocates were strongly opposed, and they marshalled all their strength to prevent it. In the first rank stood George Grenville, the late prime minister. In the debate on the subject of repeal, among other things, he said, "much against their will, the ministers have laid before this house, the disturbances and audacious enormities of the Americans; for they began in July, and now we are in the middle of January; lately they were only *occurrences;* they are now grown to disturbances, tumults, and riots. I doubt they border on open rebellion; and if the doctrine I have heard this day, be confirmed, I fear they will lose that name, to take that of revolution."—"When I proposed to tax America, I asked the house, if any gentleman would object to the right? I repeatedly asked it; and no man would attempt to deny it. And tell me, when the Americans were *emancipated?* When they want the protection of this kingdom, they are always very ready to ask it. This protection has always been granted them, in the fullest manner; and now they refuse to contribute their mite towards the public expenses. For let not gentlemen deceive themselves, with regard to the rigour of the tax; it would not suffice even for the necessary expenses of the troops stationed in America: but a *pepper-corn in acknowledgment of the right is of more value than millions without.* Yet, notwithstanding the slightness of the tax, and the urgency of our situation, the Americans grow sullen, and instead of concurring in assisting to meet expenses arising from themselves, they renounce your authority, insult your officers, and break out, I might almost say, into open rebellion.

"There was a time when they would not have proceeded thus; but they are now supported by the artifice of these young gentlemen; inflammatory petitions are handed about against us, and in their favour. Even within this house, in this sanctuary of the laws, sedition has found its defenders. Resistance to the laws is applauded; obstinacy encouraged; disobedience extolled; rebellion pronounced a virtue."

In reply to Grenville, William Pitt, now venerable for his age, and still more venerable for the important services which he had rendered his country, rose and said: "I know not whether I ought most to rejoice, that the infirmities which have been wasting, for so long a time, a body, already bowed by the weight of years, of late suspending their ordinary violence, should have allowed me, this day, to behold these walls, and to discuss, in the presence of this august assembly, a subject of such high importance, and which so nearly concerns the safety of our country; or to grieve at the rigour of destiny, in contemplating this country, which, within a few years had arrived at such a pinnacle of splendour and majesty, and become formidable to the universe from the immensity of its power, now wasted by an intestine evil, a prey to civil discords, and madly hastening to the brink of the abyss, into which the united force of the most powerful nations of Europe struggled in vain to plunge it. Would to heaven, that my health had permitted my attendance here, when it was first proposed to tax America! If my feeble voice should not have been able to avert the torrent of calamities, which has fallen upon us, and the tempest which threatens us, at least my testimony would have attested, that I had no part in them.

"It is now an act that has passed; I would speak with decency of every act of this house, but I must beg the indulgence of the house to speak of it with freedom. There is an idea in some, that the Americans are virtually represented in this house; but I would fain know by what province, county, city, or borough, they are represented here? No doubt by some province, county, city, or borough, never seen or known by them, or their ancestors, and which they never will see or know.

"The commons of America, represented in their several assemblies, have ever been in possession of the exercise of this, their constitutional right, of giving and granting their own money. They would have been slaves if they had not enjoyed it.

"I come not here, armed at all points with law cases, and acts of parliament, with the statute book doubled down in dog's ears, as my valiant adversary has done. But I know, at least, if we are to take example from ancient facts, that, even under the most arbitrary reigns, parliaments were ashamed of taxing a people without their consent, and allowed them representatives; and in our own times, even those who send no members to parliament, are all at least inhabitants of Great Britain Many have it in their option to be actually represented. They have connexions with those that elect, and they have influence over them. Would to heaven that all were better represented than they are! It is the vice of our constitution; perhaps the day will arrive, and I rejoice in the hope, when the mode of representation, this essential part of our organization, and principal safeguard of our liberty, will be carried to that perfection which every good Englishman must desire.

"I hear it said that America is obstinate, America is almost in open rebellion. I rejoice that America has resisted. Three millions of people, so dead to all the feelings of liberty as voluntarily to submit to be slaves, would have been fit instruments to make slaves of ourselves. The honourable member has said also, for he is fluent in words of bitterness, that America is ungrateful: he boasts of his bounties towards her; but are not these bounties intended, finally, for the benefit of this kingdom? And how is it true, that America is ungrateful? Does she not voluntarily hold a good correspondence with us? The profits to Great Britain, from her commerce with the colonies, are two millions a year. This is the fund that carried you triumphantly through the last war. The estates that were rented at two thousand pounds a year, seventy years ago, are at three thousand at present. You owe this to America. This is the price she pays for your protection. I omit the increase of population in the colonies; the migration of new inhabitants from every part of Europe; and the ulterior progress of American commerce, should it be regulated by judicious laws. And shall we hear a miserable financier come with a boast that he can fetch a pepper-corn into the exchequer to the loss of millions to the nation? The gentleman complains that he has been misrepresented in the public prints. I can only say, it is a misfortune common to all that fill high stations, and take a leading part in public affairs. He says, also, that when he first asserted the right of parliament to tax America, he was not contradicted. I know not how it is, but there is a modesty in this house, which does not choose to contradict a minister. If gentlemen do not get the better of this modesty, perhaps the collective body may begin to abate of its respect for the representative. A great deal has been said without doors, and more than is discreet, of the power, of the strength of America. But, in a good cause, or a sound bottom, the force of this country can crush America to atoms; but on the ground of this tax, when it is wished to prosecute an evident injustice, I am one who will lift my hands and my voice against it.

"In such a cause, your success would be deplorable, and victory hazardous. America, if she fell, would fall like the strong man. She would embrace the pillars of the state, and pull down the constitution along with her. Is this your boasted peace?—not to sheath the sword in its scabbard, but to sheath it in the bowels of your countrymen? Will you quarrel with yourselves, now the whole house of Bourbon is against you? While France disturbs your fisheries in Newfoundland, embarrasses your slave trade with Africa, and withholds from your subjects in Canada their property, stipulated by treaty? While the ransom for the Manillas is denied by Spain, and its gallant conqueror traduced into a mean plunderer? The Americans have not acted in all things with prudence and temper. They have been wronged. They have been driven to madness by injustice. Will you punish them for the madness you have occasioned? Rather let prudence and benignity come first from the strongest side. Excuse their errors; learn to honour their virtues. Upon the whole, I will beg leave to tell the house what is really my opinion. I consider it most consistent with our dignity, most useful to our liberty, and in every respect the safest for this kingdom, that the stamp act be repealed, absolutely, totally, and immediately At the same time, let the sovereign authority of this country over the colonies be asserted in as strong terms as can be devised, and be made to extend to every point of legislation whatsoever, that we may bind their trade, confine their manufactures, and exercise every power whatsoever, except that of taking their money out of their pockets without their consent."

The impression made by this speech of Mr. Pitt, pronounced, as it was, with a firm and solemn tone, was deep and effectual. Much resentment was, indeed, manifested by all on account of the excesses committed by the Americans; but conviction had settled on the minds of a majority of parliament, that at least a partial retrocession on their part was necessary. Accordingly, on the putting of the question, February 22d, the repeal of the stamp act was carried in the house by a majority of 265 to 167. The vote in the house of peers was 155 to 61. On the 19th of March, the act of repeal received the royal assent.

Thus was put at rest, for a time, a question which had deeply agitated not only the colonies of America, but England itself; and had excited much attention throughout continental Europe. But it is more than probable, that even at this time the repealing act would not have passed, had it not been accompanied by a *declaratory act*, that the parliament had the *right* to make laws and statutes to bind the colonies in all cases whatsoever.

The joy produced throughout England at this result, was greater than could have been anticipated, and no demonstrations were omitted which could testify the public sense of the kindness of the king, and the wisdom of the parliament. The flags of the ships were spread in token of felicitation, a general illumination of the city of London was made; salutes were fired; and bonfires kindled in every quarter.

But it was in America that a still higher joy prevailed, and still greater demonstrations of that joy were made. In the house of representatives in Massachusetts, a vote of gratitude to the king, and of thanks to Mr. Pitt, the Duke of Grafton, and others, was passed. By the house of burgesses in Virginia, it was resolved to erect a statue in honour of the king, and an obelisk in honour of all those, whether of the house of peers or of commons, who had distinguished themselves in favour of the rights of the colonies.

In the midst of this joy, the *declaratory act*, above mentioned, appears to have been little regarded. The extent and inadmissible character of its principles for a time remained unscrutinised. It was considered as appended to the act of repeal, to soften the prejudices of the opposition, and to save national honour from the imputation of being too greatly tarnished. But, in reality, it was designed as the recognition of a principle which the British politicians were unwilling to relinquish, and which they might in time have occasion to apply.

It is not, moreover, to be concealed, that universal and sincere as was the joy of the Americans, consequent on the repeal of the stamp act; the same cordiality was never felt by the colonies, as before the late disturbances. A strong disgust—a deep resentment, had fixed itself in the hearts of many ; and a secret wish began to be felt, that the yoke were entirely removed. Perhaps, even at this early day, the hope was indulged, that the time would arrive, when this wish would become a reality.

In July, 1766, the administration of the Marquis of Rockingham was dissolved, and a new one formed, under the direction of Mr. Pitt. Unfortunately it was composed of men of different political principles, and attached to different parties. The Duke of Grafton was placed at the head of the treasury; Lord Shelburne was joined with General Conway as one of the secretaries of state , Charles Townshend was made chancellor of the exchequer, Camden, lord chancellor, Pitt, now created Earl of Chatham, had the privy seal, and Lord North and George Cooke were joint pay-masters.

If the prejudices of many in the colonies were not yet done away, much more was this the fact with the ex-minister Grenville, and his adherents in England. Disappointed as to the popularity of his administration, and remembering as one cause of it, his measures against America, he was ready to call into view, on every occasion, her obstinacy and ingratitude, and to enter anew upon efforts to tax the colonies.

To him, therefore, is attributed the plan which, under the last formed administration, was brought forward in the parliament of 1767, to impose taxes upon the colonies. The articles enumerated in the bill, upon which duties were laid, were glass, paper, paste board, white and red lead, painters colours, and tea.

Mr. Pitt, during the discussion of this bill, was confined by indisposition, and hence, unable to raise his voice against it. Without much opposition, it passed both houses, and on the 29th of June, received the royal assent. At the same time were passed two other acts;—the one establishing a new board of custom-house officers in America; and the other restraining the legislature of the province of New-York from *passing any act whatever*, until they should furnish the king's troops with several required articles.

These three acts reached America at the same time, and again excited universal alarm. The first and second were particularly odious. The new duties, it was perceived, were only a new mode of drawing money from the colonies, and the same strong opposition to the measure was exhibited, which had prevailed against the stamp act. Several of the colonies, through their colonial assemblies, expressed their just abhorrence of these enactments, and their determination never to submit to them.

Soon after the establishment of the new board of custom house officers, at Boston, under the above act, a fit occasion presented itself, for an expression of the public indignation. This was the arrival at that port, in May, 1668, of the sloop Liberty, belonging to Mr. Hancock, and laden with wines from Madeira.

During the night, the most of her cargo was unladen, and put into stores; on the following day the sloop was entered at the custom house, with a few pipes only. A discovery being made of these facts, by the custom-house officers, the vessel was seized, and by their order removed along side of the Romney, a ship of war, then in the harbour.

The conduct of the custom-house officers in this transaction roused the indignant feelings of the Bostonians, who unwarrantably attacked the houses of the officers, and even assaulted their persons. No prosecutions, however, could be sustained, from the excited state of public feeling.

Finding themselves no longer safe in the town, the officers prudently sought protection on board the Romney, and subsequently retired to Castle Williams.

INTRODUCTION. 43

The public excitement was soon after increased, by the arrival in the harbour of two regiments of troops, under the command of Colonel Dalrymple. These were designed to assist the civil magistrates in the preservation of peace, and the custom-house officers in the execution of their functions. Both these regiments were encamped within the town—the one on the commons, the other in the market hall and state house.

This measure of the governor, under order of the British ministry, was eminently fitted to rouse the public indignation to the highest pitch. To be thus watched, as if in a state of open rebellion—to see their common a place of encampment—and their halls of justice, with the chambers of their assembly, thronged with armed soldiers, was more than the inhabitants were willing to endure. Frequent quarrels and collisions occurred between the citizens and soldiers, which every day threatened to terminate in bloodshed.

During the session of parliament in 1770, the Duke of Grafton, first lord of the treasury, resigned, and was succeeded in that office by the afterwards celebrated Lord North. In March, this latter gentleman introduced a bill abolishing the duties imposed by the act of 1767, on all the articles except *tea*. This partial suspension of the duties served to soften the feelings of the Americans in a degree; but the exception in relation to tea, it was quite apparent, was designed as a salvo to the national honour, and as an evidence which the British ministry were unwilling to relinquish, of the right of parliament to tax the colonies.

The above relaxation in respect to certain duties was, however, unaccompanied by any other indications of a more kindly feeling towards the colonies. The troops were still continued in Boston, and the acts of trade enforced with singular strictness. At length, on the evening of the 5th of March, 1770, in a quarrel between a party of soldiers and citizens, eleven of the latter were killed or wounded, by a guard, under command of a Captain Preston.

The news of this rencontre was spread in every direction over the city—the bells were rung, the alarm of "fire" was given, the drums were beat, and the citizens every where called to arms. Thousands soon assembled, and demanded the removal of the troops from the town. With the assurance that the affair should be settled to their satisfaction in the morning, they were induced to retire. When the morning came, however, Hutchinson, the lieutenant governor, for a long time refused to order the removal of the troops, and was only driven to this measure, by evidence too strong to be doubted, that his own personal safety depended upon it.

The men who were killed, were regarded as martyrs in the cause of liberty; and at their interment no mark of public sympathy or appropriate funeral ceremony was omitted. The anniversary of this tragical event, which was called "the Boston massacre," was long observed with great solemnity, and gave occasion to warm and patriotic addresses, well adapted to excite a revolutionary spirit.

Captain Preston and his guard were arraigned before a judicial tribunal; but for the honour of the colony they were all acquitted, except two, who were found guilty of manslaughter. For this acquittal, the prisoners, as well as the colony, were indebted to the independent zeal and powerful eloquence of John Adams and Josiah Quincy, Jun. than whom none were warmer friends to the colony, or had acted a more conspicuous part against the imperious demands of the British ministry. Odious to the community as the prisoners were, these honest and intrepid champions appeared in their defence, and proved to the world, that while Americans could resist the usurpations of a tyrannical ministry, they could also stand forth, when justice required, for the protection and defence of their irresponsible servants.

Allusion has been made to the requirement of his British majesty, in former years, that the colonies should provide for the support of the royal governors by a *permanent* salary, and their refusal to yield to the royal wishes. In the year 1772, it was officially announced to the assembly of Massachusetts, that provision had been made for the payment of their governor's salary by the *crown*, independent of any grant from them. The former dispute on this subject had given birth to many angry feelings; but language can scarcely describe the excitement occasioned by the renewal of the subject, and the application of the revenue of the colony to the above purpose. independent of the assembly. The house of representatives immediately declared the appropriation an infraction of their charter—a dangerous innovation, and the preliminary to a despotic administration of government.

While this dispute was going forward in Massachusetts, a bold opposition to the measures of the British ministry appeared (June, 1772) in the colony of Rhode Island. A British armed schooner, called the Gaspee, had been stationed in that colony to assist the board of customs in the execution of the revenue and trade laws. Desirous of displaying his authority, and of humbling the pride of the colonists, the captain obliged the masters of packets, navigating the bay, to lower their colours on passing the schooner; and, in case of refusal, would chase them, and fire upon them. To a requirement so humiliating, a master of one of the Providence packets refused to submit, and was chased by the schooner, which venturing too far inland, ran aground.

Intelligence of her situation was immediately communicated to the inhabitants of Providence; and several who were characterized for a love of daring enterprise, repaired to the spot. Under cover of night, they took the vessel by force, and burnt her to the water's edge. Such a bold opposition to the laws, was not suffered to pass unnoticed. But although commissioners were appointed to investigate the affair, and a reward of 500*l*. was offered for a discovery of the offenders, all efforts to detect them were futile.

The opposition to the royal provision for the salary of the governor, which we noticed in a preceding paragraph, was not confined to the assembly of Massachusetts. Numerous meetings were called in the various towns of the provinces, in relation, as well to this particular measure, as to other oppressive acts of the British parliament.

In these meetings, the town of Boston took the lead. A committee was appointed to address the several towns in the colony, and to urge upon them the importance of an unanimous expression of their feelings with regard to the conduct of the British ministry. "We have abundant reason to apprehend," said this committee, in their address, "that a *plan of despotism* has been concerted, and is hastening to a *completion*, the late measures of the administration have a direct tendency to deprive us of every thing valuable as men, as christians, and as subjects, entitled to the rights of native Britons."—"We are not afraid of poverty," said they, in conclusion,—"but we *disdain slavery*. Let us consider, we are struggling for our best birth rights and inheritance, which, being infringed, renders all our blessings precarious in their enjoyment, and trifling in their value."

The proceedings of the assembly, and of the towns in Massachusetts, were communicated to the house of burgesses in Virginia, in March of 1773. Similar sentiments prevailed in that ancient and patriotic colony. It was apparent to that body, and began to be a prevailing opinion throughout the country, that to remain much longer in that particular state, was impossible. The future was indeed indistinct. But the wild confusion of the elements gave indications of an approaching storm. A portentous cloud hung over the country. It was the part of wisdom, at least, to think of preparation, and to ascertain in what attitude things stood in different sections of the country, together with the support the directing officers might expect, should the threatening tempest actually burst.

With these views, no doubt, the house of burgesses in Virginia, on the 12th of March, 1773, passed the following resolutions:

"Be it resolved, that a standing committee of correspondence and inquiry be appointed, to consist of eleven persons, to wit: the honourable Peyton Randolph, Esquire, Robert Carter Nicholas, Richard Bland, Richard Henry Lee, Benjamin Harrison, Edmund Pendleton, Patrick Henry, Dudley Diggs, Dabney Carr, Archibald Cary, and Thomas Jefferson, Esquires, any six of whom to be a committee, whose business it shall be to obtain the most early and authentic intelligence of such acts and resolutions of the British parliament, or proceedings of administration, as may relate to, or affect the British colonies; and to keep up and maintain a correspondence and communication with our sister colonies, respecting these important considerations, and the result of their proceedings from time to time to lay before the house."

Upon the recommendation of Virginia, similar committees of correspondence and inquiry were appointed by the different colonial assemblies; and a confidential interchange of opinions was thus kept up between the colonies. Great unity of sentiment was the consequence; and the value of the measure was fully developed, in the struggle which afterwards ensued between the colonies and the parent country.

By a series of direct oppressions, and through the resident officers of the crown, the hostility of the people of Massachusetts had become a settled principle; and about this time, it received additional strength, from the discovery and publication of certain letters, addressed to a member of parliament, in the years 1768 and 1769, by Mr. Hutchinson the governor, and Mr. Oliver the chief justice of the province.

The existence of these letters was communicated to Dr. Franklin, who at that time resided in England, by a gentleman of his acquaintance, with the assurance that they contained statements calculated to prejudice the ministry and parliament against the people of Massachusetts, and to widen the breach between the two countries; and that they moreover recommended the employment of force to reduce the colonies to order and obedience.

The letters were, at length, shown by this gentleman to Dr. Franklin, who obtained copies of them to be sent to America, only upon the express condition, that they should be confidentially shown to a few, and should not be again copied.

On their arrival in America, they were confidentially shown to the "few;" but it was scarcely possible that they should not be made the subject of conversation. By some means, the existence of such letters became known, beyond the original intention; and so intense was the curiosity excited by the subject, that on the 2d of June, 1773, some of them were communicated by Samuel Adams to the assembly of Massachusetts, then sitting with closed doors, under the restriction that they should not be copied or published.

Notwithstanding the above restrictions, the contents of the letters were so extraordinary and so fully evidential of a design to subvert the constitution of the province by the introduction of arbitrary power, that the house, upon further deliberation, directed the whole to be published. They were induced to this course, by the fact, that several copies had got into circulation, from which it might be *inferred*, that the consent of the original owner had been obtained for that purpose.

The letters contained exaggerated statements and deliberate misrepresentations of occurrences in the colony, and recommended an alteration of the charter of Massachusetts, together with the institution of an order of patricians. They even hinted at the expediency of " taking off some of the *original incendiaries.*"

The governor, unable to deny his own signature, presented the poor excuse that they were " confidential letters," and were written without any such object as was ascribed to them. But now, " proof was heaped upon the shoulders of demonstration," that Hutchinson, Oliver, and their adherents, had attempted to alienate the affections of the king and ministry from the colonies. The house of representatives, in an address to the king, broadly asserted this fact; and solicited, though in vain, that Hutchinson and Oliver might be removed from their places *forever*.

During these transactions in America, a plan was devising by the British ministry, to introduce tea into the colonies. The duty on this article, as already noticed, had been retained, for the purpose of maintaining the supremacy of parliament, and its *right* to impose taxes. Little of the article, however, had been imported into the country from Great Britain; the people having firmly resolved not to submit to the payment of the duty. In consequence of a strict adherence to this resolution, the teas of the East India Company had accumulated in their warehouses; and legislative aid became necessary to relieve them of their embarrassments.

In 1773, the minister introduced a bill into parliament, allowing the company to export their teas to America, with a drawback of all the duties paid in England. By this regulation, tea would in fact become cheaper in America than in Great Britain, and it was expected that this consideration would induce the Americans to pay the small duty upon it.

On the passage of this bill, the company made a shipment of large quantities of tea to Charleston, Philadelphia, New-York, and Boston. Before its arrival, the resolution had been formed by the inhabitants of those places, that, if possible, it should not even be landed. That cargo destined for Charleston was, indeed, landed and stored; but was not permitted to be offered for sale. The vessels which brought tea to Philadelphia and New-York, were compelled to return to England with their cargoes, without even having made an entry at the custom-house.

It was designed by the leading patriots of Boston to make a similar disposition of the cargoes which were expected at that place; but on its arrival, the consignees were found to be the relations, or friends, of the governor, and they could not be induced to resign their trust. Several town meetings were held on the subject, and spirited resolutions passed, that no considerations would induce the inhabitants to permit the landing of the tea. Orders were at the same time given to the captains to obtain clearances at the custom-house, without the usual entries; but this the collector pertinaciously refused.

It was in this state of things, that the citizens of Boston again assembled, to determine what measures to adopt. During the discussions had on the posture of affairs, and while a captain of a vessel was gone to wait upon the governor, for the last time, to request a passport, Josiah Quincy, Jun. rose, and addressed the assembly in the following eloquent style: "It is not the spirit that vapours within these walls, that must stand us in stead. The exertions of this day will *call forth events*, which will make a very different spirit necessary for our salvation. Look to the end. Whoever supposes, that shouts and hosannas will terminate the trials of the day, entertains a childish fancy. We must be grossly ignorant of the importance and value of the prize, for which we contend ; we must be equally ignorant of the powers of those who have combined against us ; we must be blind to that malice, inveteracy and insatiable revenge, which actuate our enemies, public and private, abroad and in our bosoms, to hope we shall end this controversy without the sharpest, sharpest conflicts ; to flatter ourselves, that popular resolves, popular harangues, popular acclamations, and popular vapour, will vanquish our fears. Let us consider the issue. Let us look to the end. Let us *weigh* and *consider*, before we advance to those measures which must bring on the *most trying* and *terrible struggle* this country ever saw."

The captain of the vessel at length returned, to say that the governor refused the requested passport. The meeting was immediately dissolved. A secret plan had been formed to mingle the tea with the waters of the ocean. Three different parties soon after sallied out, in the costume of Mohawk Indians, and precipitately made their way to the wharves.

At the same time, the citizens were seen in crowds directing their course to the same place, to become spectators of a scene, as novel as the enterprise was bold. Without noise, without the tumult usual on similar occasions, the tea was taken from the vessel, by the conspirators, and expeditiously offered as an oblation " to the watery God."

Nothing could exceed the surprise of the British ministry, on learning the issue of their plan to introduce tea into the colonies. Their indignation was particularly severe against the inhabitants of Boston, for their " violent and outrageous conduct." In the following March, 1774, the whole affair was presented to parliament by Lord North, and a determination was formed to punish both the citizens of Boston, and the inhabitants of the colony.

Accordingly, a bill was soon introduced into the house of commons, usually called the " *Boston port bill*," which prohibited the *landing or shipping* of any goods at that port, after the first of June following. By a second act, which followed, the charter of the colony was so altered, as to make the appointment of the council, justices, judges, sheriffs, and even jurors, dependent upon the king or his agent; and restraining all town meetings, except the annual meeting, without *leave* of the governor in writing, with a statement of the special business of the meeting. To these enactments a third was added, authorising the governor, with the advice of the council, to send any person for trial to any other colony, or to Great Britain, who should be informed against, or indicted for any act done in violation of the laws of the *revenue.*

On the arrival of the Boston port bill, which was brought over by a new governor, General Gage, the citizens of Boston, in an assembly which was convened to consider the subject, declared, "that the *impolicy, injustice, inhumanity,* and *cruelty* of the act, exceeded all their powers of expression; and, therefore," said they, "we leave it to the consciences of others, and appeal to God and the world."—At the same time they adopted the following resolution: "That if the other colonies come into a joint resolution to stop all *importations* from, and exportations to Great Britain, and every part of the West Indies, till the act be repealed, the same would prove the salvation of North America and her liberties."

Copies of these proceedings were immediately circulated through the colonies. A universal sympathy for the inhabitants of Boston was expressed. In Virginia, this sympathy was manifested by the house of burgesses, in the observance of the 1st of June, the day the port of Boston was to be shut, as a "day of fasting, humiliation, and prayer."

Arrangements having been made for the meeting of the second continental congress, on the 5th of September, 1774, that body assembled at Philadelphia. All the colonies were represented, except Georgia. Peyton Randolph, a delegate from Virginia, was elected president, and Charles Thompson, a citizen of Philadelphia, was chosen secretary.

The attention of this celebrated congress was at an early date turned towards the province of Massachusetts, and the city of Boston; and the following resolutions were adopted, expressive of the sympathy they felt for that colony, in its distress, and the high sense which the congress entertained of the wisdom and fortitude which the colony exhibited. "It is assembly deeply feels the sufferings of their countrymen in the Massachusetts Bay, under the operation of the late unjust, cruel, and oppressive acts of the British parliament; at the same time, they most thoroughly approve the wisdom and fortitude with which opposition to these wicked ministerial measures has hitherto been conducted; and they earnestly recommend to their brethren a perseverance in the same firm and temperate conduct, trusting that the effect of the united efforts of North America, in their behalf, will carry such conviction to the British nation, of the unwise, unjust, and ruinous policy of the present administration, as quickly to introduce better men and wiser measures."

Congress further addressed a letter to General Gage, earnestly praying him to put a stop to the hostile preparations which he had commenced, especially the fortifications around Boston, as the surest means of maintaining public tranquillity in that quarter, and preventing the horrors of a civil war. At the same time, they urged upon the citizens of that town all the forbearance within their power; that they should "conduct themselves peaceably towards his excellency, General Gage, and his majesty's troops stationed in Boston, as far as could possibly be consistent with the immediate safety and security of the town."

Congress next proceeded to publish a declaration of rights. These rights were set forth in the following articles:

"1. That they are entitled to life, liberty, and property; and they have never ceded to any foreign power whatever, a right to dispose of either, without their consent.

"2. That our ancestors, who first settled these colonies, were, at the time of their emigration from their mother country, entitled to all the rights, liberties, and immunities of free and natural born subjects within the realm of England

"3. That by such emigration, they by no means forfeited, surrendered, or lost any of those rights, but that they were, and their descendants now are, entitled to the exercise and enjoyment of such of them, as their local and other circumstances enable them to exercise and enjoy.

"4. That the foundation of English liberty and of all free

INTRODUCTION. 53

governments, is a right in the people to participate in their legislative council; and as the English colonists are not represented, and, from their local and other circumstances, cannot properly be represented in the British parliament, t ey are entitled to as free and *exclusive power of legislation,* in their several provincial legislatures, where their right of representation can alone be preserved, in all cases of *taxation and internal policy,* subject only to the negative of their sovereign, in such a manner as has been heretofore used and accustomed. But from the *necessity* of the case, and a regard to the mutual interest of both countries, we cheerfully consent to the operation of such acts of the British parliament as are *bona fide* restrained to the regulation of our external commerce, for the purpose of securing the commercial advantages of the whole empire to the mother country, and the commercial benefits of its respective members; excluding every idea of taxation, internal or external, for raising a *revenue,* on the subjects in America, without their consent.

"5. That the respective colonies are entitled to the common law of England, and more especially, to the great and inestimable privilege of being tried by their peers of the vicinity, according to the course of that law.

"6. That they are entitled to the benefit of such of the English statutes as existed at the time of their colonization; and which they have by experience respectfully found to be applicable to their several local and other circumstances.

"7. That these his majesty's colonies, are likewise entitled to all the immunities and privileges, granted and confirmed to them by royal charters, or secured by their several codes of provincial laws.

"8. That they have a right peaceably to assemble, consider of their grievances, and petition the king; and all prosecutions, prohibitory proclamations, and commitments for the same, are illegal.

"9. That the keeping a standing army in these colonies in times of peace, without the consent of the legislature of that colony, in which such an army is kept, is against law.

"10. It is indispensably necessary to good government,

rendered essential by the English constitution, that the constituent branches of the legislature be independent of each other; that, therefore, the exercise of legislative power, in several colonies, by a council appointed during pleasure by the crown, is unconstitutional, dangerous, and destructive to the freedom of American legislation."

In relation to the above particulars, they expressed themselves in the following language:

"All and each of which, the aforesaid deputies, in behalf of themselves and their constituents, do claim, demand, and insist on, as their indubitable rights and liberties, which cannot be legally taken from them, altered, or abridged, by any power whatever, without their consent by their representatives in their several provincial legislatures."

It was also deemed of importance to adopt measures to stop commercial intercourse with Great Britain. An agreement was, therefore, entered into, to suspend all importation of merchandise from Great Britain and its dependencies, from the 1st of December, 1774; and, unless the wrongs of which the Americans complained should be redressed, to suspend in like manner all exportation from the 10th of September, 1775, with the single exception of rice.

At the same time it was urged upon the colonies to adopt a system of rigid economy; to encourage industry, and to promote agriculture, arts, and manufactures, and especially the manufacture of wool.

Having attended to these important concerns, congress closed their session on the 26th of October, after adopting addresses to the people of Great Britain, to the king, and to the French inhabitants of Canada.

The congress which then terminated its session, has justly been celebrated from that time to the present, and its celebrity will continue while wisdom finds admirers, and patriotism is regarded with veneration. The tone and temper of their various resolutions, the style of their addresses, and the composition of the several public papers, contributed, in every particular, to excite the admiration of the world. Born and educated in the wilds of a new world, unpractised in the arts of polity, most of them unexperienced in the arduous duties of legislation, differing in religion, manners, customs, and habits, as they did in their views of the nature of their connexion with Great Britain :—that such an assembly, so constituted, should display so much wisdom, sagacity, foresight, and knowledge of the world; such skill in argument; such force of reasoning; such firmness and soundness of judgment; so profound an acquaintance with the rights of men; such genuine patriotism; and, above all, such unexampled union of opinion, was indeed a political phenomenon to which history has furnished no parallel.* Both at home and abroad, they were spoken of in terms of the highest admiration. *Abroad,* the Earl of Chatham, in one of his brilliant speeches, remarked of them :— " History, my lords, has been my favourite study, and in the celebrated writings of antiquity have I often admired the patriotism of Greece and Rome; but, my lords, I must declare and avow, that in the master tales of the world, I know not the people, or the senate, who, in such a complication of difficult circumstances, can stand in preference to the delegates of America assembled in general congress at Philadelphia." At *home*, they were celebrated by a native and popular bard,† in an equally elevated strain:

>"Now meet the fathers of this western clime,
>   Nor names more noble graced the rolls of fame,
> When Spartan firmness braved the wrecks of time,
>   Or Rome's bold virtues fann'd the heroic flame.
>
> Not deeper thought the immortal sage inspired,
>   On Solon's lips when Grecian senates hung;
> Nor manlier eloquence the bosom fired,
>   When genius thundered from the Athenian tongue."

While this congress were in session, nearly all the colonies had taken measures to call provincial assemblies, for the purpose of better securing their ancient rights of government. In Massachusetts, the people had determined to hold a provincial congress on the 15th of October, which induced General Gage, with a view to prevent the intended meeting, to

* Allen.   † M'Fingal.

convoke the general court of the province at Salem, on the 5th. of the same month. Before the arrival of this latter day, however, he issued his proclamation, forbidding that assembly. The members, nevertheless, convened on the appointed day, and adjourned to Concord, where, after electing John Hancock for their president, they further adjourned to meet at Cambridge, on the 17th instant. At the latter place, they proceeded to exercise the powers of government, and to take the necessary measures for placing the province in a state of defence. They appointed a committee of safety, and a committee of supplies. One fourth of the militia were ordered to be enlisted as *minute men*, to be frequently drilled, and held in readiness for service at a minute's warning.

In other colonies also, before the close of the year, the note of preparation was heard. The horizon every day became more lowering; and as its darkness thickened, the activity and vigilance of the colonists increased.

The British parliament met on the 29th of November. The moderation evinced by the congress at Philadelphia had encouraged the mass of the American people to hope, that on the meeting of that body, conciliatory measures would be adopted, so as to restore peace and harmony between the two countries. Similar sentiments were entertained by the friends of America, in England. They saw nothing in the proceedings of the American congress, in their resolutions, manifestoes, or addresses, to which an Englishman, proud of his birthright, could justly object. It now remained with the British government to adopt a plan of reconciliation, or to lose the affections of the colonies forever.

The tone of his majesty's speech, on the opening of the session, was unexpectedly lofty, and gave little encouragement to the hopes of reconciliation. After alluding to the spirit of disobedience which was abroad in his American colonies, and to the daring resistance to law which characterized the people of Massachusetts, he informed parliament of his firm determination to resist every attempt to impair the supreme authority of parliament, throughout the dominions of the crown.

To the mind of Lord Chatham, no object, at this time, seemed more important, than the restoration of peace between the two countries. The period had arrived, when a reconciliation must take place, if ever such an event could be effected. Hence, on the assembling of parliament, after the usual recess, January 20th, 1775, when the minister had laid the papers relating to America before the house, Lord Chatham rose, and moved, " that an humble address be presented to his majesty, to direct the removal of his majesty's troops from Boston, in order to open the way towards a settlement of the dangerous troubles in America."

" My lords," says Chatham, " these papers from America, now laid by the administration for the first time before your lordships, have been, to my knowledge, five or six weeks in the pocket of the minister. And notwithstanding the fate of this kingdom hangs upon the event of this great controversy, we are but this moment called to a consideration of this important subject.

" My lords, I do not wish to look into one of these papers. I know their contents, well enough, already. I know, that there is not a member in this house, but is acquainted with their purport, also. There ought, therefore, to be no delay in entering upon this matter. We ought to proceed to it immediately. We ought to seize the first moment to open the door of reconciliation. The Americans will never be in a temper or state to be reconciled—they ought not to be—till the troops are withdrawn. The troops are a perpetual irritation to those people; they are a bar to all confidence, and all cordial reconcilement.

" The way," he said, " must be immediately opened for reconciliation. It will soon be too late. I know not who advised the present measures; I know not who advises to a perseverance and enforcement of them; but this I will say, that whoever advises them, ought to answer for it at his utmost peril. I know that no one will avow that he advised, or that he was the author of these measures; every one shrinks from the charge. But somebody has advised his majesty to these measures, and if he continues to hear such evil coun-

H

sellors, his majesty will be undone. His majesty may, indeed, wear his crown, but the American jewel out of it, it will not be worth the wearing. What more shall I say? I must not say, the king is betrayed; but this I will say, the nation is ruined. What foundation have we for our claims over America? What is our right to persist in such cruel and vindictive measures, against that loyal, respectable people?

"My lords, deeply impressed with the importance of taking some healing measures, at this most alarming, distracted state of our affairs, though bowed down with a cruel disease, I have crawled to this house, to give you my best counsel and experience: and my advice is, to beseech his majesty to withdraw his troops. This is the best I can think of. It will convince America, that you mean to try her cause, in the spirit, and by the laws of freedom and fair inquiry, and not by codes of blood. How can she now trust you, with the bayonet at her breast? She has all the reason in the world, now, to believe you mean her death or bondage. Thus entered on the threshold of this business, I will knock at your gates for justice, without ceasing, unless inveterate infirmities stay my hand. My lords, I pledge myself never to leave this business. I will pursue it to the end in every shape. I will never fail of my attendance on it, at every step and period of this great matter, unless nailed down to my bed by the severity of disease. My lords, there is no time to be lost: every moment is big with dangers. Nay, while I am now speaking, the decisive blow may be struck, and millions involved in the consequences. The very first drop of blood will make a wound, that will not easily be skinned over. Years, perhaps ages, will not heal it: it will be *immedicabile vulnus:* a wound of that rancorous, malignant, corroding, festering nature, that in all probability, it will mortify the whole body. Let us then, my lords, set to this business in earnest! not take it up by bits and scraps, as formerly, just as exigencies pressed, without any regard to general relations, connexions, and dependencies. I would not, by any thing I have said, my lords, be thought to encourage America to proceed beyond the right line. I reprobate all acts of violence by her mobility. But when her inherent constitutional rights are invaded, those rights she has an equitable claim to enjoy by the fundamental laws of the English constitution, and which are engrafted thereon by the unalterable laws of nature; then I own myself an American, and feeling myself such, shall to the verge of my life vindicate those rights against all men, who strive to trample upon, or oppose them."

This motion of Lord Chatham, offered not less from a regard to the welfare of England, than from a conviction of her impolitic and cruel oppression of the colonists,—and supported by all the eloquence of which that distinguished orator was master, was, nevertheless, rejected by a large majority. Although thus defeated, he was still determined, if possible, to save his country from the evils which his prophetic glance saw in certain prospect, unless they should be timely averted. Hence, shortly afterwards, he introduced into parliament his conciliatory bill. While this bill maintained the dependence of the colonies upon the imperial crown, and the right of parliament to make laws to bind them in all cases, touching the general interests of the British empire, it declared that that body had no right to tax the colonies without their consent.

To such a proposition the ministry were not prepared to listen. They were determined to admit no bill, which had for its object the relinquishment of any of their favourite doctrines, or which, by implication, should impeach the wisdom or justice of the course they had pursued. Nay, they had now formed their plan, and were prepared to announce it. Coercion was to be their motto, until, in the spirit of submission, America should lay herself down at their feet.

In accordance with the above declaration, a bill was soon after passed by the parliament, restricting the trade of the colonies of Massachusetts, Connecticut, New-Hampshire, and Rhode Island, to Great Britain, Ireland, and the West Indies, and prohibiting their carrying on any fisheries on the banks of Newfoundland, and other places for a limited time. The same restrictions were soon after extended to all the colonies, represented in the congress at Philadelphia, with the exception of New-York and North Carolina. By these restrictions, it was thought to starve the colonies into obedience and submission, from a mistaken apprehension that the people were dependent upon the *fisheries* for their support.

It was a general understanding among the colonists, that hostilities should not be commenced by them. It was, indeed, apparent, that the day of blood was not far distant, but that blood was to be first shed by the hands of the English. In the mean time, they were not inactive in the work of preparation. The munitions of war were collected and stored at different points, as necessity and safety seemed to require. Among the places of deposite in Massachusetts, were Worcester and Concord, and thither considerable stores of arms and provisions had been conveyed.

In the mean time, the vigilance of General Gage was not abated. Excited by the loyalists, who had persuaded him that he would find no resistance from the *cowardice of the patriots*, he resolved to send a few companies to Concord, in a secret manner, to seize the military stores deposited there; and either to transport them to Boston, or to destroy them. Accordingly, on the evening of the 18th of April, 1775, a detachment moved from Boston for this purpose, and the next day occurred the memorable battle of Lexington, in which the British were the aggressors, by first firing on the militia collected at that place.

The details of this opening scene of the revolutionary war are too well known, to require a recital in this place. Repulsed, harassed, and fatigued, the British, with no inconsiderable loss, returned to Boston, after having accomplished their object.

The provincial congress of Massachusetts was, at this time, in session at Watertown, ten miles distant from Boston. They immediately resolved that a levy of thirteen thousand men should be made. At the same time, the treasurer was directed to borrow 100,000*l.* for the use of the province; and they declared the citizens were absolved from all obligations of obedience to Govenor Gage. As the news of the battle of

Lexington spread round the country, a universal ardour inflamed the minds of the inhabitants; and shortly after, were assembled, in the neighbourhood of Boston, thirty thousand men, ready, should occasion require, to do justice to themselves and their country.

In this critical state of public affairs, congress again assembled at Philadelphia, on the 10th of May. An official account of the late aggressions of his majesty's troops in Massachusetts, was soon after laid before them; upon which it was unanimously resolved to place the colonies in a state of defence. To the colony of New-York, which had solicited the advice and direction of congress, in anticipation of the speedy arrival of foreign troops, they recommended a course of action entirely on the defensive. They were, however, advised to remove all military stores, and to provide a place of retreat for their women and children; to hold themselves in readiness for the protection of the city; and, in the event of hostilities, to meet the enemy with promptness and decision.

To some of the members of congress, it appeared desirable to make yet another attempt at reconciliation with the British government. Justice, indeed, required no such advance; and by many the measure was considered only as a work of supererogation. They were willing, however, while raising the sword with one hand, to extend the olive branch with the other; and, though driven to the necessity of forcibly vindicating their rights, they were still disposed to secure them, if possible, by a firm remonstrance. Yielding, therefore, to the pacific wishes of several members, they prepared an address to the king, by way of solemn appeal, and a second address to the people of Great Britain.

Towards the king, they yet used the language of loyalty and affection; and assured him, notwithstanding the injuries they had sustained, and the grievous oppressions under which they were suffering, they still wished for peace; and if redressed in respect to their wrongs, and secured in the just rights of subjects, they would manifest towards him all the affection and devotion which a sovereign could require.

In their address to the inhabitants of Great Britain, after

recapitulating former injuries, and stating more recent acts of hostility. they ask: "Can the descendants of Britain tamely submit to this? No, we never will; while we revere the memory of our gallant and virtuous ancestors, we never can surrender those glorious privileges for which they fought, bled, and conquered. Admit that your fleets and armies can destroy our towns, and ravage our coasts: these are inconsiderable objects, things of no moment, to men whose bosoms glow with the ardour of liberty. We can retire beyond the reach of your navy, and, without any sensible diminution of the necessaries of life, enjoy a luxury which, from that period, you will want—the luxury of being free." They again repel the charge of aiming at independence:

"Our enemies," say they, "charge us with sedition. In what does it consist? In our refusal to submit to unwarrantable acts of injustice and cruelty? If so, show us a period in your history in which you have not been equally seditious.

"We are accused of aiming at independence; but how is this accusation supported? By the allegations of your ministers, not by our actions. Abused, insulted, and contemned, what steps have we pursued to obtain redress? We have carried our dutiful petitions to the throne. We have applied to your justice for relief. We have retrenched our luxury, and withheld our trade.

"The advantages of our commerce were designed as a compensation for your protection: when you ceased to protect, for what were we to compensate?

"What has been the success of our endeavours? The clemency of our sovereign is unhappily diverted; our petitions are treated with indignity; our prayers answered by insults. Our application to you remains unnoticed, and leaves us the melancholy apprehension of your wanting either the will, or the power, to assist us."

After reminding them, that the loss of liberty in America would only be a prelude to its loss in Great Britain, they conclude: "A cloud hangs over your head and ours; ere this reaches you, it may probably burst upon us; let us then, (before the remembrance of former kindness is obliterated,) once more repeat these appellations, which are ever grateful to our ears ; let us entreat heaven to avert our ruin, and the destruction that threatens our friends, brethren, and countrymen, on the other side of the Atlantic."

Having thus done all which the most scrupulous conscience could demand, congress proceeded to adopt measures to place the country in a proper attitude of defence, by organizing an army, and appointing the necessary military officers. On the 15th of June, George Washington, by the united voice of congress, was appointed commander-in-chief of the army then raised, or to be raised, for the defence of American liberty.

Washington was, at that time, a member of congress, and in a measure prepared to decide on the important question of acceptance. On the day following, he appeared in the house, and, standing in his place, said, that he thanked congress for the honour they had conferred upon him ; but that he felt great distress, from a consciousness that his abilities and military experience were not equal to the extensive and important trust ; "however, as the congress desire it, I will enter upon the momentous duty, and exert every power I possess in their service, and for the support of the glorious cause. I beg they will accept my most cordial thanks for this distinguished testimony of their approbation.

" But lest some unlucky event should happen, unfavourable to my reputation, I beg it may be remembered by every gentleman in the room, that I this day declare, with the utmost sincerity, I do not think myself equal to the command I am honoured with.

" As to pay, sir, I beg leave to assure the congress, that as no pecuniary consideration could have tempted me to accept this arduous employment, at the expense of my domestic ease and happiness, I do not wish to make any profit from it; I will keep an exact account of my expenses. These, I doubt not, they will discharge, and that is all I desire."

During the winter of 1776, the subject of a DECLARATION OF INDEPENDENCE, occupied the attention of many men in all parts of the country. The ablest pens also were employed on this momentous subject. The propriety and necessity of the measure was enforced in the numerous gazettes, and in pamphlets. Among the latter, Common Sense, from the popular pen of Thomas Paine, produced a wonderful effect in the different colonies in favour of independence. Influential individuals urged it as a step absolutely necessary to preserve the rights and liberties of America, and effectually secure her happiness and prosperity.

In the ensuing spring, several of the colonies, by means of their assemblies, expressed their sentiments in favour of independence, and instructed their delegates in the general congress to propose to that respectable body, to declare the united colonies free and independent states.

On the seventh of June, Richard Henry Lee, one of the delegates from Virginia, brought the great question of independence before the house, by submitting the following resolution : " That these united colonies are, and of right ought to be, free and independent states ; that they are absolved from all allegiance to the British crown, and that all political connexion between them and the state of Great Britain is, and ought to be, totally dissolved."

This resolution was postponed until the next day, when it was debated in committee of the whole. On the 10th, it was adopted by a bare majority of the colonies. To give time for greater unanimity, the resolution was postponed in the house, until the first of July. In the mean time, a committee, consisting of Mr. Jefferson, John Adams, Dr. Franklin, Mr. Sherman, and R. R. Livingston, was appointed to prepare a declaration of independence. The committee thus appointed, selected Mr. Adams and Mr. Jefferson, as a sub-committee. The draft made by Mr. Jefferson, was the one reported to congress. It was discussed on the second, and third, and fourth days of the month, in committee of the whole , and on the last of those days, being reported from that committee, it received the final approbation and sanction of congress. It was ordered at the same time, that copies be sent to the several states, and that it be proclaimed at the head of the army. The declaration thus published, did not bear the names of the members, for as yet it had not been signed by them. It was authenticated, like other papers of the congress, by the signatures of the president and secretary. On the 19th of July, as appears by the secret journal, congress "*Resolved*, That the declaration, passed on the fourth, be fairly engrossed on parchment, with the title and style of 'The unanimous declaration of the thirteen United States of America;' and that the same, when engrossed, be signed by every member of congress." And on the second day of August following, the declaration being engrossed and compared at the table, was signed by the members.

The declaration thus adopted, and which gave birth to a new empire, was as follows :

"WHEN, in the course of human events, it becomes necessary for one people to dissolve the political bands which have connected them with another, and to assume, among the powers of the earth, the separate and equal station to which the laws of nature and of nature's God entitle them, a decent respect to the opinions of mankind, requires that they should declare the causes which impel them to the separation.

"We hold these truths to be self-evident :—that all men are created equal, that they are endowed by their Creator with certain unalienable rights; that among these are life, liberty, and the pursuit of happiness. That to secure these rights, governments are instituted among men, deriving their just powers from the consent of the governed; that whenever any form of government becomes destructive of these ends, it is the right of the people to alter or to abolish it, and to institute a new government, laying its foundation on such principles, and organizing its powers in such form, as to them shall seem most likely to effect their safety and happiness. Prudence, indeed, will dictate, that governments long established should not be changed for light and transient causes; and accordingly all experience hath shown, that mankind are more disposed to suffer while evils are sufferable, than to right themselves by abolishing the forms to which they are accustomed. But when a long train of abuses and usurpations, pursuing invariably the same object, evinces a design to reduce them under absolute despotism, it is their right, it is their duty, to throw off such government, and to provide new guards for their future security. Such has been the patient sufferance of these colonies; and such is now the necessity which constrains them to alter their former systems of government. The history of the present king of Great Britain, is a history of repeated injuries and usurpations, all having in direct object the establishment of an absolute tyranny over these states. To prove this, let facts be submitted to a candid world.

"He has refused his assent to laws the most wholesome and necessary for the public good.

"He has forbidden his governors to pass laws of immediate and pressing importance, unless suspended in their operation, till his assent should be obtained; and when so suspended, he has utterly neglected to attend to them. He has refused to pass other laws for the accommodation of large districts of people, unless those people would relinquish the right of representation in the legislature—a right inestimable to them, and formidable to tyrants only.

"He has called together legislative bodies at places unusual, uncomfortable, and distant from the repository of their public records, for the sole purpose of fatiguing them into compliance with his measures.

"He has dissolved representative houses repeatedly, for opposing, with manly firmness, his invasions on the rights of the people.

"He has refused, for a long time after such dissolutions, to cause others to be elected; whereby the legislative powers, incapable of annihilation, have returned to the people at large, for their exercise, the state remaining, in the mean time, exposed to all the dangers of invasion from without, and convulsions within.

"He has endeavoured to prevent the population of these states, for that purpose obstructing the laws for naturalization of foreigners; refusing to pass others to encourage their migration hither, and raising the conditions of new appropriations of lands.

"He has obstructed the administration of justice, by refusing his assent to laws for establishing judiciary powers.

"He has made judges dependent on his will alone, for the tenure of their offices, and the amount and payment of their salaries.

"He has erected a multitude of new offices; and sent hither swarms of officers, to harass our people, and eat out their substance.

"He has kept among us, in times of peace, standing armies, without the consent of our legislatures.

"He has affected to render the military independent of, and superior to, the civil power.

"He has combined with others to subject us to a jurisdiction foreign to our constitution, and unacknowledged by our laws; giving his assent to their acts of pretended legislation:

"For quartering large bodies of armed troops among us:

"For protecting them, by a mock trial, from punishment for any murders which they should commit on the inhabitants of these states:

"For cutting off our trade with all parts of the world:

"For imposing taxes on us without our consent:

"For depriving us, in many cases, of the benefits of trial by jury:

"For transporting us beyond seas to be tried for pretended offences:

"For abolishing the free system of English laws in a neighbouring province, establishing therein an arbitrary government, and enlarging its boundaries, so as to render it at once an example and fit instrument for introducing the same absolute rule into the...

"For taking away our charters, abolishing our most valuable laws, and altering, fundamentally, the forms of our governments:

"For suspending our own legislatures, and declaring themselves invested with power to legislate for us in all cases whatsoever.

"He has abdicated government here, by declaring us out of his protection, and waging war against us.

"He has plundered our seas, ravaged our coasts, burnt our towns, and destroyed the lives of our people.

"He is at this time transporting large armies of foreign mercenaries to complete the works of death, desolation, and tyranny, already begun, with circumstances of cruelty and perfidy, scarcely paralleled in the most barbarous ages, and totally unworthy the head of a civilized nation.

"He has constrained our fellow-citizens, taken captive on the high seas, to bear arms against their country, to become the executioners of their friends and brethren, or to fall themselves by their hands.

"He has excited domestic insurrections amongst us, and has endeavoured to bring on the inhabitants of our frontiers the merciless Indian savages, whose known rule of warfare is an undistinguished destruction of all ages, sexes, and conditions.

"In every stage of these oppressions we have petitioned for redress in the most humble terms: our repeated petitions have been answered only by repeated injury. A prince, whose character is thus marked by every act which may define a tyrant, is unfit to be the ruler of a free people.

"Nor have we been wanting in attentions to our British brethren. We have warned them, from time to time, of attempts by their legislature to extend an unwarrantable jurisdiction over us. We have reminded them of the circumstances of our emigration and settlement here. We have appealed to their native justice and magnanimity, and we have conjured them by the ties of our common kindred to disavow these usurpations, which would inevitably interrupt our connexions and correspondence. They too have been deaf to the voice of justice and of consanguinity. We must, therefore, acquiesce in the necessity which denounces our separation, and hold them, as we hold the rest of mankind—enemies in war, in peace friends.

"We, therefore, the representatives of the United States of America, in general congress assembled, appealing to the Supreme Judge of the world for the rectitude of our intentions, do, in the name and by the authority of the good people of these colonies, solemnly publish and declare, that these united colonies are, and of right ought to be, free and independent states; that they are absolved from all allegiance to the British crown, and that all political connexion between them and the state of Great Britain is, and ought to be, totally dissolved; and that, as free and independent states, they have full power to levy war, conclude peace, contract alliances, establish commerce, and to do all other acts and things, which independent states may of right do. And for the support of this declaration, with a firm reliance on the protection of Divine Providence, we mutually pledge to each other our lives, our fortunes, and our sacred honour."

John Hancock

THE MASSACHUSETTS DELEGATION.

JOHN HANCOCK,
SAMUEL ADAMS,
JOHN ADAMS,
ROBERT TREAT PAINE,
ELBRIDGE GERRY.

JOHN HANCOCK.

The events leading to the declaration of independence, which have been rapidly passed in review, in the preceding pages, have brought us to the more particular notice of those distinguished men, who signed their names to that instrument, and thus identified themselves with the glory of this American republic.

If the world has seldom witnessed a train of events of a more novel and interesting character, than those which led to the declaration of American independence, it has, perhaps, never seen a body of men, placed in a more difficult and responsible situation, than were the signers of that instrument. And certainly, the world has never witnessed a more brilliant exhibition of political wisdom, or a brighter example of firmness and courage.

The first instant the American colonies gave promise of future importance and respectability, the jealousy of Great Britain was excited, and the counsels of her statesmen were employed to keep them in humble subjection. This was the object, when royalty grasped at their charters; when restrictions were laid upon their commerce and manufactures; when, by taxation, their resources were attempted to be withdrawn, and the doctrine inculcated, that it was rebellion for them to think and act for themselves.

It was fortunate for the Americans, that they understood their own rights, and had the courage to assert them. But even at the time of the declaration of independence, just as was the cause of the colonies, it was doubtful how the contest would terminate. The chance of eventual success was against them. Less than three millions of people constituted their population, and these were scattered over a widely extended territory. They were divided into colonies, which had no political character, and no other bond of union than common sufferings, common danger, and common necessities. They had no veteran army, no navy, no arsenals filled with the munitions of war, and no fortifications on their extended coast. They had no overflowing treasuries; but in the outset, were to depend upon loans, taxation, and voluntary contributions.

Thus circumstanced, could success in such a contest be reasonably anticipated? Could they hope to compete with the parent country, whose strength was consolidated by the lapse of centuries, and to whose wealth and power so many millions contributed? That country directed, in a great measure, the destinies of Europe: her influence extended to every quarter of the world. Her armies were trained to the art of war; her navy rode in triumph on every sea; her statesmen were subtle and sagacious; her generals skilful and practised. And more than all, her pride was aroused by the fact, that all Europe was an interested spectator of the scene, and was urging her forward to vindicate the policy she had adopted, and the principles which she had advanced.

But what will not union and firmness, valour and patriotism, accomplish? What will not *faith* accomplish? The colonies were, indeed, aware of the crisis at which they had arrived. They saw the precipice upon which they stood. National existence was at stake. Life, and liberty, and peace, were at hazard; not only those of the generation which then existed, but of the unnumbered millions which were yet to be born. To heaven they could, with pious confidence, make their solemn appeal. They trusted in the arm of Him, who had planted their fathers in this distant land, and besought Him to guide the men, who in his providence were called to preside over their public councils.

It was fortunate for them, and equally fortunate for the cause of rational liberty, that the delegates to the congress of 1776, were adequate to the great work which devolved upon them. They were not popular favourites, brought into notice during a season of tumult and violence; nor men chosen in times of tranquillity, when nothing is to be apprehended from a mistaken selection. "But they were men to whom others might cling in times of peril, and look up to in the revolution of empires, men whose countenances in marble, as on canvass, may be dwelt upon by after ages, as the history of the times." They were legislators and senators by birth, raised up by heaven for the accomplishment of a special and important object; to rescue a people groaning under oppression, and with the aid of their illustrious compeers, destined to establish rational liberty on a new basis, in an American republic.

They, too, well knew the responsibility of their station, and the fate which awaited themselves, if not their country, should their experiment fail. They came, therefore, to the question of a declaration of independence, like men who had counted the cost; prepared to rejoice, without any unholy triumph, should God smile upon the transaction; prepared also, if defeat should follow, to lead in the way to martyrdom.

A signature to the declaration of independence, without reference to general views, was, to each individual, a personal consideration of the most momentous import. It would be regarded in England as *treason*, and expose any man to the halter or the block. The only signature, which exhibits indications of a trembling hand, is that of *Stephen Hopkins*, who had been afflicted with the palsy. In this work of treason, *John Hancock* led the way, as president of the congress, and by warrantable. But the transaction contributed greatly to bring him into notice, and to increase his popularity.

This, and several similar occurrences, served as a pretext to the governor to introduce into Boston, not long after, several regiments of British troops; a measure which was fitted more than all others to irritate the inhabitants. Frequent collisions, as might be expected, soon happened between the soldiers and the citizens, the former of whom were insolent, and the latter independent. These contentions not long after broke out into acts of violence. An unhappy instance of this violence occurred on the evening of the 5th of March, 1770, at which time, a small party of British soldiers was assailed by several of the citizens, with balls of snow, and other weapons. The citizens were fired upon by order of the commanding officer: a few were killed, and several others were wounded.

Although the provocation, in this instance, was given by the citizens, the whole town was simultaneously aroused to seek redress. At the instigation of Samuel Adams, and Mr. Hancock, an assembly of the citizens was convened the following day, and these two gentlemen, with some others, were appointed a committee to demand of the governor the removal of the troops. Of this committee, Mr. Hancock was the chairman.

A few days after the above affray, which is usually termed "the Boston massacre," the bodies of the slain were buried with suitable demonstrations of public grief. In commemoration of the event, Mr. Hancock was appointed to deliver an address. After speaking of his attachment to a righteous government, and of his enmity to tyranny, he proceeded in the following animated strain: "The town of Boston, ever faithful to the British crown, has been invested by a British fleet; the troops of George the third have crossed the Atlantic, not to engage an enemy, but to assist a band of traitors in trampling on the rights and liberties of his most loyal subjects; those rights and liberties, which, as a father, he ought ever to regard, and as a king, he is bound in honour to defend from violation, even at the risk of his own life.

"These troops, upon their first arrival, took possession of our senate house, pointed their cannon against the judgment hall, and even continued them there, whilst the supreme court of the province was actually sitting to decide upon the lives and fortunes of the king's subjects. Our streets nightly resounded with the noise of their riot and debauchery; our peaceful citizens were hourly exposed to shameful insults, and often felt the effects of their violence and outrage. But this was not all; as though they thought it not enough to violate our civil rights, they endeavoured to deprive us of the enjoyment of our religious privileges; to vitiate our morals, and thereby render us deserving of destruction. Hence the rude din of arms, which broke in upon your solemn devotions in your temples, on that day hallowed by heaven, and set apart by God himself for his peculiar worship. Hence, impious oaths and blasphemies, so often tortured your unaccustomed ear Hence, all the arts which idleness and luxury could invent, were used to betray our youth of one sex into extravagance and effeminacy, and of the other to infamy and ruin; and have they not succeeded but too well? Has not a reverence for religion sensibly decayed? Have not our infants almost learned to lisp curses, before they knew their horrid import? Have not our youth forgotten they were Americans, and regardless of the admonitions of the wise and aged, copied, with a servile imitation, the frivolity and vices of their tyrants? And must I be compelled to acknowledge, that even the noblest, fairest part of all creation, have not entirely escaped their cruel snares?—or why have I seen an honest father clothed with shame; why a virtuous mother drowned in tears?

"But I forbear, and come reluctantly to the transactions of that dismal night, when in such quick succession we felt the extremes of grief, astonishment, and rage; when heaven in anger, for a dreadful moment suffered hell to take the reins; when satan, with his chosen band, opened the sluices of New-England's blood, and sacrilegiously polluted our land with the dead bodies of her guiltless sons.

"Let this sad tale of death never be told, without a tear; let not the heaving bosom cease to burn with a manly indigna tion at the relation of it, through the long tracks of future time; let every parent tell the shameful story to his listening children, till tears of pity glisten in their eyes, or boiling passion shakes their tender frames.

"Dark and designing knaves, murderers, parricides! How dare you tread upon the earth, which has drunk the blood of slaughtered innocence shed by your hands? How dare you breathe that air, which wafted to the ear of heaven the groans of those who fell a sacrifice to your accursed ambition?—But if the labouring earth doth not expand her jaws; if the air you breathe is not commissioned to be the minister of death; yet, hear it, and tremble! The eye of heaven penetrates the darkest chambers of the soul; and you, though screened from human observation, must be arraigned, must lift your hands, red with the blood of those whose death you have procured, at the tremendous bar of God.

"But I gladly quit this theme of death—I would not dwell too long upon the horrid effects, which have already followed, from quartering regular troops in this town; let our misfortunes instruct posterity to guard against these evils. Standing armies are sometimes, (I would by no means say generally, much less universally,) composed of persons who have rendered themselves unfit to live in civil society; who are equally indifferent to the glory of a George, or a Louis: who for the addition of one penny a day to their wages, would desert from the Christian cross, and fight under the crescent of the Turkish sultan; from such men as these what has not a state to fear? With such as these, usurping Cæsar passed the Rubicon; with such as these he humbled mighty Rome, and forced the mistress of the world to own a master in a traitor. These are the men whom sceptred robbers now employ to frustrate the designs of God, and render vain the bounties which his gracious hand pours indiscriminately upon his creatures."

Previously to this address, doubts had been entertained by some, as to the perfect patriotism of Mr. Hancock. It was said that the governor of the province had, either by studied civilities, or by direct overtures, endeavoured to attach him to the royal cause. For a time insinuations of this derogatory character were circulated abroad, highly detrimental to his fame. The manners and habits of Mr. Hancock had, not a little, contributed to countenance the malicious imputations His fortune was princely. His mansion displayed the magnificence of a courtier, rather than the simplicity of a republican. Gold and silver embroidery adorned his garments, and on public occasions, his carriage and horses, and servants in livery, emulated the splendour of the English nobility The eye of envy saw not this magnificence with indifference, nor was it strange that reports unfriendly to his patriotic integrity should have been circulated abroad; especially as from his wealth and fashionable intercourse, he had more connexion with the governor and his party than many others.

The sentiments, however, expressed by Hancock in the above address, were so explicit and so patriotic, as to convince the most incredulous; and a renovation of his popularity was the consequence.

Hancock, from this time, became as odious to the royal governor and his adherents, as he was dear to the republican party. It now became an object of some importance to the royal governor, to get possession of the persons of Mr. Hancock and Samuel Adams; and this is said to have been intended in the expedition to Concord, which led to the memorable battle of Lexington, the opening scene of the revolutionary war. Notwithstanding the secrecy with which that expedition was planned, these patriots, who were at the time members of the provincial congress at Concord, fortunately made their escape; but it was only at the moment the British troops entered the house where they lodged. Following this battle, Governor Gage issued his proclamation, offering a general pardon to all who should manifest a proper penitence for their opposition to the royal authority, excepting the above two gentlemen, whose guilt placed them beyond the reach of the royal clemency.

In October, 1774, Hancock was unanimously elected to the presidential chair of the provincial congress of Massachusetts. The following year, the still higher honour of the presidency of the continental congress was conferred upon him. In this body, were men of superior genius, and of still greater experience than Hancock. There were Franklin, and Jefferson, and Dickinson, and many others, men of pre-eminent abilities and superior political sagacity; but the recent proclamation of Governor Gage, proscribing Hancock and Adams, had given those gentlemen great popularity, and presented a sufficient reason to the continental congress, to express their respect for them, by the election of the former to the presidential chair.

In this distinguished station Hancock continued till October, 1777; at which time, in consequence of infirm health, induced by an unremitted application to business, he resigned his office, and, with a popularity seldom enjoyed by any individual, retired to his native province.

Of the convention, which, about this time, was appointed to frame a constitution for the state of Massachusetts, Hancock was a member. Under this constitution, in 1780, he was the first governor of the commonwealth, to which office he was annually elected, until the year 1785, when he resigned. After an interval of two years, he was re-elected to the same office, in which he was continued to the time of his death, which took place on the 8th of October, 1793, and in the 55th year of his age.

Of the character of Mr. Hancock, the limits which we have prescribed to ourselves, will permit us to say but little more. It was an honourable trait in that character, that while he possessed a superfluity of wealth, to the unrestrained enjoyment of which he came at an unguarded period of life, he avoided excessive indulgence and dissipation. His habits, through life, were uniformly on the side of virtue. In his disposition and manners, he was kind and courteous. He claimed no superiority from his advantages, and manifested no arrogance on account of his wealth.

His enemies accused him of an excessive fondness for popularity; to which fondness, envy and malice were not backward in ascribing his liberality on various occasions. Whatever may have been the justice of such an imputation, many examples of the generosity of his character are record-

Saml Adams

ed. Hundreds of families, it is said, in times of distress, were daily fed from his munificence. In promoting the liberties of his country, no one, perhaps, actually expended more wealth, or was willing to make greater sacrifices. An instance of his public spirit, in 1775, is recorded, much to his praise.

At that time, the American army was besieging Boston, to expel the British, who held possession of the town. To accomplish this object, the entire destruction of the city was proposed by the American officers. By the execution of such a plan, the whole fortune of Mr. Hancock would have been sacrificed. Yet he immediately acceded to the measure, declaring his readiness to surrender his all, whenever the liberties of his country should require it.

It is not less honourable to the character of Mr. Hancock, that while wealth and independence powerfully tempted him to a life of indolence, he devoted himself for many years, almost without intermission, to the most laborious service of his country. Malevolence, during some periods of his public life, aspersed his character, and imputed to him motives of conduct to which he was a stranger. Full justice was done to his memory at his death, in the expressions of grief and affection which were offered over his remains, by the multitudes who thronged his house while his body lay in state, and who followed his remains to the grave.

SAMUEL ADAMS.

Among those who signed the declaration of independence, and were conspicuous in the revolution, there existed, of course, a great diversity of intellectual endowments; nor did all render to their country, in those perilous days, the same important services. Like the luminaries of heaven, each contributed his portion of influence; but, like them, they differed, as star differeth from star in glory. But in the constellation of great men, which adorned that era, few shone with more brilliancy, or exercised a more powerful influence, than *Samuel Adams.*

This gentleman was born at Quincy, in Massachusetts, September 22d, 1722, in the neighbourhood afterwards rendered memorable as the birth place of Hancock, and as the residence of the distinguished family which has given two presidents to the United States. His descent was from a respectable family, which emigrated to America with the first settlers of the land.

In the year 1736, he became a member of Harvard University, where he was distinguished for an uncommon attention to all his collegiate exercises, and for his classical and scientific attainments. On taking the degree of master, in 1743, he proposed the following question, "Whether it be lawful to resist the supreme magistrate, if the commonwealth cannot be otherwise preserved?" He maintained the affirmative; and in this collegiate exercise furnished no dubious evidence of his attachment to the liberties of the people.

On leaving the university, he began the study of law, for which profession his father designed him; but at the solicitation of his mother, this pursuit was relinquished, and he became a clerk in the counting house of Thomas Cushing, at that time a distinguished merchant. But his genius was not adapted to mercantile pursuits; and in a short time after commencing business for himself, partly owing to the failure in business of a friend, and partly to injudicious management, he lost the entire capital which had been given him by his father.

The genius of Adams was naturally bent on politics. It was with him an all engrossing subject. From his earliest youth, he had felt its inspiration. It occupied his thoughts, enlivened his conversation, and employed his pen. In respect to his private business, this was an unfortunate trait of character; but most fortunate for his country, since he thus acquired an extensive knowledge of those principles of rational liberty, which he afterwards asserted with so much energy, in opposition to the arbitrary conduct of the British government.

In 1763 it was announced, that the British ministry had it in view to "tax the colonies, for the purpose of raising a revenue, which was to be placed at the disposal of the crown." This news filled the colonies with alarm. In Massachusetts, a committee was appointed by the people of Boston to express the public sentiment in relation to this contemplated measure, for the guidance of the representatives to the general court. The instructions of this committee were drawn by Mr. Adams. They formed, in truth, a powerful remonstrance against the injustice of the contemplated system of taxation; and they merit the more particular notice, as they were the first recorded public document, which denied the right of taxation to the British parliament. They also contained the first suggestion of the propriety of that mutual understanding and correspondence among the colonies, which laid the foundation of their future confederacy. In these instructions, after alluding to the evils which had resulted from the acts of the British parliament, relating to trade, Mr. Adams observes:—"If our trade may be taxed, why not our lands? Why not the produce of our lands, and every thing we possess, or use? This we conceive annihilates our charter rights to govern and tax ourselves. It strikes at our British privileges, which, as we have never forfeited, we hold in common with our fellow subjects, who are natives of Britain. If taxes are laid upon us in any shape, without our having a legal representation, where they are laid, we are reduced from the character of free subjects, to the state of tributary slaves. We, therefore, earnestly recommend it to you, to use your utmost endeavours to obtain from the general court, all necessary advice and instruction to our agent, at this most critical juncture." "We also desire you to use your endeavours, that the other colonies, having the same interests and rights with us, may add their weight to that of this province; that by united application of all who are agreed, all may obtain redress!"

The deep interest which Mr. Adams felt and manifested for

the rights of the colonies, soon brought him into favour with the patriotic party. He became a leader in their popular assemblies, and was bold in denouncing the unjust acts of the British ministry.

In 1765 he was elected a representative to the general court of Massachusetts, from the town of Boston. From this period, during the whole revolutionary struggle, he was the bold, persevering, and efficient supporter of the rights of his oppressed country. As a member of the court, he soon became conspicuous, and was honoured with the office of clerk to that body. In the legislature, he was characterized for the same activity and boldness which he had manifested in the town. He was appointed upon almost every committee, assisted in drawing nearly every report, and exercised a large share of influence, in almost every meeting, which had for its object the counteraction of the unjust plans of the administration.

But it was not in his legislative capacity alone, that Mr. Adams exhibited his hostility to the British government, and his regard for rational freedom. Several able essays on these subjects were published by him: and he was the author of several plans for opposing, more successfully, the unjust designs of the mother country. He has the honour of having suggested the first congress at New-York, which prepared the way for a Continental Congress, ten years after, and at length for the union and confederacy of the colonies.

The injudicious management of his private affairs, already alluded to, rendered Mr. Adams poor. When this was known in England, the partisans of the ministry proposed to bribe him, by the gift of some lucrative office. A suggestion of this kind was accordingly made to Governor Hutchinson, to which he replied in a manner highly complimentary to the *integrity* of Mr. Adams. "Such is the *obstinacy* and *inflexible disposition* of the man, that he never can be conciliated by any office or gift whatever." The offer, however, it is reported, was actually made to Mr. Adams, but neither the allurements of fortune or power could for a moment tempt him to abandon the cause of truth, or to hazard the liberties of the people.

He was indeed poor; but he could be tempted neither by British gold, nor by the honours or profits of any office within the gift of the royal governor. Such patriotism has not been common in the world; but in America it was to be found in many a bosom, during the revolutionary struggle. The knowledge of facts like this, greatly diminishes the wonder, which has sometimes been expressed, that America should have successfully contended with Great Britain. Her physical strength was comparatively weak; but the moral courage of her statesmen, and her soldiers, was to her instead of numbers, of wealth, and fortifications.

Allusion has been made, both in our introduction, and in our notice of Hancock, to the Boston massacre, in 1770, an event which will long remain memorable in the annals of the revolution, not only as it was the first instance of bloodshed between the British and the Americans, but as it conduced to increase the irritation, and to widen the breach between the two countries.

Our limits forbid a more particular account of this tragical affair; and it is again alluded to only for the purpose of bringing more distinctly into view, the intrepid and decisive conduct of Samuel Adams on that occasion.

On the morning following this night of bloodshed, a meeting of the citizens of Boston was called. Mingled emotions of horror and indignation pervaded the assembly. Samuel Adams first arose to address the listening multitude. Few men could harangue a popular assembly with greater energy, or exercise a more absolute control over their passions and affections. On that occasion, a Demosthenes, or a Chatham, could scarcely have addressed the assembled multitude with a more impressive eloquence, or have represented in a more just and emphatic manner, the fearful crisis to which the affairs of the colonies were fast tending. A committee was unanimously chosen to wait upon Governor Hutchinson, with a request that the troops might be immediately removed from the town. To the request of this committee, the governor, with his usual prevarication, replied, that the troops were not subject to his order. Mr. Adams, who was one of this committee, strongly represented to the governor the danger of retaining the troops longer in the capital. His indignation was aroused, and in a tone of lofty independence, he declared, that the removal of the troops would alone satisfy his insulted and indignant townsmen, it was, therefore, at the governor's peril, that they were continued in the town, and that he alone must be answerable for the fatal consequences, which it required no gift of prophecy to predict must ensue.

It was now dark. The meeting of the citizens was still undissolved. The greatest anxiety pervaded the assembly and scarcely were they restrained from going in a body to the governor, to learn his determination. Aware of the critical posture of affairs, aware of the personal hazard which he encountered by refusing a compliance, the governor at length gave his consent to the removal of the troops, and stipulated that the necessary preparations should commence on the following morning. Thus, through the decisive and spirited conduct of Samuel Adams, and a few other kindred spirits, the obstinacy of a royal governor was subdued, and further hostilities were for a still longer time suspended.

The popularity and influence of Mr. Adams were rapidly increasing, and the importance of his being detached from the popular party became every day more manifest. We have already noticed the suggestion to Governor Hutchinson to effect this, by the gift of some lucrative office. Other offers of a similar kind, it is reported, were made to him, at different times, by the royal authorities, but with the same ill success. About the year 1773, Governor Gage renewed the experiment. At that time Colonel Fenton was requested to wait upon Mr. Adams, with the assurance of Governor Gage, that any benefits would be conferred upon him which he should demand, on the condition of his ceasing to oppose the measures of the royal government. At the same time, it was not obscurely hinted, that such a measure was necessary, on personal considerations. He had incurred the royal displeasure, and already, such had been h... ... ... w... in the power of th...

governor to send him to England for trial, on a charge of treason. It was suggested that a change in his political conduct, might save him from this disgrace, and even from a severer fate; and might elevate him, moreover, from his circumstances of indigence, to the enjoyment of affluence.

To this proposal, Mr. Adams listened with attention; but as Col. Fenton concluded his communication, with all the spirit of a man of honour, with all the integrity of the most incorrupted and incorruptible patriotism, he replied; "Go tell Governor Gage, that my peace has long since been made with the King of kings, and that it is the advice of Samuel Adams to him, no longer to *insult the feelings of an already exasperated people.*"

The independence and sterling integrity of Mr. Adams, might well have secured to him the respect, and even confidence of Governor Gage; but with far different feelings did he regard the noble conduct of this high minded patriot. Under the irritation excited by the failure of a favourite plan, Governor Gage issued a proclamation, which comprehended the following language: "I do hereby," he said, "in his majesty's name, offer and promise his most gracious pardon to all persons, who shall forthwith lay down their arms, and return to the duties of peaceable subjects: excepting only from the benefits of such pardon, SAMUEL ADAMS, and JOHN HANCOCK, whose offences are of too flagitious a nature to admit of any other consideration but that of condign punishment."

Thus these independent men were singled out as the objects of peculiar vengeance, and even their lives endangered, for honourably resisting a temptation, to which, had they yielded, they would have merited the reproach of their countrymen, and the scorn of the world.

Mr. Adams was a member of the first continental congress, which assembled in Philadelphia on the 5th of September, 1774; and continued a member of that body until the year 1781. During this period, no delegate acted a more conspicuous or manly part. No one exhibited a more indefatigable zeal, or a firmer tone of character. He early saw that the conte͏͏ ͏ ͏ould probably not be decided ͏ ͏ ͏ ͏ ͏ ͏ ͏ ͏ ͏ ͏ ͏d.

He was himself prepared for every extremity, and was willing that such measures should be adopted, as should lead to an early issue of the controversy. He was accordingly among the warmest advocates for the declaration of American independence. In his view, the die was cast, and a further friendly connexion with the parent country was impossible. "I am perfectly satisfied," said he, in a letter written from Philadelphia, to a friend in Massachusetts, in April, 1776, "of the necessity of a public and explicit declaration of independence. I cannot conceive what good reason can be assigned against it. Will it widen the breach? This would be a strange question, after we have raised armies, and fought battles with the British troops; set up an American navy; permitted the inhabitants of these colonies to fit out armed vessels, to capture the ships, &c. belonging to any of the inhabitants of Great Britain; declaring them the enemies of the United Colonies; and torn into shivers their acts of trade, by allowing commerce, subject to regulations to be made by ourselves, with the people of all countries, except such as are subject to the British king. It cannot surely, after all this, be imagined that we consider ourselves, or mean to be considered by others, in any other state, than that of independence."

The independence of America was at length declared, and gave a new political character, and an immediate dignity to the cause of the colonies. But notwithstanding this measure might itself bear the aspect of victory, a formidable contest yet awaited the Americans. The year following the declaration of independence, the situation of the colonies was extremely gloomy. The stoutest hearts trembled within them, and even doubts were expressed, whether the measures which had been adopted, particularly the declaration of independence, were not precipitate. The neighbourhood of Philadelphia became the seat of war; congress, now reduced to only twenty-eight members, had resolved to remove their session to Lancaster. At this critical period, Mr. Adams accidentally fell in company with several other members, by whom the subject of the state of the country was freely and confidentially discussed.

pervade their minds, and the greatest anxiety was expressed as to the issue of the contest.

To this conversation, Mr. Adams listened with silent attention. At length he expressed his surprise, that such desponding feelings should have settled upon *their* hearts, and such desponding language should be even *confidentially* uttered by *their* lips. To this it was answered, "The chance is desperate." "Indeed, indeed, it is desperate," said Mr. Adams, "if this be *our* language. If *we* wear long faces, others will do so too; if we despair, let us not expect that others will hope; or that they will persevere in a contest, from which their leaders shrink. But let not such feelings, let not such language, be ours." Thus, while the hearts of others were ready to faint, Samuel Adams maintained his usual firmness. His unshaken courage, and his calm reliance upon the aid and protection of heaven, contributed in an eminent degree to inspire his countrymen with a confidence of their final success. A higher encomium could not have been bestowed on any member of the continental congress, than is expressed in relation to Mr. Adams by Mr. Galloway, in his historical and political reflections on the rise and progress of the American rebellion, published in Great Britain, 1780. "He eats little," says the author, "drinks little, sleeps little, thinks much, and is most indefatigable in the pursuit of his object. It was this man, who by his superior application, managed at once the factions in congress at Philadelphia, and the factions of New-England."

In 1781, Mr. Adams retired from congress; but it was to receive from his native state, additional proofs of her high estimation of his services, and of the confidence which she reposed in his talents and integrity. He had already been an active member of the convention that formed her constitution, and after it went into effect, he was placed in the senate of the state, and for several years presided over that body. In 1789, he was elected lieutenant governor, and held that office till 1794; when, upon the death of Hancock, he was chosen governor, and was annually re-elected till 1797, when he retired from public life. This retirement, however,

M 8*

he did not long enjoy, as his death occurred on October 2d, 1803, at the advanced age of 82.

From the foregoing sketches of Mr. Adams, it will not be difficult for the reader to form a tolerably correct opinion of his character and disposition. In his person, he is said to have been only of the middle size, but his countenance indicated a noble genius within, and a more than ordinary inflexibility of character and purpose. Great sincerity and simplicity marked his manners and deportment. In his conversation, he was at once interesting and instructive; and those who shared his friendship had seldom any reason to doubt his affection and constancy. His writings were voluminous, but unfortunately, as they generally related to the temporary politics of the day, most of them are lost. Those which remain furnish abundant proof of his superiority as a writer, of the soundness of his political creed, and of the piety and sincerity of his character. As an orator, he was eminently fitted for the stormy times in which he lived. His elocution was concise and impressive, partaking more of the logical than the figurative, and rather calculated to enlighten the understanding, than to excite the feelings. Yet no man could address himself more powerfully to the passions, than he did, on certain occasions. As a statesman, his views were broad and enlightened; what his judgment had once matured, he pursued with inflexible firmness, and patriotic ardour. While others desponded, he was full of hope; where others hesitated, he was resolute; where others were supine, he was eager for action. His circumstances of indigence led him to habits of simplicity and frugality; but beyond this, he was naturally averse to parade and ostentation.

"Mr. Adams was a christian. His mind was early imbued with piety, as well as cultivated by science. He early approached the table of the Lord Jesus, and the purity of his life witnessed the sincerity of his profession. On the christian sabbath, he constantly went to the temple, and the morning and evening devotions in his family proved, that his religion attended him in his seasons of retirement from the world. The last production of his pen was in favour of Christian truth. He died in the faith of the gospel."

In his opposition to British tyranny, no man was more conscientious, he detested royalty, and despised the ostentation and contemptible servility of the royal agents; his patriotism was of a pure and lofty character. For his country he laboured both by night and by day, with a zeal which was scarcely interrupted, and with an energy that knew no fatigue. Although enthusiastic, he was still prudent. He would persuade, petition, and remonstrate, where these would accomplish his object; but when these failed, he was ready to resist even unto blood, and would sooner have sacrificed his life than yielded with dishonour. "Had he lived in any country or epoch," says his biographer, "when abuses of power were to be resisted, he would have been one of the reformers. He would have suffered excommunication, rather than have bowed to papal infallibility, or paid tribute to St. Peter; he would have gone to the stake, rather than submit to the prelatic ordinances of Laud; he would have mounted the scaffold, sooner than pay a shilling of illegal ship-money; he would have fled to a desert, rather than endure the profligate tyranny of a Stuart; he was proscribed, and would sooner have been condemned as a traitor, than assent to an illegal tax, if it had been only a sixpenny stamp or an insignificant duty on tea; and there appeared to be no species of corruption by which this inflexibility could have been destroyed."

In the delegation of political power, he may be said to have been too cautious, since our constitutions, as he would have modelled them, would not have had sufficient inherent force for their own preservation. One of his colleagues thus honourably described him: "Samuel Adams would have the state of Massachusetts govern the union; the town of Boston govern Massachusetts; and that he should govern the town of Boston, and then the whole would not be intentionally ill governed."

With some apparent austerity, there was nothing of the spirit of gloom or arrogance about him. In his demeanour, he combined mildness with firmness, and dignity with condescension. If sometimes an advocate for measures which might be thought too strong, it was, perhaps, because his comprehension extended beyond ordinary minds, and he had more energy to effect his purposes, than attaches to common men. In addition to these qualities, he manifested an uncommon indifference to pecuniary considerations; he was poor while he lived, and had not the death of an only son relieved his latter day poverty, Samuel Adams, notwithstanding his virtues, his patriotism, his unwearied zeal, and his acknowledged usefulness, while he lived, would have had to claim a burial at the hand of charity, or at the public expense.

JOHN ADAMS.

JOHN ADAMS was born at Quincy, then part of the ancient town of Braintree, on the 19th day of October, old style, 1735. He was a descendant of the Puritans, his ancestors having early emigrated from England, and settled in Massachusetts. Discovering early a strong love of reading and of knowledge, proper care was taken by his father to provide for his education. His youthful studies were prosecuted in Braintree, under Mr. Marsh, a gentleman whose fortune it was to instruct several children, who in manhood were destined to act a conspicuous part in the scenes of the revolution.

He became a member of Harvard College, 1751, and was graduated in course in 1755: with what degree of reputation he left the university is not now precisely known; we only know that he was distinguished in a class of which the Reverend Dr. Hemmenway was a member, who bore honourable testimony to the openness and decision of his character, and to the strength and activity of his mind.

Having chosen the law for his profession, he commenced and prosecuted its studies under the direction of Samuel Putnam, a barrister of eminence at Worcester. By him he was introduced to the celebrated Jeremy Gridley, then attorney general of the province of Massachusetts Bay. At the first interview they became friends, Gridley at once proposed Mr. Adams for admission to the bar of Suffolk, and took him into special favour. Soon after his admission, Mr. Gridley led his young friend into a private chamber with an air of secrecy, and, pointing to a book case, said, "Sir, there is the secret of my eminence, and of which you may avail yourself as you please." It was a pretty good collection of treatises of the civil law. In this place Mr. Adams spent his days and nights, until he had made himself master of the principles of the code.

From early life, the bent of his mind was towards politics, a propensity which the state of the times, if it did not create, doubtless very much strengthened. While a resident at Worcester, he wrote a letter of which the following is an extract. The letter was dated October 12th, 1755. "Soon after the reformation, a few people came over into this new world for conscience sake: perhaps this apparently trivial incident may transfer the great seat of empire into America. It looks likely to me; for, if we can remove the turbulent Gallicks, our people, according to the exactest computations, will in another century become more numerous than England itself. Should this be the case, since we have, I may say, all the naval stores of the nation in our hands, it will be easy to obtain a mastery of the seas; and the united force of all Europe will not be able to subdue us. The only way to keep us from setting up for ourselves is to disunite us.

"Be not surprised that I am turned politician. This whole town is immersed in politics. The interests of nations and all the *dira* of war make the subject of every conversation. I sit and hear, and after having been led through a maze of sage observations, I sometimes retire, and lay things together, and form some reflections pleasing to myself. The produce of one of these reveries you have read."

This prognostication of independence, and of so vast an increase of numbers, and of naval force, as might defy all Europe, is remarkable, especially as coming from so young a man, and so early in the history of the country. It is more remarkable that its author should have lived to see fulfilled to the letter, what would have seemed to others at the time, but the extravagance of youthful fancy. His early political feelings were thus strongly American, and from this ardent attachment to his native soil he never departed.

In 1758 he was admitted to the bar, and commenced business in Braintree. He is understood to have made his first considerable effort, or to have obtained his most signal success, at Plymouth, in a jury trial, and a criminal cause. In 1765, Mr. Adams laid before the public his "Essay on the Canon and Feudal Law," a work distinguished for its power and eloquence. The object of this work was to show, that our New-England ancestors, in consenting to exile themselves from their native land, were actuated mainly by the desire of delivering themselves from the power of the hierarchy, and from the monarchical, aristocratical, and political system of the other continent; and to make this truth bear with effect on the politics of the times. Its tone is uncommonly bold and animated for that period. He calls on the people not only to defend, but to study and understand their rights and privileges; and urges earnestly the necessity of diffusing general knowledge.

In conclusion, he exclaims, "let the *pulpit* resound with the doctrines and sentiments of religious liberty. Let us hear the danger of thraldom to our consciences, from ignorance, extreme poverty and dependence, in short, from civil and political slavery. Let us see delineated before us, the true map of man—let us hear the dignity of his nature, and the noble rank he holds among the works of God! that consenting to slavery is a sacrilegious breach of trust, as offensive in the sight of God, as it is derogatory from our own honour, or interest, or happiness; and that God Almighty has promulgated from heaven, liberty, peace, and good will to man.

"Let the *bar* proclaim the laws, the rights, the generous plan of power delivered down from remote antiquity; inform the world of the mighty struggles and numberless sacrifices made by our ancestors in the defence of freedom. Let it be known that British liberties are not the grants of princes or parliaments, but original rights, conditions of original contracts, cocqual with prerogative, and coeval with government. That many of our rights are inherent and essential, agreed on as maxims and established as preliminaries even before a parliament existed. Let them search for the foundation of British laws and government in the frame of human nature, in the constitution of the intellectual and moral world. There let us see that truth, liberty, justice, and benevolence, are its everlasting basis; and if these could be removed, the superstructure is overthrown of course.

"Let the *colleges* join their harmony in the same delightful concert. Let every declamation turn upon the beauty of liberty and virtue, and the deformity, turpitude, and malignity of slavery and vice. Let the public disputations become researches into the grounds, nature, and ends of government, and the means of preserving the good and demolishing the evil. Let the dialogues and all the exercises become the instruments of impressing on the tender mind, and of spreading and distributing far and wide the ideas of right, and the sensations of freedom."

In 1766, Mr. Adams removed his residence to Boston, still continuing his attendance on the neighbouring circuits, and not unfrequently called to remote parts of the province.

In 1770 occurred, as has already been noticed, the "Boston massacre." Mr. Adams was solicited by the British officers and soldiers to undertake their defence, on the indictment found against them, for their share in that tragical scene. This was a severe test of his professional firmness. He was well aware of the popular indignation against these prisoners, and he was at that time a representative of Boston in the general court, an office which depended entirely upon popular favour. But he knew that it was due to his profession, and to himself, to undertake their defence, and to hazard the consequences. "The trial was well managed. The captain was severed in his trial from the soldiers, who were tried first, and their defence rested in part upon the orders, real or supposed, given by the officer to his men to in a good measure successful. On the trial of Capt. Preston, no such order to fire could be proved. The result was, as it should have been, an acquittal. It was a glorious thing that the counsel and jury had nerve sufficient to breast the torrent of public feeling. It showed Britain that she had not a mere mob to deal with, but resolute and determined men, who could restrain themselves. *Such men are dangerous to arbitrary power.*"

The event proved, that as he judged well for his own reputation, so he judged well for the interest and permanent fame of his country. The same year he was elected one of the representatives in the general assembly, an honour to which the people would not have called him, had he lost their confidence and affection.

In the year 1773, and 1774, he was chosen a counsellor by the members of the general court; but was rejected by Governor Hutchinson, in the former of these years, and by Governor Gage, in the latter.

In this latter year, he was appointed a member of the continental congress, from Massachusetts. "This appointment was made at Salem, where the general court had been convened by Governor Gage, in the last hour of the existence of a house of representatives, under the provincial charter While engaged in this important business, the governor having been informed of what was passing, sent his secretary with a message, dissolving the general court. The secretary finding the door locked, directed the messenger to go in, and inform the speaker that the secretary was at the door, with a message from the governor. The messenger returned, and informed the secretary that the orders of the house were, that the doors should be kept fast; whereupon the secretary soon after read a proclamation, dissolving the general court, upon the stairs. Thus terminated, forever, the actual exercise of the political power of England in or over Massachusetts."

On the meeting of congress in Philadelphia, 1774, Mr. Adams appeared and took his seat. To talents of the highest order, and the most commanding eloquence, he added an honest devotion to the cause of his country, and a firmness of character, for which he was distinguished through life. Prior to that period he had, upon all occasions, stood forth openly in defence of the rights of his country, and in opposition to the injustice and encroachments of Great Britain. He boldly opposed them by his advice, his actions, and his eloquence; and, with other worthies, succeeded in spreading among the people a proper alarm for their liberties. Mr. Adams was placed upon the first and most important committees. During the first year, addresses were prepared to the king, to the people of England, of Ireland, Canada, and Jamaica. The name of Mr. Adams is found upon almost all those important committees. His firmness and eloquence in debate, soon gave him a standing among the highest in that august body.

The proceedings of this congress have already passed in review. Among the members, a variety of opinions seem to have prevailed, as to the probable issue of the contest, in which the country was engaged. On this subject, Mr. Adams, a few years before his death, expressed himself, in a letter to a friend, as follows: "When congress had finished their business, as they thought, in the autumn of 1774, I had with Mr. Henry, before we took leave of each other, some familiar conversation, in which I expressed a full conviction that our resolves, declaration of rights, enumeration of wrongs, petitions, remonstrances, and addresses, associations, and non-importation agreements, however they might be viewed in America, and however necessary to cement the union of the colonies, would be but waste water in England. Mr. Henry said, they might make some impression among the people of England, but agreed with me, that they would be totally lost upon the government. I had but just received a short and hasty letter, written to me by Major Joseph Hawley, of Northampton, containing a few broken hints, as he called them, of what he thought was proper to be done, and concluding with these words, 'after all, we must *fight*.' This letter I read to Mr. Henry, who listened with great attention, and as soon as I had pronounced the words, 'after all, we must fight,' he raised his head, and, with an energy and vehemence that I can never forget, broke out with, 'I am of that man's mind.' I put the letter into his hand, and when he had read it he returned it to me, with an equally solemn asseveration, that he agreed entirely in opinion with the writer.

"The other delegates from Virginia returned to their state in full confidence that all our grievances would be redressed. The last words that Mr. Richard Henry Lee said to me, when we parted, were, 'we shall infallibly carry all our points You will be completely relieved; all the offensive acts will be repealed; the army and fleet will be recalled, and Britain will give up her foolish project.'

"Washington only was in doubt. He never spoke in public. In private, he joined with those who advocated a non-exportation, as well as a non-importation agreement. With both, he thought we should prevail; without either, he thought it doubtful. Henry was clear in one opinion, Richard Henry Lee in an opposite opinion, and Washington doubted between the two."

On the 15th day of June, the continental congress appointed General Washington commander in chief of the American armies. To Mr. Adams is ascribed the honour of having suggested and advocated the choice of this illustrious man. When first suggested by Mr. Adams, to a few of his confidential friends in Congress, the proposition was received with a marked disapprobation. Washington, at this time, was almost a stranger to them; and, besides, to elevate a man who had never held a higher military rank than that of colonel, over officers of the highest grade in the militia, and those, too, already in the field, appeared not only irregular, but likely to produce much dissatisfaction among them, and the people at large. To Mr. Adams, however, the greatest advantage appeared likely to result from the choice of Washington, whose character and peculiar fitness for the station he well understood. Samuel Adams, his distinguished colleague, coincided with him in these views, and through their instrumentality this felicitous choice was effected. When a majority in congress had been secured, Mr. Adams introduced the subject of appointing a commander in chief of the armies, and having sketched the qualifications which should be found in the man to be elevated to so responsible a station, he concluded by nominating George Washington, of Virginia, to the office.

To Washington, himself, nothing could have been more unexpected. Until that moment he was ignorant of the intended nomination. The proposal was seconded by Samuel Adams, and the following day it received the unanimous approbation of congress.

When Mr. Adams was first made a member of the continental congress, it was hinted that he, at *that time*, inclined to a separation of the colonies from England, and the establishment of an independent government. On his way to Philadelphia, he was warned, by several advisers, not to introduce a subject of so delicate a character, until the affairs of the country should wear a different aspect. Whether Mr. Adams needed this admonition or not, will not, in this place, be determined. But in 1776, the affairs of the colonies, it could no longer be questioned, demanded at least the candid discussion of the subject. On the 6th of May, of that year, Mr. Adams offered, in committee of the whole, a resolution that the colonies should form governments independent of the crown. On the 10th of May, this resolution was adopted, in the following shape: "That it be recommended to all the colonies, which had not already established governments suited to the exigencies of their case, to adopt such governments as would, in the opinion of the representatives of the people, best conduce to the happiness and safety of their constituents in particular, and Americans in general."

"This significant vote was soon followed by the direct proposition, which RICHARD HENRY LEE had the honour to submit to congress, by resolution, on the 7th day of June. The published journal does not expressly state it, but there is no doubt that this resolution was in the same words, when originally submitted by Mr. Lee, as when finally passed. Having been discussed on Saturday the 8th, and Monday the

10th of June, this resolution was, on the last mentioned day, postponed for further consideration to the first day of July, and at the same time it was voted, that a committee be appointed to prepare a DECLARATION, to the effect of the resolution. This committee was elected by ballot on the following day, and consisted of THOMAS JEFFERSON, JOHN ADAMS, BENJAMIN FRANKLIN, ROGER SHERMAN, and ROBERT R. LIVINGSTON."

It is usual when committees are elected by ballot, that their members are arranged in order, according to the number of votes which each has received. Mr. Jefferson, therefore, probably received the highest, and Mr. Adams the next highest number of votes. The difference is said to have been but a single vote.

Mr. Jefferson and Mr. Adams, standing thus at the head of the committee, were requested by the other members, to act as a sub-committee to prepare the draft, and Mr. Jefferson drew up the paper. The original draft, as brought by him from his study, and submitted to the other members of the committee, with interlineations in the hand writing of Dr. Franklin, and others in that of Mr. Adams, was in Mr. Jefferson's possession at the time of his death. The merit of this paper is Mr. Jefferson's. Some changes were made in it, on the suggestion of other members of the committee, and others by Congress, while it was under discussion. But none of them altered the tone, the frame, the arrangement, or the general character of the instrument. As a composition, the declaration is Mr. Jefferson's. It is the production of his mind, and the high honour of it belongs to him clearly and absolutely.

"While Mr. Jefferson was the author of the declaration itself, Mr. Adams was its great supporter on the floor of Congress. This was the unequivocal testimony of Mr. Jefferson. 'John Adams,' said he, on one occasion, 'was our Colossus on the floor; not graceful, not elegant, not always fluent in his public addresses, he yet came out with a power, both of thought and of expression, that moved us from our seats;" and at another time, he said, 'John Adams was the pillar of its suppo defender against the multifarious assaults, which were made against it.'"

On the second day of July, the resolution of independence was adopted, and on the fourth, the declaration itself was unanimously agreed to. Language can scarcely describe the transport of Mr. Adams at this time. He has best described them himself, in a letter written the day following, to his wife. "Yesterday," says he, "the greatest question was decided that was ever debated in America; and greater, perhaps, never was or will be decided among men. A resolution was passed, without one dissenting colony, 'That these United States are, and of right ought to be, free and independent states.' The day is passed. The 4th of July, 1776, will be a memorable epoch in the history of America. I am apt to believe it will be celebrated by succeeding generations as the great anniversary festival. It ought to be commemorated as the day of deliverance, by solemn acts of devotion to Almighty God. It ought to be solemnized with pomp, shows, games, sports, guns, bells, bonfires, and illuminations, from one end of the continent to the other, from this time forward, forever. You will think me transported with enthusiasm, but I am not. I am well aware of the toil, and blood, and treasure, that it will cost to maintain this declaration, and support and defend these states; yet through all the gloom, I can see the rays of light and glory. I can see that the end is worth more than all the means; and that posterity will triumph, although you and I may rue, which I hope we shall not."

About the time of the declaration of independence, occurred the disastrous battle of Flatbush on Long Island. The victory thus gained by the British, was considered by Lord Howe as a favourable moment for proposing to congress an accommodation; and for this purpose, he requested an interview with some of the members. In the deliberations of congress, Mr. Adams opposed this proposal, on the ground that no accommodation could thus be effected.

A committee, however, was appointed to wait on Lord Howe, consisting of himself, Dr. Franklin, and Mr. Rutledge. On being apprised of their intended interview, Lord Howe sent one of his principal officers as a hostage, but the commissioners taking him with them, fearlessly repaired to the British camp. On their arrival, they were conducted through an army of twenty thousand men, drawn up for the purpose of show and impression. But the display was lost on the commissioners, who studiously avoided all signs of wonder or anxiety. As had been predicted by Mr. Adams, the interview terminated without any beneficial result. On being introduced, Lord Howe informed them that he could not treat with them as a committee of congress, but only as private gentlemen of influence in the colonies; to which Mr. Adams replied, "You may view me in any light you please, sir, except that of a British subject."

During the remainder of the year 1776, and all 1777, Mr. Adams was deeply engaged in the affairs of congress. He served as a member of ninety different committees, and was chairman of twenty-five committees. From his multiform and severe labours he was relieved in December of the latter year, by the appointment of commissioner to France, in the place of Silas Deane.

In February, 1778, he embarked for that country on board of the frigate Boston. On his arrival in France, he found that Dr Franklin, and Arthur Lee, who had been appointed commissioners the preceding year, and were then in France, had already concluded a treaty with the French government. Little business, therefore, of a public nature was left him to do. In the summer of 1779, he returned to America.

About the time of his arrival, the people of Massachusetts were adopting measures for calling a convention to form a new state constitution. Of this convention he was elected a member, and was also a member of the committee appointed by the convention to report a plan for their consideration. A plan which he drew up was accepted, and was made the basis of the constitution of that state.

In the August following, in consequence of an informal suggestion from the court of St. James, he received the appointment of minister plenipotentiary for negotiating a treaty of peace, and a treaty of commerce, with Great Britain. A salary of twenty-five hundred pounds sterling was voted him. In the month of October, he embarked on board the French ship La Sensible, and after a tedious voyage was landed at Ferrol, in Spain, whence he proceeded to Paris, where he arrived in the month of February. He there communicated with Dr. Franklin, who was at that time envoy of the United States at the court of France, and with the Count de Vergennes, the French prime minister. But the British government, it was found, were not disposed to peace, and the day seemed far distant when any negotiation could be opened with a hope of success. Mr. Adams, however, was so useful in various ways, that towards the close of the year, congress honoured him by a vote of thanks, "for his industrious attention to the interest and honour of these United States abroad."

In June, 1780, congress being informed that Mr. Laurens, who had been appointed to negotiate a loan in Holland for the United States, had been taken prisoner by the English, forwarded a commission to Mr. Adams to proceed to Holland, for the above purpose. To this, soon after, was added the new appointment of commissioner to conclude a treaty of amity and commerce with the States General of Holland; and, at the same time, authority was given him to pledge the faith of the United States to the "armed neutrality" proposed by the Russian government.

Mr. Adams repaired with promptitude to Holland, and engaged with great zeal in the business of his commission. From this station he was suddenly summoned by the Count de Vergennes, to consult, at Paris, with regard to a project for a general peace, suggested by the courts of Vienna and St. Petersburgh.

This was one of the most anxious periods in the eventful life of Mr. Adams. France was, indeed, ready to fulfil her guaranty of independence to the United States; but it was the politic aim of the Count de Vergennes, to secure important advantages for his own country, in the settlement of American difficulties. Hence, no effort was spared to make Mr. Adams, in this important matter, the subordinate agent of the French cabinet. He, on the other hand, regarded solely the interests of the United States, and the instructions of congress; and his obstinate independence, unshaken by the alternate threats and blandishments of the court of Versailles, occasioned an effort by the Count de Vergennes to obtain, through the French minister in Philadelphia, such a modification of the instructions to Mr. Adams, as should subject him to the direction of the French cabinet.

The effect of this artful and strenuous measure was, a determination on the part of congress, that Mr. Adams should hold the most confidential intercourse with the French ministers; and should "undertake nothing in the negotiation of a peace, or truce, without their knowledge and concurrence."

Under these humiliating restrictions, the independent and decisive spirit of Mr. Adams was severely tried. The imperial mediators proposed an armistice, but without any withdrawal of troops from America. Mr. Adams firmly opposed this stipulation; and the negotiation proceeded no further at that time.

It was, obviously, the policy of the French minister, not to facilitate the peace between Great Britain and the United States, without previously securing to France a large share in the fisheries, and at the same time so establishing the western boundary, as to sacrifice the interests of the United States to those of Spain.

Finding all attempts at negotiation unavailing, Mr. Adams returned to Holland.

Meantime, the apprehensions of congress being much excited by the insinuations of the French minister in Philadelphia, they added to the commission for forming a treaty with Great Britain, Dr. Franklin, then plenipotentiary at Paris; Mr. Jay, the minister at Madrid; Mr. Henry Laurens, who had recently been appointed special minister to France; and Mr. Jefferson. The whole were instructed to govern themselves by the advice and opinion of the ministers of the king of France. This unaccountable and dishonourable concession, in effect, made the Count de Vergennes minister plenipotentiary for the United States.

But the indefatigable exertions of Mr. Adams in Holland, had a most important bearing upon the proposed negotiations. By a laborious and striking exhibition of the situation and resources of the United States, he succeeded in so far influencing public opinion, as to obtain a loan of eight millions of guilders, on reasonable terms. This loan, effected in the autumn of 1782, was soon followed by a treaty of amity and commerce with Holland, recognizing the United States as independent and sovereign states.

The disposition towards peace, on the part of the English ministry, was wonderfully quickened by the favourable negotiation of this loan. During Lord Shelburne's administration, the independence of the states was unconditionally acknowledged, and the first effectual steps were taken to put an end to the war.

During the negotiations that followed, the disposition of France again evinced itself, to cut off the United States from a share of the fisheries, and to transfer a portion of the American territory to Spain. The American commissioners, therefore, were not a little embarrassed by their instructions from congress, to govern themselves by the opinion and advice of the French minister. But, as Mr. Adams had, on a former occasion, found it necessary to depart from instructions of a similar import; the other commissioners now joined with him, in the determination to secure the best interests of their country, regardless of the interference of the French minister, and of the inconsiderate restrictions imposed on them by congress.

Accordingly, provisional articles were signed by them, on the 30th of November, 1782; and this measure was followed by an advantageous definitive treaty in September, 1783.

Mr. Adams spent a part of the year 1784 in Holland, but returned eventually to Paris, on being placed at the head of a commission, with Dr. Franklin and Mr. Jefferson as coadjutors, to negotiate several commercial treaties with different foreign nations.

Near the commencement of the year 1785, congress resolved to send a minister plenipotentiary to represent the

United States at the court of St. James. To this responsible station, rendered peculiarly delicate by the fact that the United States had so recently and reluctantly been acknowledged as an independent nation, Mr. Adams was appointed. It was doubtful in what manner and with what spirit an American minister would be received by the British government. On leaving America, Mr. Jay, the then secretary of state, among other instructions, used the following language " The manner of your reception at that court, and its temper, views, and dispositions respecting American objects. are matters concerning which particular information might be no less useful than interesting. Your letters will, I am persuaded, remove all suspense on those points."

In accordance with this direction, Mr. Adams subsequently forwarded to Mr. Jay the following interesting account of his presentation to the king.

"During my interview with the marquis of Carmarthen, he told me it was customary for every foreign minister, at his first presentation to the king, to make his majesty some compliments conformable to the spirit of his credentials; and when Sir Clement Cottrel Dormer, the master of ceremonies, came to inform me that he should accompany me to the secretary of state, and to court, he said, that every foreign minister whom he had attended to the queen, had always made an harangue to her majesty, and he understood, though he had not been present, that they always harangued the king. On Tuesday evening, the Baron de Lynden (Dutch ambassador) called upon me, and said he came from the Baron de Nolkin, (Swedish envoy,) and had been conversing upon the singular situation I was in, and they agreed in opinion that it was indispensable that I should make a speech, and that it should be as complimentary as possible. All this was parallel to the advice lately given by the Count de Vergennes to Mr. Jefferson. So that finding it was a custom established at both these great courts. that this court and the foreign ministers expected it, I thought I could not avoid it, although my first thought and inclination had been to deliver my credentials silently and retire. At one, on Wednesday the first of June, the master of ceremonies called at my house, and went with me to the secretary of state's office, in Cleveland Row, where the marquis of Carmarthen received me, and introduced me to Mr. Frazier, his under secretary, who had been, as his lordship said, uninterruptedly in that office through all the changes in administration for thirty years, having first been appointed by the earl of Holderness. After a short conversation upon the subject of importing my effects from Holland and France, free of duty, which Mr. Frazier himself introduced, Lord Carmarthen invited me to go with him in his coach to court. When we arrived in the antichamber, the œil-de-bœuf of St. James's, the master of the ceremonies met me, and attended me, while the secretary of state went to take the commands of the king. While I stood in this place, where it seems all ministers stand on such occasions, always attended by the master of ceremonies, the room very full of courtiers, as well as the next room, which is the king's bed chamber, you may well suppose, that I was the focus of all eyes.

"I was relieved, however, from the embarrassment of it by the Swedish and Dutch ministers, who came to me and entertained me in a very agreeable conversation during the whole time. Some other gentlemen whom I had seen before came to make their compliments too, until the marquis of Carmarthen returned, and desired me to go with him to his majesty: I went with his lordship through the levee room into the king's closet; the door was shut, and I was left with his majesty and the secretary of state alone. I made the three reverences, one at the door, another about half way, and the third before the presence, according to the usage established at this and all the northern courts of Europe, and then addressed myself to his majesty in the following words.

"'Sir, the United States have appointed me their minister plenipotentiary to your majesty, and have directed me to deliver to your majesty this letter, which contains the evidence of it. It is in obedience to their express commands, that I have the honour to assure your majesty of their unanimous disposition and desire to cultivate the most friendly and liberal intercourse between your majesty's subjects and their citizens, and of their best wishes for your majesty's health and happiness, and for that of your royal family.

"The appointment of a minister from the United States to your majesty's court, will form an epoch in the history of England and America. I think myself more fortunate than all my fellow citizens, in having the distinguished honour to be the first to stand in your majesty's royal presence in a diplomatic character; and I shall esteem myself the happiest of men, if I can be instrumental in recommending my country more and more to your majesty's royal benevolence, and of restoring an entire esteem, confidence, and affection, or in better words, 'the old good nature, and the old good humour,' between people who, though separated by an ocean, and under different governments, have the same language, a similar religion, and kindred blood. I beg your majesty's permission to add, that although I have sometimes before been entrusted by my country, it was never, in my whole life, in a manner so agreeable to myself.'

"The king listened to every word I said, with dignity, it is true, but with an apparent emotion. Whether it was the nature of the interview, or whether it was my visible agitation, for I felt more than I did or could express, that touched him, I cannot say, but he was much affected, and answered me with more tremor than I had spoken with, and said:

"'Sir, the circumstances of this audience are so extraordinary, the language you have now held is so extremely proper, and the feelings you have discovered so justly adapted to the occasion, that I must say, that I not only receive with pleasure the assurances of the friendly disposition of the people of the United States, but that I am very glad the choice has fallen upon you to be their minister. I wish you, sir, to believe, and that it may be understood in America, that I have done nothing in the late contest but what I thought myself indispensably bound to do, by the duty which I owed to my people. I will be very frank with you. I was the last to conform to the separation; but the separation having been made, ar say now, that I would be the first to meet the friendship of the United States, as an independent power. The moment I see such sentiments and language as yours prevail, and a disposition to give this country the preference, that moment I shall say, let the circumstances of language, religion, and blood, have their natural and full effect.'

" I dare not say that these were the king's precise words, and it is even possible that I may have, in some particular, mistaken his meaning; for although his pronunciation is as distinct as I ever heard, he hesitated sometimes between his periods, and between the members of the same period. He was, indeed, much affected, and I was not less so ; and, therefore, I cannot be certain that I was so attentive, heard so clearly, and understood so perfectly, as to be confident of all his words or sense ; this I do say, that the foregoing is his majesty's meaning, as I then understood it, and his own words, as nearly as I can recollect."

The year following, 1788, Mr. Adams requested permission to resign his office, which, being granted, after an absence of between eight and nine years, he returned to his native country. The new government was, at that time, about going into operation. In the autumn of 1788, he was elected vice president of the United States, a situation which he filled, with reputation for eight years.

On the retirement of General Washington from the presidency, in 1796, Mr. Adams was a candidate for that elevated station. At this time, two parties had been formed in the United States. At the head of one stood Mr. Hamilton and Mr. Adams, and at the head of the other stood Mr. Jefferson. After a close contest between these two parties, Mr. Adams was elected president, having received seventy-one of the electoral votes, and Mr. Jefferson sixty-eight. In March, 1797, these gentlemen entered upon their respective offices of president and vice president of the United States.

Of the administration of Mr. Adams we shall not, in this place, give a detailed account. Many circumstances conspired to render it unpopular. An unhappy dispute with France had arisen a little previously to his inauguration. In the management of this dispute, which had reference to aggressions by France upon American rights and commerce. the popularity of Mr. Adams was in no small degree affected, although the measures which he recommended for upholding the national character, were more moderate than congress, and a respectable portion of the people, thought the exigencies of the case required. Other circumstances, also, conspired to diminish his popularity. Restraints were imposed upon the press, and authority vested in the president to order aliens to depart out of the United States, when he should judge the peace and safety of the country required. To these measures. acts were added for raising a standing army, and imposing a direct tax and internal duties. These, and other causes, combined to weaken the strength of the party to whom he owed his elevation, and to prevent his re-election. He was succeeded by Mr. Jefferson, in 1801.

On retiring from the presidency he removed to his former residence at Quincy, where, in quiet, he spent the remainder of his days. In 1820, he voted as elector of president and vice president; and, in the same year, at the advanced age of 85, he was a member of the convention of Massachusetts, assembled to revise the constitution of that commonwealth.

Mr. Adams retained the faculties of his mind, in remarkable perfection, to the end of his long life. His unabated love of reading and contemplation, added to an interesting circle of friendship and affection, were sources of felicity in declining years, which seldom fall to the lot of any one.

"But," to use the language of a distinguished eulogist,* "he had other enjoyments. He saw around him that prosperity and general happiness, which had been the object of his public cares and labours. No man ever beheld more clearly, and for a longer time, the great and beneficial effects of the services rendered by himself to his country. That liberty, which he so early defended, that independence, of which he was so able an advocate and supporter, he saw, we trust, firmly and securely established. The population of

* Webster.

the country thickened around him faster, and extended wider, than his own sanguine predictions had anticipated; and the wealth, respectability, and power of the nation, sprang up to a magnitude, which it is quite impossible he could have expected to witness, in his day. He lived, also, to behold those principles of civil freedom, which had been developed, established, and practically applied in America, attract attention, command respect, and awaken imitation, in other regions of the globe; and well might, and well did he exclaim, 'Where will the consequences of the American revolution end!'

"If any thing yet remains to fill this cup of happiness, let it be added, that he lived to see a great and intelligent people bestow the highest honour in their gift, where he had bestowed his own kindest parental affections, and lodged his fondest hopes.

"At length the day approached when this eminent patriot was to be summoned to another world, and, as if to render that day forever memorable in the annals of American history, it was the day on which the illustrious Jefferson was himself, also, to terminate his distinguished earthly career. That day was the fiftieth anniversary of the declaration of independence.

"Until within a few days previous, Mr. Adams had exhibited no indications of a rapid decline. The morning of the fourth of July, 1826, he was unable to rise from his bed. Neither to himself, or his friends, however, was his dissolution supposed to be so near. He was asked to suggest a toast, appropriate to the celebration of the day. His mind seemed to glance back to the hour in which, fifty years before, he had voted for the declaration of independence, and with the spirit with which he then raised his hand, he now exclaimed, 'Independence forever.' At four o'clock in the afternoon he expired. Mr. Jefferson had departed a few hours before him."

We close this imperfect sketch of the life of this distinguished man in the language of one* who, from the relation in which

* President Adams's Message.

he stood to the subject of this memoir, must have felt, more than any other individual, the impressiveness of the event. "They, (Mr. Adams and Mr. Jefferson,) departed cheered by the benediction of their country, to whom they left the inheritance of their fame, and the memory of their bright example. If we turn our thoughts to the condition of their country, in the contrast of the first and last day of that half century, how resplendent and sublime is the transition from gloom to glory! Then, glancing through the same lapse of time, in the condition of the individuals, we see the first day marked with the fulness and vigour of youth, in the pledge of their lives, their fortunes, and their sacred honour, to the cause of freedom and of mankind. And on the last, extended on the bed of death, with but sense and sensibility left to breathe a last aspiration to heaven of blessing upon their country, may we not humbly hope, that to them, too, it was a pledge of transition from gloom to glory; and that while their mortal vestments were sinking into the clod of the valley, their emancipated spirits were ascending to the bosom of their God!"

ROBERT TREAT PAINE.

ROBERT TREAT PAINE was a native of Boston, where he was born, in the year 1731. His parents were pious and respectable. His father was for some years the settled pastor of a church in Weymouth, in the vicinity of Boston. His health failing him, however, he removed with his family to the latter place; where he entered into mercantile pursuits. His mother was the grand-daughter of Governor Treat of Connecticut.

At the early age of fourteen, he became a member of Harvard College; but of his collegiate course, little has been recorded. On leaving the university, he was engaged for some time in a public school. As the fortune of his father had, from various circumstances, become much reduced, the support of his parents, with some other relations, seemed to devolve upon himself. In the acquisition of more ample means for their maintenance, he made a voyage to Europe. It was an honourable trait in his character, thus in the morning of life to exhibit such filial affection; a kindness of disposition, which he continued to manifest during his father's life.

Previously to his commencing the study of law, he devoted some time to the subject of theology, which tended to enlarge his views of Christianity, and to confirm his belief of its truth. In 1755, he served as chaplain to the troops of the province at the northward, and afterwards preached a few times in other places.

At length he directed his attention to the study of law, during which period, having no pecuniary assistance, he was obliged to resort again to the keeping of a school for his support. By most persons such a course would be deemed a serious evil; but experience has shown, that those who are obliged to depend upon their own energies for the means of education, generally enter upon their profession, if not with higher attainments, with more courage to encounter the difficulties with which almost every one meets, and they are more likely to attain to a high elevation, than those whose resources are abundant.

On being qualified for the practice of law, Mr. Paine established himself at Taunton, in the county of Bristol, where he resided for many years. We necessarily pass over several years of his life, during which we meet no occurrences of sufficient importance to merit a notice in these pages. It may be remarked, however, that at an early period, he took a deep interest in the various disputes which arose between the colonies and the British government. He was a delegate from Taunton, to a convention called by leading men of Boston, in 1768, in consequence of the abrupt dissolution of the general court by Governor Bernard. This convention the governor attempted to break up, but it continued in session several days, and adopted many spirited resolutions, design ᵕ to awaken in the people a greater attention to their rights, and to show to the ministry of England, that if those rights were violated, the provincial assembly would act independently of the governor.

Mr. Paine was engaged in the celebrated trial of Captain Preston, and his men, for the part they acted in the well known "Boston massacre" of 1770. On this occasion, in the absence of the attorney general, he conducted the prosecution on the part of the crown. Although only a fragment of his address to the jury, at this time, has been preserved, it appears that he managed the cause with the highest reputation to himself, both in regard to his honour as a faithful advocate, and at the same time as a friend to the just rights of those against whom he acted as council.

From this time, Mr. Paine appeared still more conspicuously as the friend of liberty, in opposition to the tyrannical and oppressive measures of the British administration. In 1773, he was elected a representative to the general assembly, from the town of Taunton. It was now becoming a period of great alarm in the colonies. Men of principle and talent were selected to guard the ancient rights of the colonies, and to point to those measures which, in the approaching crisis, it was proper to pursue. It was a high honour, therefore, for any one to be elected a representative of the people. The rights, the liberties, and even the lives of their constituents were placed in their hands; it was of the utmost importance that they should be men of sagacity, patriotism, and principle. Such, fortunately for the colonies, *were* the men who represented them in their provincial assemblies, and in the continental congress.

Of this latter body, Mr. Paine was elected a member in 1774. A general account of the proceedings of this assembly has already been given. At that time a separation from the parent country was not generally contemplated, although to more discerning minds, such an event appeared not improbable, and that at no distant day. The congress of 1774, were appointed mainly to deliberate and de termine upon the measures proper to be pursued, to secure the enjoyment and exercise of rights guaranteed to the colonies by their charters, and for the restitution of union and harmony between the two countries, which was still desired by all. Accordingly they proceeded no farther at that time, than to address the people of America, petition the king, state their grievances, assert their rights, and recommend the suspension of importations from Great Britain into the colonies.

The assembling of such a body, and for objects of so questionable a character, was a bold step; and bold must have been the men, who could thus openly appear on the side of the colonies, in opposition to the British ministry, and the royal power. In concluding their session, in October of the same year, they presented a solemn appeal to the world, stating that innovation was not their object, but only the preservation and maintenance of the rights which, as subjects of Great Britain, had been granted to them by their ancient charters. "Had we been permitted," say they, " to enjoy in quiet the inheritance left us by our fathers, we should, at this time, have been peaceably, cheerfully, and usefully employed in recommending ourselves, by every testimony of devotion to his majesty, and of veneration to the state from which we derive our origin. Though now exposed to unexpected and unnatural scenes of distress, by a contention with that nation, in whose general guidance, on all important occasions, we have hitherto with filial reverence constantly trusted, and therefore can derive no instruction, in our present unhappy and perplexing circumstances, from any former experience; yet we doubt not, the purity of our intentions, and the integrity of our conduct, will justify us at that great tribunal, before which all mankind must submit to judgment. We ask but for peace, liberty, and safety. We wish not a diminution of the royal prerogatives; nor do we solicit the grant of any new right in our favour."

To the continental congress, which met at Philadelphia in May, 1775, Mr. Paine was again a delegate from Massachusetts. At that time, the colonies were greatly in want of gunpowder. The manufacture of salt petre, one of its constituents, was but imperfectly understood. Congress appointed a committee, of which Mr. Paine was chairman, to introduce the manufacture of it. In this particular, he rendered essential service to his country, by making extensive inquiries into the subject, and by inducing persons in various parts of the provinces to engage in the manufacture of the article. The following is among the letters which he wrote on this subject, which, while it shows his indefatigable attention to the subject, will convey to the present generation some idea of the multiform duties of the patriots of the revolution. Mr. Paine also rendered himself highly useful, as a member of a committee for the encouragement of the manufacture of cannon, and other implements of war.

Philadelphia, June 10th, 1775.

My very dear Sir,

I cannot express to you the surprise and uneasiness I received on hearing the *congress express* respecting the want of gunpowder; it was always a matter that lay heavy on my mind; but the observation I made of your attention to it, and your alertness and perseverance in every thing you undertake, and your repeatedly expressing it as your opinion that we had probably enough for this summer's campaign, made me quite easy. I rely upon it that measures are taken in your parts of the continent to supply this defect. The design of your express will be zealously attended to, I think. I have seen one of the powder mills here, where they make excellent powder, but have worked up all the nitre; one of our members is concerned in a powder mill at New-York, and has a man at work making nitre. I have taken pains to inquire into the method Dr. Franklin has seen salt-petre works at Hanover and Paris; and it strikes me to be as unnecessary, after a certain time, to send abroad for gunpowder, as for bread; provided people will make use of common understanding and industry; but for the present we must import from abroad. Major Foster told me, at Hartford, he suspected he had some land that would yield nitre, pray converse with him about it. Dr

Franklin's account is much the same as is mentioned in one of the first of the American magazines, the sweeping of the streets, and rubbish of old buildings, are made into mortar, and built into walls, exposed to the air, and once in about two months scraped and lixiviated, and evaporated; when I can describe the method more minutely, I will write you; meanwhile, give me leave to condole with you the loss of Colonel Lee. Pray remember me to Colonel Orne, and all other our worthy friends. Pray take care of your important health, that you may be able to stand stiff as a pillar in our new government.

I must now subscribe, with great respect and affection,
Your humble servant,
R. T. PAINE.

Of the congress of 1776, Mr. Paine was also a member; and to the declaration of independence, which that body published to the world, he gave his vote, and affixed his name. In the December following, the situation of congress became justly alarming. The British army were, at this time, making rapid advances through New-Jersey, towards Philadelphia. The troops of Washington, amounting to scarcely one third of the British force, it was thought would not be able to resist their progress, or prevent their taking possession of Philadelphia. During the alarm excited by an approaching foe, congress adjourned to Baltimore. Of the state of congress, at this time, the following letter of Mr. Paine gives an interesting account.

"Our public affairs have been exceedingly agitated since I wrote you last. The loss of fort Washington made way for that of fort Lee; and the dissolution of our army happening at the same time, threw us into a most disagreeable situation. The interception of an express gave the enemy full assurance of what they must have had some knowledge of before, the state of our army; and they took the advantage of it. In two days after the possession of fort Lee, on the 20th of November, where we lost much baggage, and the chief of our battering cannon, they marched to the Hackensack, and thence to Newark, driving General Washington before them, with his 3000 men; thence to Elizabethtown. General Washington supposed, from the best information he could get, that they were 10,000 strong; marching with a large body of horse in front, and a very large train of artillery. We began to be apprehensive they were intended for Philadelphia; and congress sat all Sunday in determining proper measures on the occasion. I cannot describe to you the situation of this city. The prospect was really alarming. Monday, 9th, yesterday, General Washington crossed the Delaware, and the enemy arrived at Trenton on this side, thirty miles from this place; close quarters for Congress! It obliges us to move; we have resolved to go to Baltimore."

For the years 1777 and 1778, Mr. Paine was a member of congress, during the intervals of whose sessions, he filled several important offices in the state of Massachusetts. In 1780, he was called to take a part in the deliberations of the convention, which met for the purpose of forming a constitution for the commonwealth. Of the committee which framed that excellent instrument, he was a conspicuous member. Under the government organized according to this constitution, he was appointed attorney general, an office which he continued to hold until 1790, when he was transferred to a seat on the bench of the supreme judicial court. In this situation he remained till the year 1804, at which time he had attained to the advanced age of 73 years. As a lawyer, Mr. Paine ranked high among his professional brethren. His legal attainments were extensive. In the discharge of his duties as attorney general, he had the reputation of unnecessary severity; but fidelity in that station generally provokes the censure of the lawless and licentious. Towards the abandoned and incorrigible he *was indeed severe*, and was willing that the law in all its penalties should be visited upon them. But where crime was followed by repentance, he could be moved to tenderness; and while, in the discharge of his official duty, he took care that the law should not fall into disrespect through his inefficiency, he at the same time was ever ready to recommend such as might deserve it to executive clemency.

The important duties of a judge, he discharged with honour and great impartiality for the space of fourteen years During the latter part of this time, he was affected with a deafness, which, in a measure, impaired his usefulness on the bench. Few men have rendered more important services to the literary and religious institutions of a country, than did Judge Paine. He gave them all the support and influence of his office, by urging upon grand jurors the faithful execution of the laws, the support of schools, and the preservation of a strict morality.

The death of Judge Paine occurred on the eleventh of May, 1814, having attained to the age of 84 years. Until near the close of life, the vigour of his mental faculties continued unimpaired. In quickness of apprehension, liveliness of imagination, and general intelligence, he had few superiors. His memory was of the most retentive character, and he was highly distinguished for a sprightly and agreeable turn in conversation. A witty severity sometimes excited the temporary disquietude of a friend; but if he was sometimes inclined to indulge in pleasant raillery, he was willing to be the subject of it in his turn.

As a scholar, he ranked high among literary men, and was distinguished for his patronage of all the useful institutions of the country. He was a founder of the American Academy established in Massachusetts in 1780, and active in its service until his death. The honorary degree of doctor of laws was conferred upon him by Harvard University.

Judge Paine was a firm believer in the divine origin of the Christian religion. He gave full credence to the scriptures, as a revelation from God, designed to instruct mankind in a knowledge of their duty, and to guide them in the way to eternal happiness.

ELBRIDGE GERRY.

Elbridge Gerry was born at Marblehead, in the state of Massachusetts, on the seventeenth day of July, 1744. His father was a native of Newton, of respectable parentage and connexions. He emigrated to America in 1730, soon after which, he established himself as a merchant in Marblehead, where he continued to reside until his death, in 1774. He was much esteemed and respected, as a man of judgment and discretion.

Of the early habits or manners of young Elbridge, little is known. He became a member of Harvard College before he had completed his fourteenth year; and of course was too young at the university to acquire any decided character.

Mr. Gerry was originally destined to the profession of medicine, to which his own inclination strongly attached him. But soon after leaving college, he engaged in commercial affairs, under the direction of his father, and for some years followed the routine of mercantile business in his native town. Great success attended his commercial enterprise; and within a few years, he found himself in the enjoyment of a competent fortune.

It is natural to suppose that the superior education of Mr. Gerry, added to the respectable character he sustained, as a man of probity and judgment, gave him influence over the people among whom he resided. In May, 1772, the people of Marblehead manifested their respect and confidence by sending him a representative to the general court of the province of Massachusetts. In May of the following year, Mr. Gerry was re-elected to the same office. During the session of the general court that year, Mr. Samuel Adams introduced his celebrated motion for the appointment of a standing committee of correspondence and inquiry.

In accordance with this motion, committees of correspondence were appointed throughout the province, by means of which intelligence was freely circulated abroad, and a spirit of patriotism was infused through all parts of the country.

Though one of the youngest members, Mr. Gerry was appointed by the house of representatives, a member of this committee; in all the proceedings of which, he took an active and prominent part.

In the month of June, the celebrated letters of Governor Hutchinson to persons in England, were laid before the house by Mr. Adams. The object of these letters, as noticed in a preceding page, was to encourage the British administration in maintaining their arbitrary measures. In the debates which ensued on the disclosure of these letters, Mr. Gerry distinguished himself, and was indefatigably engaged through the year, in forwarding the resolute measures, which combined to overthrow the royal government of the province. He was also particularly active in the scenes which marked the year 1774. He united in the opposition to the importation of tea, and to the Boston port bill; and heartily concurred in the establishment of a system of non-intercourse with the parent country.

In the month of August, Governor Gage issued his precepts to the several towns, to choose representatives to meet at Salem, the first week in October. Before the arrival of that day, the governor had countermanded their meeting. Notwithstanding this prohibition, delegates assembled at Salem on the seventh of October. There having formed themselves into a provincial congress, they adjourned to Concord, and proceeded to business. Of this congress Mr. Gerry was an active and efficient member.

On the organization of the assembly, a committee was appointed to consider the state of the province. Fourteen of the most distinguished members of the congress, among whom was Mr. Gerry, composed this committee. They published a bold and energetic appeal, which, in the form of an address to Governor Gage, was calculated to justify the authority they had assumed, to awaken their constituents to a sense of the dangers they feared, and the injuries they had sustained.

They next appointed a committee of safety, and adopted measures to obtain a supply of arms and ammunition; of which the province was lamentably deficient. They re-organized the militia, appointed general officers, and took such other measures as the approaching crisis seemed to render necessary.

In February, 1775, a new provincial congress, of which Mr. Gerry was a member, assembled in Cambridge. This congress, like the former one, published an appeal to the people, designed to excite and regulate that patriotic spirit, which the emergency required. A general apprehension prevailed, that a pacific termination of the existing troubles was not to be expected. They avowed their abhorrence of actual hostilities, but still maintained their right to arm in defence of their country, and to prepare themselves to resist with the sword.

In the spring of 1775, the prospect of open war every day increased. A strong apprehension prevailed, that an attempt would be made by the royal governor to destroy such military stores as had been collected, particularly at Concord and Worcester. The committee of safety, in their solicitude on this subject, stationed a watch at each of these places, to give an alarm to the surrounding country should such an attempt be made.

A short period only elapsed, before the apprehensions of the people proved not to be without foundation. The expedition to Concord, and the bloody scenes which occurred both there and at Lexington, ushered in the long expected contest. "Among the objects of this expedition," observes Mr. Austin, in his life of Mr. Gerry, "one was to seize the persons of some of the influential members of Congress, and to hold them as hostages for the moderation of their colleagues, or send them to England for trial as traitors, and thus strike dismay and terror into the minds of their associates and friends.

"A committee of congress, among whom were Mr. Gerry, Colonel Orne, and Colonel Hancock, had been in session on the day preceding the march of the troops, in the village of Menotomy, then part of the township of Cambridge, on the road to Lexington.

was over, had gone to Lexington. Mr. Gerry and Mr. Orne remained at the village, the other members of the committee had dispersed.

"Some officers of the royal army had been sent out in advance, who passed through the villages just before dusk, in the afternoon of the 18th of April, and although the appearance of similar detachments was not uncommon, these so far attracted the attention of Mr. Gerry, that he despatched an express to Colonel Hancock, who, with Samuel Adams, was at Lexington. The messenger passed the officers, by taking a by-path, and delivered his letter. The idea of personal danger does not seem to have made any strong impression on either of these gentlemen. Mr. Hancock's answer to Mr. Gerry bears marks of the haste with which it was written, while it discovers that habitual politeness on the part of the writer, which neither haste or danger could impair.

Lexington, April 18*th*, 1775.

Dear Sir,

I am much obliged for your notice. It is said the officers are gone to Concord, and I will send word thither. I am full with you, that we ought to be serious, and I hope your decision will be effectual. I intend doing myself the pleasure of being with you to-morrow. My respects to the committee.

I am your real friend,
JOHN HANCOCK.

Mr. Gerry and Colonel Orne retired to rest, without taking the least precaution against personal exposure, and they remained quietly in their beds, until the British advance were within view of the dwelling house. It was a fine moonlight night, and they quietly marked the glittering of its beams, on the polished arms of the soldiers, as the troops moved with the silence and regularity of accomplished discipline. The front passed on. When the centre were opposite to the house, occupied by the committee, an officer and file of men ... ...ly ... nd marched towards it. It was not until this moment they entertained any apprehension of danger. While the officer was posting his files, the gentlemen found means, by their better knowledge of the premises, to escape, half dressed as they were, into an adjoining cornfield, where they remained concealed for more than an hour, until the troops were withdrawn. Every apartment of the house was searched 'for the members of the rebel congress;' even the beds in which they had lain were examined. But their property, and among other things, a valuable watch of Mr. Gerry's, which was under his pillow, was not disturbed."

A few days after the skirmishes at Lexington and Concord, the provincial congress re-assembled. It was now apparent that the controversy must be decided by force of arms. At this time, it was found that almost every article of a military kind was yet to be procured. The province possessed no magazines of arms, and had little ammunition. No contracts for provision or clothing had yet been made. To meet these exigencies, a committee, at the head of which was Mr. Gerry, was immediately appointed, and clothed with the proper power. The article most needed was that of gunpowder, to procure which, Mr. Gerry was specially commissioned by the committee. In the discharge of this duty, he wrote many letters to gentlemen in different parts of the country, from whom he received others in reply. One of these will be found in the life of Robert Treat Paine, in a preceding page. Mr. Gerry did more: in many cases he hesitated not to advance his own funds, where immediate payment was required. In the progress of the war, the evidence of these payments was lost, or mislaid, and their final settlement was attended with heavy pecuniary loss.

On the 17th day of June, was fought the celebrated battle of Bunker Hill. The provincial congress was at that time in session, at Watertown. Before the battle, Dr. Joseph Warren, president of the congress, who was the companion and room mate of Mr. Gerry, communicated to the latter his intention of mingling in the expected contest. The night preceding the doctor's departure in the same bed with Mr. Gerry. In the morning, in reply to the admonitions of his friend, as he was about to leave him, he uttered the well known words, "*Dulce et decorum est, pro patria mori.*"*

Mr. Gerry, on that day, attended the provincial congress. His brave friend, as is well known, followed where his duty called him, to the memorable "heights of Bunker," where he fell fighting for the cause of liberty and his country.

At an early period in 1775, Mr. Gerry submitted a proposal in the provincial congress of Massachusetts, for a law to encourage the fitting out of armed vessels, and to provide for the adjudication of prizes. This was a step of no small importance. To grant letters of marque and of reprisal, is the prerogative of the sovereign. For a colony to authorise such an act, was rebellious, if not treasonable. The proposal was sustained, though not without opposition. Mr. Gerry was chairman of the committee appointed to prepare the act to authorise privateering, and to establish admiralty courts. Governor Sullivan was another member of it, and on these two gentlemen devolved the task of drawing the act, which they executed in a small room under the belfry of the Watertown meeting house, in which the provincial congress was holding its session. This law, John Adams pronounced one of the most important measures of the Revolution. Under the sanction of it, the Massachusetts cruizers captured many of the enemy's vessels, the cargoes of which furnished various articles of necessity to the colonies.

Of the court of admiralty, established in pursuance of the law proposed by Mr. Gerry, that gentleman himself was appointed a judge, for the counties of Suffolk, Middlesex, and Essex. This honour, however, he declined, from a determination to devote himself to more active duties.

To such duties, he was not long after called, by the suffrages of his fellow citizens, who elected him a delegate from Massachusetts to the continental congress, in which body he took his seat, on the 9th of February, 1776. For this distinguished station he was eminently fitted; and of this

* It is sweet and glorious to lay down life for one's country.

body he continued a member with few intervals, until September, 1785. Our limits preclude a minute notice of the various duties which he there discharged. On various occasions he was appointed to serve on committees, whose business required great labour, and whose results involved the highest interests of the country. He assisted in arranging the plan of a general hospital, and of introducing a better discipline into the army, and regulating the commissary's departments. In several instances, he was appointed, with others, to visit the army, to examine the state of the money and finances of the country, and to expedite the settlement of public accounts. In the exercise of his various official functions, no man exhibited more fidelity, or a more unwearied zeal. He sustained the character of an active and resolute statesman, and retired from the councils of the confederacy, with all the honours which patriotism, integrity, and talents, could acquire in the service of the state. Before leaving New-York, he married a respectable lady, who had been educated in Europe, with whom he now returned to Massachusetts, and fixed his residence at Cambridge, a few miles from Boston.

From the quiet of retirement, Mr. Gerry was again summoned in 1787, by his native state, as one of its representatives to a convention, called for the "sole and express purpose of revising the articles of confederation, and reporting to congress, and to the several legislatures, such alterations and provisions as shall render the federal constitution adequate to the exigencies of government, and the preservation of the union."

On the meeting of this convention, little difference of opinion prevailed, as to the great principles which should form the basis of the constitution; but on reducing these principles to a system, perfect harmony did exist. To Mr. Gerry, as well as others, there appeared strong objections to the constitution, and he declined affixing his signature to the instrument. These objections he immediately set forth, in a letter addressed to his constituents, in which he observes:

"My principal ob   th pla   , that there is no

adequate provision for a representation of the people; that they have no security for the right of election; that some of the powers of the legislature are ambiguous, and others indefinite and dangerous; that the executive is blended with, and will have an undue influence over, the legislature; that the judicial department will be oppressive; that treaties of the highest importance may be formed by the president, with the advice of two thirds of a quorum of the senate; and that the system is without the security of a bill of rights. These are objections which are not local, but apply equally to all the states.

"As the convention was called for 'the sole and express purpose of revising the articles of confederation, and reporting to congress and to the several legislatures, such alterations and provisions as shall render the federal constitution adequate to the exigencies of government, and the preservation of the union,' I did not conceive that these powers extended to the formation of the plan proposed; but the convention being of a different opinion, I acquiesced in it; being fully convinced, that to preserve the union, an efficient government was indispensably necessary; and that it would be difficult to make proper amendments to the articles of confederation."

"The constitution proposed has few, if any, federal features, but is rather a system of national government; nevertheless, in many respects, I think it has great merit, and, by proper amendments, may be adapted to 'the exigencies of government,' and the preservation of liberty."

When the constitution was submitted to the state convention of Massachusetts, of three hundred and sixty members, of which that body consisted, a majority of nineteen only were in favour of its ratification. Although so many coincided with Mr. Gerry in his views of the constitution, he was highly censured by its advocates, who, under the excitement of party feelings, imputed to him motives by which he, probably, was not actuated.

Under the new constitution, Mr. Gerry was chosen by the inhabitants of the district in which he resided, as their representative to congress. In this station he served his constituents for four years; and, although he had formerly opposed the adoption of the constitution, he now cheerfully united in carrying it into effect, since it had received the sanction of his country. Indeed, he took occasion, on the floor of congress, not long after taking his seat in that body, to declare, "that the federal constitution having become the supreme law of the land, he conceived the salvation of the country depended on its being carried into effect."

At the expiration of the above period, although again proposed as a delegate to congress, he declined a re-election, and again retired to his family at Cambridge.

On the fourth of March, 1797, Mr. Adams, who had previously been elected to succeed General Washington in the presidency, entered upon that office. France had already commenced her aggressions on the rights and commerce of the United States, and General Pinckney had been dispatched to that country, to adjust existing differences.

Immediately upon succeeding to the presidency, Mr. Adams received intelligence that the French republic had announced to General Pinckney its determination "not to receive another minister from the United States, until after the redress of grievances."

In this state of things, the president convened congress by proclamation, on the fifteenth of June. Although keenly sensible of the indignity offered to the country by the French government, Mr. Adams, in his speech to congress, informed that body, "that as he believed neither the honour, nor the interests of the United States, absolutely forbade the repetition of advances for securing peace and friendship with France, he should institute a fresh attempt at negociation."

Upon his recommendation, therefore, three envoys extraordinary, Mr. Gerry, General Pinckney, and Mr. Marshall, were dispatched to carry into effect the pacific dispositions of the United States. On their arrival at Paris, the French directory, under various pretexts, delayed to acknowledge them in their official capacity. In the mean time, the tools of that government, addressed the ————, in explicit terms, a large sum of money, as the condition of any negociation. This being refused, an attempt was next made to excite their fears for themselves, and their country. In the spring of 1798, two of the envoys, Messrs. Pinckney and Marshall, were ordered to quit the territories of France, while Mr. Gerry was invited to remain, and resume the negociation which had been suspended.

Although Mr Gerry accepted the invitation to remain, yet he uniformly and resolutely refused to resume the negociation. His object in remaining in France was to prevent an immediate rupture with that country, which, it was apprehended, would result from his departure. Although he was censured, at the time, for the course he took, his continuance seems to have resulted in the good of his country. "He finally saved the peace of the nation," said the late President Adams, " for he alone discovered and furnished the evidence that X. Y. and Z. were employed by Talleyrand; and he alone brought home the direct, formal, and official assurances upon which the subsequent commission proceeded, and peace was made."

On his return to America, in October, 1798, Mr. Gerry was solicited, by the republican party in Massachusetts, to become their candidate for the office of governor. At that period, much excitement prevailed on the subject of politics, throughout the country. Although at first unsuccessful, his party, in 1805, for the first time, obtained the governor of their choice.

In the following year, Mr. Gerry retired. But in 1810, he was again chosen chief magistrate of that commonwealth, in which office he was continued for the two following years. In 1812, he was recommended to the people of the United States, by the republican members of congress, to fill the office of vice president. To a letter addressed to him, by a committee announcing his nomination, he replied, "The question respecting the acceptance, or non-acceptance of this proposition, involved many considerations of great weight, in my mind; as they related to the nation, to this state, and to my domestic concerns. But it is neither expedient or necessary to state the points, since one was paramount to the rest, that 'in a republic, the service of each citizen is due to the state, even in profound peace, and much more so when the nation stands on the threshold of war.' I have the honour frankly to acknowledge this distinguished testimony of confidence, on the part of my congressional friends and fellow citizens, gratefully to accept their proffer, and freely to assure them of every exertion in my power, for meriting in office, the approbation of themselves and of the public."

The nomination of Mr. Gerry, thus made, was followed by his election, and on the fourth of March, 1813, he was inaugurated vice president of the United States. Providence, however, had not destined him to the long enjoyment of the dignified station which he now held. While attending to his duties, at Washington, he was suddenly summoned from the scene of his earthly labours. A beautiful monument, erected at the national expense, covers his remains, and records the date and circumstances of his death.

THE TOMB OF
ELBRIDGE GERRY,
Vice President of the United States,
Who died suddenly, in this city, on his way to the
Capitol, as President of the Senate,
November 23d, 1814.
Aged 70.

THE
NEW-HAMPSHIRE DELEGATION.

JOSIAH BARTLETT,
WILLIAM WHIPPLE,
MATTHEW THORNTON.

JOSIAH BARTLETT.

JOSIAH BARTLETT, the first of the New-Hampshire delegation who signed the declaration of independence, was born in Amesbury, Massachusetts, in 1729. He was the fourth son of Stephen Bartlett, whose ancestors came from England during the seventeenth century, and settled at Beverly.

The early education of young Bartlett appears to have been respectable, although he had not the advantages of a collegiate course At the age of sixteen he began the study of medicine, for which he had a competent knowledge of the Greek and Latin languages.

On finishing his preliminary studies, which were superintended by Dr. Ordway, of Amesbury, and to which he devoted himself with indefatigable zeal for five years, he commenced the practice of his profession at Kingston, in the year 1750.

Two years from the above date, he was attacked by a fever, which for a time seriously threatened his life. From an injudicious application of medicines, and too close a confinement to his chamber, life appeared to be rapidly ebbing, and all hopes of his recovery were relinquished. In this situation, one evening, he strongly solicited his attendants to give him some cider. At first they were strongly reluctant to comply with his wishes, under a just apprehension, that serious and even fatal consequences might ensue. The patient, however, would not be pacified, until his request was granted. At length they complied with his request, and of the cider thus given him, he continued to drink at intervals during the night. The effect of it proved highly beneficial. It mitigated the febrile symptoms, a copious perspiration ensued, and from this time he began to recover.

This experiment, if it may be called an experiment, was treasured up in the mind of Dr. Bartlett, and seems to have led him to abandon the rules of arbitrary system, for the more just principles of nature and experience. He became a skilful and distinguished practitioner. To him is ascribed the first application of Peruvian bark in cases of canker, which before, was considered an inflammatory, instead of a putrid disease, and as such had been unsuccessfully treated.

This disease, which was called the throat distemper, first appeared at Kingston, in the spring of 1735. The first person afflicted with it, was said to have contracted the disease from a hog, which he skinned and opened, and which had died of a distemper of the throat. The disease which was supposed thus to have originated, soon after spread abroad through the town, and to children under ten years of age it proved exceedingly fatal. Like the plague, it swept its victims to the grave, almost without warning, and some are said to have expired while sitting at play handling their toys. At this time, medical skill was baffled; every method of treatment pursued, proved ineffectual. It ceased its ravages only where victims were no longer to be found.

In the year 1754, Kingston was again visited with this malignant disease. Doctor Bartlett was at this time a physician of the town. At first he treated it as an inflammatory disease; but at length, satisfied that this was not its character, he administered Peruvian bark to a child of his own who was afflicted with the disease, and with entire success. From this time the use of it became general, as a remedy in diseases of the same type.

A man of the distinguished powers of Doctor Bartlett, and of his d unnoticed, in times which tried men's souls. The public attention was soon directed to him, as a gentleman in whom confidence might be reposed, and whose duties, whatever they might be, would be discharged with promptness and fidelity.

In the year 1765, Doctor Bartlett was elected to the legislature of the province of New-Hampshire, from the town of Kingston. In his legislative capacity, he soon found occasion to oppose the mercenary views of the royal governor. He would not become subservient to the will of a man whose object, next to the display of his own authority, was the subjection of the people to the authority of the British administration.

The controversy between Great Britain and her colonies, was now beginning to assume a serious aspect. At this time, John Wentworth was the royal governor, a man of no ordinary sagacity. Aware of the importance of attaching the distinguished men of the colony to the royal cause, among other magistrates, he appointed Dr. Bartlett to the office of justice of the peace. This was indeed an inconsiderable honour: but as an evidence of the governor's respect for his talents and influence, was a point of some importance. Executive patronage, however, was not a bait by which such a man as Dr. Bartlett would be seduced. He accepted the appointment, but was as firm in his opposition to the royal governor as he had been before.

The opposition which was now abroad in America against the British government, and which continued to gather strength until the year 1774, had made equal progress in the province of New-Hampshire. At this time, a committee of correspondence, agreeably to the recommendation and example of other colonies, was appointed by the house of representatives. For this act, the governor immediately dissolved the assembly. But the committee of correspondence soon after re-assembled the representatives, by whom circulars were addressed to the several towns, to send delegates to a convention, to be held at Exeter, for the purpose of selecting deputies to the continental congress, which was to meet at Philadelphia in the ensuing September.

In this convention, Dr. Bartlett, and John Pickering, a lawyer, of Portsmouth, were appointed delegates to congress. The former of these having a little previously lost his house by fire, was under the necessity of declining the honour. The latter gentleman wishing also to be excused, other gentlemen were elected in their stead.

Dr. Bartlett, however, retained his seat in the house of representatives of the province. Here, as in other colonies, the collisions between the royal governor and the people continued to increase. The former was more arbitrary in his proceedings, the latter better understood their rights, and were more independent. The conspicuous part which Dr. Bartlett took on the patriotic side, the firmness with which he resisted the royal exactions, rendered him highly obnoxious to the governor, by whom he was deprived of his commission as justice of the peace, and laconically dismissed from his command in the militia.

From this time, the political difficulties in New-Hampshire greatly increased. At length, Governor Wentworth found it necessary for his personal safety to retire on board the Favey man of war, then lying in the harbour of Portsmouth. From this he went to Boston, and thence to the Isle of Shoals, where he issued his proclamation, adjourning the assembly till the following April. This act, however, terminated the royal government in the province of New-Hampshire. A provincial congress, of which Matthew Thornton was president, was soon called, by which a temporary government was organized, and an oath of allegiance was framed, which every individual was obliged to take. Thus, after subsisting for a period of ninety years, the British government was forever annihilated in New-Hampshire.

In September, 1775, Dr. Bartlett, who had been elected to the continental congress, took his seat in that body. In this new situation, he acted with his accustomed energy, and rendered important services to his country. At this time, congress met at nine in the morning, and continued its session until four o'clock in the afternoon. The state of the country required this incessant application of the members. But anxiety and fatigue they could endure without repining. The lives and fortunes of themselves and families, and fellow citizens, were in jeopardy. Liberty, too, was in jeopardy. Like faithful sentinels, therefore, they sustained with cheerfulness their laborious task; and, when occasion required, could dispense with the repose of nights. In this unwearied devotion to business, Dr. Bartlett largely participated; in consequence of which, his health and spirits were for a time considerably affected.

In a second election, in the early part of the year 1776, Dr. Bartlett was again chosen a delegate to the continental congress. He was present on the memorable occasion of taking the vote on the question of a declaration of independence. On putting the question, it was agreed to begin with the northernmost colony. Dr. Bartlett, therefore, had the honour of being called upon for an expression of his opinion, and of first giving his vote in favour of the resolution.

On the evacuation of Philadelphia, by the British, in 1778, congress, which had for some time held its sessions at Yorktown, adjourned to meet at the former place, within three days, that is, on the second day of July. The delegates now left Yorktown, and in different companies proceeded to the place of adjournment. Dr. Bartlett, however, was attended only by a single servant. They were under the necessity of passing through a forest of considerable extent; it was reported to be the lurking place of a band of robbers, by whom several persons had been waylaid, and plundered of their effects. On arriving at an inn, at the entrance of the wood, Dr. Bartlett was informed of the existence of this band of desperadoes, and cautioned against proceeding, until other travellers should arrive. While the doctor lingered for the purpose of refreshing himself and horses, the landlord, to corroborate the statement which he had made, and to heighten still more the apprehension of the travellers, related the following anecdote. "A paymaster of the army, with a large quantity of paper money, designed for General Washington, had attempted the passage of the wood, a few weeks before. On arriving at the skirts of the wood, he was apprised of his danger, but as it was necessary for him to proceed, he laid aside his military garb, purchased a worn out horse, and a saddle and bridle, and a farmer's saddlebags of corresponding appearance: in the latter, he deposited his money, and with a careless manner proceeded on his way. At some distance from the skirt of the wood, he was met by two of the gang, who demanded his money. Others were skulking at no great distance in the wood, and waiting the issue of the interview. To the demand for money, he replied, that he had a small sum, which they were at liberty to take, if they believed they had a better right to it than himself and family. Taking from his pocket a few small pieces of money, he offered them to them; at the same time, in the style and simplicity of a quaker, he spoke to them of the duties of religion. Deceived by the air of honesty which he assumed, they suffered him to pass, without further molestation, the one observing to the other, that so poor a quaker was not worth the robbing. Without any further interruption, the poor quaker reached the other side of the wood, and at length delivered the contents of his saddlebags to General Washington."

During the relation of this anecdote, several other members of congress arrived, when, having prepared their arms, they proceeded on their journey, and in safety passed over the infested territory.

On the evacuation of Philadelphia, it was obvious from the condition of the city, that an enemy had been there. In a letter to a friend, Dr. Bartlett describes the alterations and ravages which had been made. "Congress," he says, "was obliged to hold its sessions in the college hall, the state house having been left by the enemy in a condition which could scarcely be described. Many of the finest houses were converted into stables; parlour floors cut through, and the dung shovelled through into the cellars. Through the country, north of the city, for many miles, the hand of desolation had marked its way. Houses had been consumed, fences carried off, gardens and orchards destroyed. Even the great roads were scarcely to be discovered, amidst the confusion and desolation which prevailed."

In August, 1778, a new election took place in New-Hampshire, when Dr. Bartlett was again chosen a delegate to congress; he continued, however, at Philadelphia, but an inconsiderable part of the session, his domestic concerns requiring his attention. During the remainder of his life, he resided in New-Hampshire, filling up the measure of his usefulness in a zealous devotion to the interests of the state.

In the early part of the year 1779, in a letter to one of the delegates in congress, Dr. Bartlett gives a deplorable account of the difficulties and sufferings of the people in New-Hampshire. The money of the country had become much depreciated, and provisions were scarce and high. Indian corn was sold at ten dollars a bushel. Other things were in the same proportion. The soldiers of the army could scarcely subsist on their pay and the officers, at times, found it difficult to keep them together.

During the same year, Dr. Bartlett was appointed chief justice of the court of common pleas. In 1782, he became an associate justice of the supreme court, and in 1788, he was advanced to the head of the bench. In the course of this latter year, the present constitution was presented to the several states, for their consideration. Of the convention in New-Hampshire, which adopted it, Dr. Bartlett was a member, and by his zeal was accessory to its ratification. In 1789, he was elected a senator to congress; but the infirmities of age induced him to decline the office. In 1793, he was elected first governor of the state, which office he filled, with his accustomed fidelity, until the infirm state of his health obliged him to resign the chief magistracy, and to retire wholly from public business. In January, 1794, he expressed his determination to close his public career in the following letter to the legislature:

"Gentlemen of the Legislature—After having served the public for a number of years, to the best of my abilities, in the various offices to which I have had the honour to be appointed, I think it proper, before your adjournment, to signify to you, and through you to my fellow citizens at large, that I now find myself so far advanced in age, that it will be expedient for me, at the close of the session, to retire from the cares and fatigues of public business, to the repose of a private life, with a grateful sense of the repeated marks of trust and confidence that my fellow citizens have reposed in me, and with my best wishes for the future peace and prosperity of the state."

The repose of a private life, however, which must have become eminently desirable to a man whose life had been past in the toils and troubles of the revolution, was destined to be of short duration. This eminent man, and distinguished patriot, closed his earthly career on the nineteenth day of May, 1795, in the sixty-sixth year of his age.

To the sketches of the life of this distinguished man, little need be added, respecting his character. His patriotism was of a singularly elevated character, and the sacrifices which he made for the good of his country were such as few men are willing to make. He possessed a quick and penetrating mind, and, at the same time, he was distinguished for a sound and accurate judgment. A scrupulous justice marked his dealings with all men, and he exhibited great fidelity in his engagements. Of his religious views we are unable to speak with confidence, although there is some reason to believe that his principles were less strict, than pertained to the puritans of the day. He rose to office, and was recommended to the confidence of his fellow citizens, not less by the general probity of his character, than the force of his genius. Unlike many others, he had no family, or party connexions, to raise him to influence in society; but standing on his own merits, he passed through a succession of offices which he sustained with uncommon honour to himself, and the duties of which he discharged not only to the satisfaction of his fellow citizens, but with the highest benefit to his country.

WILLIAM WHIPPLE.

William Whipple was the eldest son of William Whipple, and was born at Kittery, Maine, in the year 1730. His father was a native of Ipswich, and was bred a maltster; but for several years after his removal to Kittery, he followed the sea. His mother was the daughter of Robert Cutts, a distinguished shipbuilder, who established himself at Kittery, where he became wealthy, and at his death left a handsome fortune to his daughter.

The education of young Whipple was limited to a public school, in his native town. It was respectable, but did not embrace that variety and extent of learning, which is generally obtained at some higher seminary.

On leaving school, he entered on board a merchant vessel, and for several years devoted himself to commercial business, on the sea. His voyages were chiefly confined to the West-Indies, and proving successful, he acquired a considerable fortune.

In 1759, he relinquished a seafaring life, and commenced business with a brother at Portsmouth, where they continued in trade, until within a few years of the revolution.

Mr. Whipple early entered with spirit into the controversy between Great Britain and the colonies, and being distinguished for the general probity of his character, as well as for the force of his genius, was frequently elected by his townsmen to offices of trust and responsibility. In the provincial congress, which met at Exeter, January, 1775, for the purpose of electing delegates to the continental congress in Philadelphia, he represented the town of Portsmouth. He also represented that town in the provincial congress, which was assembled at Exeter the following May, and by that body was appointed one of the provincial committee of safety. In 1776 he was appointed a delegate to the general congress, of which body he continued a member until the middle of September, 1799.

In this important situation, he was distinguished for great

activity, and by his perseverance and application commended himself to the respect of the national assembly, and to his constituents at home. He was particularly active as one of the superintendants of the commissary's and quartermaster's departments, in which he was successful in correcting many abuses, and in giving to those establishments a proper correctness and efficiency.

"The memorable day which gave birth to the declaration of independence afforded, in the case of William Whipple," as a writer observes, "a striking example of the uncertainty of human affairs, and the triumphs of perseverance. The cabin boy, who thirty years before had looked forward to a command of a vessel as the consummation of all his hopes and wishes, now stood amidst the congress of 1776, and looked around upon a conclave of patriots, such as the world had never witnessed. He whose ambition once centered in inscribing his name as commander upon a crew-list, now affixed his signature to a document, which has embalmed it for posterity."

In the year 1777, while Mr. Whipple was a member of congress, the appointment of brigadier general was bestowed upon him, and the celebrated John Stark, by the assembly of New-Hampshire. Great alarm at this time prevailed in New-Hampshire, in consequence of the evacuation of Ticonderoga by the Americans, its consequent possession by the British, and the progress of General Burgoyne, with a large force, toward the state. The militia of New-Hampshire were expeditiously organised into two brigades, the command of which was given to the above two generals. The intrepid conduct of General Stark, in the ever memorable defence of Bennington, must be only alluded to in this place. The advantage thus gained, laid the foundation of the still more signal victory which was obtained in the October following by General Gates, over the distinguished Burgoyne and his veteran soldiers, at Saratoga; since it was here proved to the militia, that the Hessians and Indians, so much dreaded by them, were not invincible. The career of conquest which had before animated the troops of Burgoyne was checked. For the first time, General Burgoyne was sensible of the danger of his situation. He had regarded the men of New-Hampshire, and the Green Mountains, with contempt. But the battle of Bennington taught him both to fear and respect them. In a letter addressed about this time to Lord Germaine, he remarks: "The New-Hampshire Grants, till of late but little known, hang like a cloud on my left."

The ill bodings of Burgoyne were realised too soon, for his own reputation. The militia from the neighbouring states hastened to reinforce the army of General Gates, which was now looking forward to an engagement with that of General Burgoyne. This engagement soon after took place, as already noticed, at Saratoga. and ended in the surrender of the royal army to the American troops. In this desperate battle, General Whipple commanded the troops of New-Hampshire. On that occasion, his meritorious conduct was rewarded by his being jointly appointed with Colonel Wilkinson, as the representative of General Gates, to meet two officers from General Burgoyne, and settle the articles of capitulation. He was also selected as one of the officers, who were appointed to conduct the surrendered army to their destined encampment, on Winter Hill, in the vicinity of Boston. On this expedition, General Whipple was attended by a faithful negro servant, named Prince, a native of Africa, and whom the general had imported several years before. "Prince," said the general, one day, as they were proceeding to their place of destination, "we may be called into action, in which case, I trust you will behave like a man of courage, and fight bravely for the country." "Sir," replied Prince, in a manly tone, "I have no wish to fight, and no inducement; but had I my liberty, I would fight in defence of the country to the last drop of my blood." "Well," said the general, "Prince, from this moment you are free."

In 1778, General Whipple, with a detachment of New-Hampshire militia, was engaged, under General Sullivan, in executing a plan which had for its object the retaking of Rhode Island from the British. By some misunderstanding, the French fleet, under Count D'Estaing, which was destined to co-operate with General Sullivan, failed of rendering the expected assistance, in consequence of which General Sullivan was obliged to retreat. General Sullivan, with his troops, occupied a position on the north end of the island One morning, while a number of officers were breakfasting in the general's quarters, a detachment of British troops were perceived on an eminence, at the distance of about three quarters of a mile. A field piece was soon after discharged by the enemy, the ball of which, after killing one of the horses at the door, passed through the side of the house, into the room where the officers were sitting, and so shattered the leg of the brigade major of General Whipple, that immediate amputation became necessary.

During the remaining years of Mr. Whipple's life, he filled several important offices. In 1780, he was elected a representative to the general assembly of New-Hampshire, the duties of which office he continued to discharge during several re-elections, with much honour to himself, and to the general acceptance of his constituents.

In 1782, he received the appointment of receiver of public moneys for the state of New-Hampshire, from Mr. Morris, the superintendant of finance. The appointment was accepted by Mr. Whipple. but the duties devolving upon him were both arduous and unpopular. The collection of money was, at that time, extremely difficult. Mr. Whipple experienced many vexations in the exercise of his commission; and at length, in 1784, found it necessary, on account of the infirm state of his health, to relinquish his office. About the same time that he received the above appointment, he was created a judge of the superior court of judicature. He began now, however, to be afflicted with strictures in the breast, which prevented him from engaging in the more active scenes of life. He was able, however, to ride the circuits of the court for two or three years, but owing to an affection of the heart, he was unable to sum up the arguments of council, or state a cause to the jury.

In the fall of 1785, while riding the circuit, his disorder so rapidly increased, that he was obliged to return home. From this time he was confined to his room, until the 28th day of November, when he expired, in the 55th year of his age.

The mind of Mr. Whipple was naturally strong, and his power of discrimination quick. In his manners, he was easy and unassuming; in his habits correct, and in his friendships constant. Although his early education was limited, his subsequent intercourse with the world, united to his natural good sense, enabled him to fill with ability the various offices to which he was appointed.

Few men have exhibited a more honest and persevering ambition to act a worthy part in the community, and few, with his advantages, have been more successful in obtaining the object of their ambition.

MATTHEW THORNTON.

MATTHEW THORNTON was the son of James Thornton, a native of Ireland, and was born in that country, about the year 1714. When he was two or three years old, his father emigrated to America, and after a residence of a few years at Wiscasset, in Maine, he removed to Worcester, in Massachusetts.

Here young Thornton received a respectable academical education, and subsequently pursued his medical studies, under the direction of Doctor Grout, of Leicester. Soon after completing his preparatory course, he removed to Londonderry, in New-Hampshire, where he commenced the practice of medicine, and soon became distinguished, both as a physician and a surgeon.

In 1745, the well known expedition against Cape Breton was planned by Governor Shirley. The co-operation of New-Hampshire being solicited, a corps of five hundred men was raised in the latter province. Dr. Thornton was selected to accompany the New-Hampshire troops, as a surgeon.

The chief command of this expedition was entrusted to Colonel William Pepperell. On the 1st of May, he invested the city of Louisburg. Lieutenant Colonel Vaughan conducted the first column, through the woods, within sight of Louisburg, and saluted the city with three cheers. At the head of a detachment, chiefly of New-Hampshire troops, he marched in the night, to the northeast part of the harbour, where they burned the warehouses, containing the naval stores, and staved a large quantity of wine and brandy. The smoke of this fire, being driven by the wind into the grand battery, so terrified the French, that, spiking the guns, they retired into the city.

The next morning, as Colonel Vaughan, with his men, consisting of only thirteen, was retiring, he accidentally discovered that the battery was deserted. Upon this, he hired a Cape Cod indian to creep into an embrasure and open the gate. Thus he obtained possession of the place, and immediately dispatched a messenger to the commanding general, with the following note · "May it please your honour to be informed, that, by the grace of God, and the courage of thirteen men, I entered the royal battery about nine o'clock, and am waiting for a reinforcement and a flag."

In the mean time, the news of Vaughan's capture of the battery being communicated to the French, a hundred men were dispatched to retake it; but the gallant colonel succeeded in preventing their design, until reinforcements arrived.

The capture of Louisburg followed after a long and perilous siege. It was here that cannons were drawn by men, for fourteen nights, with straps over their shoulders, from the landing place through a deep morass, into which they sunk, at every step, up to their knees in mud.

Few expeditions in the annals of American history, will compare with this. Louisburg was the "Dunkirk" of America; yet it surrendered to the valour of our troops. It is recorded to the praise of Dr. Thornton, and as an evidence of his professional abilities, that of the corps of five hundred men, of whom he had cha……… only six died of sickness, previous to the surrender of the city, although they were among those who assisted in dragging the cannon over the abovementioned morass.

Under the royal government, he was invested with the office of justice of the peace, and commissioned as colonel of the militia. But when the political crisis arrived, when that government in America was dissolved, Colonel Thornton abjured the British interest, and, with a patriotic spirit, adhered to the glorious cause of liberty. In 1775, the royal governor was obliged to flee from the province of New-Hampshire. A provincial convention was at this time in session at Exeter, for temporary purposes, of which Colonel Thornton was president. In this capacity we find him addressing the inhabitants of the colony of New-Hampshire in the following manner:

"Friends and brethren, you must all be sensible that the affairs of America have, at length, come to a very affecting and alarming crisis. The horrors and distresses of a civil war, which, till of late, we only had in contemplation, we now find ourselves obliged to realize. Painful beyond expression, have been those scenes of blood and devastation, which the barbarous cruelty of British troops have placed before our eyes. Duty to God, to ourselves, to posterity, enforced by the cries of slaughtered innocents, have urged us to take up arms in our own defence. Such a day as this was never before known, either to us or to our fathers. You will give us leave, therefore, in whom you have reposed special confidence, as your representative body, to suggest a few things, which call for the serious attention of every one, who has the true interest of America at heart. We would, therefore, recommend to the colony at large, to cultivate that christian union, harmony, and tender affection, which is the only foundation upon which our invaluable privileges can rest with any security, or our public measures be pursued with the least prospect of success."

After enjoining an inviolable observance of the measures recommended by the congress of 1774, lest they should cross the *general plan*, he proceeds to recommend, " that the most industrious attention be paid to the cultivation of lands and American manufactures, in their various branches, especially the linen and woollen, and that the husbandry might be managed with a particular view thereto; accordingly, that the farmer raise flax, and increase his flock of sheep to the extent of his ability.

"We further recommend a serious and steady regard to the rules of temperance, sobriety, and righteousness; and that those laws which have, heretofore, been our security and defence from the hand of violence, may still answer all their former valuable purposes, though persons of vicious and corrupt minds would willingly take advantage from our present situation.

"In a word, we seriously and earnestly recommend the practice of that pure and undefiled religion, which embalmed the memory of our pious ancestors, as that alone upon which we can build a solid hope and confidence in the Divine protection and favour, without whose blessing all the measures of safety we have, or can propose, will end in our shame and disappointment."

The next year he was chosen a delegate to the continental congress, and took his seat on the fourth of November following. He was, therefore, not a member of that illustrious body which planned and published the declaration of independence. This was true, also, of Benjamin Rush. George Clymer. James Wilson, George Ross, and George Taylor. But all these gentlemen acceding to the declaration, were permitted to affix their signatures to the engrossed copy of that instrument.

During the same year, he was appointed chief justice of the court of common pleas; and not long after was raised to the office of judge of the superior court of New-Hampshire, in which office he remained until 1782. In 1780, he purchased a farm, pleasantly situated on the banks of the Merrimack, near Exeter, where, in connexion with his other diversified occupations, he devoted himself to the business of agriculture. Although advanced in life, he cheerfully granted his pr..

and they were at all times highly appreciated. In the municipal affairs of the town, he took a lively interest. Of the general court he was a member for one or two years, and a senator in the state legislature, and served as a member of the council in 1785, under President Langdon.

Dr. Thornton was a man of strong powers of mind, and on most subjects to which he directed his attention, was able to elicit light and information. In private life, he was peculiarly instructive and agreeable. The young were delighted with his hilarity and humour. His memory was well stored with entertaining and instructive anecdotes, which he was able to apply upon any incident or subject of conversation. He often illustrated his sentiments by fable. He delighted to amuse a circle of an evening by some fictitious narrative, in which he greatly excelled. At such times, placing his elbows upon his knees, and supporting his head with his hands, he would rivet the attention of his auditors, and astonish them by his powers of invention. In satire he was scarcely equalled. And though he sometimes employed his power immoderately, he was universally beloved, and occupied a large share of the confidence of his neighbours. A single fault of his character should not pass unnoticed. It is asserted, that he betrayed some traits of an avaricious disposition, and sometimes enforced his rights, when if justice did not require, charity dictated a relinquishment of them. If, however, he was severe in his pecuniary claims, he was also strict in the payment of his debts.

The powers of Dr. Thornton's mind continued unusually vigorous to a late period of his life. After he was eighty years of age, he wrote political essays for the newspapers, and about this period of life prepared for the press a metaphysical work, comprised in seventy-three manuscript pages in quarto, and entitled, "Paradise Lost; or, the Origin of the Evil called Sin, examined, or how it ever did, or ever can come to pass, that a creature should or could do any thing unfit or improper for that creature to do," &c. This work was never published; but those who have had access to the manuscript, pronounce it a very singular production

It is not a little remarkable, that, although a physician, and consequently often exposed to the whooping cough, he did not take that disease until he had passed his eightieth year. Although at this time enfeebled by years, he survived the attack, and even continued his medical practice.

In stature, Dr. Thornton exceeded six feet in height, but he was remarkably well formed. His complexion was dark, and his eyes black and piercing. His aspect was uncommonly grave, especially for one who was naturally given to good humour and hilarity.

Dr. Thornton died while on a visit at Newburyport, Massachusetts, on the 24th of June, 1803, in the 89th year of his age. In the funeral sermon by Rev. Dr. Burnap, we are furnished with the following sketch. "He was venerable for his age, and skill in his profession, and for the several very important and honourable offices he had sustained; noted for the knowledge he had acquired, and his quick penetration into matters of abstruse speculation, exemplary for his regard for the public institutions of religion, and for his constancy in attending the public worship, where he trod the courts of the house of God, with steps tottering with age and infirmity. Such is a brief outline of one who was honoured in his day and generation; whose virtues were a model for imitation, and while memory does her office, will be had in grateful recollection."

THE RHODE ISLAND DELEGATION.

Stephen Hopkins,
William Ellery.

STEPHEN HOPKINS

STEPHEN HOPKINS was a native of tha part of Providence which is now called Scituate, where he was born on the 7th of March, 1707. His parentage was very respectable, being a descendant of Benedict Arnold, the first governor of Rhode Island.

His early education was limited, being confined to the instruction imparted in the common schools of the country. Yet it is recorded of him, that he excelled in a knowledge of penmanship, and in the practical branches of mathematics, particularly surveying.

For several years he followed the profession of a farmer. At an early period, he was elected town clerk of Scituate, and some time after was chosen a representative from that town to the general assembly. He was subsequently appointed a justice of the peace, and a justice of one of the courts of common pleas. In 1733, he became chief justice of that court.

In 1742, he disposed of his estate in Scituate, and removed to Providence, where he erected a house, in which he continued to reside till his death. In this latter place he entered into mercantile business, and was extensively engaged in building and fitting out vessels.

When a representative from Scituate, he was elected speaker of the house of representatives. To this latter office he was again chosen after his removal to Providence, and continued to occupy the station for several successive years, being a representative from the latter town. In 1751, he was chosen chief justice of the superior court, in which office he continued till the year 1754.

In this latter year he was appointed a commissioner from Rhode Island, to the celebrated convention which met at Albany; which had for its object the securing of the friendship of the five nations of Indians, in the approaching French war, and an union between the several colonies of America.

In 1756, he was elected chief magistrate of the colony of Rhode Island, which office he continued to hold, with but few intervals, until the year 1767. In the discharge of the duties of this responsible station, he acted with dignity and decision. The prosperity of his country lay near his heart, nor did he hesitate to propose and support the measures, which appeared the best calculated to promote the interests of the colonies in opposition to the encroachments of British power.

At an early period of the difficulties between the colonies and Great Britain, he took an active and decided part in favour of the former. In a pamphlet, entitled, "The rights of colonies examined," he exposed the injustice of the stamp act, and various other acts of the British government. This pamphlet was published by order of the general assembly, in 1765.

The siege of fort William Henry, by the Marquis de Montcalm, 1757, and its surrender to the force under that general, with the subsequent cruel outrages and murders committed by the savages of the French army, are too well known to need a recital in this place. It is necessary only to state, that the greatest excitement prevailed throughout all the colonies. In this excitement, the inhabitants of Rhode Island largely participated. An agreement was entered into by a volunteer corps, couched in the following terms:

"Whereas the British colonies in America are invaded by a large army of French and Indian enemies, who have already possessed themselves of fort William Henry, and are now on their march to penetrate further into the country, and from whom we have nothing to expect, should they succeed in their enterprise, but death and devastation; and as his majesty's principal officers in the parts invaded, have in the most pressing and moving manner, called on all his majesty's faithful subjects, for assistance to defend the country:—Therefore, we, whose names are underwritten, thinking it our duty to do every thing in our power, for the defence of our liberties, families, and property, are willing, and have agreed to enter voluntarily into the service of our country, and go in a warlike manner against the common enemy; and hereby call upon and invite all our neighbours, who have families and property to defend, to join with us in this undertaking, promising to march as soon as we are two hundred and fifty in number, recommending ourselves and our cause to the favourable protection of Almighty God."

To this agreement, Mr. Hopkins was the first to affix his name, and was chosen to command the company thus raised, which consisted of some of the most distinguished men in Providence. Preparations for a speedy departure for the field of action were made, but on the eve of their march, intelligence arrived, that their services were no longer necessary, as the progress of hostilities towards the south was not to be expected.

In 1774, Mr. Hopkins received the appointment of a delegate from Rhode Island to the celebrated congress, which met at Philadelphia that year. In this assembly he took his seat on the first day of the session, where he became one of the most zealous advocates of the measures adopted by that illustrious body of men.

In the year 1775 and 1776, he again represented Rhode Island in the continental congress. In this latter year he had the honour of affixing his name to the imperishable instrument, which declared the colonies to be free, sovereign, and independent states. He recorded his name with a trembling hand, the only instance in which a tremulous hand is visible among the fifty-six patriots who then wrote their names. But it was in this case only that the flesh was weak. Mr. Hopkins had for some time been afflicted with a paralytic affection, which compelled him, when he wrote, to guide his right hand with his left. The spirit of the man knew no fear, in a case where life and liberty were at hazard.

In 1778, Mr. Hopkins was a delegate to congress for the last time. But in several subsequent years, he was a member of the general assembly of Rhode Island. The last year in which he thus served, was that of 1779, at which time he was seventy-two years of age.

Mr. Hopkins lived to the 13th of July, 1785, when he closed his long, and honourable and useful life, at the advanced age of 78. His last illness was long, but to the period of his dissolution, he retained the full possession of his faculties A vast assemblage of persons, consisting of judges of the courts, the president, professors and students of the college, together with the citizens of the town, and inhabitants of the state, followed the remains of this eminent man to his resting place in the grave.

Although the early education of Mr. Hopkins was limited, as has already been observed, the vigour of his understanding enabled him to surmount his early deficiencies, and an assiduous application to the pursuit of knowledge, at length, placed him among the distinguished literary characters of the day. He delighted in literature and science. He was attentive to books, and a close observer of mankind, thus he went on improving, until the period of his death As a public speaker, he was always clear, precise, pertinent, and powerful.

As a mathematician, Mr. Hopkins greatly excelled. Till in advanced age, he was extensively employed in surveying lands. He was distinguished for great exactness in his calculations, and an unusual knowledge of his business.

As a statesman and a patriot, he was not less distinguished. He was well instructed in the science of politics; had an extensive knowledge of the rights of his country, and proved himself, through a longer life than falls to the lot of most men, an unshaken friend of his country, and an enemy to civil and religious intolerance. He went to his grave honoured as a skilful legislator, a righteous judge, an able representative, a dignified and upright governor. Charity was an inmate of his habitation. To the cry of suffering his ear was ever open, and in the relief of affliction he ever delighted.

WILLIAM ELLERY.

William Ellery, the son of a gentleman of the same name, was born at Newport, on the 22d day of December, 1727. His ancestors were originally from Bristol, in England, whence they emigrated to America during the latter part of the seventeenth century, and took up their residence at Newport, in Rhode Island.

The early education of the subject of this memoir, was received almost exclusively from his father, who was a graduate of Harvard university; and who although extensively engaged in mercantile pursuits, found leisure personally to cultivate the mind of his son. At the age of sixteen, he was qualified for admission to the university, of which his father had been a member before him. In his twentieth year, he left the university, having sustained, during his collegiate course, the character of a faithful and devoted student. In a knowledge of the Greek and Latin languages, he is said to have particularly excelled, and through the whole bustle of his active life, until the very hour of dissolution, he retained his fondness for them.

On his return to Newport, he commenced the study of the law, and after the usual preparatory course, he entered upon the practice, which for twenty years he pursued with great zeal. During this period, no other particulars have been recorded of him, than that he succeeded in acquiring a competent fortune, and receiving the esteem and confidence of his fellow citizens.

U

At an early period of the controversy between Great Britain and the colonies, Rhode Island strongly enlisted herself in the patriotic cause. She was not backward in expressing her disapprobation of the arbitrary measures of the parent country. Indeed, it is doubtful whether Rhode Island is not equally entitled, with Virginia and Massachusetts, to the honour which they claim, of being earliest in the measures leading to the revolution. Among the great scenes which led the way to actual resistance, two occurred in Narraganset bay. The first of these was an attack by the people of Rhode Island, upon the armed revenue sloop, Liberty, in the harbour of Newport, June 17th, 1769. The second was the memorable affair of the Gaspee, June 9th, 1772, and in which it may be said, was shed the first blood in the revolution. This latter occurrence excited an unusual alarm among the royal party in the provinces, and gave occasion to Governor Hutchinson to address the following letter to Commodore Gambier. "Our last ships carried you the news of the burning of the Gaspee schooner, at Providence. I hope, if there should be another like attempt, some concerned in it may be taken prisoners, and carried directly to England. A few punished at *execution dock*, would be the only effectual preventive of any further attempts."

By other acts did the people of Rhode Island, at an early period, evince their opposition to the royal government. On the arrival in the year 1774 of the royal proclamation prohibiting the importation of fire arms from England, they dismantled the fort at Newport, and took possession of forty pieces of cannon. Again, on the occurrence of the battle of Lexington, they simultaneously roused to the defence of their fellow citizens, in the province of Massachusetts. Within three days after that memorable event, a large number of her militia were in the neighbourhood of Boston, ready to cooperate in measures either of hostility or defence. In the same year she sent twelve hundred regular troops into the service, and afterwards furnished three state regiments to serve during the war.

No so···· ·· ··· form·tion of a continental congress sup

gested, than Rhode Island took measures to be represented in that body, and elected as delegates two of her most distinguished citizens, Governor Hopkins and Mr. Ward.

During these movements in Rhode Island, Mr. Ellery, the subject of this notice, was by no means an idle spectator. The particular history of the part which he took in these transactions is, indeed, not recorded; but the tradition is, that he was not behind his contemporaries either in spirit or action.

In the election for delegates to the congress of 1776, Mr. Ellery was a successful candidate, and in that body took his seat, on the seventeenth of May. Here, he soon became an active and influential member, and rendered important services to his country, by his indefatigable attention to duties assigned him, on several committees. During this session, he had the honour of affixing his name to the declaration of independence. Of this transaction he frequently spoke, and of the notice he took of the members of congress when they signed that instrument. He placed himself beside secretary Thompson, that he might see how they *looked*, as they put their names to their *death warrant*. But while all appeared to feel the solemnity of the occasion, and their countenances bespoke their awe, it was *unmingled with fear*. They recorded their names as *patriots*, who were ready, should occasion require, to lead the *way to martyrdom*.

In the year 1777, the marine committee of congress, of which Mr. Ellery was a member, recommended the plan, and it is supposed, at his suggestion, of preparing fire ships, and sending them out from the state of Rhode Island. Of this plan, the journals of congress speak in the following terms:

"If upon due consideration, jointly had by the navy board for the eastern department, and the governor and council of war for the state of Rhode Island, and for which purpose the said navy board are directed to attend upon the said governor and council of war, the preparing fire ships be judged practicable, expedient, and advisable, the said navy board immediately purchase, upon as reasonable terms as possible, six ships, or square rigged v ls, at Provi   , the state of Rhode I nd and Pr i n Plantati n   e st calculated for fire ships, with all possible expedition ; that the said navy board provide proper materials for the same, and employ a proper captain or commander, one lieutenant, and a suitable number of men for each of the said ships, or vessels, of approved courage and prudence ; and that notice be given to all the commanders of the continental ships and vessels in the port of Providence, to be in readiness to sail at a moment's warning : that as soon as the said fire ships are well prepared, the first favourable wind be embraced to attack the British ships and navy in the rivers and bays of the state of Rhode Island and Providence Plantations: that the officers of the continental navy there, favour, as much as possible, the design, and use their utmost efforts to get out to sea, and proceed to such cruise, or to such ports, as the said navy board, or the marine committee, shall appoint or order."

During the year that the British army under General Piggot took possession of Newport, where they fortified themselves, and continued their head quarters for some time, the inhabitants sustained much injury in their property. Mr. Ellery shared in the common loss, his dwelling house being burned, and other destruction of property occasioned.

Mr. Ellery continued a member of congress until the year 1785, and indeed, through that year, when he retired to his native state. Soon after, however, he was elected by congress, a commissioner of the continental loan office, to which was subsequently added, by the citizens of Rhode Island, the office of chief justice of their superior court, a station which he did not continue to hold long. On the organization of the federal government, he received from General Washington the appointment of collector of the customs for the town of Newport, an office which he retained during the remainder of his life.

On the 15th of February, 1820, this venerable man—venerable for his age, which had been prolonged to ninety-two years, and venerable for the services which he had rendered his country, was summoned to his account. His death was in unison with his life. He wasted gradually and almost imperceptibly, until the powers of nature were literally worn out by use. On the day on which his death occurred, he had risen, as usual, and rested in his old flag bottomed chair, the relict of half a century, he had employed himself in reading Tully's offices in Latin.

While thus engaged, his family physician called to see him. On feeling his pulse, he found that it had ceased to beat. A draught of wine and water quickened it into life, however, again, and being placed and supported on the bed, he continued reading, *until the lamp of life, in a moment of which his friends were ignorant, was extinguished.*

> "Of no distemper, of no blast he died,
> But fell like autumn fruit that mellowed long,
> E'en wonder'd at because he falls no sooner.
> Fate seem'd to wind him up for fourscore years,
> Yet freshly ran he on twelve winters more.
> Till, like a clock worn out with eating time,
> The wheels of weary life at last stood still."

In the character of Mr. Ellery there was much to admire. He was, indeed, thought by some to have been too tenacious of his opinion, and not always free from asperity to others. But years mellowed down these unpleasant traits of his character, and showed that he had exercised a watchfulness over himself, not entirely in vain. He manifested an uncommon disregard of the applause of men. It was often upon his lips: "humility rather than pride becomes such creatures as we are." He looked upon the world and its convulsions with religious serenity, and in times of public danger, and of public difficulty, he comforted himself and others, with the pious reflection of the psalmist, "The Lord reigneth."

In conversation, Mr. Ellery was at once interesting and instructive. His advice was often sought, and his opinions regarded with great reverence. In letter writing he excelled, as he did in fine penmanship, which latter would be inferred from his signature to the declaration of independence. In stature, he was of middling height, and carried in his person the indications of a sound frame and an easy mind. In the courtesies of life, he kept pace with the improvements of the age; but his conversation and dress, and habits of life, plainly showed that he belonged to a more primitive generation.

THE

CONNECTICUT DELEGATION.

ROGER SHERMAN,
SAMUEL HUNTINGTON,
WILLIAM WILLIAMS,
OLIVER WOLCOTT.

ROGER SHERMAN.

ROGER SHERMAN, the subject of the present memoir, was a native of Newton, Massachusetts, where he was born on the 19th of April, 1721. His ancestors were from Dedham, in England, whence they removed to America about the year 1635, and settled at Watertown in the same state. The father of Mr. Sherman, whose name was William, was a respectable farmer, but from his moderate circumstances was unable to give his son the advantages of an education, beyond those which were furnished by a parochial school.

He was early apprenticed to a shoemaker, which occupation he followed for some time after he was twenty-two years of age. It is recorded of him, however, that he early evinced an uncommon thirst for knowledge, and was wont, even while at work on his seat, to have a book open before him, upon which he would employ every moment, not necessarily devoted to the duties of his calling.

The father of Mr. Sherman died in the year 1741, leaving his family, which was quite n   .   , i.   cum-tances of dependence. The care of th   ed upon Roger, his older brother having sometime before removed to New-Milford, in Connecticut. This was a serious charge for a young man only nineteen years of age. Yet, with great kindness and cheerfulness did he engage in the duties which devolved upon him. Towards his mother, whose life was protracted to a great age, he continued to manifest the tenderest affection, and assisted two of his younger brothers to obtain a liberal education. These, afterwards, became clergymen of some distinction in Connecticut.

It has already been observed, that an older brother had established himself in New-Milford, Connecticut. In 1743, it was judged expedient for the family, also, to remove to that place. Accordingly, having disposed of their small farm, they became residents of New-Milford, in June of that year. This journey was performed by young Roger on foot, with his tools on his back.

At New-Milford, he commenced business as a shoemaker; but not long after he relinquished his trade, having entered into partnership with his older brother, in the more agreeable occupation of a country merchant.

Mr. Sherman early evinced, as has already been observed, an unusual thirst for knowledge. This led him to seize with avidity every opportunity to acquire it. The acquisitions of such a mind, even with the disadvantages under which he laboured, must have been comparatively easy, and his improvement was rapid. The variety and extent of his attainments, even at this early age, are almost incredible. He soon became known in the county of Litchfield, where he resided, as a man of more than ordinary talents, and of unusual skill in the science of mathematics. In 1745, only two years after his removal into the above county, and at the age of twenty-four, he was appointed to the office of county surveyor. At this time it appears, also, he had made no small advance in the science of astronomy. As early as 1748, he supplied the astronomical calculations for an almanac, published in the city of New-York, and continued this supply for several succeeding years.

In 1749 he was married to Miss Elizabeth Hartwell, of

Stoughton, in Massachusetts. After her decease, in 1760, he married Miss Rebecca Prescot, of Danvers, in the same state. By these wives he had fifteen children, seven by the former, and eight by the latter.

In 1754, Mr. Sherman was admitted as an attorney to the bar. It is a trite remark, that great effects often proceed from small causes, and that not unfrequently some apparently trivial occurrence, exercises a controling influence over the whole after life of an individual. Both these remarks are eminently verified in the history of Mr. Sherman. While yet a young man, and, it is believed before he had relinquished his mechanical occupation, he had occasion to go to a neighbouring town to transact some business for himself. A short time previous to this, a neighbour of his, in settling the affairs of a person deceased, became involved in a difficulty which required the assistance of legal counsel. The neighbour stated the case to young Sherman, and authorized him to seek the advice of the lawyer of the town to which he was going.

As the subject was not without intricacy, Sherman committed the case to paper, and on his arrival in the town, proceeded with his manuscript to the lawyer's office. In stating the case to the lawyer, he had frequent occasion to recur to his manuscript. This was noticed by the lawyer, and, as it was necessary to present a petition in the case to some court, Sherman was requested to leave the paper, as an assistance in framing the petition. The modesty of young Sherman would scarcely permit him to comply with this request. "The paper," he said, "was only a memorandum drawn by himself to assist his memory." He gave it, however, into the hands of the lawyer, who read it with surprise. He found it to contain a clear statement of the case, and remarked, that with some slight verbal alterations, it would be equal to any petition which he himself could draft.

The conversation now passed to the situation and circumstances of young Sherman. The lawyer urged him seriously to think upon the profession of law. At this time, he was deeply involved in the care of his father's family, which, as before noticed, were left in a great measure destitute at his decease. The suggestion, however, appears not to have been lost upon him. A new direction was given to his thoughts. A stronger impulse was added to his energies. His leisure hours were devoted to the acquisition of legal knowledge, and in 1754, as already remarked, he entered upon a professional career, in which few have attained to greater honour and distinction.

From this date, Mr. Sherman soon became distinguished as a judicious counsellor, and was rapidly promoted to offices of trust and responsibility. The year following his admission to the bar, he was appointed a justice of the peace for New-Milford, which town he also represented the same year in the colonial assembly. In 1759, he was appointed judge of the court of common pleas for the county of Litchfield, an office which he filled with great reputation for the two following years.

At the expiration of this time, that is in 1761, he became a resident of New-Haven, of which town he was soon after appointed a justice of the peace, and often represented it in the colonial assembly. To these offices was added, in 1765, that of judge of the court of common pleas. About the same time he was appointed treasurer of Yale College, which institution bestowed upon him the honorary degree of Master of Arts.

In 1766, he was elected by the freemen of the colony a member of the upper house, in the general assembly of Connecticut. The members of the upper house were called *assistants*. This body held their deliberations with closed doors. The precise rank, therefore, which Mr. Sherman held among his colleagues, or the services which he rendered his country, cannot now be ascertained. Few men, however, were better fitted for a deliberative assembly. During the same year, the confidence of his fellow-citizens was still farther expressed, by his appointment to the office of judge of the superior court. The offices, thus conferred upon him, during the same year, were not then considered as incompatible. He continued a member of the upper house for nineteen years, until 1785, at which time the two offices which he held being considered as incompatible, he relinquished his seat at the council board, preferring his station as a judge. This latter office he continued to exercise until 1789, when he resigned it, on being elected to congress under the federal constitution.

At an early stage of the controversy between Great Britain and her American colonies, Mr. Sherman warmly espoused the cause of his country. This was to be expected of him. A man of so much integrity and consistency of character, of such firmness and solidity, would not be likely to be wanting in the day of trial. It was fortunate for America that she had some such men in her councils, to balance and keep in check the feverish spirits which, in their zeal, might have injured, rather than benefitted the cause. Mr. Sherman was no enthusiast, nor was he to be seduced from the path of duty by motives of worldly ambition, or love of applause. He early perceived, that the contest would have to be terminated by a resort to arms. Hence, he felt the paramount importance of union among the colonies. He felt the full force of the sentiment, " United we stand, divided we fall." From the justice or clemency of Great Britain, he expected nothing; nor, at an early day, could he perceive any rational ground to hope that the contest could be settled, but by the entire separation of American and British interests. He was, therefore, prepared to proceed, not rashly, but with deliberate firmness, and to resist, even unto blood the unrighteous attempts of the British parliament to enthral and enslave the American colonies.

Of the celebrated congress of 1774, Mr. Sherman was a conspicuous member. He was present at the opening of the session; and continued uninterruptedly a member of that body for the long space of nineteen years, until his death in 1793.

Of the important services which he rendered his country, during his congressional career, it is difficult and even impossible to form an estimate. He served on various committees, whose deliberations often involved the interest of the country. During the continuance of the war of the revolution, the duties of committees were frequently arduous and fatiguing. No man adventured upon these duties with more courage; no one exercised a more indefatigable zeal than did Mr. Sherman. He investigated every subject with uncommon particularity, and formed his judgment with a comprehensive view of the whole. This, together with the well known integrity of his character, attracted universal confidence. He naturally became, therefore, one of the leading and most influential members of congress, during the whole period of his holding a seat in that body.

Of the congress of 1775, Mr. Sherman was again a member; but of this day of clouds and darkness, when the storm which had long lowered, began to burst forth on every side, we can take no further notice than to mention, with gratitude and admiration, the firmness of those assembled sages who, with courage, breasted themselves to the coming shock. They calmly and fearlessly applied themselves to the defence of the liberties of their country, having counted the cost, and being prepared to surrender their rights only with their lives.

In the congress of 1776, Mr. Sherman took a distinguished part. He assisted on committees appointed to give instructions for the military operations of the army in Canada; to establish regulations and restrictions on the trade of the United States; to regulate the currency of the country; to furnish supplies for the army; to provide for the expenses of the government; to prepare articles of confederation between the several states, and to propose a plan of military operations for the campaign of 1776.

During this year, also, he received the most flattering testimony of the high estimation in which he was held by congress, in being associated with Adams, Jefferson, Franklin. and Livingston, in the responsible duty of preparing the declaration of independence.

The reputation of Mr. Sherman abroad, was cordially reciprocated in the state in which he resided. Few men were ever more highly esteemed in Connecticut. The people understood his worth. They respected him for his abilities, but still more for his unbending integrity. During the war he belonged to the governor's council of safety; and from the year 1784 to his death, he held the mayoralty of the city of New-Haven. In 1783, he was appointed, with the honourable Richard Law, both of whom were at this time judges of the superior court, to revise the statutes of the state. This service, rendered doubly onerous to the committee from their being instructed to digest all the statutes relating to the same subject into one, and to reduce the whole to alphabetical order, was performed with great ability. Many useless statutes were omitted; others were altered to correspond to the great changes which had then recently taken place in the state of the country, and the whole reduced to comparative order and simplicity.

Another expression of the public confidence awaited Mr Sherman in 1787. Soon after the close of the war, the inefficacy of the old confederation between the states was apparent. The necessity of a federal constitution, by which the powers of the state governments and of the general government should be more nicely balanced, became every day more obvious. Accordingly, in 1787, a general convention of the states, for forming a new constitution, was called, and Mr. Sherman, in connexion with the learned Mr. Ellsworth and Dr. Johnson, were appointed to attend it, on the part of Connecticut. In this assemblage of patriots, distinguished for their political wisdom, Mr. Sherman was conspicuous, and contributed, in no small degree, to the perfection of that constitution, under which the people of America have for more than forty years enjoyed as much civil liberty and political prosperity as is, probably, compatible with the lapsed condition of the human race. Many of the convention, who warmly advocated the adoption of the constitution, were not, indeed, well pleased with every feature of that instrument. To this number Mr. Sherman belonged. He was of the opinion, however, as were others, that it was the best which, under existing circumstances, the convention could have framed. On his return to Connecticut, when the question respecting the adoption of the constitution came before the convention of that state, its adoption, according to the testimony of the late Chief Justice Ellsworth, was, in no small degree, owing to the influence of Mr. Sherman. On that occasion, he appeared before the convention, and, with great plainness and perspicuity, entered into an explanation of the probable operation of the principles of the constitution.

Under this new constitution, he was elected a representative to congress, from the state of Connecticut. At the expiration of two years, a vacancy occurring in the senate, he was elevated to a seat in that body, an office which he continued to hold, and the duties of which he continued to discharge with honour and reputation to himself, and with great usefulness to his country, until the 23d day of July, 1793, when he was gathered to his fathers, in the 73d year of his age.

In estimating the character of Mr. Sherman, we must dwell a moment upon his practical wisdom. This, in him, was a predominant trait. He possessed, more than most men, an intimate acquaintance with human nature. He understood the springs of human action in a remarkable degree, and well knew in what manner to touch them, to produce a designed effect. This practical wisdom, another name for common sense, powerfully contributed to guide him to safe results, on all the great political questions in which he was concerned, and assisted him to select the means which were best adapted to accomplish the best ends. With the habits and opinions, with the virtues and vices, the prejudices and weaknesses of his countrymen, he was also well acquainted. Hence, he understood, better than many others, who were superior to him in the rapidity of their genius, what laws and principles they would bear, and what they would not bear, in government. Of the practical wisdom of Mr. Sherman, we might furnish many honourable testimonies and numerous illustrations. We must content ourselves, however, with recording a remark of President Jefferson, to the late Dr. Spring, of Newburyport. During the sitting of Congress at Philadelphia, the latter gentleman, in company with Mr. Jefferson, visited the national hall. Mr. Jefferson pointed out to the doctor several of the members, who were most conspicuous. At length, his eye rested upon Roger Sherman. "That," said he, pointing his finger, "is Mr Sherman of Connecticut, *a man who never said a foolish thing in his life.*" Not less complimentary was the remark of Mr. Macon, the aged and distinguished senator, who has recently retired from public life: "Roger Sherman had more common sense than any man I ever knew."

Another distinguishing trait in the character of Roger Sherman, was his unbending integrity. No man, probably, ever stood more aloof from the suspicion of a selfish bias, or of sinister motives. In both his public and private conduct, he was actuated by principle. The opinion which appeared correct, he adopted, and the measure which appeared the best, he pursued, apparently uninfluenced by passion, prejudice, or interest. It was probably owing to this trait in his character, that he enjoyed such extraordinary influence in those deliberative bodies of which he was a member. In his speech, he was slow and hesitating. He had few of the graces of oratory; yet no man was heard with deeper attention. This attention arose from the solid conviction of the hearers, that he was an honest man. What he said, was indeed always applicable to the point, was clear, was weighty; and, as the late President Dwight remarked, was generally new and important. Yet the weight of his observations, obviously, sprung from the integrity of the man. It was this trait in his character, which elicited the observation of the distinguished Fisher Ames. "If I am absent," said he, "during the discussion of a subject, and consequently know not on which side to vote, I always look at Roger Sherman, for I am sure *if I vote with him I shall vote right.*"

To the above excellent traits in the character of Mr. Sherman, it may be added, that he was eminently a pious man. He was long a professor of religion, and one of its brightest ornaments. Nor was his religion that which appeared only on occasions. It was with him a principle and a habit. It appeared in his closet, in the family, on the bench, and in the senate house. Few men had a higher reverence for the bible, few men studied it with deeper attention; few were more intimately acquainted with the doctrines of the gospel, and the metaphysical controversies of the day. On these subjects, he maintained an extended correspondence with some of the most distinguished divines of that period, among whom were Dr. Edwards, Dr. Hopkins, Dr. Trumbull, President Dickenson, and President Witherspoon, all of whom had a high opinion of him as a theologian, and derived much instruction from their correspondence with him.

If the character of a man's religion is to be tested by the fruits it produces, the religion of Mr. Sherman must be admitted to have been not of this world. He was naturally possessed of strong passions; but over these he at length obtained an extraordinary control. He became habitually calm, sedate, and self-possessed. The following instance of his self-possession is worthy of being recorded.

Mr. Sherman was one of those men who are not ashamed to maintain the forms of religion in his family. One morning he called them together, as usual, to lead them in prayer to God: the " old family bible" was brought out, and laid on the table. Mr. Sherman took his seat, and beside him placed one of his children, a small child, a child of his old age; the rest of the family were seated round the room; several of these were now grown up. Besides these, some of the tutors of the college, and it is believed, some of the students, were boarders in the family, and were present at the time alluded to. His aged, and now superanuated mother, occupied a corner of the room, opposite to the place where the distinguished judge of Connecticut sat. At length he opened the bible, and began to read. The child which was seated beside him, made some little disturbance, upon which Mr. Sherman paused, and told it to be still. Again he proceeded, but again he paused, to reprimand the little offender, whose playful disposition would scarcely permit it to be still. At this time, he gently tapped its ear. The blow, if it might be called a blow, caught the attention of his aged mother, who with some effort rose from her seat, and tottered across the room.

At length, she reached the chair of Mr. Sherman, and in a moment most unexpected to him, she gave him a blow on the ear, with all the power she could summon. "*There*," said she, "*you strike your child, and I will strike mine.*"

For a moment, the blood was seen rushing to the face of Mr. Sherman; but it was only for a moment, when all was as mild and calm as usual. He paused—he raised his spectacles—he cast his eye upon his mother—again it fell upon the book, from which he had been reading. Perhaps he remembered the injunction, "honour thy mother," and he did honour her. Not a word escaped him; but again he calmly pursued the service, and soon after sought in prayer ability to set an example before his household, which should be worthy their imitation. Such self-possession is rare. Such a victory was worth more than the proudest victory ever achieved in the field of battle.

We have room only to add the inscription, which is recorded upon the tablet which covers the tomb of this truly excellent man:

In memory of
THE HON. ROGER SHERMAN, ESQ.
Mayor of the city of New-Haven,
and Senator of the United States.
He was born at Newton, in Massachusetts,
April 19th, 1721,
And died in New-Haven, July 23d, A, D. 1793,
aged LXXII.
Possessed of a strong, clear, penetrating mind,
and singular perseverance,
he became the self-taught scholar,
eminent for jurisprudence and policy.
He was nineteen years an assistant,
and twenty-three years a judge of the superior court,
in high reputation.
He was a Delegate in the first Congress,
signed the glorious act of Independence,
and many years displayed superior talents and ability
in the national legislature.
He was a member of the general convention,
approved the f[e]deral co[n]stitution
And served [four years with fidelity [and hono]ur,
in the H[o]u[se] of Rep[resent]at[ive]s.

and in the Senate of the United States.
He was a man of approved integrity,
a cool, discerning Judge;
a prudent, sagacious Politician;
a true, faithful, and firm Patriot
He ever adorned
the profession of christianity
which he made in youth,
and distinguished through life
for public usefulness,
died in the prospect of a blessed immortality.

SAMUEL HUNTINGTON.

SAMUEL HUNTINGTON was born in Windham, Connecticut, on the 2d day of July, 1732. His ancestors were respectable; they came to America at an early period of the country, and settled in Connecticut.

The father of the subject of the present memoir was Nathaniel Huntington, who resided in the town of Windham, where he was a plain but worthy farmer. His mother was distinguished for her many virtues. She was a pious, discreet woman, and endued with a more than ordinary share of mental vigour. A numerous family of children cemented the affection of this worthy pair. Several of the sons devoted themselves to the gospel ministry, and attained to a highly respectable standing in their profession. Of those who thus devoted themselves to the clerical profession, Dr. Joseph Huntington was one. He is well known as the author of a posthumous work, on universal salvation. It was entitled, "Calvinism Improved, or the Gospel illustrated as a system of real Grace, issuing in the salvation of all men." This work was afterwards ably answered by Dr. Nathan Strong, of Hartford.

In the benefits of a public education, which were thus con

ferred on several of his brothers, Samuel Huntington did not share. He was the eldest son, and his father needed his assistance on the farm. Indeed, his opportunities for obtaining knowledge were extremely limited, not extending beyond those furnished by the common schools of that day.

Mr. Huntington, however, possessed a vigorous understanding, and, when released from the toils of the field, he devoted himself with great assiduity to reading and study. Thus, the deficiencies of the common school were more than supplied. He became possessed of an extensive fund of information upon various subjects, and by the time he was twenty-one years of age, he probably fell little short in his acquisitions of those who had received a collegiate education, except in some particular branches. His knowledge was less scientific, but more practical and useful.

Although not averse to husbandry, he early manifested a fondness for legal pursuits, and at the age of twenty-two he relinquished the labours of the field, for the more agreeable study of the law. Pecuniary circumstances prevented his availing himself of legal tuition in the office of a lawyer. But he was contented to explore the labyrinths of the profession unaided, except by his own judgment. The library of a respectable lawyer in a neighbouring town, furnished him with the necessary books, and his diligence and perseverance accomplished the rest.

Mr. Huntington soon obtained a competent knowledge of the principles of law, to commence the practice of the profession. He opened an office in his native town, but in 1760, removed to Norwich, where a wider field presented itself, for the exercise of his talents. Here, he soon became eminent in his profession. He was distinguished by a strict integrity, and no man exceeded him in punctuality. These traits of character, united to no ordinary legal attainments, and strong common sense, insured him the respect of the community, and a large share of professional business.

In 1764, Mr. Huntington represented the town of Norwich in the general assembly. This was the commencement of his political career. In the year following he was ap pointed to the office of king's attorney, the duties of which he continued to discharge, with great fidelity, for several years. In 1774, he became an associate judge in the superior court, and soon after an assistant in the council of Connecticut.

Mr. Huntington was among those who early and strongly set themselves in opposition to the claims and oppressions of the British parliament. In his opinions on national subjects, he was eminently independent; nor was he backward in expressing those opinions, on every suitable occasion. His talents and patriotism recommended him to public favour, and in October, 1775, he was appointed by the general assembly of Connecticut to represent that colony in the continental congress. In the January following, in conjunction with his distinguished colleagues, Roger Sherman, Oliver Wolcott, &c. he took his seat in that venerable body. In the subsequent July he voted in favour of the declaration of independence.

Of the continental congress, Mr. Huntington continued a member until the year 1781, when the ill state of his health required the relinquishment of the arduous services in which he had been engaged for several years. These services had been rendered still more onerous by an appointment, in 1779, to the presidency of the congress, in which station he succeeded Mr. Jay, on the appointment of the latter as minister plenipotentiary to the court of Madrid. The honourable station of president, Mr. Huntington filled with great dignity and distinguished ability. " In testimony of their approbation of his conduct in the chair, and in the execution of public business," congress, soon after his retirement, accorded to him the expression of their public thanks.

Thus relieved from the toils which his high official station in congress had imposed upon him, Mr. Huntington was soon able to resume his judicial functions in the superior court of Connecticut, and his duties as an assistant in the council of that state, both of which offices had been kept vacant during his absence.

The public however, were unwilling long to dispense with his services in the great national assembly. Accordingly, in

1782, he was re-elected a delegate to congress; but either feeble health, or his duties as a judge, prevented his attendance for that year. He was re-appointed the following year to the same office, and in July resumed his seat in congress, where he continued a conspicuous and influential member, until November, when he finally retired from the national assembly.

Soon after his return to his native state, he was placed at the head of the superior court, and the following year, 1785, was elected lieutenant governor of the state. The next year he succeeded Governor Griswold in the office of chief magistrate of the state, and to this office he was annually re-elected during the remainder of his life.

The death of this excellent and distinguished man occurred on the 5th of January, 1796, in the 64th year of his age. His departure from the world, as might be expected, from the even tenor of his life, and from the decided christian character and conversation which he had manifested, was tranquil. He had for many years been a professor of religion, and a devoted attendant upon the ordinances of the gospel. His seat in the house of God was seldom vacant, and, when occasion required, he was ready to lead in an address to the throne of grace, and was able to impart instruction to the people, drawn from the pure oracles of God.

Such, in few words, was the religious character of Governor Huntington. His domestic character was not less excellent To strangers, he might appear formal. He possessed a dignity, and a natural reserve, which repressed the advances of all, except his intimate friends; but to these he was ever accessible and pleasant. Few men ever possessed a greater share of mildness and equanimity of temper. Sentiments of anger seem to have found no place in his breast; nor was he scarcely ever known to utter a word which could wound the feelings of another, or asperse the good name of an absent person.

To show and parade, Mr. Huntington was singularly averse. In early life he had acquired rigid habits of economy, which appear to have continued during his life. Hence in his domestic arrangements, in his diet, in his dress, his simplicity was such as to bring upon him the charge of parsimony. The justice or injustice of this charge, we have not the means of determining; but the private beneficence of Mr. Huntington is so amply attested to, that the charge of parsimony was probably brought against him only by the profuse.

Mr. Huntington was not connected in life until the 30th year of his age. At that time he married a daughter of Ebenezer Devotion, the worthy minister of the town of Windham. Having no children, Mr. Huntington adopted two of the children of his brother, the Reverend Joseph Huntington, one of whom afterwards became governor of Ohio; and the other is at present the wife of the Reverend Doctor Griffin, president of Williams' College, in Massachusetts. The death of Mrs. Huntington preceded that of her husband about two years.

On the public character, or the public services of Governor Huntington, it is unnecessary to enlarge. It is pleasant, however, to mark the progress of such a man, from obscurity to the exalted and dignified walks of life, and from the humble occupation of a plough boy, to the deep and learned investigations of the judge, and to the wise and sagacious plans of the statesman. What was true of Mr. Huntington, in this respect, was true of a great proportion of that phalanx of patriots who, during the days of our revolutionary struggle, opposed themselves with success to British exactions and British oppressions. They came from humble life. They rose by the force of their native genius. Obstacles served only to rouse their latent strength. They threw aside discouragements, as the skilful swimmer dashes aside the waters which impede his course.

Mr. Huntington was one of these men. He had not the advantage of family patronage, or the benefit of a liberal education; nor did hereditary wealth lend him her aid. But, instead of these, he had genius, courage, and perseverance. With the united assistance of these, he entered upon his professional course, and afterwards, on his political career. He rendered services to his country, which will long be remembered with gratitude; he attained to honours with which a high ambition might have been satisfied; and, at length, went down to the grave, cheered with the prospect of a happy immortality.

WILLIAM WILLIAMS.

The family of William Williams is said to have been originally from Wales. A branch of it came to America in the year 1630, and settled in Roxbury, Massachusetts. His grandfather, who bore the same name, was the minister of Hatfield, Massachusetts; and his father, Solomon Williams, D.D. was the minister of a parish in Lebanon, where he was settled fifty-four years. Solomon Williams, the father, married a daughter of Colonel Porter, of Hadley, by whom he had five sons and three daughters. The sons were all liberally educated. Of these, Eliphalet was settled, as a minister of the gospel, in East-Hartford, where he continued to officiate for about half a century. Ezekiel was sheriff of the county of Hartford for more than thirty years; he died a few years since at Wethersfield, leaving behind him a character distinguished for energy and enterprise, liberality and benevolence

William Williams, the subject of this memoir, was born in Lebanon, Connecticut, on the eighth of April, 1731. At the age of sixteen, he entered Harvard college. During his collegiate course, he was distinguished for a diligent attention, and, at the proper period, was honourably graduated. From the university he returned home, and, for a considerable time, devoted himself to theological studies, under the direction of his father.

In September, 1755, was fought, at the head of Lake George, a celebrated battle between the provincial troops, under command of major general, afterwards Sir William Johnson, aided by a body of indians led by the celebrated Hendrick, and a body of French Canadians and indians, commanded by Monsieur le Baron de Dieskau. At this time, Colonel Ephraim Williams commanded a regiment of provincial troops, raised by Massachusetts, with which he was engaged in the above battle. William Williams, the subject of our memoir, belonged to his staff.

Colonel Williams was an officer of great merit. He was much beloved by his soldiers, and highly respected by the people of Massachusetts, in the place where he resided. Williams' college owes its existence to him. As he was proceeding through Albany, to the head of Lake George, he made his will in that city. In this instrument, after giving certain legacies to his connexions, he directed that the remainder of his land should be sold at the discretion of his executors, within five years after an established peace, and that the interest of the monies arising from the sale, together with some other property, should be applied to the support of a free school, in some township in the western part of Massachusetts. This was the origin of Williams' college. Both the college, and the town in which it is situated, were named after their distinguished benefactor.

Previous to the battle of Lake George, Colonel Williams was despatched with a party of twelve hundred men, to observe the motions of the French and Indian army, under Baron Dieskau. He met the enemy at Rocky Brook, four miles from Lake George. A tremendous battle now ensued. The English soldiers fought with great courage, but at length they were overpowered, and obliged to retreat. During the contest, Colonel Williams was shot through the head by an Indian, and killed. The command of the detachment now devolved upon Colonel Whiting, of New-Haven, who succeeded in joining Sir William Johnson, with the force which had escaped the power of the enemy. The issue of this day is well known. The French army was finally repulsed, and the Baron Dieskau was both wounded and taken prisoner.

Soon after the death of Colonel Williams, the subject of

this memoir, returned to Lebanon, where he resolved to fix his permanent residence. In 1756, at the age of twenty-five years, he was chosen clerk of the town of Lebanon, an office which he continued to hold for the space of forty-five years. About the same time, he was appointed to represent the town in the general assembly of Connecticut. In this latter capacity, he served a long succession of years, during which he was often chosen clerk of the house, and not unfrequently filled, and always with dignity and reputation, the speaker's chair. In 1780, he was transferred to the upper house, being elected an assistant; an office to which he was annually re-elected for twenty-four years. It was recorded of him, what can probably be recorded of few, and perhaps of no other man, that for more than *ninety* sessions, he was scarcely absent from his seat in the legislature, excepting when he was a member of the continental congress, in 1776 and 1777.

During the years last mentioned, he was a member of the national council; and in the deliberations of that body took a part, during the memorable period, when the charter of our independence received the final approbation of congress.

At an early period of the revolution, he embarked with great zeal in the cause of his country. During the campaign of 1755, while at the north, he had learned a lesson, which he did not forget. He was at that time disgusted with the British commanders, on account of the haughtiness of their conduct, and the little attachment which they manifested for his native country. The impression was powerful and lasting. At that time he adopted the opinion, that America would see no days of prosperity and peace, so long as British officers should manage her affairs. On the arrival of the day, therefore, when the revolutionary struggle commenced, and a chance was presented of release from the British yoke, Mr. Williams was ready to engage with ardour, in bringing about this happy state of things. He had for several years been interested in mercantile pursuits. These he now relinquished, that he might devote himself to the cause of his country. He powerfully contributed to awaken public feeling, by several essays on political subjects and when an occasion called him to speak in public, his patriotic zeal and independent spirit were manifested, in a powerful and impressive eloquence.

Nor was Mr. Williams one of those patriots with whom words are all. He was ready to make sacrifices, whenever occasion required. An instance of his public spirit is recorded, in the early part of the revolution. At this time the paper money of the country was of so little value, that military services could not be procured for it. Mr. Williams, with great liberality, exchanged more than two thousand dollars in specie, for this paper, for the benefit of his country. In the issue, he lost the whole sum.

A similar spirit of liberality marked his dealings, in the settlement of his affairs, on the eve and during the course of the revolution. He was peculiarly kind to debtors impoverished by the war, and from the widow and the fatherless, made so by the struggle for freedom, he seldom made any exactions, even though he himself suffered by his kindness.

At the commencement of the war, it is well known, there was little provision made for the support of an army. There were no public stores, no arsenals filled with warlike instruments, and no clothing prepared for the soldiers. For many articles of the first necessity, resort was had to private contributions. The selectmen in many of the towns of Connecticut volunteered their services, to obtain articles for the necessary outfit of new recruits, for the maintenance of the families of indigent soldiers, and to furnish supplies even for the army itself.

Mr. Williams was, at this time, one of the selectmen of the town of Lebanon, an office which he continued to hold during the whole revolutionary war. No man was better fitted for such a station, and none could have manifested more unwearied zeal than he did, in soliciting the benefactions of private families for the above objects. Such was his success, that he forwarded to the army more than one thousand blankets. In many instances, families parted with their last blanket, for the use of the soldiers in the camp; and bullets were made from the lead taken from the weights of clocks Such was the patriotism of the fathers and mothers of the land, in those days of trial. There were no comforts, which they could not cheerfully forego, and no sacrifices which they did not joyfully make, that the blessings of freedom might be theirs, and might descend to their posterity.

In confirmation of the above evidence of the firmness and patriotism of Mr. Williams, the following anecdote may be added. Towards the close of the year 1776, the military affairs of the colonies wore a gloomy aspect, and strong fears began to prevail that the contest would go against them. In this dubious state of things, the council of safety for Connecticut was called to sit at Lebanon. Two of the members of this council, William Hillhouse and Benjamin Huntington, quartered with Mr. Williams.

One evening, the conversation turned upon the gloomy state of the country, and the probability that, after all, success would crown the British arms. "Well," said Mr. Williams, with great calmness, "if they succeed, it is pretty evident what will be my fate. I have done much to prosecute the contest, and one thing I have done, which the British will never pardon—I have signed the Declaration of Independence. *I shall be hung.*" Mr. Hillhouse expressed his hope, that America would yet be successful, and his confidence that this would be her happy fortune. Mr Huntington observed, that in case of ill success, *he* should be exempt from the gallows, as his signature was not attached to the declaration of independence, nor had he written any thing against the British government. To this Mr. Williams replied, his eye kindling as he spoke, "Then, sir, you deserve to be hanged, for not having done your duty."

At the age of 41, he became settled in domestic life, having connected himself with the daughter of Jonathan Trumbull, at that time governor of the state. His lady, it is believed, is still living. Three children were the offspring of this marriage. Of these children, Solomon, the eldest, died in New-York, in 1810, a man greatly beloved by all who had the pleasure to know him. The only daughter is respectably connected in Woodstock, and the remaining son resides in Lebanon.

The demise of his eldest son was a great affliction to the aged and infirm father. The intelligence produced a shock from which he never recovered. From this time, he gradually declined. Four days before his death, he lost the power of utterance, nor was it expected that he would again speak on this side the grave. A short time, however, previously to his death, he called aloud for his deceased son, and requested him to attend his dying parent. In a few moments he closed his life. This event occurred on the 2d day of August, 1811, in the 81st year of his age.

To this biographical sketch of Mr. Williams, we have only to add a word, respecting his character as a Christian. He made a profession of religion at an early age, and through the long course of his life, he was distinguished for a humble and consistent conduct and conversation. While yet almost a youth, he was elected to the office of deacon, in the congregational church to which he belonged, an office which he retained during the remainder of his life. His latter days were chiefly devoted to reading, meditation, and prayer. At length the hour arrived, when God would take him to himself. He gave up the ghost, in a good old age, and was gathered to his fathers.

OLIVER WOLCOTT.

Few families have been more distinguished in the annals of Connecticut, than the Wolcott family. The ancestor of this family was Henry Wolcott, an English gentleman of considerable fortune, who was born in the year 1578. During the progress of the Independents in England, he embraced the principles of that sect, and hence becoming obnoxious to the British government, he found it expedient to emigrate to America. His emigration, with his family, took place in 1630. They settled for a time at Dorchester, in Massachusetts.

Mr. Wolcott is represented to have been a man of talents and enterprise. Possessing an ample fortune, he associated himself with John Mason, Roger Ludlow, Mr. Stoughton, and Mr. Newberry, who were also men of wealth, in the settlement of Windsor, in Connecticut. About the same time, as is well known, settlements were made at Hartford and Wethersfield.

In 1639, the first general assembly of Connecticut was holden at Hartford. It was composed of delegates from the above towns. Among these delegates was Henry Wolcott. Since that date, down to the present time, some of the members of this distinguished family have been concerned in the civil government of the state.

Simon Wolcott was the youngest son of Henry Wolcott. Roger Wolcott, who is distinguished both in the civil and military annals of the state, was the youngest son of Simon Wolcott. Oliver Wolcott, the subject of the present memoir, was the youngest son of Roger Wolcott. He was born in the year 1726, and graduated at Yale College in 1747. In this latter year he received a commission as captain in the army, in the French war. At the head of a company, which was raised by his own exertions, he proceeded to the defence of the northern frontiers, where he continued until the peace of Aix-la-Chapelle.

At this time he returned to Connecticut, and commenced the study of medicine. He, however, never entered into the practice of the profession, in consequence of receiving the appointment of sheriff of the county of Litchfield, which was organized about the year 1751.

In 1774 he was appointed an assistant in the council of the state. This may be considered as the commencement of his political career. To the office of assistant, he continued to be annually re-elected till 1786. In the interval, he was for some time chief judge of the court of common pleas for the county, and judge of the court of probate for the district of Litchfield

In the revolutionary contest, Mr. Wolcott was one of the strong pillars of the American cause. He inherited much of the independent feeling of the ancestor of the family, of whom we have spoken in the commencement of this memoir. In 1776, he was summoned by his native state to represent it in the national congress in Philadelphia. He had the honour of participating in the deliberations of that body, on the declaration of independence, and of recording his vote in favour of its adoption.

Immediately after the adoption of that instrument, he returned to Connecticut, and was now invested with the command of fourteen regiments of the state militia, which were raised for the defence of New-York. In November, he resumed his seat in congress, and on the adjournment of that body to Baltimore, he accompanied them, and there spent the winter of 1777. In the ensuing summer, he was engaged in several military movements, after which, he joined the northern army, under General Gates, with a corps of several hundred volunteers, and assisted in the memorable defeat of the British army under General Burgoyne. From this period, until 1786, he was either in attendance upon congress, in the field in defence of his country, or, as a commissioner of indian affairs for the northern department, he was assisting in settling the terms of peace with the six nations. In 1786 he was elected lieutenant governor, an office to which he was annually elected for ten years, when he was raised to the chief magistracy of the state. This latter office, however, he enjoyed but a little time, death putting an end to his active and laborious life, on the first of December, 1797, in the 72d year of his age.

The life of Mr. Wolcott was extended beyond the common age of man, but it was well filled with honourable services for his country. He merited and received the confidence of his fellow citizens. In his person, he was tall, and had the appearance of great muscular strength. His manners were dignified. He had great resolution of character, and might be said to be tenacious of his own opinions; yet he could surrender them, in view of evidence, and was ready to alter a course which he had prescribed for himself, when duty and propriety seemed to require it.

In 1755, he was married to a Miss Collins, of Guilford, with whom he enjoyed great domestic felicity, for the space of forty years. Few women were better qualified for the discharge of domestic duties, than was Mrs. Wolcott. During the long absence of her husband, she superintended the education of her children, and by her prudence and frugality administered to the necessities of her family, and rendered her house the seat of comfort and hospitality.

Mr. Wolcott never pursued any of the learned professions, yet his reading was various and extensive. He cultivated an acquaintance with the sciences, through the works of some of the most learned men of Europe, and was intimately acquainted with history, both ancient and modern. He has the reputation, and it is believed justly, of having been an accomplished scholar.

Mr. Wolcott was also distinguished for his love of order and religion. In his last sickness he expressed, according to Dr. Backus, who preached his funeral sermon, a deep sense of his personal unworthiness and guilt. For several days before his departure, every breath seemed to bring with it a prayer. At length, he fell asleep. He was an old man, and full of years, and went to his grave distinguished for a long series of services rendered both to his state and nation. The memory of his personal worth, of his patriotism, his integrity, his christian walk and conversation, will go down to generations yet unborn.

THE

NEW-YORK DELEGATION.

WILLIAM FLOYD,
PHILIP LIVINGSTON,
FRANCIS LEWIS,
LEWIS MORRIS,
HENRY MISNER.[*]

WILLIAM FLOYD.

WILLIAM FLOYD, who was the first delegate from New-York that signed the Declaration of Independence, was born on Long Island, on the 17th of December, 1734. His father was Nicoll Floyd, an opulent and respectable landholder, whose ancestors came to America from Wales, about the year 1680, and settled on Long Island. The father of William died while his son was young, and left him heir to a large estate.

The early education of young Floyd, by no means corresponded to the wealth and ability of his father. His studies were limited to a few of the useful branches of knowledge, and these were left unfinished, in consequence of the death of that gentleman. The native powers of Floyd were, however, respectable, and his house being the resort of an exten

---

[*] This gentleman was present when congress expressed their approbation of the D....... n of Independen.e, and voted in favour of it. but, before the engr...... py was signed by th................ Mr. ..... r left congress......... failed of affixing his name to that ....rt.

sive circle of connexions and acquaintance, which included many intelligent and distinguished families, his mind, by the intercourse which he thus enjoyed with those who were enlightened and improved, became stored with rich and varied knowledge. His wealth enabled him to practice a generous hospitality, and few enjoyed the society of friends with more pleasure.

At an early period in the controversy between Great Britain and the colonies, the feelings of Mr. Floyd were strongly enlisted in the cause of the latter. He was a friend to the people; and, with zeal and ardour, entered into every measure which seemed calculated to ensure to them their just rights. These sentiments on his part excited a reciprocal confidence on the part of the people, and led to his appointment as a delegate from New-York to the first continental congress, which met in Philadelphia on the fifth of September, 1774. In the measures adopted by that body, so justly eulogized by the advocates of freedom, from that day to the present, Mr. Floyd most heartily concurred.

In the following year, he was again elected a delegate to congress, and continued a member of that body until after the Declaration of American Independence. On that occasion, he assisted in dissolving the political bonds which had united the colonies to the British government, and in consequence of which, they had suffered numberless oppressions for years. Into other measures of congress, Mr. Floyd entered with zeal. He served on numerous important committees, and by his fidelity rendered essential service to the patriotic cause.

It was the lot of not a few, while thus devoted to the public good, to experience the destructive effects of the war upon their property, or the serious inconveniences arising from it in relation to their families. In both these respects Mr. Floyd suffered severely. While at Philadelphia, attending upon congress, the American troops evacuated Long Island, which was taken possession of by the British army. On this latter event, the family of Mr. Floyd were obliged to flee for safety to Connecticut. His house was occupied by company of horsemen, which made it the place of their rendezvous during the remainder of the war. Thus, for nearly seven years, Mr. Floyd and his family were refugees from their habitation. nor did he, during this long period, derive any benefit from his landed estate.

In the year 1777, General Floyd (we give him this military appellation, from the circumstance of his having some time before been appointed to the command of the militia on Long Island) was appointed a senator of the state of New-York, under the new constitution. In this body, he assisted to organize the government, and to accommodate the code of laws to the changes which had recently been effected in the political condition of the state.

In October, 1778, he was again elected to represent the state of New-York in the continental congress. From this time, until the expiration of the first congress, under the federal constitution, General Floyd was either a member of the national assembly, or a member of the senate of New-York. In this latter body, he maintained a distinguished rank, and was often called to preside over its deliberations, when the lieutenant governor left the chair.

In 1784, he purchased an uninhabited tract of land upon the Mohawk River. To the clearing and subduing of this tract, he devoted the leisure of several successive summers. Under his skilful management, and persevering labours, a considerable portion of the tract was converted into a well cultivated farm; and hither, in 1803, he removed his residence. Although, at this time, he was advanced in life, his bodily strength and activity were much greater than often pertain to men of fewer years. He enjoyed unusual health, until a year or two before his death. The faculties of his mind continued unimpaired to the last. A little previous to his death, he appeared to be affected with a general debility, which continuing to increase, the lamp of life was at length extinguished. This event occurred on the 4th of August, 1821, and when he had attained to the extraordinary age of eighty-seven years.

In his person General Floyd was of a middle stature. He

possessed a natural dignity, which seldom failed to impress those into whose company he was thrown. He appeared to enjoy the pleasures of private life, yet in his manners he was less familiar, and in his disposition less affable, than most men. Few men, however, were more respected. He was eminently a practical man. The projects to which he gave his sanction, or which he attempted, were those which judgment could approve. When his purposes were once formed, he seldom found reason to alter them. His firmness and resolution were not often equalled.

In his political character, there was much to admire. He was uniform and independent. He manifested great candour and sincerity towards those from whom he happened to differ; and such was his well known integrity, that his motives were rarely, if ever, impeached. He seldom took part in the public discussion of a subject, nor was he dependent upon others for the opinions which he adopted. His views were his own, and his opinions the result of reason and reflection. If the public estimation of a man be a just criterion by which to judge of him, General Floyd was excelled by few of his contemporaries, since, for more than fifty years he was honoured with offices of trust and responsibility by his fellow citizens.

PHILIP LIVINGSTON.

Philip Livingston was born at Albany, on the fifteenth of January, 1716. His ancestors were highly respectable, and for several generations the family have held a distinguished rank in New-York. His great grandfather, John Livingston, was a divine of some celebrity in the church of Scotland, from which country he removed to Rotterdam in the year 1663. In 1772, or about that time, his son Robert emigrated to America, and settled in the colony of New-York. He was fortunate in obtaining a grant of a tract of land in that colony, delightfully situated on the banks of the Hudson. This tract, since known as the Manor of Livingston, has been in possession of the family from that time to the present.

Robert Livingston had three sons, Philip, Robert, and Gilbert. The first named of these, being the eldest, inherited the manor. The fourth son of this latter is the subject of the present memoir.

The settlement of New-York, it is well known, was commenced by the Dutch. For many years scarcely any attention was paid by them to the subject of education. They had few schools, few academies, and, until the year 1754, no college in the territory. Such gentlemen as gave their sons a liberal education, sent them either to New-England, or to some foreign university. But the number of liberally educated men was extremely small. As late as 1746, their number did not exceed fifteen in the whole colony. The subject of this memoir, and his three brothers, were included in the number. The author is ignorant where the brothers of Mr. Livingston received their education, but he was himself graduated at Yale College, 1737.

Soon after leaving college he settled in the city of New-York, where he became extensively engaged in commercial operations. Mercantile life was, at this time, the fashionable pursuit Mr. Livingston followed it with great ardour; and, having the advantage of an excellent education, and being distinguished for a more than ordinary share of integrity and sagacity, he was prosperous in an eminent degree.

In 1754, he was elected an alderman in the city of New-York. This was his first appearance in public life. The office was important and respectable. The population of the city was ten thousand eight hundred and eighty-one souls. Mr. Livingston continued to be elected to this office for nine successive years, by his fellow citizens, to whom he gave great satisfaction, by his faithful attention to their interests.

In 1759, Mr. Livingston was returned a member from the city of New-York to the general assembly of the colony, which was convened on the thirty-first of January of that year. This body consisted of twenty-seven members, representing a population of about one hundred thousand inhabitants, the number which the colony at that time contained.

At this period, Great Britain was engaged in a war with France. A plan had been formed for the reduction of Canada by the United Colonies. For this object, it was proposed to raise twenty thousand men. The quota of New-York was two thousand six hundred and eighty. This number the general assembly directed to be raised, and appropriated one hundred thousand pounds for the support of the troops, and ordered an advance of one hundred and fifty thousand pounds to the British commissariat, for the general objects of the expedition. Similar measures were adopted by the other colonies, which, together with the assistance of the mother country, led to the capture of several important posts in Canada; and, in the following year, to the subjugation of the whole territory to the British power.

In this assembly, Mr. Livingston acted a distinguished part. His talents and education gave him influence, which was powerfully exerted in promoting the above important measures. He also suggested several plans, which were calculated to improve the condition of the colony, particularly in relation to agriculture and commerce. He was deeply impressed with the importance of giving to the productions of the country a high character in the markets abroad, and of increasing the facilities of communication with other countries. In respect to these and other subjects, he possessed a well informed mind, and was desirous of pursuing a most liberal policy.

Previous to the revolution, it was usual for the respective colonies to have an agent in England, to manage their individual concerns with the British government. This agent was appointed by the popular branch of the colonial assemblies. In 1770, the agent of the colony of New-York dying, the celebrated Edmund Burke was chosen in his stead. Between this gentleman and a committee of the colonial assembly, a correspondence was maintained. As the agent of the colony, he received a salary of five hundred pounds. He represented the colony in England, and advocated her rights. Hence the office was one of great importance. Not less important were the duties of the committee of correspondence. Upon their representations, the agent depended for a knowledge of the state of the colony. Of this committee Mr. Livingston was a member. From his communications, and those of his colleagues, Mr. Burke doubtless obtained that information of the state of the colonies, which he sometimes brought forward, to the perfect surprise of the house of commons, and upon which he often founded arguments, and proposed measures, which were not to be resisted.

The patriotic character and sentiments of Mr. Livingston, led him to regard, with great jealousy, the power of the British government over the colonies. With other patriots, he was probably willing to submit to the authority of the mother country, while that authority was confined to such acts as reason and justice approved. But, when the British ministers began to evince a disposition to oppress the colonies, by way of humbling them, no man manifested a stronger opposition than Mr. Livingston. His sentiments on this subject may be gathered from an answer, which he reported in 1764, to the speech of Lieutenant Governor Colden. In the extract we give, may be seen the very spirit of the revolution, which led to American independence.

"But nothing can add to the pleasure we receive from the information your honour gives us, that his majesty, our most gracious sovereign, distinguishes and approves our conduct. When his service requires it, we shall ever be ready to exert ourselves with loyalty, fidelity, and zeal; and as we have always complied, in the most dutiful manner, with every requisition made by his directions, we, with all humility, hope tha his majesty, who, and whose ancestors, have long been the guardians of British liberty, will so protect us in our rights, as to prevent our falling into the abject state of being forever hereafter incapable of doing what can merit either his distinction or approbation. Such must be the deplorable state of that wretched people, who (being taxed by a power subordinate to none, and in a great degree unacquainted with their circumstances) can call nothing their own. This we speak with the greatest deference to the wisdom and justice of the British parliament, in which we confide. Depressed with this prospect of inevitable ruin, by the alarming information we have from home, neither we nor our constituents can attend to improvements, conducive either to the interests of our mother country, or of this colony. We shall, however, renew the act for granting a bounty on hemp, still hoping that a stop may be put to those measures, which, if carried into execution, will oblige us to think that nothing but extreme poverty can preserve us from the most insupportable bondage. We hope your honour will join with us in an endeavour to secure that great badge of English liberty, of *being taxed only with our own consent;* which we conceive all his majesty's subjects at home and abroad equally entitled to."

The colony of New-York, it is well known, was, for a time, more under the influence of the British crown than several others, and more slowly, as a colony, adopted measures which hastened forward the revolution. But all along, there were individuals in that colony, of kindred feelings with those who acted so conspicuous a part in Massachusetts and Virginia.

Among these individuals, none possessed a more patriotic spirit, or was more ready to rise in opposition to British aggressions, than Philip Livingston. The sentiments which he had avowed, and the distinguished part which he had all along taken, in favour of the rights of the colonies, marked him out as a proper person to represent the colony in the important congress of 1774. In the deliberations of this body he bore his proper share, and assisted in preparing an address to the people of Great Britain.

Of the equally distinguished congress of 1776, Mr. Livingston was a member, and had the honour of giving his vote in favour of that declaration, which, while it was destined to perpetuate the memory of the illustrious men who adopted it, was to prove the charter of our national existence. In the following year, he was re-elected to congress by the state convention, which, at this time, tendered to him and his colleagues an expression of public thanks, for the long and faithful services which they had rendered to the colony of the state of New-York.

The constitution of the state of New-York was adopted at Kingston, on the twentieth of April, 1777. Under this constitution, Mr. Livingston, in May following, was chosen a senator for the southern district, and in that capacity attended the first meeting of the first legislature of the state of New-York.

In October of the same year, an election took place for members of congress, under the new constitution. Among the number chosen, Mr. Livingston was one. On the 5th of May, 1778, he took his seat in that body. This was an eminently critical and gloomy period in the history of the revolution. The British had taken possession of Philadelphia, compelling congress to retire from that city. They had agreed to hold a session at York.

At this time, the health of Mr. Livingston was exceedingly precarious. And such was the nature of his complaint, which was a dropsy in the chest, that no rational prospect existed of his recovery. Indeed, he was daily liable to be summoned from the active scenes of life to his final account. Yet, in this dubious and anxious state, his love to his country continued strong and unwavering. For her good he had made many sacrifices; and, now that her interests seemed to require his presence in congress, he hesitated not to relinquish the comforts of home, and those attentions which, in his feeble and declining state, he peculiarly needed from a beloved family.

Previous to his departure, he visited his friends in Albany, whom he now bid a final farewell, as he expected to see them no more. His family, at this time, were at Kingston, whither they had been obliged to flee to escape the British army. To these, also, he bid an affectionate adieu, at the same time expressing his conviction, that he should no more return.

These sad anticipations proved too true. On the fifth of May, he took his seat in congress, from which time his decline was rapid. On the twelfth of June, he ended his valuable life. Although deprived of the consolations of home, he was attended, during the few last days of his illness, by his son, Henry, who was at that time a member of General Washington's family. Hearing of the illness of his father, he hastened to administer such comforts as might be in his power, and to perform the last duties to a dying parent.

On the day of his decease, his death was announced in the hall of congress, and by that body the following resolutions adopted:

"Congress being informed that Mr. P. Livingston, one of the delegates for the state of New-York, died last night, and that circumstances require that his corpse be interred this evening,

"Resolved, that congress will in a body attend the funeral this evening, at six o'clock, with a crape round the arm, and will continue in mourning for the space of one month.

"Ordered, that Mr. Lewis, Mr. Duer, and Mr. G. Morris, be a committee to superintend the funeral; and that the Rev. Mr. Duffield, the attending chaplain, be notified to officiate on the occasion."

Mr. Livingston married the daughter of Colonel Dirck Ten Broeck, by whom he had several children. His family has furnished several characters who have adorned society, and whose virtues have imparted dignity to human nature. Mr. Livingston is said to have been naturally silent and reserved, and, to strangers, to have appeared austere. Yet he was uncommonly mild and affectionate to his family and friends. He was a firm believer in the great truths of the Christian system, and a sincere and humble follower of the divine Redeemer.

FRANCIS LEWIS.

Francis Lewis was a native of Landaff, in South Wales, where he was born in the year 1713. His father was a clergyman, belonging to the established church. His mother was the daughter of Dr. Pettingal, who was also a clergyman of the episcopal establishment, and had his residence in North Wales. At the early age of four or five years, being left an orphan, the care of him devolved upon a maternal maiden aunt, who took singular pains to have him instructed in the native language of his country. He was afterwards sent to Scotland, where, in the family of a relation, he acquired a knowledge of the Gaelic. From this, he was transferred to the school of Westminster, where he completed his education; and enjoyed the reputation of being a good classical scholar.

Mercantile pursuits being his object, he entered the counting room of a London merchant; where, in a few years, he acquired a competent knowledge of the profession. On attaining to the age of twenty-one years, he collected the property which had been left him by his father, and having converted it into merchandise, he sailed for New-York, where he arrived in the spring of 1735.

Leaving a part of his goods to be sold in New-York, by Mr. Edward Annesly, with whom he had formed a commercial connexion, he transported the remainder to Philadelphia. whence, after a residence of two years, he returned to the former city, and there became extensively engaged in navigation and foreign trade. About this time he connected himself by marriage with the sister of his partner, by whom he had several children.

Mr. Lewis acquired the character of an active and enterprising merchant. In the course of his commercial transactions, he traversed a considerable part of the continent of Europe. He visited several of the seaports of Russia, the Orkney and Shetland Islands, and twice suffered shipwreck of the Irish coast.

During the French or Canadian war, Mr. Lewis was, for a time, agent for supplying the British troops. In this capacity, he was present at the time, when, in August, 1756, the fort of Oswego was surrendered to the distinguished French general, de Montcalm. The fort was, at that time, commanded by the British Colonel Mersey. On the tenth of August, Montcalm approached it with more than five thousand Europeans, Canadians, and Indians. On the twelfth, at midnight, he opened the trenches, with thirty-two pieces of cannon, besides several brass mortars and howitzers. The garrison having fired away all their shells and ammunition, Colonel Mersey ordered the cannon to be spiked, and crossed the river to Little Oswego Fort, without the loss of a single man. Of the deserted fort, the enemy took immediate possession, and from it began a fire, which was kept up without intermission. The next day, Colonel Mersey was killed while standing by the side of Mr. Lewis.

The garrison, being thus deprived of their commander, their fort destitute of a cover, and no prospect of aid presenting itself, demanded a capitulation, and surrendered as prisoners of war. The garrison consisted at this time of the regiments of Shirley and Pepperell, and amounted to one thousand and four hundred men. The conditions required, and acceded to, were, that they should be exempted from plunder, conducted to Montreal, and treated with humanity. The services rendered by Mr. Lewis, during the war, were held in such consideration by the British government, that at the close of it he received a grant of five thousand acres of land.

The conditions, upon which the garrison at Fort Oswego surrendered to Montcalm, were shamefully violated by that commander. They were assured of kind treatment; but no sooner had the surrender been made, than Montcalm allowed the chief warrior of the Indians, who assisted in taking the fort, to select about thirty of the prisoners, and do with them as he pleased. Of this number Mr. Lewis was one. Placed thus at the disposal of savage power, a speedy and cruel death was to be expected. The *tradition* is, however that he soon discovered that he was able to converse with the indians, by reason of the similarity of the ancient language of Wales, which he understood, to the indian dialect. The ability of Mr. Lewis, thus readily to communicate with the chief, so pleased the latter, that he treated him kindly; and on arriving at Montreal, he requested the French governor to allow him to return to his family, without ransom. The request, however, was not granted, and Mr. Lewis was sent as a prisoner to France, from which country, being some time after exchanged, he returned to America.

This tradition as to the *cause* of the liberation of Mr. Lewis, is incorrect; no such affinity existing between the *Cymreag*, or ancient language of Wales, and the language of any of the indian tribes found in North America. The cause might have been, and probably was, some unusual occurrence, or adventure; but of its precise nature we are not informed.

Although Mr. Lewis was not born in America, his attachment to the country was coeval with his settlement in it. He early espoused the patriotic cause, against the encroachments of the British government, and was among the first to unite with an association, which existed in several parts of the country, called the "sons of liberty," the object of which was to concert measures against the exercise of an undue power on the part of the mother country.

The independent and patriotic character which Mr. Lewis was known to possess, the uniform integrity of his life, the distinguished intellectual powers with which he was endued, all pointed him out as a proper person to assist in taking charge of the interest of the colony in the continental congress. Accordingly, in April, 1775, he was unanimously elected a delegate to that body. In this honourable station he was continued by the provincial congress of New-York, through the following year, 1776; and was among the number who declared the colonies forever absolved from their allegiance to the British crown, and from that time entitled to the rank and privileges of free and independent states.

In several subsequent years, he was appointed to represent

the state in the national legislature. During his congressional career, Mr. Lewis was distinguished for a becoming zeal in the cause of liberty, tempered by the influence of a correct judgment and a cautious prudence. He was employed in several secret services; in the purchase of provisions and clothing for the army; and in the importation of military stores, particularly arms and ammunition. In transactions of this kind, his commercial experience gave him great facilities. He was also employed on various committees, in which capacity, he rendered many valuable services to his country.

In 1775, Mr. Lewis removed his family and effects to a country seat which he owned on Long Island. This proved to be an unfortunate step. In the autumn of the following year, his house was plundered by a party of British light horse. His extensive library and valuable papers of every description were wantonly destroyed. Nor were they contented with this ruin of his property. They thirsted for revenge upon a man, who had dared to affix his signature to a document, which proclaimed the independence of America. Unfortunately Mrs. Lewis fell into their power, and was retained a prisoner for several months. During her captivity, she was closely confined, without even the comfort of a bed to lie upon, or a change of clothes.

In November, 1776, the attention of congress was called to her distressed condition, and shortly after a resolution was passed that a lady, who had been taken prisoner by the Americans, should be permitted to return to her husband, and that Mrs. Lewis be required in exchange. But the exchange could not at that time be effected. Through the influence of Washington, however, Mrs. Lewis was at length released; but her sufferings during her confinement had so much impaired her constitution, that in the course of a year or two, she sunk into the grave.

Of the subsequent life of Mr. Lewis, we have little to record. His latter days were spent in comparative poverty, his independent fortune having in a great measure been sacrificed on the altar of patriotism, during his country's struggle for independence. The life of this excellent man, and distinguished patriot, was extended to his ninetieth year. His death occurred on the 30th day of December, 1803.

LEWIS MORRIS.

LEWIS MORRIS was born at the manor of Morrisania, in the state of New York, in the year 1726. His family was of ancient date; the pedigree of it has been preserved; but it is too extended to admit of a particular notice in these pages. Richard Morris, an ancestor of the family, beyond whom it is unnecessary to trace its genealogy, was an officer of some distinction in the time of Cromwell. At the restoration, however, he left England, and came to New-York; soon after which he obtained a grant of several thousand acres of land, in the county of West-Chester, not far from the city. This was erected into a manor, and invested with the privileges, which usually pertain to manorial estates.

Richard Morris died in the year 1673, leaving an infant child by the name of Lewis, who afterwards held the office of chief justice of the province of New-York, and became governor of New-Jersey. In both these offices he was much respected, and exercised an enviable influence in both these colonies. The sons of Lewis were not less eminent; one being appointed a judge of the court of vice admiralty; another chief justice of New-Jersey; and a third lieutenant governor of the state of Pennsylvania.

From one of these sons, Lewis Morris, the subject of the present memoir, was descended. He was the eldest of four brothers. Staats became an officer in the British service, and for some time a member of parliament. Richard and Governeur both settled in the state of New-York, and both became men of considerable distinction; the former as judge of the of the vice admiralty court, and chief justice of the state, and the latter as a representative in congress.

The early education of Lewis was respectable. At the age of sixteen he was fitted for college, and was entered at Yale college, the honours of which he received in due course, having acquired the reputation of good scholarship, and a strict morality. Immediately on leaving college, he returned to his father's residence, where he devoted himself to the pursuits of agriculture. As he entered upon manhood, he seems to have possessed every thing which naturally commands the respect, and attracts the admiration of men. His person was of lofty stature, and of fine proportions, imparting to his presence an uncommon dignity, softened, however, by a disposition unusually generous and benevolent, and by a demeanor so graceful, that few could fail to do him homage.

Although thus apparently fitted for the enjoyment of society, Mr. Morris found his greatest pleasure in the endearments of domestic life, and in attention to his agricultural operations. He was early married to a Miss Walton, a lady of fortune and accomplishments, by whom he had a large family of six sons and four daughters

The condition of Mr. Morris, at the time the troubles of the colonies began, was singularly felicitous. His fortune was ample; his pursuits in life consonant to his taste; his family and connexions eminently respectable, and eminently prosperous. No change was, therefore, likely to occur which would improve his condition, or add to the happiness which he enjoyed. On the contrary, every collision between the royal government and the colonies, was likely to abridge some of his privileges, and might even strip his family of all their domestic comforts, should he participate in the struggle which was likely to ensue.

These considerations, no doubt, had their influence at times upon the mind of Mr. Morris. He possessed, however, too great a share of patriotism, to suffer private fortune, or individual happiness, to come in competition with the interests of his country. He could neither feel indifferent on a subject of so much magnitude, nor could he pursue a course of neutrality. He entered, therefore, with zeal into the growing controversy; he hesitated not to pronounce the measures of the British ministry unconstitutional and tyrannical, and beyond peaceful endurance. As the political condition of the country became more gloomy, and the prospect of a resort to arms increased, his patriotic feeling appeared to gather strength; and although he was desirous that the controversy should be settled without bloodshed, yet he preferred the latter alternative, to the surrender of those rights which the God of nature had given to the American people.

About this time, the celebrated congress of 1774 assembled at New-York. Of this congress Mr. Morris was not a member. He possessed a spirit too bold and independent, to act with the prudence which the situation of the country seemed to require. The object of this congress was not war, but peace. That object, however, it is well known, failed, notwithstanding that an universal desire pervaded the country, that a compromise might be effected between the colonies and the British government, and was made known to the latter, by a dignified address, both to the king and to the people of Great Britain.

In the spring of 1775, it was no longer doubtful that a resort must be had to arms. Indeed, the battle of Lexington had opened the war; shortly after which the New-York convention of deputies were assembled to appoint delegates to the general congress. Men of a zealous, bold, and independent stamp, appeared now to be required. It was not singular, therefore, that Mr. Morris should have been elected.

On the 15th of May, he took his seat in that body, and eminently contributed, by his indefatigable zeal, to promote the interests of the country. He was placed on a committee of which Washington was the chairman, to devise ways and means to supply the colonies with ammunition and military stores, of which they were nearly destitute. The labours of this committee were exceedingly arduous.

During this session of congress, Mr. Morris was appointed to the delicate and difficult task of detaching the western indians from a coalition with the British government, and securing their co-operation with the American colonies. Soon after his appointment to this duty, he repaired to Pittsburg, in which place, and the vicinity, he continued for some time zealously engaged in accomplishing the object of his mission. In the beginning of the year 1776, he resumed his seat in congress, and was a member of several committees, which were appointed to purchase muskets and bayonets, and to encourage the manufacture of salt-petre and gunpowder.

During the winter of 1775 and 1776, the subject of a Declaration of Independence began to occupy the thoughts of many in all parts of the country. Such a declaration seemed manifestly desirable to the leading patriots of the day, but an unwillingness prevailed extensively in the country, to destroy all connexion with Great Britain. In none of the colonies was this unwillingness more apparent than in New-York.

The reason which has been assigned for this strong reluctance in that colony, was the peculiar intimacy which existed between the people of the city and the officers of the royal government. The military officers, in particular, had rendered themselves very acceptable to the citizens, by their urbanity; and had even formed connexions with some of the most respectable families.

This intercourse continued even after the commencement of hostilities, and occasioned the reluctance which existed in that colony to separate from the mother country. Even as late as the middle of March, 1776, Governor Tryon, although he had been forced to retreat on board a British armed vessel in the harbour for safety, had great influence over the citizens, by means of artful and insinuating addresses, which he caused to be published and spread through the city. The following extract from one of these addresses, will convey to the reader some idea of the art employed by this minister of the crown, to prevent the people of that colony from mingling in the struggle.

"It is in the clemency and authority of Great Britain only that we can look for happiness, peace, and protection; and I have it in command from the king, to encourage, by every means in my power, the expectations in his majesty's well-disposed subjects in this government, of every assistance and protection the state of Great Britain will enable his majesty to afford them, and to crush every appearance of a disposition, on their part, to withstand the tyranny and misrule, which accompany the acts of those who have but too well, hitherto, succeeded in the total subversion of legal government. Under such assurances, therefore, I exhort all the friends to good order, and our justly admired constitution, still to preserve that constancy of mind which is inherent in the breasts of virtuous and loyal citizens, and, I trust, a very few months will relieve them from their present oppressed, injured, and insulted condition.

"I have the satisfaction to inform you, that a door is still open to such honest, but deluded people, as will avail themselves of the justice and benevolence, which the supreme legislature has held out to them, of being restored to the king's grace and peace; and that proper steps have been taken for passing a commission for that purpose, under the great seal of Great Britain, in conformity to a provision in a late act of parliament, the commissioners thereby to be appointed having, also, power to inquire into the state and condition of the colonies for effecting a restoration of the public tranquillity."

To prevent an intercourse between the citizens and the fleet, so injurious to the patriotic cause, timely measures were adopted by the committee of safety; but for a long time no efforts were availing, and even after General Washington had established his head-quarters at New-York, he was obliged to issue his proclamation, interdicting all intercourse and correspondence with the ships of war and other vessels belonging to the king of Great Britain.

But, notwithstanding this prevalent aversion to a separation from Great Britain, there were many in the colony who believed that a declaration of independence was not only a point of political expediency, but a matter of paramount duty. Of this latter class, Mr. Morris was one; and, in giving his vote for that declaration, he exhibited a patriotism and disinterestedness which few had it in their power to display. He was at this time in possession of an extensive domain, within a few miles of the city of New-York. A British army had already landed from their ships, which lay within cannon shot of the dwelling of his family. A signature to the Declaration of Independence would insure the devastation of the former, and the destruction of the latter. But, upon the ruin of his individual property, he could look with comparative indifference, while he knew that his honour was untarnished, and the interests of his country were safe. He voted, therefore, for a separation from the mother country, in the spirit of a man of honour, and of enlarged benevolence.

It happened as was anticipated. The hostile army soon spread desolation over the beautiful and fertile manor of Morrisania. His tract of woodland of more than a thousand acres in extent, and, from its proximity to the city, of incalculable value, was destroyed; his house was greatly injured; his fences ruined; his stock driven away; and his family obliged to live in a state of exile. Few men during the revolution were called to make greater sacrifices than Mr. Morris; none made them more cheerfully. It made some amends for his losses and sacrifices, that the colony of New-York, which had been backward in agreeing to a Declaration of Independence, unanimously concurred in that measure by her convention, when it was learned that congress had taken that step.

It imparts pleasure to record, that the three eldest sons of Mr. Morris followed the noble example of their father, and gave their personal services to their country, during the revolutionary struggle. One served for a time as aid-de-camp to General Sullivan, but afterwards entered the family of General Greene, and was with that officer during his brilliant campaign in the Carolinas; the second son was appointed aid-de-camp to General Charles Lee, and was present at the gallant defence of Fort Moultrie, where he greatly distinguished himself. The youngest of these sons, though but a youth, entered the army as a lieutenant of artillery, and honourably served during the war.

Mr. Morris left congress in 1777, at which time, he received, together with his colleagues, the thanks of the provincial convention, "for their long and faithful services rendered to the colony of New-York, and the said state."

In subsequent years, Mr. Morris served his state in various ways. He was often a member of the state legislature, and rose to the rank of major general of the militia.

The latter years of Mr. Morris were passed at his favourite residence at Morrisania, where he devoted himself to the noiseless, but happy pursuit of agriculture; a kind of life to which he was much attached, and which was an appropriate mode of closing a long life, devoted to the cause of his country. He died on his paternal estate at Morrisania, in the bosom of his family, January, 1798, at the good old age of seventy-one years.

THE NEW-JERSEY DELEGATION.

RICHARD STOCKTON,
JOHN WITHERSPOON,
FRANCIS HOPKINSON,
JOHN HART,
ABRAHAM CLARK.

RICHARD STOCKTON.

The first of the New-Jersey delegation, who signed the Declaration of Independence, was Richard Stockton. He was born near Princeton, on the 1st day of October, 1730. His family was ancient and respectable. His great grandfather, who bore the same name, came from England, about the year 1670, and after residing a few years on Long Island, removed with a number of associates to an extensive tract of land, of which the present village of Princeton is nearly the centre. This tract consisted of six thousand and four hundred acres. This gentleman died in the year 1705, leaving handsome legacies to his several children; but the chief portion of his landed estate to his son, Richard. The death of Richard followed in 1720. He was succeeded in the family seat by his youngest son, John; a man distinguished for his moral and religious character, for his liberality to the college of New-Jersey, and for great fidelity in the discharge of the duties of public and private life.

Richard Stockton, the subject of the present memoir, was the eldest son of the last mentioned gentleman. His early education was highly respectable, being superintended by that accomplished scholar, Rev. Dr. Samuel Finley, in a celebrated academy at West-Nottingham. His preliminary studies being finished, he entered the college of New-Jersey, whose honours he received in 1748. He was even at this time greatly distinguished for intellectual superiority; giving promise of future eminence in any profession he might choose.

On leaving college, he commenced the study of law with the honourable David Ogden, of Newark, at that time at the head of the legal profession in the province. At length, Mr. Stockton was admitted to the bar, and soon rose, as had been anticipated, to great distinction, both as a counsellor and an advocate. He was an able reasoner, and equally distinguished for an easy, and, at the same time, impressive eloquence.

In 1766 and 1767, he relinquished his professional business, for the purpose of visiting England, Scotland, and Ireland. During his tour through those countries, he was received with that attention to which he was eminently entitled, by the estimable character which he had sustained at home, and his high professional reputation. He was presented at court, by a minister of the king, and had the honour of being consulted on American affairs, by the Marquis of Rockingham, by the Earl of Chatham, and many other distinguished personages.

On visiting Edinburgh, he was received with still greater attention. He was complimented with a public dinner, by the authorities of that city, the freedom of which was unanimously conferred upon him, as a testimony of respect for his distinguished character.

A short time previous, the presidency of New-Jersey college had been conferred upon the Reverend Dr. Witherspoon, a distinguished divine, of the town of Paisley, in the vicinity of Glasgow. This appointment Dr. Witherspoon had been induced to decline, by reason of the reluctance of the female members of his family to emigrate to America. At the request of the trustees of the college, Mr. Stockton visited Dr. Witherspoon, and was so fortunate in removing objections, that not long after the latter gentleman accepted the appointment, and removed to America, where he became a distinguished supporter of the college over which he presided, a friend to religion and science in the country, and one of the strong pillars in the temple of American freedom.

The following instances in which Mr. Stockton narrowly escaped death, during his absence, deserve notice. While he was in the city of Edinburgh, he was waylaid one night by a furious robber. He defended himself, however, by means of a small sword, and even succeeded in wounding the desperado. He was not materially injured himself, but was not so fortunate as to prevent the escape of his assailant In the other case, he was designing to cross the Irish channel, and had actually engaged a passage in a packet for that purpose. The unseasonable arrival of his baggage, however, detained him, and fortunate it was that he was thus detained, for the packet, on her voyage, was shipwrecked during a storm, and both passengers and crew found a watery grave.

The following year he was appointed one of the royal judges of the province, and a member of the executive council. At that time he was high in the royal favour, and his domestic felicity seemed without alloy. He possessed an ample fortune, was surrounded by a family whom he greatly loved, and held a high and honourable station under the king of Great Britain.

But the time at length arrived, when the question arose, whether he should renounce his allegiance to his sovereign, and encounter the sacrifices which such a step must bring upon him, or continue that allegiance, and forfeit his character as a friend to his country.

Situated as was Mr. Stockton, the above question could not long remain unsettled; nor was it for any length of time doubtful into which scale he would throw the weight of his influence and character. The sacrifices which he was called upon to make, were cheerfully endured He separated himself from the royal council, of which he was a member in New-Jersey, and joyfully concurred in all those measures of the day, which had for their object the establishment of

American rights, in opposition to the arbitrary and oppressive acts of the British ministry.

On the twenty-first of June, 1776, he was elected by the provincial congress of New-Jersey a delegate to the general congress, then sitting in the city of Philadelphia. On the occurrence of the question relating to a declaration of independence, it is understood that he had some doubts as to the *expediency* of the measure. These doubts, however, were soon dissipated by the powerful and impressive eloquence of John Adams, the great Colossus on this subject on the floor of congress. Mr. Stockton was not only convinced of the importance of the measure, but even addressed the house in its behalf, before the close of the debate. It is needless to detain the reader by a particular mention of the many important services which Mr. Stockton rendered his country, while a member of congress. In all the duties assigned to him, which were numerous and often arduous, he acted with an energy and fidelity alike honourable to him as a man and a patriot.

On the thirtieth of November he was unfortunately taken prisoner by a party of refugee royalists. He was dragged from his bed by night, and carried to New-York. During his removal to the latter place he was treated with great indignity, and in New-York he was placed in the common prison, where he was in want of even the necessaries of life. The news of his capture and sufferings being made known to congress, that body unanimously passed the following resolution:

"Whereas congress hath received information that the honourable Richard Stockton, of New-Jersey, and a member of this congress, hath been made a prisoner by the enemy, and that he hath been ignominiously thrown into a common goal, and there detained—*Resolved*, that General Washington be directed to make immediate inquiry into the truth of this report, and if he finds reason to believe it well founded, that he send a flag to General Howe, remonstrating against this departure from that humane procedure which has marked the conduct of these states to prisoners who have fallen into their hands; and to know of General Howe whether he chooses this shall be the future rule for treating all such, on both sides, as the fortune of war may place in the hands of either party."

Mr. Stockton was at length released; but his confinement had been so strict, and his sufferings so severe, that his constitution could never after recover the shock. Besides this, his fortune, which had been ample, was now greatly reduced. His lands were devastated; his papers and library were burnt, his implements of husbandry destroyed; and his stock seized and driven away. He was now obliged to depend, for a season, upon the assistance of friends, for even the necessaries of life. From the time of his imprisonment his health began to fail him; nor was it particularly benefitted by his release, and a restoration to the society of his friends. He continued to languish for several years, and at length died at his residence, at Princeton, on the 28th of February, 1781, in the fifty-third year of his age.

His death made a wide chasm among the circle of his friends and acquaintance. He was, in every respect, a distinguished man; an honour to his country, and a friend to the cause of science, freedom, and religion, throughout the world. The following extract from the discourse delivered on the occasion of his interment, by the Rev. Dr. Samuel S. Smith, will convey to the reader a just account of this distinguished man:

"Behold, my brethren, before your eyes, a most sensible and affecting picture of the transitory nature of mortal things, in the remains of a man who hath been long among the foremost of his country for power, for wisdom, and for fortune, whose eloquence only wanted a theatre like Athens, to have rivalled the Greek and the Roman fame, and who, if what honours this young country can bestow, if many and great personal talents, could save man from the grave, would not thus have been lamented here by you. Behold there 'the end of all perfection.'

"Young gentlemen, (the students of the College,) and others of the fathers of learning and long nursing me. He w before in the same path in which you are now treading, and hath since long presided over, and helped to confirm the footsteps of those who were here labouring up the hill of science and virtue. While you feel and deplore his loss as a guardian of your studies, and as a model upon which you might form yourselves for public life, let the memory of what he *was* excite you to emulate his fame; let the sight of what he *is*, teach you that every thing human is marked with imperfection.

"At the bar he practised for many years with unrivalled reputation and success. Strictly upright in his profession, he scorned to defend a cause that he knew to be unjust. A friend to peace and to the happiness of mankind, he has often with great pains and attention reconciled contending parties, while he might fairly, by the rules of his profession, have drawn from their litigation no inconsiderable profit to himself. Compassionate to the injured and distressed, he hath often protected the poor and helpless widow unrighteously robbed of her dower, hath heard her with patience, when many wealthier clients were waiting, and hath zealously promoted her interest, without the prospect of reward, unless he could prevail to have right done to her, and to provide her an easy competence for the rest of her days.

"Early in his life, his merits recommended him to his prince and to his country, under the late constitution, who called him to the first honours and trusts of the government. In council he was wise and firm, but always prudent and moderate. Of this he gave a public and conspicuous instance, almost under your own observation, when a dangerous insurrection in a neighbouring county had driven the attorneys from the bar, and seemed to set the laws at defiance. Whilst all men were divided betwixt rash and timid counsels, he only, with wisdom and firmness, seized the prudent mean, appeased the rioters, punished the ringleaders, and restored the laws to their regular course.

"The office of a judge of the province, was never filled with more integrity and learning than it was by him, for several years before the revolution. Since that period, he hath represented New-Jersey in the congress of the United States. But a declining health, and a constitution worn out with application and with service, obliged him, shortly after, to retire from the line of public duty, and hath at length dismissed him from the world.

"In his private life, he was easy and graceful in his manners; in his conversation, affable and entertaining, and master of a smooth and elegant style even in his ordinary discourse. As a man of letters, he possessed a superior genius, highly cultivated by long and assiduous application. His researches into the principles of morals and religion were deep and accurate, and his knowledge of the laws of his country extensive and profound. He was well acquainted with all the branches of polite learning, but he was particularly admired for a flowing and persuasive eloquence, by which he long governed in the courts of justice.

"As a christian, you know that, many years a member of this church, he was not ashamed of the gospel of Christ. Nor could the ridicule of licentious wits, nor the example of vice in power, tempt him to disguise the profession of it, or to decline from the practice of its virtues. He was, however, liberal in his religious principles. Sensible, as became a philosopher, of the rights of private judgment, and of the difference in opinion that must necessarily arise from the variety of human intellects; he was candid, as became a christian, to those who differed from him, where he observed their practice marked with virtue and piety. But if we follow him to the last scene of his life, and consider him under that severe and tedious disorder which put a period to it, there the sincerity of his piety, and the force of religion to support the mind in the most terrible conflicts, was chiefly visible. For nearly two years he bore with the utmost constancy and patience, a disorder that makes us tremble only to think of it. With most exquisite pain it preyed upon him, until it reached the passages by which life is sustained: yet, in the midst of as much as human nature could endure, he always discovered a submission to the will of heaven, and a resign"

Illman & Pilbrow Sc.

Jno Witherspoon

tion to his fate, that could only flow from the expectation of a better life.

"Such was the man, whose remains now lie before us, to teach us the most interesting lessons that mortals have to learn, the vanity of human things; the importance of eternity; the holiness of the divine law; the value of religion; and the certainty and rapid approach of death."

JOHN WITHERSPOON.

JOHN WITHERSPOON, a man alike distinguished as a minister of the gospel, and a patriot of the revolution, was born in the parish of Yester, a few miles from Edinburgh, on the 5th of February, 1722. He was lineally descended from John Knox, the Scottish reformer, of whom Mary, queen of Scots, said, "she was more afraid of his prayers, than of an army of ten thousand men."

The father of Mr. Witherspoon was the minister of the parish of Yester. He was a man, eminent for his piety and literature, and for a habit of great accuracy in his writings and discourses. The example of the father contributed, in no small degree, to form in his son that love of taste and simplicity, for which he was deservedly distinguished.

He was sent, at an early age, to the public school at Haddington, where he soon acquired a high reputation for the native soundness of his judgment, his close application to study, and the quick and clear conceptions of his mind. Many, who at that time were the companions of his literary toils, afterwards filled some of the highest stations in the literary and political world.

At the age of fourteen, he was removed to the university of Edinburgh. Here he was distinguished, as he had been at the school of Haddington, for his great diligence and rapid literary attainments. In the theological hall, particularly he exhibited an uncommon taste in sacred criticism, and an unusual precision of thought, and perspicuity of expression. At the age of twenty-one, he finished his collegiate studies, and commenced preaching.

Immediately on leaving the university, he was invited to become the minister of Yester, as colleague with his father, with the right of succeeding to the charge. He chose, rather, however, to accept an invitation from the parish of Beith, in the west of Scotland, and here he was ordained and settled, by the unanimous consent of his congregation.

Soon after his settlement at Beith, a circumstance occurred of too interesting a nature to be omitted. On the 17th of January, 1746, was fought the battle of Falkirk. Of this battle, Dr. Witherspoon and several others were spectators. Unfortunately, they were taken prisoners by the rebels, and shut up in close confinement in the castle of Doune. In the same room in which he was confined, were two cells, in one of which were five members of a military company from Edinburgh, who had also been taken prisoners, and two citizens of Aberdeen, who had been threatened to be hanged as spies. In the other cell were several others who had been made prisoners, under circumstances similar to those of Dr. Witherspoon.

During the night which followed their imprisonment, the thoughts of the prisoners, who were able to communicate with one another, were turned on the best means of making their escape. The room where they were confined was the highest part of the castle, not far from the battlements, which were seventy feet high. It was proposed to form a rope of some blankets which they had purchased, and by means of this to descend from the battlements to the ground.

A rope was accordingly made, in the best manner they were able, and about one o'clock in the morning they commenced descending upon it. Four reached the ground in safety. Just as the fifth touched the ground the rope broke, about twenty feet above. This unfortunate occurrence was communicated to those who remained on the battlements, and warning was given to them not to attempt the hazardous descent In disregard, however, of the advice, the next one whose turn it was to descend, immediately went down the rope. On reaching the end of it, his companions below perceiving him determined to let go his hold, put themselves in a posture to break his fall. They succeeded, however, only in part The poor fellow was seriously injured, having one of his ancles dislocated, and several ribs broken. His companions, however, succeeded in conveying him to a village on the borders of the sea, whence he was taken, by means of a boat, to a sloop of war lying in the harbour.

The other volunteer, and Dr. Witherspoon, were left behind. The volunteer now drew the rope up, and to the end of it attached several blankets. Having made it sufficiently long, he again let it down and began his descent. He reached the place where the rope was originally broken, in safety; but the blankets, which he had attached to it, being too large for him to span, like his predecessor, he fell, and was so much wounded, that he afterwards died. The fate of these unhappy men induced Dr. Witherspoon to relinquish the hope of escape in this way, and to wait for a safer mode of liberation.

From Beith, Dr. Witherspoon was translated, in the course of a few years, to the flourishing town of Paisley, where he was happy in the affections of a large congregation, among whom he was eminently useful, until the period of his emigrating to America, to take charge, as president, of the college of New-Jersey.

The election of Dr. Witherspoon to the presidency of the above college, occurred in the year 1766. This appointment, however, he was induced to decline, in the first instance, from the reluctance of the female members of his family, and especially of Mrs. Witherspoon, to leave the scene of their happiness and honour, for a land of strangers. and that land so distant from her father's sepulchres.

At a subsequent period, however, Dr. Witherspoon again took the subject into consideration; and at length, through the influence and representations of Mr. Stockton, of whom we have spo..the wishes of the tru...It reflects no small honour upon Dr. Witherspoon, that he should consent to cross the ocean, and take charge of a college in a new country, leaving behind him a sphere of great respectability, comfort, and usefulness. Having previously declined, it is understood, an urgent invitation to an honourable station in Dublin, in Rotterdam, and in the town of Dundee, in his own country. It deserves also to be mentioned, that a little previous to his embarking for America, and while still in a state of suspense, respecting his duty, an unmarried gentleman of considerable fortune, and a relation of the family, offered to make him his heir, provided he would remain in Scotland.

Dr. Witherspoon arrived in America in August, 1768, and in the same month was inaugurated president of the college. The fame of his literary character caused an immediate accession to the number of students, and an increase of the funds of the college. At that time it had not been patronized by the state. It had been founded and supported by private liberality. At the period of Dr. Witherspoon's arrival, the finances of the college were in a low and declining condition. His reputation, however, in connexion with his personal exertions, excited the generosity of all parts of the country, from Massachusetts to Virginia; in consequence of which, the finances of the institution were soon raised to a flourishing state. During the war of the revolution, the college was broken up, and its resources nearly annihilated. Yet it can scarcely be estimated how much the institution owed, at that time, to the enterprise and talents of Dr. Witherspoon.

"But the principal advantages it derived," says Dr. Rogers, in a discourse occasioned by his death, " were from his literature, his superintendency, his example as a happy model of good writing, and from the tone and taste which he gave to the literary pursuits of the college."

He made great alterations in every department of instruction. "He endeavoured," says the same writer, "to establish the system of education in this institution, upon the most extensive and respectable basis that its circumstances and its finances would admit. Formerly, the course of instruction had been too superficial: and its metaphysics and philosophy were too much tinctured with the dry and uninstructive forms of the schools. This, however, was by no means to be imputed as a defect to those great and excellent men who had presided over the institution before him, but rather to the recent origin of the country, the imperfection of its state of society, and to the state of literature in it. Since his presidency, mathematical science has received an extension that was not known before in the American seminaries. He introduced into philosophy all the most liberal and modern improvements of Europe. He extended the philosophical course to embrace the general principles of policy and public law; he incorporated with it sound and rational metaphysics, equally remote from the doctrines of fatality and contingency, from the barrenness and dogmatism of the schools, and from the excessive refinements of those contradictory, but equally impious sects of scepticism, who wholly deny the existence of matter, or maintain that nothing but matter exists in the universe.

"He laid the foundation of a course of history in the college, and the principles of taste, and the rules of good writing, were both happily explained by him, and exemplified in his *manner*." He possessed an admirable faculty for governing, and was very successful in exciting a good degree of emulation among the pupils committed to his care. Under his auspices, many were graduated, who became distinguished for their learning, and for the eminent services which they rendered their countrymen as divines, as legislators, and patriots.

On the occurrence of the American war, the college was broken up, as has already been noticed, and the officers and students were dispersed. Dr. Witherspoon now appeared in a new attitude before the American public. Although a foreigner, he had laid aside his prejudices on becoming a citizen of the country, and now warmly espoused the cause of the Americans against the English ministry. His distinguished abilities pointed him out to the citizens of New Jersey, as one of the most proper delegates to that convention which formed their republican constitution. In this respect able assembly he appeared, to the astonishment of all the professors of the law, as profound a civilian as he had before been known to be a philosopher and divine.

Early in the year 1776, he was elected a representative to the general congress, by the people of New-Jersey. He took his seat a few days previously to the fourth of July, and assisted in the deliberations on the momentous question of a declaration of independence. Of this measure he was an advocate. It was a happy reply which he made to a gentleman who, in opposing the measure, declared that the country was not yet ripe for a declaration of independence. "Sir," said he, " in my judgment the country is not only *ripe*, but *rotting*."

For the space of seven years, Dr. Witherspoon continued to represent the people of New-Jersey in the general congress. He was seldom absent from his seat, and never allowed personal considerations to prevent his attention to official duties. Few men acted with more energy and promptitude; few appeared to be enriched with greater political wisdom; few enjoyed a greater share of public confidence; few accomplished more for the country, than he did, in the sphere in which he was called to act. In the most gloomy and formidable aspect of public affairs, he was always firm, discovering the greatest reach and presence of mind, in the most embarrassing situations.

It is impossible here to particularise all, or even a small part of the important services which he rendered his country, during his continuance in the grand legislative council. He served on numerous committees, where his judgment and experience were of eminent importance. He seldom took part in the discussions of public measures, until, by reason and reflection, he had settled his ideas on the subject. He would then come forward with great clearness and power, and seldom did he fail to impart light to a subject, and cause even his opponents to hesitate. His speeches were usually composed in closet, and committed to memory. His memory was unusually tenacious. He could repeat verbatim a sermon, or a speech, composed by himself, by reading it three times.

Dr. Witherspoon, it must be admitted, was a sagacious politician. He indeed adopted views which, in some respects, differed from those of his brethren in congress; yet his principles have been justified by the result. A few examples may be mentioned. He constantly opposed the expensive mode of supplying the army by commission. For several years this was the mode adopted. A certain commission per cent. on the money that the commissioners expended, was allowed them, as a compensation. A strong temptation was thus presented to purchase at extravagant prices, since the commissioners correspondingly increased their compensation.

In consequence of this mode of supplying the army, the expenses of the country became alarmingly great. Much dissatisfaction, from time to time, existed in reference to the management of the commissary general's department, and a reform was loudly demanded by many judicious men in the country. Among those who loudly complained on this subject, and who deemed a change essential to the salvation of the country, Dr. Witherspoon was one. This change, so useful and economical, was at length agreed to, July 10th, 1781. The superintendent of finance was authorized to procure all necessary supplies for the army and navy of the United-States by contract, *i. e.* by allowing a certain sum to the purchaser for every ration furnished.

Another point on which Dr. Witherspoon differed from many of his brethren in congress, was the emission of a paper currency. After the first or second emission, he strongly opposed the system, predicting the wound which would be ultimately given to public credit, and the private distress which must necessarily follow. Instead of emissions of an unfunded paper beyond a certain quantum, Dr. Witherspoon urged the propriety of making loans and establishing funds for the payment of the interest. Happy had it been for the country, had this better policy been adopted. At a subsequent date, at the instance of some of the very gentlemen who opposed him in congress, he published his ideas on the nature, value, and uses of money, in one of the most clear and judicious essays that perhaps was ever written on the subject.

At the close of the year 1779, Dr. Witherspoon voluntarily retired from congress, desirous of spending the remainder of his life, as he said, in "*otio cum dignitate.*" Accordingly, he resigned his house in the vicinity of the college to his son-in-law, the Rev. Dr. Samuel Smith, to whom was committed the care and instruction of the students, who now began to return from their dispersion. Dr. Witherspoon retired to a country seat, at the distance of about one mile from Princeton. His name, however, continued to add celebrity to the institution, which not long after recovered its former reputation.

But he was not long allowed the repose which he so much desired. In 1781, he was again elected a representative to congress. But at the close of the following year, he retired from political life. In the year 1783, he was induced, through his attachment to the institution over which he had so long presided, to cross the ocean to promote its benefit. He was now in his sixtieth year, and strong must have been his regard for the interests of learning, to induce him, at this advanced age, to brave the dangers of the ocean. Much success could scarcely be expected in an undertaking of this kind, considering the hostility which still subsisted between England and America. The pecuniary assistance which he obtained exceeded only, by a little, his necessary expenses, although he was not wanting in enterprise and zeal in relation to the object of his voyage.

After his return to this country, in 1784, finding nothing to obstruct his entering on that retirement which was now becoming dear to him, he withdrew, in a great measure, except on some important occasions, from the exercise of those public functions that were not immediately connected with the duties of his office, as president of the college, or his character as a minister of the gospel.

Although Dr. Witherspoon was peculiarly fitted for political life, he appeared with still more advantage as a minister of the gospel, and particularly as a minister in the pulpit. "He was, in many respects," says Dr. Rogers, "one of the best models on which a young preacher could form himself. It was a singular felicity to the whole college, but especially to those who had the profession of the ministry in contemplation, to have such an example constantly in view. Religion, by the manner in which it was treated by him, always commanded the respect of those who heard him, even when it was not able to engage their hearts. An admirable textuary; a profound theologian, perspicuous and simple in his manner; an universal scholar, acquainted with human nature; a grave, dignified, solemn speaker;—he brought all the advantages derived from these sources, to the illustration and enforcement of divine truth."

The social qualities of Dr. Witherspoon rendered him one of the most companionable of men. He possessed a rich fund of anecdote, both amusing and instructive. His moments of relaxation were as entertaining as his serious ones were fraught with improvement. The following anecdote presents a specimen of his pleasantry. On the surrender of the British army to General Gates, at Saratoga, that officer dispatched one of his aids to convey the news to congress. The interesting character of the intelligence would have prompted most men to have made as expeditious a journey as possible; but the aid proceeded so leisurely, that the intelligence reached Philadelphia three days before his arrival. It was usual for congress, on such occasions, to bestow some mark of their esteem upon the person who was the bearer of intelligence so grateful; and it was proposed, in this case, to bestow upon the messenger an elegant sword. During the conversation on this subject in the hall, Dr. Witherspoon rose, and begged leave to amend the motion, by substituting for an elegant sword, a *pair of golden spurs*.

Another interesting trait in his character, was his attention to young persons. He never suffered an opportunity to escape him of imparting the most useful advice to them, according to their circumstances, when they happened to be in his company. And this was always done with so much kindness and suavity, that they could neither be inattentive to it or easily forget it.

In domestic life, he was an affectionate husband, a tender parent, a kind master, and a sincere friend. He was twice married. The first time in Scotland, at an early age, to a lady by the name of Montgomery. She was a woman distinguished for her piety and benevolence. At the time of his emigration to America, he had three sons and two daughters. James, his eldest son, was killed in the battle of Germantown. John was bred a physician, and David applied himself to the study of the law. Both were respectable men. Of the daughters, one was married to the Rev. Samuel S. Smith, the successor of Dr. Witherspoon in the presidency of the college. The other became connected with Dr. Ramsay, the celebrated historian. The second marriage of Dr. Witherspoon occurred when he was seventy years old; the lady whom he married was only twenty-three.

In his person, Dr. Witherspoon was remarkably dignified. He was six feet in height, and of fine proportion. He was distinguished for a fervent piety, and for great punctuality and exactness in his devotional exercises. "Besides his daily devotions of the closet, and the family, it was his stated practice to observe the last day of every year, with his family, as a day of fasting, humiliation, and prayer: and it was also his practice to set apart days for secret fasting and prayer, as occasion suggested."

"Bodily infirmities began at length to come upon him. For more than two years before his death, he was afflicted with the loss of sight, which contributed to hasten the progress of his other disorders. These he bore with a patience, and even with a cheerfulness, rarely to be met with in the most eminent for wisdom and piety. Nor would his active mind, and his desire of usefulness to the end, permit him, even in this situation, to desist from the exercise of his ministry, and his duties in the college, as far as his strength and health would admit. He was frequently led into the pulpit, both at home and abroad, during his blindness; and always acquitted himself with his usual accuracy, and frequently with more than his usual solemnity and animation."

At length, however, he sank under the accumulated pressure of his infirmities; and on the 15th day of November, 1794, in the seventy-third year of his age he retired to his final rest. The following epitaph is inscribed on the marble which covers his remains:

Beneath this marble lie interred
the mortal remains of
JOHN WITHERSPOON, D. D. LL. D.
a venerable and beloved President of the College of
New-Jersey
He was born in the parish of Yester, in Scotland,
on the 5th of February, 1722, O. S.
And was liberally educated in the University of Edinburgh,
invested with holy orders in the year 1743,
he faithfully performed the duties of
his pastoral charge,
during five and twenty years,
first at Beith, and then at Paisley.
Elected president of Nassau Hall,
he assumed the duties of that office on the 13th of August, 1768,
with the elevated expectations of the public
Excelling in every mental gift,
he was a man of pre-eminent piety and virtue
and deeply versed in the various branches
of literature and the liberal arts.
A grave and solemn preacher,
his sermons abounded in the most excellent doctrines and precepts,
and in lucid expositions of the Holy Scriptures.
Affable, pleasant, and courteous in familiar conversation,
he was eminently distinguished
in concerns and deliberations of the church,
and endowed with the greatest prudence
in the management and instruction of youth.
He exalted
the reputation of the college amongst foreigners,
and greatly promoted the advancement
of its literary character and taste.
He was, for a long time, conspicuous
Among the most brilliant luminaries of learning and of the Church.
At length,
universally venerated, beloved, and lamented,
he departed this life on the fifteenth of November, MDCCXCIV.
aged LXXIII years.

FRANCIS HOPKINSON

Francis Hopkinson was a native of Pennsylvania, and was born in the city of Philadelphia, in the year 1737. His father, Thomas Hopkinson, was an Englishman, who emigrated to America, but in what year is unknown to the writer. A short time previous to his emigration, he became respectably connected by marriage, with a niece of the bishop of Worcester.

On his arrival in America, he took up his residence in the city of Philadelphia, where he honourably filled several offices of distinction, under the government of his native country. Mr. Hopkinson was distinguished for his scientific attainments. He was intimate with that distinguished philosopher, Benjamin Franklin, by whom he was held in high estimation. The intimacy which subsisted between these gentlemen, seems to have arisen from a similarity of taste, particularly on philosophical subjects. To Mr. Hopkinson is attributed the first experiment of attracting the electric fluid, by means of a *pointed* instrument, instead of a blunt one. This experiment he had the pleasure of first exhibiting to Dr. Franklin. Its practical importance consisted in preventing the severe explosion, which always takes place in the passage of the electric fluid, upon a blunted instrument.

Upon the death of Mr. Hopkinson, which occurred while he was in the prime of life, the care of his interesting and numerous family devolved upon his widow. Fortunately, Mrs. Hopkinson was a lady of superior mental endowments, and well qualified to superintend the education of her children. At an early period, discovering indications of genius in her son, the subject of the present memoir, she resolved to make every sacrifice, and every effort in her power, to give him the advantages of a superior education. *Her income was comparatively limited, but a mother can relinquish every enjoyment for her children. This Mrs. Hopkinson did with the greatest pleasure; and to the practice of self-denial for her son, she added, for his benefit, the most admirable precepts.

and the most excellent example. Her efforts were crowned with singular success. She lived to see him graduate with reputation, from the college of Philadelphia, and become eminent in the profession of law. He possessed talents of a high order. His genius was quick and versatile. He penetrated the depths of science with ease, and with grave and important truths stored his capacious mind. But he by no means neglected the lighter accomplishments. In music and poetry he excelled, and had some knowledge of painting. Few men were more distinguished for their humour and satire.

In the year 1766, Mr. Hopkinson embarked for England, for the purpose of visiting the land of his fathers. Such was the estimation in which he was held in his native city, that he received a public expression of respect and affection, from the board of trustees of the college of Philadelphia, which the provost of that institution was desired to communicate to him, and wish him, in the behalf of his Alma Mater, a safe and prosperous voyage.

After a residence of more than two years in England, he returned to America, soon after which he became settled in life, having married a Miss Borden, of Bordentown, in the state of New-Jersey. His acknowledged talents soon drew the attention of the royal government, under which he received the appointment of collector of the customs, and executive counsellor.

These offices, however, he did not long enjoy, being obliged to sacrifice them in the cause of his country. He entered with strong feelings into the public measures which preceded the revolutionary contest, and having taken up his residence in New-Jersey, his abilities and patriotism pointed him out as a proper person to represent her in congress. Accordingly, in the year 1776 he received this appointment, and in this capacity he voted for the declaration of independence, and subsequently affixed his signature to the engrossed copy of that memorable instrument.

On the retirement of Mr. Ross, in 1779, the judge of the admiralty court of Pennsylvania, the president of that state nominated Mr. Hopkinson as his successor; an office to which he was unanimously appointed, and the duties of which, for ten years, until the organization of the federal government, he continued to discharge with honour to himself, and benefit to his country.

Soon after the adoption of the federal constitution, General Washington, with the advice and consent of the senate, appointed Mr. Hopkinson to the office of Judge of the United States, for the district of Pennsylvania. This was an important and dignified station, for which he was admirably fitted, and in which capacity he assisted in giving stability and dignity to the national government.

During the period of his judicial career, he conscientiously avoided mingling in party, or occasional politics. He employed his powers, however, when occasion required, in promoting the public good. He contributed in no small degree in rousing the feelings of the people, during the war of the revolution. The chief means by which he accomplished this, was the employment of his powers of satire, which he possessed in an uncommon degree. His occasional productions were quite numerous, and were well adapted to the state of the country at that time. They rendered the author justly popular at that day, and will continue to interest and amuse, while the memory of these times shall remain.

Mr. Hopkinson published several poetical pieces. His chief merit as a poet consisted in an easy versification. His poetical productions were chiefly designed to amuse. This object they effected. They attracted no small attention, throughout the country; but none was more popular than the humorous and well known ballad, called "The Battle of the Kegs."

The life of Mr. Hopkinson was suddenly terminated, while in the midst of his usefulness, on the eighth of May, 1791, in the fifty-third year of his age. He died of an apoplectic fit, which, in two hours after the attack, put a period to his mortal existence. In stature, Mr. Hopkinson was below the common size. His countenance was extremely animated, though his features were small. In speech he was fluent, and in his motions he was unusually quick. Few men were kinder in their dispositions, or more benevolent in their lives

He was distinguished for his powers of taste, and for his love and devotion to science. He possessed a library, which contained the most distinguished literary productions of the times; and in his library room was to be found a collection of scientific apparatus, with which he amused himself in his leisure hours, and added greatly to his stock of knowledge. The following anecdote furnishes evidence of the estimation in which he was held, as a philosopher, and a man of letters. Sometime during the revolutionary war, Bordentown, the place where Mr. Hopkinson and family resided, was suddenly invaded by a party of Hessians. The family had hardly time to escape before the invaders began the plunder of the house. After the evacuation of Philadelphia, by the British, a volume, which had been taken from the library of Mr. Hopkinson, at the above period, fell into his hands. On a blank leaf, the officer, who took the book, had written in German an acknowledgment of the theft, declaring that although he believed Mr. Hopkinson to be an obstinate rebel, the books and philosophical apparatus of his library were sufficient evidence, that he was a learned man.

Mr. Hopkinson, at his decease, left a widow and five children. The eldest of these, Joseph Hopkinson, who still lives, strongly resembles his father, in the endowments of his mind, and the brilliancy of his genius. He occupies an enviable rank among the advocates of the American bar.

JOHN HART.

The history of the world probably furnishes not another instance in which there was a nobler exhibition of true patriotism, than is presented in the history of the American revolution. It was certain at its commencement, in respect to numerous individuals, whose talents, wisdom and enterprise were necessary to its success, that they could derive but little, if any, individual advantage. Nay, it was certain, that instead of gain they would be subjected to great loss and suffering. The comforts of their families would be abridged, their property destroyed; their farms desolated; their houses plundered or consumed; their sons might fall in the field of battle; and, should the struggle be vain, an ignominious death would be their portion. But, then, the contest respected rights which God had given them; it respected liberty, that dearest and noblest privilege of man; it respected the happiness of generations yet to succeed each other on this spacious continent to the end of time. Such considerations influenced the patriots of the revolution. They thought comparatively little of themselves; their views were fixed on the happiness of others; on the future glory of their country; on universal liberty!

These sentiments alone could have actuated JOHN HART, the subject of the present memoir, a worthy and independent farmer of New-Jersey. He was the son of Edward Hart, of Hopewell, in the county of Hunterdon, in New-Jersey. The time of his birth is unknown to the writer, and unfortunately few incidents of his life have been preserved. He inherited from his father a considerable patrimonial estate. To this he added, by purchase, a farm of about four hundred acres. He married a Miss Scudder, a respectable and amiable lady, by whom he had a numerous family of children. He was fond of agricultural pursuits; and in the quiet of domestic life, sought those enjoyments, which are among the purest which the world affords.

The character which Mr. Hart sustained for wisdom, stability, and judgment naturally brought him into notice, and disposed the community to seek the aid of his counsel. He was often a member of the colonial assembly; and rendered important service to the section of country in which he resided, by suggesting improvements as to laying out new roads, the erection of bridges, the superior means of education and the prompt administration of justice.

At the commencement of the aggressions of the British ministry upon the rights of the colonies, Mr. Hart perceived, in common with many of the thinking men of the day, that the only alternative of the latter would be a resort to arms, or absolute slavery. Although he was not one of the most zealous men, or as easily roused to adopt strong measures, as were some of those around him, still he was not backward to express his abhorrence of the unjust conduct of the mother country, nor to enter upon a well matured system of opposition to her designs. He was particularly disgusted with the stamp act. Not that he feared pecuniary loss from its exactions; it was an inconsiderable tax; but trifling as it was, involved a principle of the greatest importance. It gave to the crown a power over the colonies, against the arbitrary exercise of which they had no security. They had in truth, upon the principles claimed by the British government, little or no control over their own property. It might be taxed in the manner, and to the extent, which parliament pleased, and not a single representative from the colonies could raise his voice in their behalf. It was not strange, therefore, that the setting up of such a claim, on the other side of the water, should have been severely felt in the American colonies, and that a spirit of opposition should have pervaded all classes, as well the humble as the elevated, the farmer in his retirement as well as the statesman in his public life.

This spirit of opposition in the colonies kept pace with the spirit of aggression in the mother country. There were few men in the community, who did not feel more intensely each succeeding month the magnitude of the subject; and who were not more and more convinced of the necessity of an united and firm opposition to the British government.

When the congress of 1774 assembled, Mr. Hart appeared. and took his seat; having been elected by a conference of committees from several parts of the colony. The precise share which he took in the deliberations of this august and venerable body, is unknown. If his habits and unambitious spirit led him to act a less conspicuous part than some others, he rendered perhaps no less valuable service, by his moderation and cool judgment.

During several succeeding sessions, Mr. Hart continued to

represent the people of New-Jersey in the continental congress. When the question respecting a Declaration of Independence was brought forward, he was at his post, and voted for the measure with unusual zeal. It was a distinguished honour to belong to this congress, under any circumstances, but the appointment of Mr. Hart must have been peculiarly flattering to him. A little time previous, the provincial congress of New-Jersey had made several changes in their delegation to the general congress. Their confidence was not entire in some of their representatives, especially in regard to that bold and decisive measure, a declaration of independence, which was now occupying the thoughts of many in the country. But the firmness of Mr. Hart, or, as he was afterwards called, "honest John Hart," they could safely trust. They knew him to be a man of tried courage, and never inclined to adopt temporizing or timorous measures. He was accordingly retained, while others were dismissed; and was instructed, "to join with the delegates of the other colonies in continental congress, in the most vigorous measures for supporting the just rights and liberties of America; and if you shall judge it necessary or expedient for this purpose, to join with them in declaring the United Colonies independent of Great Britain, entering into a confederation for union and common defence, making treaties with foreign nations for commerce and assistance, and to take such other measures as may appear to them and you necessary for those great ends, promising to support them with the whole force of this province; always observing, that whatsoever plan of confederacy you enter into, the regulating the internal police of this province is to be reserved to the colonial legislature."

Sometime during the latter part of the year 1776, New-Jersey became the theatre of war. The distress which the people suffered in consequence, was very great; and a wanton destruction of property was often occasioned by the enemy. In this destruction, the property of Mr. Hart largely participated. His children were obliged to flee, his farm was pillaged, and great exertions were made to secure him, as a prisoner. The situation of Mrs. Hart was at the time peculiarly distressing. She was afflict prevented her removal to a place of safety, and eventually caused her death. Mr. Hart continued by her side, until the enemy had nearly reached the house, when he made his escape, his wife being safer alone than if he were present. For some time, he was hunted and pursued with the most untiring zeal. He was scarcely able to elude his enemies, was often in great want of food, and sometimes destitute of a comfortable lodging for the night. In one instance, he was obliged to conceal himself, during the night, in the usual resting place of a large dog, who was his companion for the time.

The battles of Trenton and Princeton led to the evacuation of New-Jersey by the British. On this event, Mr. Hart again collected his family, and began to repair the desolation of his farm by the hand of the enemy. His constitution, however, had received an irreparable shock. His health gradually failed him; and though he lived to see brighter prospects opening before his country, he died before the contest was ended. His death occurred in the year 1780. Although the domestic peace and tranquillity of few men had been more disturbed than those of Mr. Hart, he never repented the course he had taken. He enlisted himself in a good cause; and in the darkest periods, still believed that a righteous Providence would ultimately enable that cause to prevail, and finally to triumph.

The personal appearance of Mr. Hart was uncommonly interesting; in his form he was straight and well proportioned. In stature, he was above the middling size, and, when a young man, was said to have been handsome. In his disposition he was uncommonly mild and amiable. He was greatly beloved by his family and friends, and highly respected by a large circle of acquaintance, who often appealed to his wisdom and judgment in the settlement of their local affairs. In addition to this, he enjoyed the reputation of being a sincere and humble christian. He was exceedingly liberal to the Baptist church of Hopewell, to which community he belonged; and greatly assisted them in the erection of a public house of worship; the ground for which he presented to the church, as also the ground for a burial place. Such was the life, and such the last end, of "honest John Hart."

ABRAHAM CLARK.

It is unfortunately the fact, in respect to many of the distinguished actors in the revolutionary drama, but especially in reference to the subject of this memoir, that but few incidents of their lives have been preserved. The truth is, that although men of exalted patriotism, who filled their respective duties, both in public and private life, with great honour to themselves and benefit to all around them, they were naturally unobtrusive and unambitious. The incidents of their lives were, indeed, few. Some of them lived in retirement, pursuing the "even tenor of their way," nor was the regularity of their lives often interrupted, except, perhaps, by an attendance upon congress, or by the discharge of some minor civil office in the community.

These remarks apply with some justice to Mr. Clark, but perhaps not with more force, than to several others, who stand enrolled among the signers of the declaration of independence.

Mr. Clark was a native of Elizabethtown, New-Jersey, where he was born, on the fifteenth of February, 1726. His father's name was Thomas Clark, of whom he was an only child. His early education, although confined to English branches of study, was respectable. For the mathematics and the civil law he is said to have discovered an early predilection.

He was bred a farmer; but his constitution being inadequate to the labours of the field, he turned his attention to surveying, conveyancing, and imparting legal advice. For this last service he was well qualified; and as he gave advice gratuitously, he was called, "the poor man's counsellor."

The course of Mr. Clark's life, his love of study, and the generosity of his character, naturally rendered him popular. His opinion was valued, and often sought, even beyond the immediate circle within which he lived. He was called to fill various respectable offices, the duties of which he discharged with great fidelity; and thus rendered himself highly useful in the community in which he lived.

At an early period of the revolution, as he had formed his opinion on the great question, which divided the British government and the American colonies, he was appointed one of the committee of public safety; and some time after was elected by the provincial congress, in conjunction with the gentlemen, a sketch of whose lives has already been given, a delegate to the continental congress.

Of this body he was a member, for a considerable period; and was conspicuous among his colleagues from New-Jersey. A few days after he took his seat for the first time, as a member of congress, he was called upon to vote for, or against, the proclamation of independence. But he was at no loss on which side to throw his influence. His patriotism was of the purest character. Personal considerations did not influence his decision. He knew full well that fortune and individual safety were at stake. But what were these in comparison with the honour and liberty of his country. He voted, therefore, for the declaration of independence, and affixed his name to that sacred instrument with a firm determination to meet the consequences of the noble, but dangerous action, with a fortitude and resolution becoming a free born citizen of America.

Mr. Clark frequently, after this time, represented New-Jersey in the national councils. He was also often a member of the state legislature. But in whatever capacity he acted as a public servant, he attracted the respect and admiration of the community, by his punctuality, his integrity, and perseverance.

In 1787, he was elected a member of the general convention, which framed the constitution; but in consequence of ill health, was prevented from uniting in the deliberations of that body. To the constitution, as originally proposed, he had serious objections. These, however, were removed by subsequent amendments; but his enemies took advantage of his objections, and for a time he was placed in the min*** i. t* *** *** icrs of New-Jersey. His popularity, however, again revived, and he was elected a representative in the second congress, under the federal constitution; an appointment which he continued to hold until a short time previous to his death. Two or three of the sons of Mr. Clark were officers in the army, during the revolutionary struggle. Unfortunately they were captured by the enemy. During a part of their captivity, their sufferings were extreme, being confined in the notorious prison-ship, Jersey. Painful as the condition of his sons was, Mr. Clark scrupulously avoided calling the attention of congress to the subject, excepting in a single instance. One of his sons, a captain of artillery, had been cast into a dungeon, where he received no other food than that which was conveyed to him by his fellow prisoners, through a key hole. On a representation of these facts to congress, that body immediately directed a course of retaliation in respect to a British officer. This had the desired effect, and Captain Clark's condition was improved.

On the adjournment of congress in June, 1794, Mr. Clark finally retired from public life. He did not live long, however, to enjoy even the limited comforts he possessed. In the autumn of the same year a stroke of the sun put a period to his mortal existence, in the space of two hours. He was already, however, an old man, having attained to his sixty-ninth year. The church yard at Rahway contains his mortal remains, and the church of that place will long have reason to remember his benefactions. A marble slab marks the place where this useful and excellent man lies deposited, and the following inscription upon it, records the distinguished traits of his character:

Firm and decided as a patriot,
zealous and faithful as a friend to the public,
he loved his country,
and adhered to her cause
in the darkest hours of her struggles
against oppression.

THE PENNSYLVANIA DELEGATION.

Robert Morris,
Benjamin Rush,
Benjamin Franklin,
John Morton,
Geoge Clymer,
James Smith,
George Taylor,
James Wilson,
George Ross.

ROBERT MORRIS.

Robert Morris was a native of Lancashire, England, where he was born January, 1773—4, O. S. His father was a Liverpool merchant, who had for some years been extensively concerned in the American trade. While he was yet a boy, his father removed to America; shortly after which, he sent to England for his son, who arrived in this country at the age of thirteen years.

Young Morris was placed at school in Philadelphia, but his progress in learning appears to have been small, probably from the incompetency of his teacher, as he declared to his father one day, on the latter expressing his dissatisfaction at the little progress he made, "Sir," said he, "I have learned all that he can teach me."

"During the time that young Morris was pursuing his

education at Philadelphia, he unfortunately lost his father, in consequence of a wound received from the wad of a gun, which was discharged as a compliment, by the captain of a ship consigned to him, that had just arrived at Oxford, the place of his residence, on the eastern shores of the Chesapeake Bay, and was thus left an orphan, at the age of fifteen years. In conformity to the intentions of his parent, he was bred to commerce, and served a regular apprenticeship in the counting-house of the late Mr. Charles Willing, at that time one of the first merchants of Philadelphia. A year or two after the expiration of the term for which he had engaged himself, he entered into partnership with Mr. Thomas Willing. This connexion, which was formed in 1754, continued for the long period of thirty-nine years, not having been dissolved until 1793. Previously to the commencement of the American war, it was, without doubt, more extensively engaged in commerce than any other house in Philadelphia.

"Of the events of his youth we know little. The fact just mentioned proves, that although early deprived of the benefit of parental counsel, he acted with fidelity, and gained the good will of a discerning master. The following anecdote will show his early activity in business, and anxiety to promote the interests of his friends. During the absence of Mr. Willing, at his country place, near Frankford, a vessel arrived at Philadelphia, either consigned to him, or that brought letters, giving intelligence of the sudden rise in the price of flour, at the port she left. Mr. Morris instantly engaged all that he could contract for, on account of Mr. Willing, who, on his return to the city next day, had to defend his young friend from the complaints of some merchants, that he had raised the price of flour. An appeal, however, from Mr. Willing, to their own probable line of conduct, in case of their having first received the news, silenced their complaints."

There were few men who viewed with greater indignation the encroachments of the British government upon the liberties of the people, or were more ready to resist them, than Mr. Morris. Nor did he hesitate to sacrifice his private interest for the public good, when occasion demanded it. This disposition was strikingly manifested in the year 1765, at which time he signed the non-importation agreement, entered into by the merchants of Philadelphia. The extensive mercantile concerns with England of the house of Mr. Morris, and the large importations of her manufactures and colonial produce by it, must have made this sacrifice considerable

The massacre at Lexington, April, 1775, seems to have decided the mind of Mr. Morris, as to the unalterable course which he would adopt in respect to England. The news of this measure reached Philadelphia four days after its occurrence. Robert Morris, with a large company, were at this time engaged at the city tavern, in the celebration, on George's day, of their patron saint. The news was received by the company with the greatest surprise. The tables, at which they were dining, were immediately deserted. A few only of the members, among whom was Mr. Morris, remained. To these, indeed to all, who had been present, it was evident that the die was cast—that the Lexington measure was an event which must lead to a final separation from the British government. Such an opinion Mr. Morris, at this time, expressed; he was willing it should take place, and from this time cordially entered into all the measures which seemed the most likely to effect the object.

On the third of November, 1775, Mr. Morris was elected, by the legislature of Pennsylvania, a delegate to the second congress that met at Philadelphia. "A few weeks after he had taken his seat, he was added to the secret committee of that body, which had been formed by a resolve of the preceding congress, (1775,) and whose duty it was 'to contract for the importation of arms, ammunition, sulphur, and saltpetre, and to export produce on the public account, to pay for the same.' He was also appointed a member of the committee for fitting out a naval armament, and specially commissioned to negociate bills of exchange for congress; to borrow money for the marine committee, and to manage the fiscal concerns of congress on other occasions. Independently of his enthusiastic zeal in the cause of his country, his capacity for business, and knowledge of the subjects committed to him, or his talents for managing pecuniary concerns, he was particularly fitted for such services; as the commercial credit he had established among his fellow-citizens probably stood higher than that of any other man in the community, and this he did not hesitate to avail himself of, whenever the public necessities required such an evidence of his patriotism.

A highly interesting illustration of this last remark, is furnished in the conduct of Mr. Morris in the December following the declaration of independence. For some time previous, the British army had been directing its course towards Philadelphia, from which congress had retired, leaving a committee, consisting of Mr. Morris, Mr. Clymer, and Mr. Walton, to transact all necessary continental business.

While attending to the duties of their appointment, Mr. Morris received a letter from Gen. Washington, then with his army on the Delaware, opposite Trenton, in which letter he communicated to Mr. Morris his distressed state, in consequence of the want of money. The sum he needed was ten thousand dollars, which was essentially necessary to enable him to obtain such intelligence of the movement and position of the enemy, as would authorise him to act offensively. To Mr. Morris, Gen. Washington now looked, to assist him in raising the money.

This letter he read with attention, but what could he do? The citizens generally had left the city. He knew of no one, who possessed the required sum, or who would be willing to lend it. The evening approached, and he left his counting-room to return home. On the way, he accidentally overtook an honest quaker, with whom he was acquainted. The quaker inquired of him the news. Mr. Morris replied, that he had but little news of importance to communicate, but he had a subject which pressed with great weight upon his mind. He now informed the quaker of the letter which he had received, the situation of General Washington, and the immediate necessity of ten thousand dollars. "Sir," said Mr. Morris, "you must let me have it. My *note* and my *honour* will be your only security." The quaker hesitated a moment, but at length replied, "Robert, thou shalt have it." The money was soon told, was transmitted to Washington, whom it enabled to accomplish his wishes, and to gain a signal victory over the Hessians at Trenton, thus animating the drooping spirits of patriotism, and checking in no small degree, the proud hopes and predictions of the enemy.

Another instance of patriotic liberality is recorded of Mr. Morris in 1779, or 1780. These were distressing years of the war. The army was alarmingly destitute of military stores, particularly of the essential article of lead. It was found necessary to melt down the weights of clocks and the spouts of houses; but, notwithstanding resort was had to every possible source, the army was often so destitute, that it could scarcely have fought a single battle.

In this alarming state of things, General Washington wrote to several gentlemen, and among the rest to Judge Peters, at that time secretary to the board of war, stating his necessities, and urging an immediate exertion to supply the deficiency.

This it seemed impossible to do. Mr. Peters, however, showed the letter of Washington to Mr. Morris. Fortunately, just at this juncture, a privateer belonging to the latter gentleman had arrived at the wharf, with ninety tons of lead. Half of this lead was immediately given by Mr. Morris, for the use of the army, and the other half was purchased by Mr. Peters of other gentlemen, who owned it, Mr. Morris becoming security for the payment of the debt. At a more advanced stage of the war, when pressing distress in the army had driven congress and the commander in chief almost to desperation, and a part of the troops to mutiny, he supplied the army with four or five thousand barrels of flour upon his own private credit; and on a promise to that effect, persuaded a member to withdraw an intended motion to sanction a procedure, which, although common in Europe, would have had a very injurious effect upon the cause of the country: this was no less than to authorize General Washington to seize all the provision that could be found, within a circle of twenty miles of his camp. While financier, his notes constituted, for large transactions, part of the circulating medium. Many other similar instances occurred of this patriotic interposition of his own personal responsibility for supplies which could not otherwise have been obtained.

Allusion has been made above to the gloomy posture of affairs, during the year 1780; at this time the wants of the army, particularly of provisions, were so great, as to threaten its dissolution. This state of things, being communicated to Mr. Morris, he immediately proposed the establishment of a Bank, the principal object of which was, to supply the army with provisions. This plan becoming popular, ninety-six subscribers gave their bonds, on this occasion, by which they obliged themselves to pay, if it should become necessary, in gold and silver, the amounts annexed to their names, to fulfil the engagements of the Bank. By this means, the confidence of the public in the safety of the bank was confirmed.

Mr. Morris headed the list with a subscription of 10,000*l*; others followed to the amount of 300,000*l*. The directors were authorized to borrow money on the credit of the bank, and to grant special notes, bearing interest at six per cent. The credit thus given to the bank effected the object intended, and the institution was continued until the bank of North America went into operation in the succeeding year. It was probably on this occasion, that he purchased the four or five thousand barrels of flour, abovementioned, on his own credit, for the army, before the funds could be collected to pay for it."

We have not yet spoken of the congressional career of Mr. Morris, nor is it necessary to delay the reader by a minute account of the services which he rendered the country, in the national assembly. In this capacity, no one exhibited a more untiring zeal, none more cheerfully sacrificed ease and comfort than he did. He accomplished much by his active exertions, and perhaps not less by the confidence which he uniformly manifested of ultimate success. The display of such confidence powerfully tended to rouse the desponding, to fix the wavering, and confirm the brave

In another way, Mr. Morris contributed to advance the patriotic cause. During the whole war, he maintained an extensive private correspondence with gentlemen in England by means of which he often received information of importance to this country. "These letters he read to a few select mercantile friends, who regularly met in the insurance room at the merchant's coffee house, and through them the intelligence they contained was diffused among the citizens, and thus kept alive the spirit of opposition, made them acquainted with the gradual progress of hostile movements, and convinced them how little was to be expected from the government in respect to the alleviation of the oppression and hardships against which the colonies had for a long time most humbly, earnestly, and eloquently remonstrated. This practice, which began previous to the suspension of the intercourse between the two countries, he continued during the war; and through the route of the continent, especially France and Holland, he received for a while the despatches, which had formerly come directly from England."

In the year 1781, Mr. Morris was appointed by congress, superintendant of finance, an office then for the first time established. This appointment was unanimous. Indeed it is highly probable that no other man in the country would have been competent to the task of managing such great concerns as it involved, or possessed, like himself, the happy expedient of raising supplies, or deservedly enjoyed more, if equal, public confidence among his fellow-citizens, for punctuality in the fulfilment of his engagements.

Some idea may be formed of them, when it is known that he was required to examine into the state of the public debts, expenditures, and revenue; to digest and report plans for improving and regulating the finances; and for establishing order and economy in the expenditure of public money. To him was likewise committed the disposition, management, and disbursement of all the loans received from the government of France, and various private persons in that country and Holland; the sums of money received from the different states; and of the publi expense for the support of government, civil, military, and naval; the procuring supplies of every description for the army and navy; the entire management and direction of the public ships of war; the payment of all foreign debts; and the correspondence of our ministers at European courts, on subjects of finance. In short, the whole burden of the money operations of government was laid upon him. No man ever had more numerous concerns committed to his charge, and few to greater amount; and never did any one more faithfully discharge the various complicated trusts with greater dispatch, economy, or credit, than the subject of this sketch."

Never was an appointment more judicious than the appointment of Mr. Morris as financier of this country. At this time the treasury was more than two millions and a half in arrears, and the greater part of the debt was of such a nature that the payment could not be avoided, or even delayed, and therefore, Dr. Franklin, then our minister in France, was under the necessity of ordering back from Amsterdam monies which had been sent thither for the purpose of being shipped to America. If he had not taken this step, the bills of exchange drawn by order of congress must have been protested, and a vital stab given to the credit of the government in Europe. At home, the greatest public as well as private distress existed; public credit had gone to wreck, and the enemy built their most sanguine hopes of overcoming us, upon this circumstance; and the treasury was so much in arrears to the servants in the public offices, that many of them could not, without payment, perform their duties, but must have gone to jail for debts they had contracted to enable them to live. To so low an ebb was the public treasury reduced, that some of the members of the board of war declared to Mr. Morris that they had not the means of sending an express to the army. The pressing distress for provision among the troops, has already been mentioned. The paper bills of credit were sunk so low in value, as to require a burdensome mass of them to pay for an article of clothing."

But the face of things soon began to change through the exertions of Mr. Morris. Without attempting to give the history of his wise and judicious management, it will be sufficient to say, in the language of an elegant historian of the American war, " certainly the Americans owed, and still owe, as much acknowledgment to the financial operations of Robert Morris, as to the negociations of Benjamin Franklin, or even the arms of George Washington."

To Mr. Morris, also, the country was indebted for the establishment of the bank of North America, and for all the public benefits which resulted from that institution. By means of this, public credit was greatly revived; internal improvements were promoted, and a general spring was given to trade. " The circulating medium was greatly increased by the circulation of its notes, which being convertible at will into gold or silver, were universally received equal thereto, and commanded the most unbounded confidence. Hundreds availed themselves of the security afforded by the vaults of the bank, to deposit their cash, which, from the impossibility of investing it, had long been hid from the light; and the constant current of deposits in the course of trade, authorised the directors to increase their business and the amount of their issues, to a most unprecedented extent. The consequence of this was, a speedy and most perceptible change in the state of affairs, both public and private."

We now come to an event, on account of the interest in which the name of Robert Morris should be remembered with gratitude by the American people, while republican America shall last. The campaign of 1781, respected the reduction of New-York; this was agreed upon by Washington and the French general, Count Rochambeau, and it was expected that the French fleets, under De Barras and De Grasse, would co-operate. Judge the surprise when, on the arrival of the French fleet, it was announced to Washington, that the French admiral would not enter the bay of New-York, as was anticipated, but would enter and remain for a few weeks in the Chesapeake.

This necessarily altered all the arrangements respecting the campaign. It was now obvious to Washington, that the reduction of New-York would be impracticable. In this stat—

of things, it is hinted by Dr. Mease, in his biographical sketch of Mr. Morris, in the Edinburgh Encyclopedia, to which article we are greatly indebted, that Mr. Morris suggested to Washington the attack on Cornwallis, which put a finishing stroke to the war. Whether this be so or not, certain it is, that until the news was communicated to Washington, that the French fleet would not come into New-York bay, the project of a southern campaign had not been determined upon by the commander in chief. But when, at length, it was determined upon, whether at the suggestion of Robert Morris or not, we are unable to say, it is certain that he provided the funds which enabled General Washington to move his army towards the south, and which led to the decisive battle which terminated the war.

The length to which this article is already extended, forbids any further account of the services of this distinguished patriot.

"It adds not a little, however," says Dr. Mease, "to the merit of Mr. Morris, to be able to say, that notwithstanding his numerous engagements as a public or private character, their magnitude, and often perplexing nature, he was enabled to fulfil all the private duties which his high standing in society necessarily imposed upon him. His house was the seat of elegant, but unostentatious hospitality, and he regulated his domestic affairs with the same admirable order which had so long proverbially distinguished his counting-house, and the offices of the secret committee of congress, and that of finance. The happy manner in which he conducted his official and domestic concerns, was owing, in the first case, to his own superior talents for dispatch and method in business, and, in the last, to the qualifications of his excellent partner, the sister of the esteemed bishop of Pennsylvania, Dr. White. An introduction to Mr. Morris was a matter of course, with all the strangers in good society, who, for half a century, visited Philadelphia, either on commercial, public, or private business; and it is not saying too much to assert, that during a certain period, it greatly depended upon him to do the honours of the city; and certainly no one was more qualified, or more willing to support them. Although active in the acquisition of wealth as a merchant, no one more freely parted with his gains, for public or private purposes of a meritorious nature, whether these were to support the credit of the government, to promote the objects of humanity, local improvement, the welfare of meritorious individuals in society, or a faithful commercial servant. The instances in which he shone on all these occasions were numerous. Some in reference to the three former particulars, have been mentioned, and more of his disinterested generosity in respect to the last could be given, were the present intended to be any thing more than a hasty sketch. The prime of his life was engaged in discharging the most important civil trusts to his country that could possibly fall to the lot of any man, and millions passed through his hands as a public officer, without the smallest breath of insinuation against his correctness, or of negligence amidst "the defaulters of unaccounted thousands," or the losses sustained by the reprehensible carelessness of national agents.

From the foregoing short statement, we may have some idea of the nature and magnitude of the services rendered by Mr Morris to the United States. It may be truly said, that few men acted a more conspicuous or useful part; and when we recollect, that it was by his exertions and talents, that the United States were so often relieved from their difficulties, at times of great depression and pecuniary distress, an estimate may be formed of the weight of obligations due to him from the people of the present day. The length to which this article is already extended, forbids any further particulars respecting this distinguished man. It may be proper to add, however, that the latter part of his life was rendered unhappy, by an unfortunate scheme of land speculation, in which he engaged, and by which his pecuniary affairs became exceedingly embarrassed; yet amidst his severest trials, he maintained a firmness and an independence of character, which in similar circumstances belong to but few.

At length, through public labour, and private misfortune

his constitution was literally worn out, and like a shock of corn fully ripe, he came to his end on the 8th of May 1806, in the seventy-third year of his age.

BENJAMIN RUSH.

BENJAMIN RUSH was born on the 24th of December, 1745, O. S. in the township of Byberry, twelve or fourteen miles northeast of Philadelphia. His ancestors emigrated from England to Pennsylvania, about the year 1683.

The father of young Rush died when he was six years of age. The care of his education therefore devolved upon his mother, who well understood the importance of knowledge, and early took measures to give her son a liberal education. Young Rush was sent to the academy at Nottingham, in Maryland, about sixty miles southeast from Philadelphia. This academy had long been conducted, with great reputation, by the Reverend Dr. Finley, afterwards president of Princeton college, in New-Jersey.

Under the care of this excellent man, and among the people of Nottingham, who were remarkable for their simplicity, industry, morality, and religion, Rush spent five years, in acquiring a knowledge of the Greek and Latin languages. In this retired spot, and at this early age, he is said to have been deeply impressed with a reverence for religion, with the importance of a regular life, and of diligence, industry, and a punctual attention to business; and in general, of such steady habits, as stamped a value on his character through life. The solid foundation which was thus laid for correct principles and an upright conduct, was chiefly the work of the learned and pious Dr. Finley. He was an accomplished instructor of youth. He trained his pupils for both worlds, having respect in all his intercourse with them to their future, as well as present state of existence.

After finishing his preparatory studies at Nottingham, he was entered in 1759, a student in the college of Princeton, then under the superintendence of President Davies. Such had been his progress in his classical studies at Nottingham, that he obtained the degree of bachelor of arts in 1760, and before he had completed his fifteenth year.

On leaving college, he commenced the study of medicine, under the direction of the eminent Dr. Redman, of Philadelphia. He was also one of Dr. Shippen's ten pupils, who attended the first course of anatomical lectures given in this country. In 1766, he went to Edinburgh, where he spent two years at the university in that city, and from which he received the degree of M. D. in 1768.

The next winter after his graduation he spent in London; and the following spring having visited France, in the autumn of the same year he returned to Philadelphia, and commenced the practice of medicine.

In 1769, he was elected professor of chemistry in the college of Philadelphia. This addition to Drs. Shippen, Morgan, Kuhn, and Bond, who had begun to lecture a few years before, completed the various departments, and fully organized this first medical school in America. By a subsequent arrangement in 1791, the college was merged in a university, and Dr. Rush was appointed professor of the institutes and practice of medicine, and of clinical practice, in the university of Pennsylvania.

As a lecturer on chemistry, and a practitioner, Dr. Rush became deservedly popular. During his residence abroad, his professional attainments were much enlarged, and he was successful in introducing several valuable improvements. He was particularly attached to the system of depletion, and resorted to bleeding in many new cases. Next to the lancet, he used cathartics; and upon these two remedies he chiefly depended for the cure of diseases. About the year 1790, twenty years after Dr. Rush had been a practitioner, and professor of medicine, he began to publish his new principles of medicine. These were more or less developed by him in his successive annual course of lectures, for the subsequent twenty-three years of his life.

It is not our province to settle the merits of that system, which Dr. Rush adopted. He applied his principles of medicine to the cure of consumptions, dropsies, hydrocephalus, apoplexy, gout, and other diseases of the body, and also to madness, and the diseases of the mind. He depended chiefly upon the lancet, and strongly urged the use of calomel, to which he gave the name of "the *Sampson* of the Materia Medica."

It was not to be expected that a system, in many respects so novel, should be adopted by every one. It had its strong opposers, and these opposers exist at the present day. They objected to the system of depletion, but agreed with Doctor Rush, that calomel was well entitled to the name of "Sampson," not for the reason which he assigned, but "because," said they, "*it has slain its thousands.*"

In the year 1793, Dr. Rush had an opportunity of applying his principles, in the treatment of yellow fever. In that year, Philadelphia was desolated by that tremendous scourge, after an interval of thirty-one years. The disease baffled the skill of the oldest and most judicious physicians; and they differed about the nature, and the treatment of it. "This general calamity lasted for about one hundred days, extending from July till November. The deaths in the whole of this distressing period, were four thousand and forty-four, or something more than thirty-eight each day, on an average. Whole families were confined by it. There was a great deficiency of nurses for the sick. There was likewise a great deficiency of physicians, from the desertion of some, and the sickness and death of others. At one time, there were but three physicians, who were able to do business out of their houses, and at this time there were probably not less than six thousand persons ill with the fever."

"A cheerful countenance was scarcely to be seen for six weeks. The streets every where discovered marks of the distress that p⋯⋯ ⋯ ⋯. In walking for many hundred yards, few persons were met, except such as were a quest of a physician, a nurse, a bleeder, or the men who buried the dead. The hearse alone kept up the remembrance of the noise of carriages, or carts, in the streets. A black man leading or driving a horse, with a corpse, on a pair of chair wheels, met the eye in most of the streets of the city, at every hour of the day; while the noise of the same wheels passing slowly over the pavement kept alive anguish and fear in the sick and well, every hour of the night."

For some time after the commencement of the disease, all the physicians were nearly alike unsuccessful in the management of it. At this time, Dr. Rush resorted to gentle evacuants as had been used in the yellow fever of 1762; but finding these unavailing, he applied himself to an investigation of the disease, by means of the authors who had written on the subject. He ransacked his library, and pored over every book which treated of the yellow fever. At length he took up a manuscript, which contained an account of the disease, as it prevailed in Virginia, in 1741, and which was given to him by Dr. Franklin, and had been written by Dr. Mitchell of Virginia. In this manuscript the propriety and necessity of powerful evacuants were stated and urged, even in cases of extreme debility.

These ideas led Dr. Rush to an alteration in his practice. He adopted the plan of Dr. Mitchell. He administered calomel and jalap combined, and had the happiness of curing four of the first five patients to whom he administered this medicine, notwithstanding some of them were advanced several days in the disease.

"After such a pledge of the safety and success of this new medicine," says Dr. Thatcher, in his biographical sketch of Dr. Rush, "he communicated the prescription to such of the practitioners as he met in the streets. Some of them, he found, had been in the use of calomel for several days; but as they had given it in single doses only, and had followed it by large doses of bark, wine, and laudanum, they had done little or no good with it. He imparted the prescription to the college of physicians, on the third of September, and endeavoured to remove the fears of his fellow citizens, by assuring them that the disease was no longer incurable. The credit his prescription acquired, brought him an immense accession of business. It continued to be almost uniformly effectual, in nearly all those cases which he was able to attend, either in person, or by his pupils. But he did not rely upon purges alone to cure the disease. The theory which he had adopted led him to use other remedies, to abstract excess of stimulus from the system. These were blood letting, cool air, cold drinks, low diet, and application of cold water to the body. He began by drawing a small quantity of blood at a time. The appearance of it when drawn, and its effects upon the system, satisfied him of its safety and efficacy, and encouraged him to proceed. Never did he experience such sublime joy as he now felt, in contemplating the success of his remedies It repaid him for all the toils and studies of his life. The conquest of this formidable disease was not the effect of accident, nor of the application of a single remedy ; but it was the triumph of a principle in medicine. In this joyful state of mind, he entered in his note book, dated the 10th of September, ' Thank God, out of one hundred patients whom I have visited or prescribed for this day, I have lost none '

"Being unable to comply with the numerous demands which were made upon him, for the purging powders, notwithstanding he had employed three persons to assist his pupils in putting them up, and finding himself unable to attend all the persons who sent for him, he furnished the apothecaries with the receipt for the mercurial purges, together with printed directions for giving them, and for the treatment of the disease. Had he consulted his own interest, he would silently have pursued his own plans of cure, with his old patients, who still confided in him and his new remedies, but he felt, at this season of universal distress, his professional obligations to all the citizens of Philadelphia, to be superior to private and personal considerations; and therefore determined, at every hazard, to do every thing in his power to save their lives. Under the influence of this disposition, he addressed a letter to the college of physicians, in which he stated his objections to Dr. Stevens's remedies, and defended those he had recommended. He likewise defended them in the public papers, against the attacks that were made upon them by several of the physicians of the city, and occasionally addressed such advice to the citizens as experience had suggested to be useful to prevent the disease. In none of the recommendations of his remedies did he claim the credit of their discovery. On the contrary, he constantly endeavoured to enforce their adoption by mentioning precedents in favour of their efficacy, from the highest authorities in medicine. This controversy was encouraged merely to prevent the greater evil of the depopulation of Philadelphia, by the use of remedies which had been prescribed by himself as well as others, not only without effect, but with evident injury to the sick. The repeated and numerous instances of their inefficacy, and the almost uniform success of the depleting remedies, after a while procured submission to the latter, from nearly all the persons who were affected by the fever.

"Many whole families, consisting of five, six, and, in three instances, of nine members, were recovered by plentiful purging and bleeding. These remedies were prescribed with great advantage by several of the physicians of the city But the use of them was not restricted to the physicians alone; the clergy, the apothecaries, many private citizens, several intelligent women, and two black men, prescribed them with great success. Nay, more, many persons prescribed them to themselves. It was owing to the almost universal use of these remedies, that the mortality of the disease diminished in proportion as the number of persons who were affected by it increased It is probable that not less than six thousand of the inhabitants of Philadelphia were saved from death by bleeding and purging, during the autumn of 1793.

"The credit which this new mode of treating the disease acquired in all parts of the city, produced an immense influx of patients to Dr. Rush. His pupils were constantly employed at first in putting up purging powders, but after a while only in bleeding and visiting the sick.

"Between the 8th and 15th of September, Dr. Rush visited

and prescribed for a hundred and a hundred and twenty patients a day. In the short intervals of business, which he spent at his meals, his house was filled with patients, chiefly the poor, waiting for advice. For many weeks he seldom ate without prescribing for numbers as he sat at table. To assist him, three of his pupils, Mr. Stall, Mr. Fisher, and Mr. Cox, accepted of rooms in his house, and became members of his family. Their labours now had no remission. He employed every moment in the interval of his visits to the sick, in prescribing in his house for the poor, or in sending answers to messages from his patients. Unable to comply with the numerous applications that were made to him, he was obliged to refuse many every day. His sister counted forty-seven applicants for medical aid turned off in one forenoon, before eleven o'clock. In riding through the streets, he was often forced to resist the entreaties of parents imploring a visit to their children, or of children to their parents. He was sometimes obliged to tear himself from persons who attempted to stop him, and to urge his way by driving his chair as speedily as possible beyond the reach of their cries. While he was thus overwhelmed with business, and his own life endangered, without being able to answer the numerous calls made on him, he received letters from his friends in the country, pressing him, in the strongest terms, to leave the city. To one of these letters he replied, "that he had resolved to stick to his principles, his practice, and his patients, to the last extremity."

The incessant labours of Dr. Rush, both of body and mind, during this awful visitation, nearly overpowered his health, and for a time his useful life was despaired of. By a timely application of remedies, however, he was restored, and able to return to the duties of his profession. But ill health was not the only evil he suffered, as the consequence of his activity, during the prevalence of the yellow fever in Philadelphia. His mode of treatment was called in question by many of his contemporaries, notwithstanding the great success which attended it. At length the prejudices against him infected not only physicians, but a considerable part of the community. The public journals were enlisted against him, and in numerous pamphlets his system was attacked with great severity. He was even called a murderer, and was at length threatened to be prosecuted and expelled the city.

The benefactors of mankind have not unfrequently been treated in a similar manner. They suffer for a time; but justice is at length done them. Dr. Harvey, as a consequence of publishing his account of the circulation of the blood, lost his practice; and the great Dr. Sydenham suffered in a similar manner, for introducing depleting medicine in cases of inflammatory fevers. On the termination of the fever in Philadelphia, a motion was made in a public meeting of the citizens in that city, to thank the physicians for their services during the prevalence of the fever, but no one would second it. This was high ingratitude, and especially when it is considered that eight out of thirty-five of the physicians, who continued in the city, died; and of those who remained, but three escaped the fever.

Notwithstanding the great labours of Dr. Rush as a lecturer and practitioner, he was a voluminous writer. His printed works consisted of seven volumes, six of which treat of medical subjects. One is a collection of essays, literary, moral, and philosophical. It is a matter of wonder how a physician, who had so many patients to attend—a professor, who had so many pupils to instruct—could find leisure to write so much, and at the same time so well. Our wonder will cease, when it is known that he suffered no fragments of time to be wasted, and that he improved every opportunity of acquiring knowledge, and used all practicable means for retaining and digesting what he had acquired. In his early youth he had the best instructors, and in every period of his life, great opportunities for mental improvement. He was gifted from heaven with a lively imagination, a retentive memory, a discriminating judgment, and he made the most of all these advantages. From boyhood till his last sickness, he was a constant and an indefatigable student. He read much, but thought more. His mind was constantly engrossed with at least one literary inquiry, to which, for the time, he devoted his undivided attention. To make himself master of that subject, he read, he meditated, he conversed. It was less his custom to read a book through, than to read as much of all the authors within his reach as bore on the subject of his present inquiry. His active mind brooded over the materials thus collected, compared his ideas, and traced their relations to each other, and from the whole drew his own conclusions. In these, and similar mental exercises, he was habitually and almost constantly employed, and daily aggregated and multiplied his intellectual stores. In this manner his sound judgment was led to form those new combinations, which constitute principles in science. He formed acquaintances with his literary fellow-citizens, and all well informed strangers, who visited Philadelphia, and drew from them every atom of information he could obtain, by conversing on the subjects with which they were best acquainted. He extracted so largely from the magazine of knowledge deposited in the expanded mind of Dr. Franklin, that he once mentioned to a friend, his intention to write a book with the title of Frankliniana, in which he proposed to collect the fragments of wisdom, which he had treasured in his memory, as they fell in conversation from the lips of this great original genius. To Dr. Rush, every place was a school, every one with whom he conversed was a tutor. He was never without a book, for, when he had no other, the book of nature was before him, and engaged his attention. In his lectures to his pupils, he advised them, 'to lay every person they met with, whether in a packet boat, a stage wagon, or a public road, under contribution for facts on physical subjects.' What the professor recommended to them, he practised himself. His eyes and ears were open to see, hear, and profit by every occurrence. The facts he received from persons of all capacities he improved to some valuable purpose. He illustrates one of his medical theories by a fact communicated by a butcher; another from an observation made by a madman, in the Pennsylvania Hospital. In his scientific work on the diseases of the mind, he refers frequently to poets, and particularly to Shakspeare, to illustrate the history of madness, and apologises for it in the following words. 'They (poets) view the human mind in all its operations, whether natural or morbid, with a microscopic eye, and hence many things arrest their attention, which escape the notice of physicians.' It may be useful to students to be informed, that Dr. Rush constantly kept by him a note book, consisting of two parts, in one of which he entered facts as they occurred; in the other, ideas and observations, as they arose in his own mind, or were suggested by others in conversation. His mind was under such complete discipline, that he could read or write with perfect composure, in the midst of the noise of his children, the conversation of his family, and the common interrogatories of his visiting patients. A very moderate proportion of his time was devoted to sleep, and much less to the pleasures of the table. In the latter case, sittings were never prolonged, but in conversation on useful subjects, and for purposes totally distinct from the gratifications of appetite. In the course of nearly seventy years spent in this manner, he acquired a sum of useful practical knowledge that has rarely been attained by one man, in any age or country."

Medical inquiries were the primary objects of Dr. Rush's attention; yet he by no means neglected other branches of knowledge. In the earlier part of his life, he paid great attention to politics. The subjects of a political character, which chiefly engrossed his mind, were the independence of his country, the establishment of wise constitutions for the states generally, and for his own state particularly, and the diffusion of knowledge among the American people. On these subjects he usefully employed his pen in numerous essays, which were published under a variety of names.

This political knowledge, and political integrity, were so well appreciated, that sundry offices were conferred upon him. He was a member of the celebrated congress of 1776, which declared these states free and independent. This event Dr. Rush perceived to be the harbinger of important blessings to the American people. He was not one of those who thought so much of commerce, of the influx of riches, or high rank among the nations. These, indeed, he well knew were consequences which would result from the declaration of independence. But these he viewed as a minor consideration, compared with the increase of talents and knowledge. The progress of eloquence, of science, and of mind, in all its various pursuits, was considered by him as the necessary effect of republican constitutions, and in the prospect of them he rejoiced. Nor was he disappointed; for in a lecture, delivered in November, 1799, he observes: "from a strict attention to the state of mind in this country, before the year 1774, and at the present time, I am satisfied the ratio of intellect is as twenty are to one, and of knowledge as a hundred are to one, in these states, compared with what they were before the American revolution."

In 1777, he was appointed physician general of the military hospital in the middle department, sometime after which he published his observations on our hospitals, army diseases, and the effects of the revolution on the army and people.

In 1787, he became a member of the convention of Pennsylvania for the adoption of the federal constitution. This constitution received his warmest approbation. He pronounced the federal government a masterpiece of human wisdom. From it he anticipated a degree of felicity to the American people which they have not, and probably never will, experience.

For the last fourteen years of his life, he was treasurer for the United States mint, by appointment of President Adams; an office which was conferred upon him, as a homage to his talents and learning, and by means of which something was added to his revenue.

Dr. Rush took a deep interest in the many private associations, for the advancement of human happiness, with which Pennsylvania abounds. In the establishment of the Philadelphia Dispensary, the first institution of the kind in the United States, he led the way. He was the principal agent in founding Dickinson College, in Carlisle; and through his influence, the Rev. Dr. Nisbet, of Montrose, in Scotland, was induced to remove to America to take charge of it. For some years, he was president of the society for the abolition of slavery, and, also, of the Philadelphia Medical Society. He was a founder of the Philadelphia Bible Society, and one of its vice-presidents, and a vice-president of the American Philosophical Society. He was an honorary member of many of the literary institutions, both of this country and of Europe. In 1805, he was honoured by the king of Prussia, with a medal, for his replies to certain questions on the yellow fever. On a similar account, he was presented with a gold medal in 1807, from the queen of Etruria, and in 1811, the Emperor of Russia sent him a diamond ring, as a testimony of his respect for his medical character.

Dr. Rush was a public writer for forty-nine years, and from the nineteenth to the sixty-eighth year of his age. His works, which were quite numerous, show much reading, deep investigation, and tried experience. He seems to have combined the most useful in physical science, with the most elegant in literature. Instead of being a mere collator of the opinions of others, he was constantly making discoveries and improvements of his own; and from the result of his individual experience and observation, established more principles, and added more facts to the science of medicine, than all who had preceded him in his native country. The tendency of all his writings was decidedly good.

He powerfully, and to some extent successfully, employed his pen against some of the habits and vices of mankind. His "Inquiry into the effects of ardent spirits upon the human body and mind," has been more read than any of his works. All the medical philosophy that was pertinent to the subject, was incorporated with it. Striking descriptions of the personal and family distress occasioned by that vice, and of its havoc on the minds, bodies and estates of its unhappy votaries, were given, and the means of prevention and cure pointed out. The whole was illustrated by a scale, graduated like a thermometer, showing at one view the effects of certain enumerated liquors on the body, the mind, and the condition in society of those who are addicted to them. In the last year of Dr. Rush's life, he presented to the general assembly of the Presbyterian church in the United States, one thousand copies of this popular pamphlet, to be given away among the people of their respective congregations. About the same time, that numerous and respectable body passed a resolution, enjoining on their members to exert themselves in counteracting this ruinous vice.

In his "Observations upon the influence of the habitual use of tobacco upon health, morals, and property," Dr. Rush employed his eloquent pen in dissuading from practices, which insensibly grow into habits productive of many unforeseen evils.

Dr. Rush was a great practical physician. In the treatment of diseases he was eminently successful, and in describing their symptoms and explaining their causes, he was uncommonly accurate. Nor is this matter of wonder, for he was minutely acquainted with the histories of diseases of all ages, countries, and occupations. The annals of medicine cannot produce an account of any great epidemic disease, that has visited our earth, in any age, or country, which is more minute, accurate, and completely satisfactory, than Dr Rush's description of the yellow fever of 1793, in Philadelphia. Had he never written another line, this alone would have immortalized his name. He was a physician of no common cast. His prescriptions were not confined to doses of medicine, but to the regulation of the diet, air, dress, exercise, and mental actions of his patients, so as to prevent disease, and to make healthy men and women from invalids. His pre-eminence as a physician, over so many of his contemporaries, arose from the following circumstances:

He carefully studied the climate in which he lived, and the symptoms of acute and chronic diseases therein prevalent: the different habits and constitutions of his patients, and varied his prescriptions with their strength, age, and sex.

He marked the influence of different seasons, upon the same disease; and varied his practice accordingly. He observed and recorded the influence of successive epidemic diseases upon each other, and the hurtful as well as salutary effects of his remedies, and by this added to his knowledge of the character of the reigning disease in every successive season. His notes and records of the diseases, which have taken place in Philadelphia for the last forty-four years, must be of incalculable value to such as may have access to them. In attendance upon patients, Dr. Rush's manner was so gentle and sympathising, that pain and distress were less poignant in his presence. On all occasions he exhibited the manners of a gentleman, and his conversation was sprightly, pleasant, and instructive. His letters were peculiarly excellent; for they were dictated by a feeling heart, and adorned with the effusions of a brilliant imagination. His correspondence was extensive, and his letters numerous; but every one of them, as far as can be known to an individual, contained something original, pleasant, and sprightly. I can truly say, remarks Dr. Ramsay, that in the course of thirty-five years' correspondence and friendly intercourse, I never received a letter from him without being delighted and improved; nor left his company without learning something. His observations were often original, and when otherwise, far from insipid: for he had an uncommon way of expressing common thoughts. He possessed in a high degree those talents which engage the heart. He took so lively an interest in every thing that concerned his pupils, that each of them believed himself a favourite, while his kind offices to all proved that he was the common friend and father of them all.

In lecturing to his class, Dr. Rush mingled the most abstruse investigation with the most agreeable eloquence; the sprightliest sallies of imagination, with the most profound disquisitions; and the whole was enlivened with anecdotes, both pleasant and instructive. His language was simple and always intelligible, and his method so judicious, that a consistent view of the subject was communicated, and the recollection of the whole rendered easy. His lectures were originally written on leaves alternately blank. On the blank side he entered from time to time, every new fact, idea, anecdote, or illustration, that he became possessed of, from any source whatever. In the course of about four years, the blank was generally filled, and he found it expedient to make a new set of lectures. In this way he not only enlightened the various subjects, on which it was his province to instruct his class; but the light which he cast on them, for forty-four successive years, was continually brightening. The instructions he gave to his pupils by lectures, though highly valuable, were less so than the habits of thinking and observation he, in some degree, forced upon them. His constant aim was to rouse their minds from a passive to an active state, so as to enable them to instruct themselves. Since the first institution of the medical school in Pennsylvania, its capital, Philadelphia, has been the very atmosphere of medicine, and that atmosphere has been constantly clearing from the fogs of error, and becoming more luminous from the successive and increasing diffusion of the light of truth. A portion of knowledge floated about that hallowed spot, which was imbibed by every student, without his being conscious of it, and had an influence in giving to his mind a medical texture. To this happy state of things all the professors contributed. Drs. Wistar, Barton, Physick, Dorsey, Coxe, and James, the survivors of that illustrious and meritorious body, will acknowledge that their colleague, Professor Rush, was not deficient in his quota.

We have hitherto viewed Dr. Rush as an author, a physician, a professor, and a philosopher; let us now view him as a man. From him we may learn to be good, as well as great. Such was the force of pious example and religious education in the first fifteen years of his life, that though he spent the ensuing nine in Philadelphia, Edinburgh, London, and Paris, exposed to the manifold temptations which are inseparable from great cities, yet he returned, at the age of twenty-four, to his native country, with unsullied purity of morals. The sneers of infidels, and the fascinations of pleasure, had no power to divert him from the correct principles and virtuous habits which had been ingrafted on his mind in early youth. He came home from his travels with no excessive attachment but to his books; no other ambition than that of being a great scholar; and without any desire of making a stepping-stone of his talents and education, to procure for him the means of settling down in inglorious ease, without the farther cultivation and exertion of his talents. In a conversation which he held with Dr. Ramsay, thirty-five years ago, Dr. Rush observed, that as he stepped from the ship that brought him home from Europe, he resolved that " no circumstances of personal charms, fortune, or connexions, should tempt him to perpetrate matrimony, (his own phrase,) till he had extended his studies so far that a family would be no impediment to his farther progress." To this resolution of sacrificing every gratification to his love for learning, and his desire of making a distinguished figure in the republic of letters, he steadily adhered. For this he trimmed the midnight lamp; for this, though young, gay, elegant in person and manners, and possessed of the most insinuating address, he kept aloof from all scenes of dissipation, enervating pleasure, and unprofitable company, however fashionable; and devoted himself exclusively to the cultivation of those powers which God had given him.

Piety to God was an eminent trait in the character of Dr Rush. In all his printed works, and in all his private transactions, he expressed the most profound respect and veneration for the great Eternal. At the close of his excellent observations on the pulmonary consumption, he observes, " I cannot conclude this inquiry without adding, that the author of it derived from his paternal ancestors a predisposition to pulmonary consumption; and that, between the eighteenth and forty-third year of his age, he has occasionally been afflicted with many of the symptoms of that disease which he has described. By the constant and faithful use of many of the remedies which he has now recommended, he now, in the sixty-first year of his age, enjoys nearly an uninterrupted exemption from pulmonary complaints. In humble gratitude, therefore, to that Being who condescends to be called the ' preserver of men,' he thus publicly devotes the result of his experience and inquiries to the benefit of such of his fellow creatures as may be afflicted with the same disease, sincerely wishing that they may be as useful to them as they have been to the author."

It was not only by words, but in deeds, that he expressed

his reverence for the Divine character. It was his usual practice to close the day by reading to his collected family a chapter in the Bible, and afterwards by addressing his Maker in prayer, devoutly acknowledging his goodness for favours received, and humbly imploring his continued protection and blessing. His respect for Jehovah, led him to respect his ministers, who acted consistently with their high calling. He considered their office of the greatest importance to society, both in this world and that which is to come. He strengthened their hands, and was always ready and willing to promote and encourage arrangements for their comfortable support, and for building churches, and for propagating the gospel In an address to ministers of every denomination, on subjects interesting to morals, he remarks, " If there were no hereafter, individuals and societies would be great gainers by attending public worship every Sunday. Rest from labour in the house of God winds up the machine of both soul and body better than any thing else, and thereby invigorates it for the labours and duties of the ensuing week." Dr. Rush made his first essay as an author, when an apprentice to Dr. Redman, by writing an eulogy on the Rev. Gilbert Tennent, who had been the friend and fellow labourer of the celebrated George Whitfield, and an active, useful, animated preacher of the gospel, from 1725 till 1764. On the 27th of May, 1809, he wrote to his cousin, Dr. Finley, to this effect. "The general assembly of the presbyterian church is now in session in Philadelphia. It is composed of many excellent men, some of whom are highly distinguished by talents and learning, as well as piety. I have had some pleasant visits from a number of them, and have been amply rewarded for my civilities to them, by their agreeable and edifying conversation. They remind me of the happy times when their places in the church were filled by your venerable father, and his illustrious contemporaries and friends, Messrs. Tennent, Blair, Davies, and Rodgers."

The life of Dr. Rush was terminated on the 19th of April, in the 6?th year of his age. ... his illness, which was of but few days continu... ... ... with crowds

Engraved by James W Steel

Benj Franklin

of citizens, such was the general anxiety in respect to the life of this excellent man. When, at length, he died, the news of his decease spread a deep gloom over the city, and expressions of profound sympathy were received from all parts of the country.

BENJAMIN FRANKLIN.

BENJAMIN FRANKLIN was born at Boston, on the 17th of January, 1706. His ancestors were from the county of Northampton, in England, where they had for many generations possessed a small freehold estate, near the village of Eaton. During the persecutions in the reign of Charles II., against the puritans, the father of Benjamin, who was of that persuasion, emigrated to America, and settling in Boston, had recourse for a livelihood to the business of a chandler and soap boiler. His mother's name was Folger. She was a native of Boston, and belonged to a respectable family.

At an early age, young Franklin discovered, as his parents thought, a more than ordinary genius; and they resolved to give him an education, with reference to the profession of a clergyman. Accordingly, he was placed at a grammar school, where he soon attained the reputation of a lad of industrious habits, and respectable genius.

His parents, however, at the expiration of a year, found that their slender revenues would not admit of the expense of collegiate instruction. He was, therefore, soon after taken home to prosecute the business of his father. In this occupation he was employed for two years, but it was ill adapted to his constitution, and he felt unwilling to continue cutting wicks for candles, filling moulds, and running of errands. He became uneasy, and at length resolved to embark on a seafaring life. To such a proposition, however, his parents strongly objected, as they had already lost a son at sea. He was permitted, however, to change his business, and allowed to choose an occupation which was more congenial to his inclinations.

His fondness for books had, from an early age, been singularly great. He read every thing within his reach. His father's library was itself scanty, being confined to a few such works as Defoe's Essay upon Projects, Mather's Essay on doing Good, and the Lives of Plutarch. These he perused with great attention, and they appear to have exercised a favourable influence on his mind. His love of books was frequently noticed by his father, who, at length, proposed to bind him as an apprentice to an elder brother, who was at that time a printer of a newspaper in Boston. He was accordingly thus situated, in the year 1717, when he was scarcely twelve years of age. He soon became a proficient in the mechanical part of the business, and seized every opportunity for reading books that he could borrow from his acquaintance, in which employment he spent the greater part of his nights. He soon began to indulge himself in writing ballads and other poetical pieces; but, it is said, that his father speedily satisfied him that this was not the species of composition in which he could excel. His next efforts were directed to prose composition, in which his success is well known, and duly appreciated. With a passion for reading and writing, he imbibed a kindred one for disputation, and adopting the Socratic method, he became dexterous in confuting and confounding an antagonist, by a series of questions. This course gave him a sceptical turn with regard to religion, and while he was young he took every opportunity of propagating his tenets, and with the ordinary zeal of a new convert. He was, however, soon convinced, by the effect produced on some of his companions, that it was extremely dangerous to loosen the ties of religion, without the probability of substituting other principles equally efficacious. The doubts which subsisted in his own mind, he was never able to remove; but he was not deficient in fortifying himself with such moral principles as directed him to the most valuable ends, by honourable means. The habit of self-denial, early formed, he obtained a complete dominion over his appetites, so that, at the age of sixteen, he readily discarded animal food, from the conviction produced in his mind by perusing a work on the subject, that he should enjoy a more vigorous state of health without it. He now offered his brother to maintain himself, for half the sum paid for his board; and even with this he was able to make savings to purchase what books he wanted. In his brother, he found a harsh master, and Benjamin felt indignant at the treatment which he experienced from him in the way of business. His brother had established a newspaper, in which the apprentice contrived to insert some papers and essays anonymously. These were read and highly commended by people of the best judgment and taste in the town. The young man began now to feel his importance, which was still more impressed on him by having the paper published in his own name, that of his brother, for some political offence, having been interdicted by the state.

On the release of his brother, who had for some time been imprisoned for the above political offence, Franklin was treated by him with so much severity, that at length he determined to leave him. His indentures having before this been cancelled, he secretly went on board of a vessel, bound to New-York, in which he took passage for that city. After a few days spent in New-York, having sought in vain to procure business, he proceeded on foot to Philadelphia, where he at length arrived, fatigued and destitute of all means of support. He was now but seventeen years of age, at the distance of four hundred miles from home, nearly pennyless, without employment, without a counsellor, and unacquainted with a single person in the city.

The day following his arrival he wandered through the streets of Philadelphia with an appearance little short of a beggar. His pockets were distended by his clothes, which were crowded into them; and provided with a roll of bread under each arm, he proceeded through the principal streets of the city. His uncouth appearance attracted the notice of several of the citizens, and among others of a Miss R. J.

who afterwards became his wife, and by whom, as he passed along, he was thought to present a very awkward and ridiculous appearance.

There were at this time but two printing offices in Philadelphia. Fortunately, in one of these he found employment as compositor. His conduct was very becoming; he was attentive to business, and economical in his expenses. His fidelity not only commended him to his master, but was noticed by several respectable citizens, who promised him their patronage and support.

Among others, who took much notice of him, was Sir William Keith, at that time governor of the province. The governor having become acquainted with the history of his recent adventures, professed a deep interest in his welfare, and at length proposed that he should commence business on his own account; at the same time, promising to aid him with his influence and that of his friends, and to give him the printing of the government. Moreover, the governor urged him to return to Boston, to solicit the concurrence and assistance of his father. At the same time, he gave him a letter to that gentleman, replete with assurances of affection, and promises of support to the son.

With this object in view, he sailed for Boston, and at length, after an absence of several months, he again entered his father's house. He was affectionately received by the family. To his father he communicated the letter of Governor Keith, which explained the object of his return. His father, however, judiciously advised him, on account of youth and inexperience, to relinquish the project of setting up a printing office, and wrote to this effect to his patron, Governor Keith. Having determined to follow the advice of his father, he returned to Philadelphia, and again entering the employment of his former master, pursued his business with his usual assiduous attention.

Governor Keith, on learning the advice and decision of Franklin's father, offered himself to furnish the necessary materials for a printing establishment, and proposed to Franklin to make a voyage to England to procure them. This proposal Franklin readily accepted, and with gratitude to his generous benefactor, he sailed for England in 1725, accompanied by his friend Ralph, one of his literary associates in Philadelphia.

Before his departure, he exchanged promises of fidelity with Miss Reed of Philadelphia, with whose father he had lodged. Upon his arrival in London, Mr. Franklin found that Governor Keith, upon whose letters of credit and recommendation he relied, had entirely deceived him. He was now obliged to work as a journeyman printer, and obtained employment in an office in Bartholomew-close. His friend Ralph did not so readily find the means of subsistence, and was a constant drain upon the earnings of Franklin. In that great city, the morals of the young travellers were not much improved; Ralph forgot, or acted as if he had forgotten, that he had a wife and child across the Atlantic; and Franklin was equally forgetful of his promises and engagements to Miss Reed. About this period he published, "A Dissertation on Liberty and Necessity, Pleasure and Pain," dedicated to Ralph, and intended as an answer to Wollaston's "Religion of Nature." This piece gained for him some degree of reputation, and introduced him to the acquaintance of Dr. Mandeville, author of the "Fable of the Bees," and some other literary characters. Franklin was always temperate and industrious, and his habits in this respect were eventually the means of securing his morals, as well as of raising his fortune. In the interesting account which he has left of his own life, is a narrative of the method which he took in reforming the sottish habits of his fellow-workmen in the second printing office in which he was engaged in London, and which was situated in the neighbourhood of Lincoln's-inn-fields. He tried to persuade them that there was more real sustenance in a penny roll, than in a pint of porter; at first, the plan of economy which he proposed was treated with contempt or ridicule; but in the end he was able to induce several of them to substitute a warm and nourishing breakfast, in the place of stimulating liquors.

Having resided about a year and a half in London, he

concerted a scheme with an acquaintance, to make the tour of Europe. At this juncture, however, he fell in company with a mercantile friend, who was about returning home to Philadelphia, and who now persuaded Franklin to abandon his project of an eastern tour, and to enter his service in the capacity of a clerk. On the 22d of July. 1726, they set sail for Philadelphia, where they arrived the 11th of October.

The prospects of Franklin were now brighter. He was attached to his new adopted profession, and by his assiduous attention to business gained the confidence of his employer so much, that he was about to be commissioned as supercargo to the West Indies, when of a sudden his patron died, by which, not only his fair prospects were blighted, but he was once more thrown out of all employment.

He had, however, one resource, and that was a return to the business of printing, in the service of his former master. At length, he became superintendant of the printing office where he worked, and finding himself able to manage the concern with some skill and profit, he resolved to embark in business for himself. He entered into partnership with a fellow-workman, named Meredith, whose friends were enabled to furnish a supply of money sufficient for the concern, which was no doubt very small; for Franklin has recorded the high degree of pleasure, which he experienced from a payment of five shillings only, the first fruits of their earnings. "The recollection," says this noble spirited man, "of what I felt on this occasion, has rendered me more disposed, than perhaps I might otherwise have been, to encourage young beginners in trade." His habitual industry and undeviating punctuality, obtained him the notice and business of the principal people in the place. He instituted a club under the name of "the Junto," for the purpose of the discussion of political and philosophical questions, which proved an excellent school for the mutual improvement of its several members. The test proposed to every candidate, before his admission, was this; "Do you sincerely declare that you love mankind in general, of what profession or religion soever? Do you think any p... ... ... harmed in his body, name, or goods, for mere speculative opinions, or his external way of worship? Do you love truth for truth's sake; and will you endeavour impartially to find and receive it yourself, and communicate it to others." Mr. Franklin and his partner ventured to set up a new public paper, which his own efforts as writer and printer caused to succeed, and they obtained likewise the printing of the votes and laws of the assembly. In process of time, Meredith withdrew from the partnership, and Franklin met with friends, who enabled him to undertake the whole concern in his own name, and add to it the business of a stationer.

In 1730, he married the lady to whom he was engaged before his departure for England. During his absence he forgot his promises to her, and on his return to America, he found her the wife of another man. Although a woman of many virtues, she suffered from the unkindness of her husband, who, fortunately for her, lived but a short time. Not long after his death, Franklin again visited her, soon after which they were married, and for many years lived in the full enjoyment of connubial peace and harmony.

In 1732, he began to publish "Poor Richard's Almanac," a work which was continued for twenty-five years, and which, besides answering the purposes of a calendar, contained many excellent prudential maxims, which were of great utility to that class of the community, who by their poverty or laborious occupations, were deprived of the advantages of education. Ten thousand copies of this almanac are said to have been published every year, in America. The maxims contained in it, were from time to time republished both in Great Britain, and on the continent.

The political course of Franklin began in the year 1736, when he was appointed clerk to the general assembly of Pennsylvania; an office which he held for several years, until he was, at length, elected a representative. During the same year, he assisted in the establishment of the American Philosophical Society, and of a college, which now exists under the title of the University of Pennsylvania. In the following year he was appointed to the small office of postmaster of Philadelphia. In 1738 he improved the police of the city, in respect to the dreadful calamity of fire, by forming a society called a fire company, to which was afterwards added an assurance office, against losses by fire.

In 1742 he published his treatise upon the improvement of chimnies, and at the same time contrived a stove, which is in extensive use at the present day.

In the French war of 1744, he proposed a plan of voluntary association for the defence of the country. This was shortly joined by ten thousand persons, who were trained to the use and exercise of arms. Franklin was chosen colonel of the Philadelphia regiment, but he refused the honour in favour of one, whom he supposed to be more competent to the discharge of its duties.

During the same year he was elected a member of the provincial assembly, in which body he soon became very popular, and was annually re-elected by his fellow-citizens for the space of ten years.

About this time, the attention of Mr. Franklin was particularly turned to philosophical subjects. In 1747, he had witnessed at Boston, some experiments on electricity, which excited his curiosity, and which he repeated on his return to Philadelphia, with great success. These experiments led to important discoveries, an account of which was transmitted to England, and attracted great attention throughout all Europe.

In the year 1749 he conceived the idea of explaining the phenomena of thunder gusts, and of the aurora borealis, upon electrical principles; he pointed out many particulars, in which lightning and electricity agreed, and he adduced many facts and reasonings in support of his positions. In the same year, he thought of ascertaining the truth of his doctrine by drawing down the forked lightning, by means of sharp pointed iron rods, raised into the region of the clouds. Admitting the identity of lightning and electricity, and knowing the power of points in conducting away silently the electric fluid, he suggested the idea of securing houses, ships, &c. from the damages to which they were liable from lightning, by erecting pointed iron rods, which should rise some feet above the most elevated part, and descend some feet into the ground, or the water. The effect of these, he concluded, would be either to prevent a stroke, by repelling the cloud beyond the striking distance, or by drawing off the electrical fluid, which it contained; or at least, conduct the stroke to the earth, without any injury to the building. It was not till the summer of 1752, that Mr. Franklin was enabled to complete his grand experiment. The plan which he proposed was, to erect on some high tower, or elevated place, a sort of hut, from which should rise a pointed iron rod, insulated by being fixed in a cake of resin. Electrified clouds passing over this, would, he conceived, impart to it a portion of their electricity, which might be rendered evident to the senses by sparks being emitted, when the knuckle or other conductor was presented to it. While he was waiting for the erection of a spire, it occurred to him, that he might have more ready access to the region of clouds by means of a common kite: he accordingly prepared one for the purpose, affixing to the upright stick an iron point. The string was as usual, of hemp, except the lower end, which was silk, and where the hempen part terminated, a key was fastened. With this simple apparatus, on the appearance of a thunder storm approaching, he went into the fields, accompanied by his son, to whom alone he communicated his intentions, dreading probably the ridicule which frequently awaits unsuccessful attempts in experimental philosophy. For some time no sign of electricity appeared; he was beginning to despair of success, when he suddenly observed the loose fibres of the string to start forward in an erect position. He now presented his knuckle to the key, and received a strong spark. How exquisite must his sensations have been at this moment? On this experiment depended the fate of his theory; repeated sparks were drawn from the key, a phial was charged, a shock given, and all the experiments made, which are usually performed with electricity. He immediately fixed an insulated iron rod upon his house, which drew down the lightning, and gave him an opportunity of examining whether it were positive or negative, and hence he applied his discovery to the securing of buildings from the effects of lightning.

It will be impossible to enumerate all, or even a small part of the experiments which were made by Dr. Franklin, or to give an account of the treatises which he wrote on the branches of science. Justice requires us to say, that he seldom wrote, or discoursed on any subject, upon which he did not throw light. Few men possessed a more penetrating genius, or a happier faculty of discrimination. His investigations attracted the attention, and his discoveries called forth the admiration of the learned in all parts of the world. Jealousy was at length excited in Europe, and attempts were made, not only to detract from his well earned fame, but to rob him of the merit of originality. Others claimed the honour of having first made several of his most brilliant experiments, or attempted to invalidate the truth and reality of those, an account of which he had published to the world. The good sense of Dr. Franklin led him to oppose his adversaries only by silence, leaving the vindication of his merit to the slow, but sure operations of time.

In 1753 he was raised to the important office of deputy post master general of America. Through ill management, this office had been unproductive: but soon after the appointment of Franklin, it became a source of revenue to the British crown. In this station, he rendered important services to General Braddock, in his wild and fatal expedition against fort Du Quesne. When, at length, Braddock was defeated, and the whole frontier was exposed to the incursions of the savages and the French, Franklin raised a company of volunteers, at the head of which he marched to the protection of the frontier.

At length, in 1757, the militia was disbanded by order of the British government, soon after which Franklin was appointed agent to settle the disputes which had arisen between the people of Pennsylvania, and the proprietary government. With this object in view, he left his native country once more for England. On his arrival, he laid the subject before the privy council. The point in dispute was occasioned by an effort of the proprietors to exempt their private estates from taxation ; and because this exemption was not admitted, they refused to make appropriations for the defence of the province, even in times of the greatest danger and necessity. Franklin managed the subject with great ability, and at length brought the proprietary faction to terms. It was agreed, that the proprietary lands should take their share in a tax for the public service, provided that Franklin would engage that the assessment should be fairly proportioned. The measure was accordingly carried into effect, and he remained at the British court as agent for his province. His reputation caused him also to be entrusted with the like commission from Massachusetts, Maryland, and Georgia. The molestation received by the British colonies, from the French in Canada, induced him to write a pamphlet, pointing out the advantages of a conquest of that province by the English; and the subsequent expedition against it, and its retention under the British government, at the peace, were, it is believed, much influenced by the force of his arguments on the subject. About this period, his talents as a philosopher were duly appreciated in various parts of Europe. He was admitted a fellow of the royal society of London, and the degree of doctor of laws was conferred upon him at St. Andrews, Edinburgh, and at Oxford.

In 1762 he returned to America. On his arrival the provincial assembly of Pennsylvania expressed their sense of his meritorious services by a vote of thanks ; and as a remuneration for his successful labours in their behalf, they granted him the sum of five thousand dollars. During his absence, he had annually been elected a member of the assembly, in which body he now took his seat. The following year he made a journey of sixteen hundred miles, through the northern colonies, for the purpose of inspecting and regulating the post offices.

In 1764, he was again appointed the agent of Pennsylvania, to manage her concerns in England, in which country he arrived in the month of December. About this period the famous stamp act was exciting violent commotions in America.

Against this measure, Dr. Franklin strongly enlisted himself, and on his arrival in England, he presented a petition against it, which, at his suggestion, had been drawn up by the Pennsylvania assembly. At length the tumults in America became so great, that the ministry found it necessary either to modify the act, or to repeal it entirely. Among others, Dr. Franklin was summoned before the house of commons, where he underwent a long examination. "No person was better acquainted with the circumstances and internal concerns of the colonies, the temper and disposition of the colonists towards the parent country, or their feelings in relation to the late measures of parliament, than this gentleman. His answers to the numerous questions put to him in the course of this inquiry, not only show his extensive acquaintance with the internal state of the colonies, but evince his sagacity as a statesmen. To the question, whether the Americans would submit to pay the stamp duty if the act were modified, and the duty reduced to a small amount? He answered, no, they never will submit to it. British statesmen were extremely desirous that the colonial assemblies should acknowledge the right of parliament to tax them, and rescind and erase from their journals their resolutions on this subject. To a question, whether the American assemblies would do this, Dr. Franklin answered, 'they never will do it, unless compelled by force of arms.' "

The whole of this examination on being published was read with deep interest, both in England and America. To the statements of Dr. Franklin, the repeal of the stamp act was, no doubt, in a great measure, attributable.

In the year 1766, and 1767, he made an excursion to Holland, Germany, and France, where he met with a most flattering and distinguished reception. To the monarch of the latter country, Louis XV., he was introduced, and also to other members of the royal family, by whom, as well as by the nobility and gentry at court, he was treated with great hospitality and courtesy. About this time, he was elected a member of the French Academy of Sciences, and received diplomas from several other literary societies in England, and on the continent.

Allusion has already been made, in our introduction, to the discovery and publication, in 1772, of certain letters of Governor Hutchinson, addressed by that gentleman to his friends in England, and which reflected in the severest manner upon the people of America. These letters had fallen into the hands of Dr. Franklin, and by him had been transmitted to America, where they were at length inserted in the public journals. For a time, no one in England knew through what channel the letters had been conveyed to America. In 1773, Franklin publicly avowed himself to be the person who obtained the letters and transmitted them to America. This occasioned a violent clamour against him, and upon his attending before the privy council, in the following January, to present a petition from the colony of Massachusetts, for the dismission of Mr. Hutchinson, a most violent invective was pronounced against him, by Mr. Weddeburne, afterwards Lord Loughborough. Among other abusive epithets, the honourable member called Franklin a coward, a murderer, and a thief. During the whole of this torrent of abuse, Franklin sat with a composed and unaverted aspect, or, to use his own expression, in relation to himself on another occasion, "as if his countenance had been made of wood." During this personal and public insult, the whole assembly appeared greatly amused, at the expense of Dr. Franklin. The president even laughed aloud. There was a single person present, however, Lord North, who, to his honour be it recorded, expressed great disapprobation of the indecent conduct of the assembly. The intended insult, however, was entirely lost. The dignity and composure of Franklin caused a sad disappointment among his enemies, who were reluctantly compelled to acknowledge the superiority of his character. Their animosity, however, was not to be appeased, but by doing Franklin the greatest injury within their power. They removed him from the office of deputy post master general, interrupted the payment of his salary as agent for the colonies, and finally instituted against him a suit in chancery concerning the letters of Hutchinson.

At length, finding all his efforts to restore harmony between Great Britain and the colonies useless; and perceiving that the controversy had reached a crisis, when his presence in England was no longer necessary, and his continuance personally hazardous, he embarked for America, where he arrived in 1775, just after the commencement of hostilities. He was received with every mark of esteem and affection. He was immediately elected a delegate to the general congress, in which body he did as much, perhaps, as any other man, to accomplish the independence of his country.

In 1776, he was deputed by congress to proceed to Canada, to negociate with the people of that country, and to persuade them, if possible, to throw off the British yoke; but the inhabitants of Canada had been so much disgusted with the zeal of the people of New-England, who had burnt some of their chapels, that they refused to listen to the proposals made to them by Dr. Franklin and his associates. On the arrival of Lord Howe in America in 1776, he entered upon a correspondence with him on the subject of reconciliation. He was afterwards appointed, with two others, to wait upon the English commissioners, and learn the extent of their powers; but as these only went to the granting of pardon upon submission, he joined his colleagues in considering them as insufficient. Dr. Franklin was decidedly in favour of a declaration of independence; and was appointed president of the convention assembled for the purpose of establishing a new government for the state of Pennsylvania. When it was determined by congress to open a public negociation with France, he was commissioned to visit that country, with which he negotiated the treaty of alliance, offensive and defensive, which produced an immediate war between England and France. Dr. Franklin was one of the commissioners who, on the part of the United States, signed the provincial articles of peace in 1782, and the definitive treaty in the following year. Before he left France, he concluded a treaty with Sweden and Prussia; and, from her, he obtained several most liberal and humane stipulations in favour of the freedom of commerce, and the security of private property during war, in conformity to those principles which he had ever maintained on these subjects. Having seen the accomplishment of his wishes in the independence of his country, he requested to be recalled, and after repeated solicitations, Mr. Jefferson was appointed in his stead. On the arrival of his successor, he repaired to Havre de Grace, and crossing the English channel, landed at Newport in the Isle of Wight, whence, after a favourable passage, he arrived safe at Philadelphia, in September, 1785.

The news of his arrival, was received with great joy by the citizens. A vast multitude flocked from all parts to see him, and amidst the ringing of bells, the discharge of artillery, the acclamations of thousands, conducted him in triumph to his own house. In a few days, he was visited by the members of congress, and the principal inhabitants of Philadelphia. From numerous societies and assemblies he received the most affectionate addresses. All testified their joy at his return, and their veneration of his exalted character.

This was a period in his life of which he often spoke with peculiar pleasure. "I am now," said he, "in the bosom of my family, and find four new little prattlers, who cling about the knees of their grandpapa, and afford me great pleasure. I am surrounded by my friends, and have an affectionate good daughter and son-in-law to take care of me. I have got into my *niche*, a very good house, which I built twenty-four years ago, and out of which I have been ever since kept by foreign employments."

The domestic tranquillity in which he now found himself, he was not permitted long to enjoy, being appointed president of the commonwealth of Pennsylvania, an office which he held for three years, and the duties of which he discharged very acceptably to his constituents. Of the federal convention of 1787, for organizing the constitution of the United States, he was elected a delegate, and in the intricate discussions which arose on different parts of that instrument, he bore a distinguished part.

In 1788, he withdrew from public life, his great age rendering retirement desirable, and the infirmities of his body unfitting him for the burdens of public office. On the 17th of April, 1790, in the eighty-fourth year of his age, he expired, in the city of Philadelphia. He was interred on the 21st of April. Congress directed a general mourning for him, throughout the United States, for the space of a month. The national assembly of France testified their sense of the loss which the world sustained, by decreeing that each member should wear mourning for three days. This was an honour perhaps never before paid by the national assembly of one country, to a citizen of another. Dr. Franklin lies buried in the northwest corner of Christ Church yard, in Philadelphia. In his will he directed that no monumental ornaments should be placed upon his tomb. A small marble slab only, therefore, and that, too, on a level with the surface of the earth, bearing the name of himself and wife, and the year of his death, marks the spot in the yard where he lies.

Dr. Franklin had two children, a son and a daughter. The son, under the British government, was appointed governor of New-Jersey. On the occurrence of the revolution, he left America, and took up his residence in England, where he spent the remainder of his life. The daughter was respectably married in Philadelphia, to Mr. William Bache, whose descendants still reside in that city.

In stature, Dr. Franklin was above the middle size. He possessed a healthy constitution, and was remarkable for his strength and activity. His countenance indicated a serene state of mind, great depth of thought, and an inflexible resolution.

In his intercourse with mankind, he was uncommonly agreeable. In conversation, he abounded in curious and interesting anecdote. A vein of good humour marked his conversation, and strongly recommended him to both old and young, to the learned and illiterate.

As a philosopher, his j... ranks high. In his speculations, he seldom l... ... or yielded up

his understanding either to enthusiasm or authority. He
contributed, in no small degree, to the extension of science,
and to the improvement of the condition of mankind. He
appears to have entertained, at some periods of his life, opinions which were in many respects peculiar, and which probably were not founded upon a sound philosophy. The following experiment, which he made some years after his father's death, and after an absence of several years, to ascertain whether his mother would know him, will be thought at
least curious and interesting. It was his conjecture, if not a
well settled opinion, that a mother might, by a kind of instinct or natural affection, recognize her children, even although she had lost the recollection of their particular features. It was on a visit to his native town of Boston, after
an absence of many years, that this curious incident occurred.

"To discover the existence of this instinct by actual experiment," says an unknown writer, to whom we are indebted for the story, and upon whose responsibility we give it to
our readers, "the Doctor resolved to introduce himself as a
stranger to his mother, and to watch narrowly for the moment in which she should discover her son, and then to determine, with the cool precision of the philosopher, whether
that discovery was the effect of that instinct of affection, that
intuitive love, that innate attachment, which is conjectured
to cement relatives of the same blood; and which, by according the passions of parent and child, like a well-tuned
viol, would, at the first touch, cause them to vibrate in unison, and at once evince that they were different chords of the
same instrument.

"On a sullen, chilly day, in the month of January, in the
afternoon, the Doctor knocked at his mother's door, and
asked to speak with Mrs. Franklin. He found the old lady
knitting before the parlour fire. He introduced himself, and
observing, that he understood she entertained travellers, requested a night's lodging. She eyed him with that cold look
of disapprobation which most people assume, when they imagine themselves insulted, by being supposed to exercise an

employment but one degree below their real occupation in life—assured him that he had been misinformed, that she did not keep tavern; but that it was true, to oblige some members of the legislature, she took a number of them into her family during the session; that she had four members of tne council, and six of the house of representatives. who then boarded with her; that all her beds were full; and then betook herself to her knitting. with that intense application, which expressed, as forcibly as action could do, if you have concluded your business, the sooner you leave the house the better. But upon the Doctor's wrapping his coat around him, affecting to shiver with cold, and observing that it was very chilly weather, she pointed to a chair, and gave him leave to warm himself.

"The entrance of her boarders precluded all further conversation; coffee was soon served. and the Doctor partook with the family. To the coffee, according to the good old custom of the times, succeeded a plate of pippins, pipes, and a paper of M'Intire's best, when the whole family formed a cheerful smoking semi-circle before the fire. Perhaps no man ever possessed colloquial powers to a more fascinating degree, than Dr Franklin, and never was there an occasion when he displayed those powers to greater advantage, than at this time. He drew the attention of the company, by the solidity of his modest remarks, instructing them by the varied, new, and striking lights in which he placed his subjects. and delighted them with apt and amusing anecdotes. Thus employed, the hours passed merrily along, until eight o'clock, when, punctual to a moment, Mrs. Franklin announced supper. Busied with her household affairs, she fancied the intruding stranger had quitted the house, immediately after coffee, and it was with difficulty she could restrain her resentment, when she saw him, without molestation, seat himself at the table with the freedom of a member of the family.

"Immediately after supper, she called an elderly gentleman, a member of the council, in whom she was accustomed to confide, to another room; complained bitterly of the rudeness of the stranger: told the manner of his introduction to her house; observed that he appeared like an outlandish man; and, she thought, had something very suspicious in his appearance; concluding by soliciting her friend's advice with respect to the way in which she could most easily rid herself of his presence. The old gentleman assured her, that the stranger was certainly a young man of education, and to all appearance a gentleman; that, perhaps, being in agreeable company, he had paid no attention to the lateness of the hour; and advised her to call him aside, and repeat her inability to lodge him. She accordingly sent her maid to him, and then, with as much temper as she could command, recapitulated the situation of her family, observed that it grew late, and mildly intimated that he would do well to seek himself a lodging. The Doctor replied, that he would by no means incommode her family; but that, with her leave, he would smoke one pipe more with her boarders, and then retire.

"He returned to the company, filled his pipe, and with the first whiff his powers returned with double force. He recounted the hardships, he extolled the piety and policy of their ancestors. A gentleman present mentioned the subject of the day's debate in the house of representatives. A bill had been introduced to extend the prerogatives of the royal governor. The Doctor immediately entered upon the subject, supported the colonial rights with new and forcible arguments; was familiar with the names of the influential men in the house, when Dudley was governor; recited their speeches, and applauded the noble defence of the charter of rights.

"During a discourse so appropriately interesting to the company, no wonder the clock struck eleven, unperceived by the delighted circle, and was it wonderful that the patience of Mrs. Franklin grew quite exhausted? She now entered the room, and, before the whole company, with much warmth, addressed the Doctor; told him plainly, she thought herself imposed on; observed, it was true she was a lone woman, but that she had friends who would protect her, and concluded by insisting on his leaving the house. The Doctor made a slight apology, deliberately put on his great coat and hat, took polite leave of the company, and approached the street door, lighted by the maid, and attended by the mistress. While the Doctor and his companions had been enjoying themselves within, a most tremendous snow storm had, without, filled the streets knee deep; and no sooner had the maid lifted the latch, than a roaring northeaster forced open the door, extinguished the light, and almost filled the entry with drifted snow and hail. As soon as it was re-lighted, the Doctor cast a woful look towards the door, and thus addressed his mother: 'My dear madam, can you turn me out in this dreadful storm? I am a stranger in this town, and shall certainly perish in the streets. You look like a charitable lady; I shouldn't think you could turn a dog from your door, in this tempestuous night.' 'Don't tell me of charity,' said the offended matron; 'charity begins at home. It is your own fault you tarried so long. To be plain with you, sir, I do not like your looks, or your conduct; and I fear you have some bad designs in thus introducing yourself to my family.'

"The warmth of this parley had drawn the company from the parlour, and by their united interference the stranger was permitted to lodge in the house; and as no bed could be had, he consented to rest on an easy chair before the parlour fire. Although the boarders appeared to confide, perfectly, in the stranger's honesty, it was not so with Mrs. Franklin. With suspicious caution, she collected her silver spoons, pepper-box, and porringer, from her closet; and, after securing her parlour door, by sticking a fork over the latch, carried the plate to her chamber; charged the negro man to sleep with his clothes on, to take the great lever to bed with him, and to waken and seize the vagrant at the first noise he made, in attempting to plunder the house. Having thus taken every precaution, she retired to her bed with her maid, whom she compelled to sleep in her room.

"Mrs. Franklin rose before the sun, roused her domestics, unfastened the parlour door with timid caution, and was agreeably surprised to find her guest sleeping on his own chair. A sudden transition from extreme distrust to perfect confidence, was natural. She awakened him with a cheerful good morning; inquired how he rested; invited him to partake of her breakfast, which was always served previous to that of her boarders. 'And pray, sir,' said the lady, as she sipped her chocolate, 'as you appear to be a stranger here, to what distant country do you belong?' 'I, madam, belong to the city of *Philadelphia.*' At the mention of Philadelphia, the Doctor declared he, for the first time, perceived some emotion in her. '*Philadelphia!*' said she, and all the mother suffused her eye: 'if you live in Philadelphia, perhaps you know our Ben.' 'Who, madam?' 'Why Ben Franklin—my Ben —Oh! he is the dearest child that ever blest a mother!' 'What,' said the Doctor, 'is Ben Franklin, the printer, your son; why he is my most intimate friend· he and I lodge in the same room.' 'Oh! God forgive me,' exclaimed the old lady, raising her watery eyes to heaven—'and have I suffered a friend of my Benny to sleep in this hard chair, while I myself rested on a good bed?'

"How the Doctor discovered himself to his mother, he has not informed us; but from the above experiment, he was firmly convinced, and was often afterwards heard to declare, that *natural* affection did not exist."

Few men have exhibited a more worthy conduct than did Dr. Franklin, through his long life. Through every vicissitude of fortune, he seems to have been distinguished for his sobriety and temperance, for his extraordinary perseverance and resolution. He was not less distinguished for his veracity, for the constancy of his friendship, for his candour, and his fidelity to his moral and civil obligations. In the early part of his life, he acknowledged himself to have been sceptical in religion, but he became in maturer years, according to the testimony of his intimate friend, Dr. William Smith, a believer in divine revelation. The following extract from his memoirs, written by himself, deserves to be recorded: "And here let me with all humility acknowledge, that to Divine Providence I am indebted for the felicity I have hitherto enjoyed.' It is that power alone which has furnished me with the means I have employed, and that has crowned them with success. My faith in this respect leads me to hope, though I cannot count upon it, that the divine goodness will still be exercised towards me, either by prolonging the duration of my happiness to the close of life, or by giving me fortitude to support any melancholy reverse which may happen to me as well as to many others. My future fortune is unknown but to Him, in whose hand is our destiny, and who can make our very afflictions subservient to our benefit."

We conclude our notice of this distinguished man and profound philosopher, by subjoining the following epitaph, which was written by himself, many years previously to his death:

The body of
BENJAMIN FRANKLIN, Printer,
Like the cover of an old book,
its contents torn out,
and stript of its lettering and gilding,
lies here food for worms;
Yet the work itself shall not be lost,
For it will (as he believed) appear once more
in a new
and more beautiful edition,
Corrected and amended
by the Author.

JOHN MORTON.

John Morton was a native of Ridley, in the county of Chester, now Delaware. His ancestors were of Swedish extraction, and among the first Swedish emigrants, who located themselves on the banks of the Delaware. His father, after whom he was called, died a few months previously to his birth. His mother was some time after married to an Englishman, who possessed a more than ordinary education, and who, with great kindness, on young Morton's becoming of the proper age, superintended and directed his education at home. Here his active mind rapidly expanded, and gave promise of the important part which he was destined to act in the subsequent history of his country.

About the year 1764, he was commissioned as a justice of the peace, and was sent as a delegate to the general assembly of Pennsylvania. Of this body he was for many years an active and distinguished member, and for some time the speaker of the house of representatives. The following year he was appointed by the house of representatives of Pennsylvania to attend the general congress at New-York. The object and proceedings of this congress are too well known to need a recital in this place.

In 1766, Mr. Morton was appointed sheriff of the county in which he lived, an office which he continued to hold for the three following years, and the duties of which he discharged with great satisfaction to the public. Some time after, he was elevated to a seat on the bench, in the superior court of Pennsylvania.

Of the memorable congress of 1774 he was a member, and continued to represent the state of Pennsylvania in the national assembly, through the memorable session of that body which gave birth to the declaration of American Independence.

On the occurrence of the momentous subject of independence, in the continental congress, Mr. Morton unexpectedly found himself placed in a delicate and trying situation. Previously to the 4th of July, the states of Delaware and Pennsylvania had voted in opposition to that measure. Great doubts were therefore entertained by the other members of congress, how the Pennsylvania and Delaware delegations would act. Much was obviously depending upon them, for it was justly apprehended, that should these two states decline to accede to the measure, the result might prove most unfortunate. Happily, the votes of both these states were, at length, secured in favour of independence. But, as the delegation from Pennsylvania were equally divided, it fell to Mr. Morton to give his casting vote. The responsibility which he thus assumed was great, and even fearful, should the measure be attended by disastrous results. Mr. Morton, however, was a man of firmness and decision, and, in the spirit of true patriotism, he enrolled his vote in favour of the liberty of his country. Considering his novel and solemn situation, he deserves to be remembered with peculiar respect, by the free and independent yeomanry of America.

In the following year, he assisted in organizing a system of confederation, and was chairman of the committee of the whole, at the time it was finally agreed to, on the 15th of November, 1777. During the same year, he was seized with an inflammatory fever, which, after a few days, ended his mortal existence, in the 54th year of his age. Mr. Morton was a professor of religion, and a truly excellent man. To the poor he was ever kind; and to an affectionate family, consisting of a wife, three sons, and five daughters, he was an affectionate husband and father. His only enemies were those who would not forgive him because of his vote in favour of independence. During his last sickness, and even on the verge of the eternal world, he remembered them, and requested those who stood round him, to tell them, that the hour would yet come, when it would be acknowledged, that his vote in favour of American independence was the most illustrious act of his life.

GEORGE CLYMER.

George Clymer was born in the city of Philadelphia, in the year 1739. His father was descended from a respectable family of Bristol, in England, and after his emigration to America became connected by marriage with a lady in Philadelphia. Young Clymer was left an orphan at the age of seven years, upon which event the care of him devolved upon William Coleman, a maternal uncle, a gentleman of much respectability among the citizens of Philadelphia.

The education of young Clymer was superintended by his uncle, than whom few men were better qualified for such a charge. The uncle possessed a cultivated mind, and early instilled into his nephew a love of reading. On the completion of his education, he entered the counting-room of his uncle. His genius, however, was little adapted to mercantile employments, being more inclined to literary and scientific pursuits. At a suitable period he commenced business for himself, in connexion with Mr. Robert Ritchie, and afterwards with two gentlemen, father and son, by the name of Merediths, a daughter of the former of whom he subsequently married.

Although Mr. Clymer embarked in the pursuits of commerce, and continued engaged in that business for many years, he was always decidedly opposed to it. During his mercantile operations, he found much time to read. He was distinguished for a clear and original mind; and though he never pursued any of the learned professions, he became well versed in the principles of law, history, and politics.

At the age of twenty-seven, he was married, as has already been noticed, to a daughter of Mr. Meredith, a gentleman of a generous and elevated mind, as the following anecdote of him will show. While yet a young man, General Washington had occasion to visit Philadelphia, where he was an entire stranger. Happening in at the public house where Washington lodged, Mr. Meredith observed him, inquired his name, and finding him to be a stranger in the place, invited him to the hospitalities of his house, and kindly insisted upon his continuance with his family while he remained in the city. This accidental acquaintance led to a friendship of many years continuance, and at Mr. Meredith's, Washington ever after made it his home when he visited Philadelphia.

Mr Clymer may be said to have been by nature a republican. He was, also, a firm and devoted patriot. His feelings were strongly enlisted, at an early age, against the arbitrary acts of the British government. Gifted with a sort of prescience, he foresaw what was meditated against his country, and was ready to hazard every interest in support of the pillars of American freedom. Hence, when conciliatory measures with the parent country were found unavailing, he was one of the foremost to adopt measures necessary for defence. He early accepted a captain's commission in a company of volunteers, raised for the defence of the province, and manfully opposed, in 1773, the sale of tea, which was sent out by the British government for the purpose of indirectly levying a contribution on the Americans without their consent. Never was a plan more artfully laid by the ministry of Great Britain: never was an attack upon American liberty more covert and insidious; and never was a defeat more complete and mortifying. On the arrival of the tea destined to Philadelphia, the citizens of that place, in a numerous meeting, adopted the most spirited resolutions, the object of which was to prevent the sale of it. A committee was appointed, of which Mr. Clymer was chairman, to wait upon the consignees, and to request them not to attempt to sell it. This was a delicate office: the committee, however, fearlessly and faithfully discharged the duties of their appointment; and not a single pound of tea was offered for sale in the city of Philadelphia.

In 1775, Mr. Clymer was chosen a member of the council of safety, and one of the first continental treasurers. On the 20th of July, of the following year, he was elected a member of the continental congress; and though not present when the vote was taken on the question of independence, he had the honour of affixing his signature to that instrument in the following month.

In September, Mr. Clymer was appointed to visit Ticonderoga, in conjunction with Mr. Stockton, to inspect the affairs of the northern army. In December of the same year, congress, finding it necessary to adjourn to Baltimore, in consequence of the advance of the British army towards Philadelphia, left Mr. Clymer, Robert Morris, and George Walton, a committee to transact such business in that city as might be found necessary.

In 1777, Mr. Clymer was again a member of congress. His duties during this session were particularly arduous, and owing to his unremitting exertions, he was obliged to retire for a season, for the recovery of his health.

During the fall of this distressing year, the family of Mr. Clymer, which, at that time resided in the county of Chester about twenty-five miles from Philadelphia, suffered severely, in consequence of an attack by a band of British soldiers The furniture of the house was destroyed, and a large stock of liquors shared a similar fate. Fortunately, the family made their escape. Mr. Clymer was then in Philadelphia. On the arrival of the British in that place, they sought out his residence, and were proceeding to tear it down, and were only diverted from their purpose by the information, that the house did not belong to him.

During this year, Mr. Clymer was appointed a commissioner, in conjunction with several other gentlemen, to proceed to Pittsburg, on the important and confidential service, of preserving a good understanding with several indian tribes in that country, and particularly to enlist warriors from the Shawanese and Delaware indians into the service of the United States. During his residence at Pittsburg, he narrowly escaped death from the tomahawk of the enemy, having, in an excursion to visit a friend, accidentally and fortunately taken a route which led him to avoid a party of savages, who murdered a white man at the very place where Mr. Clymer must have been, had he not chosen a different road.

In our biographical sketch of Robert Morris, we have given some account of the establishment of a bank by the patriotic citizens of Philadelphia, the object of which was the relief of the army, which, in 1780, was suffering such a combination of calamities, as was likely to lead to its disbanding. Of the advocates of this measure, Mr. Clymer was one, and from the active and efficient support which he gave to the bank, he was selected as a director of the institution. By means of this bank, the pressing wants of the army were relieved. Congress, by a resolve, testified the high sense which they entertained of the generosity and patriotism of the association, and pledged the faith of the

United States to the subscribers to the bank, for their ultimate reimbursement and indemnity.

Mr. Clymer was again elected to congress in 1780; from which time, for nearly two years, he was absent from his seat but a few weeks, so faithfully and indefatigably attentive was he to the public service. In the latter part of 1782, he removed with his family to Princeton, in New-Jersey, for the purpose of giving to his children the advantages of a collegiate education, in the seminary in that place. After the many toils and privations through which he had passed, it was a luxury, indeed, to enjoy the peace of domestic life, especially having to reflect that the glorious object for which he and his fellow-countrymen had laboured so long, was now with certainty soon to be accomplished.

In 1784, Mr. Clymer was again summoned by the citizens of Pennsylvania, to take a part in the general assembly of that state. Of this body he continued a member until the meeting of the convention to form a more efficient constitution for the general government; of which latter body he was elected a member, and after the adoption of the constitution, he represented the state of Pennsylvania, in congress, for two years; when declining a re-election, he closed his long and able legislative career.

In the year 1791, congress passed a bill imposing a duty on spirits distilled in the United States. To the southern and western part of the country, this duty was singularly obnoxious. At the head of the excise department, in the state of Pennsylvania, Mr. Clymer was placed. The duties of this office were rendered extremely disagreeable, by reason of the general dissatisfaction, which prevailed on account of the law. This dissatisfaction was particularly strong in the district of Pennsylvania lying west of the Alleghany mountains, and here the spirit of discontent broke out into acts of open opposition. At the risk of his life, Mr. Clymer made a visit to this theatre of insurrection, to ascertain the existing state of things, and if possible to allay the spirit of opposition, which was manifesting itself. His instructions, however, were so limited, that he was able to produce but little effect upon the turbulent and heated minds of the faction. Soon after his return, he was induced to resign an office, which, from the difficulty of faithfully discharging it, had become extremely disagreeable to him.

In the year 1796, Mr. Clymer was appointed, together with Colonel Hawkins and Colonel Pickins, to negotiate a treaty with the Cherokee and Creek indians, in Georgia. With this object in view, he sailed from Philadelphia for Savannah, in the month of April, accompanied by his wife. Their voyage proved not only exceedingly unpleasant, but extremely hazardous, in consequence of a violent storm, during which, the crew were for several days obliged to labour incessantly at the pumps. Having satisfactorily completed the business of his mission, he again returned to Philadelphia. At this time, he closed his political life, and retired to the enjoyment of that rest which he justly coveted, after having served his country, with but few short intervals, for more than twenty years.

At a subsequent date, he was called to preside over the Philadelphia bank, and over the Academy of Fine Arts, and was elected a vice president of the Philadelphia Agricultural Society, upon its re-organization, in 1805. These offices he held at the time of his death, which occurred on the 23d of January, 1813, in the 74th year of his age.

The following extracts from an eloquent eulogium, pronounced before the Academy of Fine Arts, upon the character of Mr. Clymer, by Joseph Hopkinson, Esq. may properly conclude this brief biographical notice. After alluding to the election of Mr. Clymer to the presidency of the Academy of Fine Arts, Mr. Hopkinson happily observes: "At different periods of our national history, from the first bold step which was taken in the march of independence, to its full and perfect consummation in the establishment of a wise and effective system of government, whenever the virtue and talents of our country were put in requisition, Mr. Clymer was found with the selected few, to whom our rights and destinies were committed.

"When posterity shall ponder on the declaration of July

1776, and admire, with deep amazement and veneration, the courage and patriotism, the virtue and self-devotion of the deed, they will find the name of *Clymer* there. When the strength and splendour of this empire shall hereafter be displayed in the fulness of maturity, (heaven grant we reach it,) and the future politician shall look at that scheme of government, by which the whole resources of a nation have been thus brought into action; by which power has been maintained, and liberty not overthrown; by which the people have been governed and directed, but not enslaved or oppressed; they will find that *Clymer* was one of the fathers of the country, from whose wisdom and experience the system emanated. Nor was the confidence, which had grown out of his political life and services, his only claim to the station which he held in this institution. Although his modest, unassuming spirit never sought public displays of his merit, but rather withdrew him from the praise, that was his due; yet he could not conceal from his friends, nor his friends from the world, the extraordinary improvement of his mind. Retired, studious, contemplative, he was ever adding something to his knowledge, and endeavouring to make that knowledge useful. His predominant passion was to promote every scheme for the improvement of his country, whether in science, agriculture, polite education, the useful or the fine arts. Accordingly, we find his name in every association for these purposes, and wherever we find him, we also find his usefulness. Possessed of all that sensibility and delicacy, essential to taste, he had of course a peculiar fondness for the fine arts, elegant literature, and the refined pursuits of a cultivated genius. It was in the social circle of friendship that his acquirements were displayed and appreciated, and although their action was communicated from this circle to a wider sphere, it was with an enfeebled force. His intellects were strong by nature, and made more so by culture and study; but he was diffident and retired. Capable of teaching, he seemed only anxious to learn. Firm, but not obstinate; independent but not arrogant; communicative, but not obtrusive; he was at once the amiable and instructive companion. His researches had been various, and, if not always profound, they were competent to his purposes, and beyond his pretensions. Science, literature, and the arts, had all a share of his attention, and it was only by a frequent intercourse with him, we discovered how much he knew of each. The members of this board have all witnessed the kindness and urbanity of his manners. Sufficiently fixed in his own opinions, he gave a liberal toleration to others, assuming no offensive or unreasonable control over the conduct of those with whom he was associated."

In a subsequent part of his discourse, Mr. Hopkinson, alluding to the value of a punctual performance of our promises, remarks: "In this most useful virtue, Mr. Clymer was pre-eminent. During the seven years he held the presidency of this academy, his attention to the duties of the station were without remission. He excused himself from nothing that belonged to his office, he neglected nothing. He never once omitted to attend a meeting of the directors, unless prevented by sickness or absence from the city; and these exceptions were of very rare occurrence. He was indeed the first to come; so that the board never waited a moment for their president. With other public bodies to which he was attached, I understand, he observed the same punctual and conscientious discharge of his duty. It is thus that men make themselves useful, and evince that they do not occupy places of this kind merely as empty and undeserved compliments, but for the purpose of rendering all the services which the place requires of them."

JAMES SMITH.

James Smith, the subject of the following memoir, was a native of Ireland; but in what year he was born is unknown. This was a secret which, even to his relations and friends, he would never communicate, and the knowledge of it was buried with him in the grave. It is conjectured, however, that he was born between the years 1715 and 1720.

His father was a respectable farmer, who removed to America with a numerous family, and settled on the west side of the Susquehanna. He died in the year 1761. James, who was his second son, received his education from the distinguished Dr. Allison, provost of the college of Philadelphia. His attainments in classical literature were respectable. In the art of surveying, which at that early period of the country was of great importance, he is said to have excelled. After finishing his education, he applied himself to the study of law, in the office of Thomas Cookson, of Lancaster. On being qualified for his profession, he took up his residence as a lawyer and surveyor, near the present town of Shippensburg; but some time after, he removed to the flourishing village of York, where he established himself, and continued the practice of his profession during the remainder of his life.

On the occurrence of the great contest between Great Britain and her American colonies, Mr. Smith entered with zeal into the patriotic cause, and on a meeting of delegates from all the counties of Pennsylvania in 1774, convened to express the public sentiment, on the expediency of abstaining from importing any goods from England, and assembling a general congress, Mr. Smith was a delegate from the county of York, and was appointed one of the committee to report a draft of instruction to the general assembly, which was then about to meet. At this time, a desire prevailed throughout the country, that the existing difficulties between the mother country and the colonies should be settled, without a resort to arms. Mr. Smith, however, it appears, was disposed to adopt vigorous and decided measures, since, on his return to York, he was the means of raising a volunteer company, which was the first volunteer corps raised in Pennsylvania, in opposition to the armies of Great Britain. Of this company he was elected captain, and when, at length, it increased to a regiment, he was appointed colonel of that regiment; a title, however, which in respect to him was honorary, since he never assumed the actual command.

In January, 1775, the convention for the province of Pennsylvania was assembled. Of this convention, Mr. Smith was a member, and concurred in the spirited declaration made by that convention, that "if the British administration should determine by force to effect a submission to the late arbitrary acts of the British parliament, in such a situation, we hold it our indispensable duty to resist such force, and at every hazard to defend the rights and liberties of America."

Notwithstanding this declaration by the convention, a great proportion of the Pennsylvanians, particularly the numerous body of Quakers, were strongly opposed, not only to war, but even to a declaration of independence. This may be inferred from the instructions given by the general assembly to their delegates, who were appointed in 1775 to the general congress, of the following tenor:—that "though the oppressive measures of the British parliament and administration, have compelled us to resist their violence by force of arms; yet we strictly enjoin you, that you, in behalf of this colony, dissent from and utterly reject any proposition, should such be made, that may cause or lead to a separation from our mother country, or a change in this form of government."

This decided stand against a declaration of independence, roused the friends of that measure to the most active exertions, throughout the province. On the 15th of May, congress adopted a resolution, which was in spirit a declaration of independence. This resolution was laid before a large meeting of the citizens of Philadelphia, assembled five days after the passage of it, and in front of the very building in which congress was assembled, digesting plans of resistance. The resolution was received by this assembly of citizens, who were decided whigs, with great enthusiasm, the instructions of the provincial assembly to the Pennsylvania delegation in congress was loudly and pointedly condemned, and a plan adopted to assemble a provincial conference to establish a new government in Pennsylvania.

Accordingly, such a conference was assembled, on the

18th of June. Of this conference, Mr. Smith was an active and distinguished member. The proceedings of the conference were entirely harmonious. Before it had assembled, the provincial assembly had rescinded their obnoxious instructions to their delegates in congress. Still, however, it was thought advisable for the conference to express in form their sentiments on the subject of a declaration of independence. The mover of a resolution to this effect, was Dr. Benjamin Rush, at that time a young man. Colonel Smith seconded the resolution, and these two gentlemen, with Thomas M'Kean, were appointed a committee to draft it. On the following morning, the resolution being reported, was unanimously adopted, was signed by the members, and on the 25th of June, a few days only before the declaration of independence by congress, was presented to that body.

This declaration, though prepared in great haste, contained the substance of that declaration, which was adopted by congress. It declared, that the king had paid no attention to the numerous petitions which had been addressed to him, for the removal of the most grievous oppressions, but (to use the language of the preamble to the resolution) he "hath lately purchased foreign troops to assist in enslaving us; and hath excited the savages of this country to carry on a war against us, as also the negroes to imbrue their hands in the blood of their masters, in a manner unpractised by civilized nations; and hath lately insulted our calamities, by declaring that he will show us no mercy, till he has reduced us. And whereas the obligations of allegiance (being reciprocal between a king and his subjects) are now dissolved, on the side of the colonists, by the despotism of the said king, insomuch that it now appears that loyalty to him is treason against the good people of this country; and whereas not only the parliament, but there is reason to believe, too many of the people of Great Britain, have concurred in the arbitrary and unjust proceedings against us; and whereas the public virtue of this colony (so essential to its liberty and happiness) must be endangered by a future political union with, or dependence on, a crown and nation, so lost to justice, patriotism, and magnanimity :" Therefore, the resolution proceeded to assert that " the deputies of Pennsylvania assembled in the conference, unanimously declare their willingness to concur in a vote of the congress, declaring the united colonies free and independent states : and that they call upon the nations of Europe, and appeal to the great Arbiter and Governor of the empires of the world, to witness, that this declaration did not originate in ambition, or in an impatience of lawful authority ; but that they are driven to it in obedience to the first principles of nature, by the oppressions and cruelties of the aforesaid king and parliament of Great Britain, as the only possible measure left to preserve and establish our liberties, and to transmit them in violate to posterity."

In the month of July, a convention was assembled in Philadelphia, for the purpose of forming a new constitution for Pennsylvania. Of this body, Colonel Smith was elected a member, and he appeared to take his seat on the 15th day of the month. On the 20th he was elected by the convention a member of congress, in which body he took his seat, after the adjournment of the convention. Colonel Smith continued a member of congress for several years, in which capacity he was active and efficient. He always entertained strong anticipations of success during the revolutionary struggle, and by his cheerfulness powerfully contributed to dispel the despondency which he often saw around him. On withdrawing from congress, in November, 1778, he resumed his professional pursuits, which he continued until the year, 1800, when he withdrew from the bar, having been in the practice of his profession for about sixty years. In the year 1806, he was removed to another world. He had three sons and two daughters, of whom only one of each survived him.

In his disposition and habits, Colonel Smith was very peculiar. He was distinguished for his love of anecdote and conviviality. His memory was uncommonly retentive, and remarkably stored with stories of a humourous and diverting character, which, on particular occasions, he related with great effect.

He was for many years a professor of religion, and very regular in his attendance on public worship. Notwithstanding his fondness for jest, he was more than most men ready to frown upon every expression which seemed to reflect on sacred subjects. It was a singular trait in the character of Mr. Smith, that he should so obstinately refuse to inform his friends of his age. The monument erected over his grave informs us, that his death occurred in the ninety-third year of his age. It is probable, however, that he was not so old by several years.

GEORGE TAYLOR.

Of the early life of George Taylor, although he acted a distinguished part in the political affairs of his time, few incidents are recorded, in any documents which we have seen, and few, it is said, are remembered by the old men of the neighbourhood in which he lived. Mr. Taylor was born in the year 1716. Ireland gave him birth. He was the son of a respectable clergyman in that country, who having a more just estimation of the importance of a good education, gave to his son an opportunity to improve his mind, beyond most youth in the country about him. At a proper age he commenced the study of medicine; but his genius not being adapted to the profession, he relinquished his medical studies, and soon after set sail for America.

On his arrival, he was entirely destitute of money, and was obliged to resort to manual labour to pay the expenses of his voyage to America. The name of the gentleman who kindly employed him, and paid his passage, was Savage. He was the owner of extensive iron works at Durham, a small village, situated on the river Delaware, a few miles from Easton.

In these works, young Taylor was for a time employed to throw coal into the furnace, when in blast. The business was, however, too severe for him, and at length Mr. Savage transferred him from this menial and arduous service, into his counting-room as a clerk. In this situation, he rendered himself very useful and acceptable, and, at length, upon the death of Mr. Savage, he became connected in marriage with his widow, and consequently the proprietor of the whole establishment. In a few years the fortune of Mr. Taylor was considerably farther increased. He was now induced to purchase a considerable estate near the river Lehigh, in the county of Northampton, where he erected a spacious mansion, and took up his permanent residence.

A few years after, Mr. Taylor was summoned by his fellow-citizens into public life. Of the provincial assembly, which met at Philadelphia, in October, 1764, he was for the first time a member, and immediately rendered himself conspicuous, by the active part which he took in all the important questions which came before that body.

From this period, until 1770, Mr. Taylor continued to represent the county of Northampton in the provincial assembly. He was uniformly placed on several standing committees, and was frequently entrusted, in connexion with other gentlemen, with the management of many important special concerns, as they continued to rise. At Northampton, Mr. Taylor entered into the business, which had so extensively occupied him, while at Durham. The business, however, at the former place was by no means as profitable as it had been at the latter. Indeed it is said, that the fortune of Mr Taylor suffered so considerably, that he was at length induced to return to Durham to repair it.

In October, 1775, he was again elected a delegate to the provincial assembly in Pennsylvania, and in the following month was appointed, in connexion with several other gentlemen, to report a set of instructions to the delegates, which the assembly had just appointed to the continental congress.

The circumstances of the colony of Pennsylvania, were at this time, in some respects, peculiar. She was far less oppressed than the other colonies in America. On the contrary, she had been greatly favoured by his British majesty. Her government, which was proprietary, was administered without the least political oppression, and her constitution was free and liberal.

In consequence of these, and other circumstances, a strong reluctance prevailed in Pennsylvania to sever the bonds of union between herself and the mother country. Hence, the measures of her public bodies were characterized by a more obvious respect for the British government than the measures of other colonies. This might be inferred from the instructions reported at this time, by Mr. Taylor and his associates, and adopted by the assembly:

"The trust reposed in you is of such a nature, and the modes of executing it may be so diversified, in the course of your deliberations, that it is scarcely possible to give you particular instructions respecting it. We, therefore, in general, direct that you, or any four of you, meet in congress the delegates of the several colonies now assembled in this city, and any such delegates as may meet in congress next year; that you consult together on the present critical and alarming state of public affairs; that you exert your utmost endeavours to agree upon, and recommend such measures as you shall judge to afford the best prospect of obtaining redress of American grievances, and restoring that union and harmony between Great Britain and the colonies, so essential to the welfare and happiness of both countries."

"Though the oppressive measures of the British parliament and administration have compelled us to resist their violence by force of arms, yet we strictly enjoin you, that you, in behalf of this colony dissent from, and utterly reject any propositions, should such be made, that may cause or lead to a separation from our mother country, or a change of the form of this government."

During the winter and spring of 1776, a great change was effected in public sentiment in the province of Pennsylvania, on the subject of the contest between the mother country and the colonies. Hence the provincial assembly rescinded their former instructions to their delegates in congress, and while they expressed an ardent desire for the termination of the unhappy controversy, they were unwilling to purchase peace by a dishonourable submission to arbitrary power. "We, therefore," said the assembly, in their instructions to their delegates in congress. "authorize you to concur with the other delegates in congress, in forming such further compacts between the united colonies, concluding such treaties with foreign kingdoms and states, and in adopting such other measures as, upon a view of all circumstances, shall be judged necessary for promoting the liberty, safety, and interests of America; reserving to the people of this colony the sole and exclusive right of regulating the internal government and police of the same.

"The happiness of these colonies has, during the whole course of this fatal controversy, been our first wish. Their reconciliation with Great Britain our next. Ardently have we prayed for the accomplishment of both. But if we must renounce the one or the other, we humbly trust in the mercies of the Supreme Governor of the universe, that we shall not stand condemned before his throne, if our choice is determined by that overruling law of self-preservation, which His divine wisdom has thought fit to implant in the hearts of his creatures."

Fortunately for the cause of American liberty, the change in public sentiment above alluded to, continued to spread, and on taking the great question of a declaration of independence, an approving vote by all the colonies was secured in its favour. The approbation of Pennsylvania, however, was only obtained by the casting vote of Mr. Morton, as has already been mentioned in our biographical notice of that gentleman. On the 20th of July, the Pennsylvania convention proceeded to a new choice of Representatives. Mr. Morton, Dr. Franklin, Mr. Morris, and Mr. Wilson, who had voted in favour of the declaration of independence, were re-elected. Those who had opposed it were at this time dropped, and the following gentlemen were appointed in their place, viz : Mr. Taylor, Mr. Ross, Mr. Clymer, Dr. Rush, and Mr. Smith. These latter gentlemen were consequently not present on the fourth of July, when the declaration was passed and proclaimed, but they had the honour of affixing their signatures to the engrossed copy, on the second of August following, at which time the members generally signed it.

Mr. Taylor retired from congress in 1777, from which time we know little of his history. He settled at Easton, where he continued to manage his affairs with much success, and to repair his fortune, which had greatly suffered during his residence on the banks of the Lehigh. Mr. Taylor died on the 23d of February, 1781, in the sixty-sixth year of his age. He had two children by his wife, a son, who became an attorney, but died before his father, and a daughter who was never married

JAMES WILSON.

James Wilson was a native of Scotland, where he was born about the year 1742. His father was a respectable farmer, who resided in the vicinity of St. Andrews, well known for its university. Though not wealthy, he enjoyed a competency, until at length, a passion for speculation nearly ruined him.

James Wilson received an excellent education. He studied successively at Glasgow, St. Andrews, and Edinburgh. He had the good fortune to enjoy the instruction of the distinguished Dr. Blair, and the not less celebrated Dr. Watts. By the former he was taught rhetoric; by the latter, both rhetoric and logic. Under these eminent men, Mr. Wilson laid the fou... ... ... and a superi...
and al... ... ...
Afte... ... ... superior advantag...s

already named, he resolved to seek in America that independence which he could scarcely hope for in his native country Accordingly, he left Scotland, and reached Philadelphia early in the year 1766. He was highly recommended to several gentlemen of that city, by one or more of whom he was introduced as a tutor to the Philadelphia college and academy. During the period that he served in this capacity, he enjoyed a reputation of being the best classical scholar who had officiated as tutor in the Latin department of the college.

He continued, however, only a few months to fill the above office, having received an offer, through the assistance of Bishop White and Judge Peters, of entering the law office of Mr. John Dickinson. In this office he continued for the space of two years, applying himself with great ardour to the study of the profession of law. At the expiration of this time, he entered upon the practice, first at Reading, but soon after removed to Carlisle, at which latter place he acquired the reputation of being an eminent counsellor previous to the revolution. From Carlisle, Mr. Wilson removed to Annapolis, in Maryland, whence, in 1778, he came to Philadelphia, where he continued to reside for the remainder of his life.

At an early day, Mr. Wilson entered with patriotic zeal into the cause of American liberty. He was an American in principle from the time that he landed on the American shore; and at no period in the revolutionary struggle, did he for a single hour swerve from his attachment to the principles which he had adopted.

Mr. Wilson, who was a member of the provincial convention of Pennsylvania, was proposed as a delegate to the congress of 1774, in conjunction with his former instructor, Mr. Dickinson. Neither, however, was elected, through the influence of the speaker, Mr. Galloway, of whom we have spoken in our introduction, and who afterwards united himself to the British on their taking possession of Philadelphia. In the following year, however, Mr. Wilson was unanimously elected a member of congress, and in that body took his seat or feeling, he was superseded, and another appointed in his stead.

In 1782, however, he was again elected to congress, and took his seat in that body, on the second of January, 1783. A few months previously to his re-election, he was appointed by the president and supreme executive council, a counsellor and agent for Pennsylvania, in the great controversy between that state and the state of Connecticut, relating to certain lands within the charter boundary of Pennsylvania. These lands the state of Connecticut claimed as belonging to her, being included within her charter. On the thirtieth of December, 1782, this great question was determined at Trenton, New-Jersey, by a court of commissioners appointed for that purpose, who unanimously decided it in favour of Pennsylvania. To the determination of the question in this manner, Mr. Wilson, it is said, greatly contributed, by a luminous and impressive argument, which he delivered before the court, and which occupied several days.

The high estimation in which Mr. Wilson was held, about this time, may be learned from his receiving the appointment of advocate general for the French government, in the United States. His commission bore date the fifth of June, 1779; and at a subsequent date was confirmed, by letters patent from the king of France. The duties of this office were both arduous and delicate. Few men, however, were better qualified for such an office than Mr. Wilson. In 1781, difficulties having arisen as to the manner in which he should be paid for his services, he resigned his commission. He continued, however, to give advice in such cases as were laid before him, by the ministers and consuls of France, until 1783. At which time, the king of France handsomely rewarded him by a gift of ten thousand livres.

The standing of Mr. Wilson, during the whole course of his attendance in congress, was deservedly high. As a man of business, Pennsylvania had, probably, at no time, any one among her delegation who excelled him. He was placed on numerous committees, and in every duty assigned him exhibited great assiduity, ability, and perseverance.

Notwithstanding this high and honourable conduct of Mr Wilson, and the active exertions which he made in favour of his adopted country, he had enemies, whose slanders he did not escape. It was especially charged against him, that he was opposed to the declaration of independence. This, however, has been amply refuted by gentlemen of the highest standing in the country, who were intimately acquainted with his views and feelings on that important subject Many who voted for the measure, and who sincerely believed in the ultimate expediency of it, were of the opinion, that it was brought forward prematurely. But when, at length, they found the voice of the nation loudly demanding such a measure, and saw a spirit abroad among the people determined to sustain it, they no longer hesitated to vote in its favour. Mr. Wilson, probably, belonged to this class. Though at first doubtful whether the state of the country would justify such a measure, he at length became satisfied that existing circumstances rendered it necessary; and accordingly it received his vote.

Notwithstanding that a declaration of independence had been spoken of for some time previously to the fourth of July, 1776, no motion was brought forward in congress respecting it, until the 7th of June. This motion was referred the following day to a committee of the whole, but it was postponed until the tenth of June. On the arrival of the tenth of that month, the following resolution was offered: " That these united colonies are, and of right ought to be, free and independent states; that they are absolved from all allegiance to the British crown; and that all political connexion between them and the state of Great Britain is, and ought to be, totally dissolved." The consideration of this resolution was postponed to the first of July, on which day it was expected that the committee which was appointed to draft a declaration, and which consisted of Mr. Jefferson, J. Adams, Dr. Franklin, and R. R. Livingston, would report.

At length, the first of July arrived, when the motion was further discussed, and the question taken in committee of the whole.

former state were four to three in the opposition; the delegates of the latter, Thomas M'Kean and George Read, were divided, the one in favour of the measure, the other opposed to it. The final question was postponed from day to day, until the fourth of July, when it was taken, and an unanimous vote of all the states was obtained. The day was rainy. Of the Pennsylvania delegation, Messrs. Morris and Dickinson were absent, and consequently the vote of Pennsylvania was now in favour of the measure, Messrs. Wilson, Franklin, and Morton, being in favour of it, and Messrs. Humphreys and Willing being opposed to it. Fortunately, at this juncture, Cæsar Rodney, a delegate from Delaware, arrived. He had been sent for by an express from Mr. M'Kean, and arrived in time to vote with that gentleman, in opposition to their colleague, George Read.

Thus, an unanimous vote of the thirteen colonies was secured. Thus, a question was decided which deeply agitated the whole American community, and the decision of which was fraught with blessings to the country, which will go down, we trust, to the end of time.

In a preceding paragraph we have intimated that a charge was brought against Mr. Wilson of being opposed to the declaration of independence. Had such been his sentiments, who could have charged him with a want of patriotism? The truth is, there were hundreds, and even thousands, at that day, in America, as strongly attached to her cause, as friendly to her liberties, and as firmly resolved never to surrender the rights which the God of nature had given them, as were those who voted in favour of a declaration of independence, but who yet thought the time had not arrived when the wisest policy dictated such a measure. Mr. Wilson was, indeed, not altogether of this class. He would perhaps not have brought forward the subject at so early a day; but when it was brought forward, he voted in favour of it, on the first of July, even in opposition to the majority of his colleagues, and on the fourth, as it happened, fortunately for the cause of his country, in a majority.

Another charge has also been brought against Mr. Wilson,

(viz.) a participation in the combination which was formed against General Washington, towards the close of the year 1777. This conspiracy, if it may be so called, originated in the discontent of many who felt envious at the exalted station which Washington occupied, and was founded, at this time, upon the high military reputation which General Gates had acquired by the capitulation of Saratoga, and the gloomy aspect of affairs in the region where Washington was in particular command. In this combination, it was supposed several members of congress, and a very few officers of the army, were concerned. Among these officers, it is believed, General Gates himself may be included. "He had not only omitted," says Marshall, in his life of Washington, "to communicate to that general the successes of his army, after the victory of the seventh of October had opened to him the prospect of finally destroying the enemy opposed to him: but he carried on a correspondence with General Conway, in which that officer had expressed himself with great contempt of the commander in chief, and on the disclosure of this circumstance, General Gates had demanded the name of the informer, in a letter expressed in terms by no means conciliatory, and which was accompanied by the very extraordinary circumstance of being passed through congress.

"The state of Pennsylvania, too, chagrined at losing its capital, and forgetful of its own backwardness in strengthening the army, which had twice fought superior numbers in its defence, furnished many discontented individuals, who supposed it to be the fault of General Washington that he had not, with an army inferior to that of the enemy in numbers, and in every equipment, effected the same result, which had been produced in the north, by a continental army, in itself much stronger than its adversary, and so re-inforced by militia as to amount to three times the number opposed to them. The legislature of that state, on the report that General Washington was moving into winter quarters, addressed a remonstrance to congress on the subject, which manifested, in very intelligible terms, their dissatisfaction with the commander in chief. About the same time, a new board of wa-

was created, of which General Gates was appointed the president; and General Mifflin, who was supposed to be also of the party unfriendly to Washington, was one of its number. General Conway, who was, perhaps, the only brigadier in the army that had joined this faction, was appointed inspector general, and was elevated above brigadiers older than himself, to the rank of major general. There were other evidences that, if the hold which the commander in chief had taken of the affections and confidence of the army, and of the nation, could be shaken, the party in congress which was disposed to change their general, was far from being contemptible in point of numbers."

Fortunately for America, it was impossible to loosen this hold. Even the northern army clung to Washington as the saviour of their country. The only effect of this combination was, to excite a considerable degree of resentment, which was directed entirely against those who were believed to be engaged in it. General Gates himself, in consequence of this, and of the disastrous battle of Camden, fell into obscurity; and General Conway, the great calumniator of General Washington, scorned by honourable men, on account of his cowardice at the battle of Germantown, and other equally unworthy conduct, resigned his commission on the 28th of April, 1778.

The charge brought against Mr. Wilson, of having been hostile to General Washington, and of having participated in the combination formed against him, was wholly unfounded. The evidence on this point is complete.

Of the celebrated convention of 1787, which was assembled in Philadelphia, for the purpose of forming the constitution of the United States, Mr. Wilson was a member. During the long deliberations of the convention on that instrument, he rendered the most important services. He possessed great political sagacity and foresight, and being a fluent speaker, he did much to settle upon just principles the great and important points which naturally arose in the formation of a new government. On the twenty-third of July, the convention resolved, " That the proceedings of the convention for the establishment of a national government, except what respects the supreme executive, be referred to a committee for the purpose of reporting a constitution, conformably to the proceedings aforesaid." In pursuance of this resolution, a committee was appointed on the following day, consisting of Messrs. Wilson, Rutledge, Randolph, Gorham, and Ellsworth, who accordingly, on the sixth of August, reported the draught of a constitution.

When the state convention of Pennsylvania assembled to ratify the federal constitution, Mr. Wilson was returned a member of that body, and as he was the only one who had assisted in forming that instrument, it devolved upon him to explain to the convention the principles upon which it was founded, and the great objects which it had in view. Thus he powerfully contributed to the ratification of the constitution in that state. The following language, which he used in conclusion of his speech, in favour of this ratification, deserves a place here: "It is neither extraordinary nor unexpected, that the constitution offered to your consideration, should meet with opposition. It is the nature of man to pursue his own interest, in preference to the public good; and I do not mean to make any personal reflection when I add, that it is the interest of a very numerous, powerful, and respectable body, to counteract and destroy the excellent work produced by the late convention. All the officers of government, and all the appointments for the administration of justice, and the collection of the public revenue, which are transferred from the individual to the aggregate sovereignty of the states, will necessarily turn the stream of influence and emolument into a new channel. Every person, therefore, who enjoys, or expects to enjoy, a place of profit under the present establishment, will object to the proposed innovation; not, in truth, because it is injurious to the liberties of his country, but because it affects his schemes of wealth and consequence. I will confess, indeed, that I am not a blind admirer of this plan of government, and that there are some parts of it which, if my wish had prevailed, would certainly have been altered. But, when I reflect how widely men differ in their opinions, and that every man, (and the observation applies likewise to every state,) has an equal pretension to assert his own, I am satisfied that any thing nearer to perfection could not have been accomplished. If there are errors, it should be remembered, that the seeds of reformation are sown in the work itself, and a concurrence of two thirds of the congress may, at any time, introduce alterations and amendments. Regarding it, then, in every point of view, with a candid and disinterested mind, I am bold to assert, that it is the *best form of government which has ever been offered to the world.*"

After the ratification of the federal constitution in Pennsylvania, a convention was called to alter the constitution of that state, to render it conformable to that of the United States. Mr. Wilson was one of the committee appointed to prepare the form of a constitution, and upon him devolved the task of making the draught.

In the year 1789, General Washington appointed Mr. Wilson a judge of the supreme court of the United States, under the federal constitution. In this exalted station he was associated with John Jay, who was placed at the head of the department, and Judge Rutledge, of South Carolina, William Cushing, of Massachusetts, Robert Harrison, of Maryland, and John Blair, of Virginia. In this office he continued until his death, which occurred on the twenty-eighth of August, 1798, at Edenton, in North Carolina, while on a circuit attending to his duties as a judge. He is supposed to have been about fifty-six years of age.

In stature, Judge Wilson was about six feet. His appearance was dignified and respectable, and in his manners he was not ungraceful. As a lawyer, he stood at the head of his profession, while he practised at the Philadelphia bar. He was not less eminent as a judge on the bench. He entered with great readiness into the causes which came before him, and seldom did he fail to throw light on points of law of the most difficult and perplexing character.

In his domestic relations, such was his happy and consistent course, as to secure the respect and affection of his family and friends. Towards all with whom he had intercourse from abroad, he was friendly and hospitable, and within his family he was affectionate and indulgent. He was distinguished for great integrity of character, and for an inviolate regard for truth. Mr. Wilson was twice married, the first time to a daughter of William Bird, of Berks county, and the second time to a daughter of Mr. Ellis Gray, of Boston. By the former wife, he had six children; and by the latter one. Two only of these children are now living, the one at Philadelphia, the other in the state of New-York. After the death of Mr. Wilson, his wife became connected in marriage with Dr. Thomas Bartlett, of Boston, whom she accompanied to England, where she died in 1807.

GEORGE ROSS.

The last gentleman who belonged to the Pennsylvania delegation, at the time the members of the revolutionary congress affixed their signatures to the declaration of independence, was GEORGE ROSS. He was the son of a clergyman by the same name, who presided over the episcopal church at New Castle, in the state of Delaware, in which town he was born in the year 1730.

At an early age, he gave indications of possessing talents of a superior order. These indications induced his father to give him the advantages of a good education. At the age of eighteen he entered upon the study of law, under the superintendence of an elder brother, who was at that time in the practice of the profession, in the city of Philadelphia.

Soon after being admitted to the bar, he established himself at Lancaster, at that time near the western limits of civilization. He soon became connected in marriage with a lady of a respectable family. For several years he continued to devote his life, with great zeal, to the duties of his profession, in which, at length, he attained a high reputation, both as a counsellor and an advocate.

Mr. Ross commenced his political career in 1768, in which year he was first returned as a representative to the assembly of Pennsylvania. Of this body he continued to be re-elected a member, until the year 1774, when he was chosen in connection with several other gentlemen, a delegate to the celebrated congress which met at Philadelphia. At the time he was appointed to a seat in this congress, he was also appointed to report to the assembly of the province, a set of instructions, by which the conduct of himself and colleagues were to be directed. The instructions thus drafted and reported, were accepted by the assembly. In concluding these instructions, the assembly observed: " that the trust reposed in you is of such a nature, and the modes of executing it may be so diversified in the course of your deliberations, that it is scarcely possible to give you particular instructions respecting it. We shall, therefore, only in general direct, that you are to meet in congress the committees of the several British colonies, at such time and place as shall be generally agreed on, to consult together on the present critical and alarming situation and state of the colonies, and that you, with them, exert your utmost endeavours to form and adopt a plan, which shall afford the best prospect of obtaining a redress of American grievances, ascertaining American rights, and establishing that union and harmony, which is most essential to the welfare and happiness of both countries. And in doing this, you are strictly charged to avoid every thing indecent or disrespectful to the mother state."

Mr. Ross continued to represent the state of Pennsylvania in the national legislature, until January, 1777, when, on account of indisposition, he was obliged to retire. During his congressional career, his conduct met the warmest approbation of his constituents. He was a statesman of enlarged views, and under the influence of a general patriotism, he cheerfully sacrificed his private interests for the public good. The high sense entertained by the inhabitants of the county of Lancaster, of his zeal for the good of his country, and of his constituents in particular, was expressed in the following resolution: "Resolved, that the sum of one hundred and fifty pounds, out of the county stock, be forthwith transmitted to George Ross, one of the members of assembly for this county, and one of the delegates for this colony in the continental congress; and that he be requested to accept the same, as a testimony from this county, of their sense of his attendance on the public business, to his great private loss, and of their approbation of his conduct. Resolved, that if it be more agreeable, Mr. Ross purchase with part of the said money, a genteel piece of plate, ornamented as he thinks proper, to remain with him, as a testimony of the esteem this county has for him, by reason of his patriotic conduct, in the great struggle of American liberty." Such a testimony of respect and affection, on the part of his constituents, must have been not a little gratifying to the feelings of Mr. Ross. He felt it his duty, however, to decline accepting the present, offering as an apology for so doing, that he considered it as the duty of every man, and especially of every representative of the people, to contribute, by every means within his power, to the welfare of his country, without expecting pecuniary rewards.

The attendance of Mr. Ross in congress, did not prevent him from meeting with the provincial legislature. Of this latter body, he was an active, energetic, and influential member. In the summer of 1775, it was found by the general assembly, that the circumstances of the state required the adoption of some decisive measures, especially in respect to putting the city of Philadelphia, and the province, in a state of defence. A committee was accordingly appointed, of which Mr. Ross was one, to report what measures were expedient In a few days that committee did report, recommending to the people to associate for the protection of their lives, and liberty, and property, and urging upon the several counties o the province the importance of collecting stores of ammunition and arms. A resolution was also offered, providing for the payment of all such associations as should be called out to repel a ⁃ atta⁃⁃s ⁃⁃⁃ by the British ⁃⁃⁃⁃⁃. T⁃ c⁃rry these pl⁃ ⁃ ⁃⁃⁃ ⁃⁃⁃⁃⁃. a ⁃en⁃ral c⁃mmitt⁃ ⁃ of ⁃⁃⁃ ⁃⁃ s⁃⁃⁃

was appointed, and clothed with the necessary authority. To this committee Mr. Ross was attached, and was one of its most active and efficient members. He also belonged to another important committee, viz. that of grievances.

On the dissolution of the proprietary government in Pennsylvania, a general convention was assembled, in which Mr. Ross represented the county of Lancaster. Here, again, he was called to the discharge of most important duties, being appointed to assist in preparing a declaration of rights on behalf of the state, for forming rules of order for the convention, and for defining and settling what should be considered high treason and misprision of treason against the state, and the punishment which should be inflicted for those offences.

In the year 1779, Mr. Ross was appointed a judge of the court of admiralty for the state of Pennsylvania. This was on the 14th of April. He was permitted to enjoy, however, the honourable station which he now filled but a short time. In the month of July following, he was suddenly and violently attacked by the gout, which terminated his useful life, in the fiftieth year of his age.

In respect to the character of Judge Ross, we have little to add to the preceding account. As a lawyer, even before the revolution, he was among the first of his profession, a rank which he continued to hold, while he practised at the bar. As a politician, he was zealous, patriotic, and consistent. As a judge, he was learned and upright, and uncommonly skilful in the despatch of business. He comprehended with ease causes of the greatest intricacy, and formed his decisions, which often displayed much legal knowledge, with great promptness. It is to be added to his honour, that while he was thus distinguished abroad, he was characterized in the fulfilment of his domestic duties, by an uncommonly kind and affectionate disposition.

THE
DELAWARE DELEGATION.

Cæsar Rodney,
George Read,
Thomas M'Kean.

CÆSAR RODNEY.

Cæsar Rodney, the first of the delegation from Delaware, was a native of that state, and was born about the year 1730. His birth-place was Dover. The family, from which he was descended, was of ancient date, and is honourably spoken of in the history of early times. We read of Sir Walter De Rodeney, of Sir George De Rodeney, and Sir Henry De Rodeney, with several others of the same name, even earlier than the year 1234. Sir Richard De Rodeney accompanied the gallant Richard Cœur de Lion in his crusade to the Holy Land, where he fell, while fighting at the seige of Acre.

In subsequent years, the wealth and power of the family continued to be great. Intermarriages took place between some of the members of it, and several illustrious and noble families of England. During the civil wars, about the time of the commonwealth, the family became considerably reduced, and its members were obliged to seek their fortunes in new employments, and in distant countries. Soon after the settlement of Pennsylvania by William Penn, William Rodney, one of the descendants of this illustrious family removed to that province and after a short residence in Philadelphia, settled in Kent, a county upon the Delaware. This gentleman died in the year 1708, leaving a considerable fortune, and eight children, the eldest of whom is the subject of the following sketch. Mr. Rodney inherited from his father a large landed estate, which was entailed upon him, according to the usages of distinguished families at that day. At the early age of twenty-eight years, such was his popularity, he was appointed high sheriff in the county in which he resided, and on the expiration of his term of service, he was created a justice of the peace, and a judge of the lower courts. In 1762, and perhaps at a still earlier date, he represented the county of Kent in the provincial legislature. In this station he entered with great zeal and activity into the prominent measures of the day. In the year 1765, the first general congress was assembled, as is well known, at New-York, to consult upon the measures which were necessary to be adopted in consequence of the stamp act, and other oppressive acts of the British government. To this congress, Mr. Rodney, Mr. M'Kean, and Mr. Kollock, were unanimously appointed by the provincial assembly of Delaware to represent that province. On their return from New-York, they reported to the assembly their proceedings, under the instructions which they had received. For the faithful and judicious discharge of the trust reposed in them, the assembly unanimously tendered them their thanks, and voted them a liberal compensation.

The tumults caused in America by the stamp act, we have had frequent occasion to notice, as well as the joy consequent upon the repeal of that odious measure. In this universal joy, the inhabitants of Delaware largely participated. On the meeting of their legislature, Mr. Rodney, Mr. M'Kean, and Mr. Read, were appointed to express their thanks to the king, for his kindness in relieving them, in common with their country, from a burden which they had considered as exceedingly oppressive. In the address which was reported by the above committee, and forwarded, by direction of the assembly, to England, we find the following language:

"We cannot help glorying in being the subjects of a king, that has made the preservation of the civil and religious rights of his people, and the established constitution, the foundation and constant rule of his government, and the safety, ease, and prosperity of his people, his chiefest care; of a king, whose mild and equal administration is sensibly felt and enjoyed in the remotest parts of his dominion. The clouds which lately hung over America are dissipated. Our complaints have been heard, and our grievances redressed; trade and commerce again flourish. Our hearts are animated with the warmest wishes for the prosperity of the mother country, for which our affection is unbounded, and your faithful subjects here are transported with joy and gratitude. Such are the blessings we may justly expect will ever attend the measures of your majesty, pursuing steadily the united and true interests of all your people, throughout your wide extended empire, assisted with the advice and support of a British parliament, and a virtuous and wise ministry. We most humbly beseech your majesty, graciously to accept the strongest assurances, that having the justest sense of the many favours we have received from your royal benevolence, during the course of your majesty's reign, and now much our present happiness is owing to your paternal love and care for your people; we will at all times most cheerfully contribute to your majesty's service, to the utmost of our abilities, when your royal requisitions, as heretofore, shall be made known; that your majesty will always find such returns of duty and gratitude from us, as the best of kings may expect from the most loyal subjects, and that you will demonstrate to all the world, that the support of your majesty's government, and the honour and interests of the British nation, are our chief care and concern, desiring nothing more than the continuance of our wise and excellent constitution, in the same happy, firm, and envied situation, in which it was delivered down to us from our ancestors, and your majesty's predecessors."

This according to the agent who presented it, was

kindly received by his majesty, who expressed his pleasure by reading it over twice.

Unfortunately for the British government, but perhaps fortunately in the issue for the America colonies, the repeal of the stamp act was followed by other oppressive measures, which caused a renewal of the former excitement in the American colonies, and led to that revolution, which deprived Great Britain of one of her fairest possessions. The inhabitants of Delaware were for a long time anxious for a reconciliation between the mother country and the American colonies; still they understood too well their unalienable rights, and had too high a regard for them, tamely to relinquish them. In a subsequent address, prepared by the same gentlemen who had drafted the former, they renewed their protestations of loyalty; but at the same time took the liberty of remonstrating against the proceedings of the British parliament:

"If our fellow-subjects of Great Britain, who derive no authority from us, who cannot in our humble opinion represent us, and to whom we will not yield in loyalty and affection to your majesty, can at their will and pleasure, of right, give and grant away our property; if they enforce an implicit obedience to every order or act of theirs for that purpose, and deprive all, or any of the assemblies on this continent, of the power of legislation, for differing with them in opinion in matters which intimately affect their rights and interests, and every thing that is dear and valuable to Englishmen, we cannot imagine a case more miserable, we cannot think that we shall have even the shadow of liberty left. We conceive it to be an inherent right in your majesty's subjects, derived to them from God and nature, handed down from their ancestors, and confirmed by your royal predecessors and the constitution, in person, or by their representatives, to give and grant to their sovereigns those things which their own labours and their own cares have acquired and saved, and in such proportions and at such times, as the national honour and interest may require. Your majesty's faithful subjects of this government have enjoyed this inestimable privilege uninterrupted from its first existence, till of late. They have at all times cheerfully contributed to the utmost of their abilities for your majesty's service, as often as your royal requisitions were made known; and they cannot now, but with the greatest uneasiness and distress of mind, part with the power of demonstrating their loyalty and affection to their beloved king."

About this time, Mr. Rodney, in consequence of ill health, was obliged to relinquish his public duties, and seek medical advice in the city of Philadelphia. A cancerous affection had some time previously made its appearance on his nose, and was fast spreading itself over one side of his face. Fortunately, the skill of the physicians of Philadelphia afforded him considerable relief, and deterred him from making a voyage to England to seek professional advice in that country. In 1769, Mr. Rodney was elected speaker of the house of representatives, an office which he continued to fill for several years. About the same time he was appointed chairman of the committee of correspondence with the other colonies. In the discharge of the duties of this latter office, he communicated with gentlemen of great influence in all parts of the country, and by the intelligence which he received from them, and which he communicated to his constituents, contributed to that union of sentiment which, at length, enabled the colonies to achieve their independence.

Among the persons which composed the well known congress of 1774, Mr. Rodney was one, having for his colleagues the gentlemen already named, viz. Thomas M'Kean and George Read. The instructions given to this delegation required them to consult and determine upon such measures as might appear most wise for the colonies to adopt, in order to obtain relief from the sufferings they were experiencing. On the meeting of this congress, on the fifth of September, in the year already named, Mr. Rodney appeared and took his seat. He was soon after appointed on several important committees, in the discharge of which he exhibited great fidelity, and as a reward for his services he received the thanks of the provincial assembly, together with a re-appointment to the same high station in the following year. He was also appointed to the office of brigadier general in the province.

At the time that the important question of independence came before congress, Mr. Rodney was absent on a tour into the southern part of Delaware, having for his object to quiet the discontent which prevailed in that section of the country, and to prepare the minds of the people to a change of their government. On the question of independence, his colleagues, Mr. M'Kean and Mr. Read, who were at this time in attendance upon congress, in Philadelphia, were divided. Aware of the importance of an unanimous vote of the states in favour of a declaration of independence. and acquainted with the views of Mr. Rodney, Mr. M'Kean dispatched a special messenger to summon him to be present in his seat on the occurrence of the trying question. With great effort, Mr. Rodney reached Philadelphia just in time to give his vote, and thus to secure an entire unanimity in that act of treason. In the autumn of 1776, a convention was called in Delaware, for the purpose of framing a new constitution, and of appointing delegates to the succeeding congress. In this convention there was a majority opposed to Mr. Rodney, who was removed from congress, and another appointed in his stead. Such ingratitude on the part of a people was not common during the revolutionary struggle. In the present instance, the removal of this gentleman was principally attributable to the friends of the royal government, who were quite numerous, especially in the lower counties, and who contrived to enlist the prejudices of some true republicans in accomplishing their object.

Although thus removed from congress, Mr. Rodney still continued a member of the council of safety, and of the committee of inspection, in both of which offices he employed himself with great diligence, especially in collecting supplies for the troops of the state, which were at that time with Washington, in the state of New-Jersey. In 1777, he repaired in person to the camp near Princeton, where he remained for nearly two months, in the most active and laborious services.

In the autumn of this year, Mr. Rodney was again appointed as a delegate from Delaware to congress, but before taking his seat he was elected president of the state. This was an office of great responsibility, demanding energy and promptness, especially as the legislature of the state was tardy in its movements, and the loyalists were not unfrequently exciting troublesome insurrections. Mr. Rodney continued in the office of president of the state for about four years. During this period, he had frequent communications from Washington, in relation to the distressed condition of the army. In every emergency, he was ready to assist to the extent of his power; and by the influence which he exerted, and by the energy which he manifested, he succeeded in affording the most prompt and efficient aid. The honourable course which he pursued, his firm and yet liberal conduct, in circumstances the most difficult and trying, greatly endeared him to the people of Delaware, who universally expressed their regret when, in the year 1782, he felt himself obliged, on account of the arduous nature of his duties, and the delicate state of his health, to decline a re-election.

Shortly after retiring from the presidency, he was elected to congress, but it does not appear that he ever after took his seat in that body. The cancer which had for years afflicted him, and which for a long time previously had so spread over his face as to oblige him to wear a green silk screen to conceal its ill appearance, now increased its ravages, and in the early part of the year 1783, brought him to the grave.

It would be unnecessary, were it in our power, to add any thing further on the character of Mr. Rodney. He was, as our biographical notice clearly indicates, a man of great integrity, and of pure patriotic feeling. He delighted, when necessary, to sacrifice his private interests for the public good. He was remarkably distinguished for a degree of good humour and vivacity; and in generosity of character was an ornament to human nature.

GEORGE READ.

George Read was a native of the province of Maryland, where he was born in the year 1734. His grandfather was an Irishman, who resided in the city of Dublin, and was possessed of a considerable fortune. His son, John Read, the father of the subject of the present memoir, having emigrated to America, took up his residence in Cecil county, where he pursued the occupation of a planter. Not long after the birth of his eldest son, he removed with his family into the province of Delaware, and settled in the county of Newcastle. Mr. Read designing his son for one of the learned professions, placed him in a seminary at Chester, in the province of Pennsylvania. Having there acquired the rudiments of the learned languages, he was transferred to the care of that learned and accomplished scholar, the Rev. Dr. Allison, a gentleman eminently qualified to superintend the education of young men. With this gentleman young Mr. Read continued his studies until his seventeenth year, when he entered the office of John Moland, Esq. a distinguished lawyer in the city of Philadelphia, for the purpose of acquiring a knowledge of the legal profession. The intense application, and the sober habits of Mr. Read, were at this time highly honourable to him. While yet a student, he gave promise of future eminence in his profession. Mr. Moland reposed so great confidence in his abilities, that even before he had finished his preparatory studies, he entrusted to him a considerable share of his attorney business.

In 1753, at the early age of nineteen years, Mr. Read was admitted to the bar. On this event he performed an act of singular generosity in favour of the other children of the family. As the eldest son, he was entitled, by the existing laws, to two shares of his father's estate, but he relinquished all his rights in favour of his brothers, assigning as a reason for this act, his belief that he had received his proper portion in the education which had been given him.

In the following year, he commenced the practice of law,

in the town of Newcastle, and although surrounded by gentlemen of high attainments in the profession, he soon acquired the confidence of the public, and obtained a respectable share of business. In 1763, he was appointed to succeed John Ross, as attorney general of the three lower counties on the Delaware. This office, Mr. Read held until the year 1775, when, on being elected to congress, he resigned it.

During the same year, Mr. Read was connected by marriage with a daughter of the Rev. John Ross, a clergyman, who had long presided over an episcopal church, in the town of Newcastle. The character of Mrs. Read was in every respect excellent. She possessed a vigorous understanding. In her person she was beautiful, and to elegant manners was added a deep and consistent piety. She was also imbued with the spirit of a pure patriotism. During the revolutionary war, she was often called to suffer many privations, and was frequently exposed with her infant family to imminent danger, by reason of the predatory incursions of the British. Yet, in the darkest hour, and amidst the most appalling danger, her fortitude was unshaken, and her courage undaunted.

In the year 1765, Mr Read was elected a representative from Newcastle county to the general assembly of Delaware, a post which he occupied for twelve years. In this station, and indeed through his whole political course, he appears to have been actuated neither by motives of self-interest nor fear. By an adherence to the royal cause, he had reason to anticipate office, honour, and wealth. But his patriotism and integrity were of too pure a character to be influenced by worldly preferment, or pecuniary reward. The question with him was, not what a worldly policy might dictate, but what reason and justice and religion would approve.

On the first of August, 1774, Mr. Read was chosen a member of the continental congress, in connexion with Cæsar Rodney, and Thomas M'Kean. To this station he was annually re-elected, during the whole revolutionary war, and was indeed present in the national assembly, except for a few short intervals, during the whole of that period.

It has already been noticed, that when the great question of independence came before congress, Mr. Read was opposed to the measure, and ultimately gave his vote against it. This he did from a sense of duty: not that he was unfriendly to the liberties of his country, or was actuated by motives of selfishness or cowardice. But he deemed the agitation of the question, at the *time*, premature and inexpedient. In these sentiments, Mr. Read was not alone. Many gentlemen in the colonies, characterized for great wisdom, and a decided patriotism, deemed the measure impolitic, and would have voted, had they been in congress, as he did. The idle bodings of these, fortunately, were never realised. They proved to be false prophets, but they were as genuine patriots as others. Nor were they, like some in similar circumstances, dissatisfied with results, differing from those which they had predicted. On the contrary, they rejoiced to find their anticipations were groundless. When, at length, the measure had received the sanction of the great national council, and the time arrived for signing the instrument, Mr. Read affixed his signature to it, with all the cordiality of those who had voted in favour of the declaration itself.

In the following September, Mr. Read was elected president of the convention which formed the first constitution of the state of Delaware. On the completion of this, he was offered the executive chair, but chose at that time to decline the honour. In 1777, the governor, Mr. M'Kinley, was captured by a detachment of British troops, when Mr. M'Kean was called to take his place in this responsible office, the duties of which he continued to discharge, until the release of the former gentleman.

In 1779, ill health required him to retire for a season from public employment. In 1782, however, he accepted the appointment of judge of the court of appeals in admiralty cases, an office in which he continued till the abolition of the court.

In 1787, he represented the state of Delaware in the convention which framed the constitution of the United States, under which he was immediately elected a member of the Senate. The duties of this exalted station he discharged till

1793, when he accepted of a seat on the bench of the supreme court of the state of Delaware, as chief justice. In this station he continued till the autumn of 1798, when he was suddenly summoned to another world.

In all the offices with which Mr. Read was entrusted by his fellow citizens, he appeared with distinguished ability; but it was as a judge that he stood pre-eminent. For this station he was peculiarly fitted, not only by his unusual legal attainments, but by his singular patience in hearing all that council might deem important to bring forward, and by a cool and dispassionate deliberation of every circumstance which could bear upon the point in question. To this day his decisions are much respected in Delaware, and are often recurred to, as precedents of no doubtful authority.

In private life, the character of Mr. Read was not less estimable and respectable. He was consistent in all the relations of life, strict in the observance of his moral duties, and characterized by an expanded benevolence towards all around him.

THOMAS M'KEAN.

Thomas M'Kean was the second son of William M'Kean, a native of Ireland, who sometime after his emigration to America, was married to an Irish lady, with whom he settled in the township of New-London, county of Chester, and the province of Pennsylvania. where Thomas was born, on the nineteenth of March, 1734.

At the age of nine years, he was placed under the care of the learned Dr. Allison, who was himself from Ireland, and of whose celebrated institution at New-London, we have already had occasion to speak, in terms of high commendation. Besides an unusually accurate and profound acquaintance with the Latin and Greek classics, Dr. Allison was well in formed in moral philosophy, history, and general literature. To his zeal for the diffusion of knowledge, Pennsylvania owes much of that taste for solid learning and classical literature, for which many of her principal characters have been so distinguished.

Under the instructions of this distinguished scholar, young M'Kean made rapid advances in a knowledge of the languages, rhetoric, logic, and moral philosophy. After finishing the regular course of studies, he was entered as a student at law, in the office of David Finney, a gentleman who was related to him, and who resided in Newcastle, in Delaware. Before he had attained the age of twenty-one years, he commenced the practice of law, in the courts of common pleas for the counties of Newcastle, Kent, and Sussex, and also in the supreme court. His industry and talents soon became known, and secured to him a respectable share of business. In 1756, he was admitted to practice in the courts of the city and county of Philadelphia. In the following year he was admitted to the bar of the supreme court in Pennsylvania. In the same year the house of assembly elected him as their clerk, and in the following year he was re-appointed to the same station.

Mr. M'Kean was as yet a young man, but at this early age, he occupied an enviable rank among men of maturer years. He had held several offices of distinction, and by his industry and assiduity, his judgment and ability, he gave promise of his future eminence.

The political career of Mr. M'Kean commenced in the year 1762, at which time he was returned a member of the assembly from the county of Newcastle, which county he continued to represent in that capacity for several successive years, although the last six years of that period he spent in Philadelphia. In 1779, Mr. M'Kean appeared at Newcastle on the day of the general election in Delaware, and after a long and eloquent speech addressed to his constituents, he requested the privilege of being considered no longer one of their candidates for the state legislature. Most unexpectedly he was now placed in a peculiarly delicate situation. His constituents, although unwilling to dispense with his services in the assembly, consented to comply with his wishes; but at the same time requested him to nominate certain gentlemen, whom they should consider as candidates for the next general assembly. This was conferring on Mr. M'Kean an honour which must have been highly flattering. It was a mark of confidence in his judgment, without a parallel within our recollection. To a compliance with this request, Mr. M'Kean delicately gave his refusal; but, it being repeated, he delivered, with much reluctance, to the committee who waited upon him, the names of seven gentlemen, who were all elected with great unanimity.

We have had frequent occasion, in these biographical notices, to speak of the congress which assembled in New-York in 1765, usually called the stamp act congress, its object being to obtain relief of the British government from the grievances generally under which the colonies were suffering, and of the stamp act in particular. Of that illustrious body Mr. M'Kean was a member, from the counties of Newcastle, Kent, and Sussex, on the Delaware. Of the proceedings of this first American congress, little has been known, or can probably be collected, except from their general declaration of rights, and their address to the king, and petitions to parliament. Yet it is known, that in that congress, there were some who were distinguished for great energy and boldness of character. Among those of this description was James Otis of Boston, who, as Cæsar Rodney afterwards said, "displayed that light and knowledge of the interest of America, which, shining like a sun, lit up those stars which shone on this subject afterwards." In original firmness and energy, Mr. M'Kean was probably not greatly inferior to Mr. Otis. His independent conduct, on the last day of the session of the above congress, reflects the highest honour upon him, and deserves a special notice in every history of his life.

A few of the members of this body appeared not only timid, but were suspected of hostility to the measures which had been adopted. Among these, was Timothy Ruggles, a representative from the province of Massachusetts, who had been elected president of the congress in preference to James Otis, by only a single vote. In conclusion of the business, and when the members were called upon to sign the proceedings, Mr. Ruggles, with a few others, refused to affix their signatures.

At this moment, Mr. M'Kean rose, and with great dignity, but with deep feeling, addressing himself to the president, requested him to assign his reasons for refusing to sign the petitions. The president refused, on the ground that he was not bound in duty to state the cause of his objections. So uncourteous a refusal, especially as unanimity and harmony had prevailed during the session, called forth a rejoinder from Mr. M'Kean, in which he pressed upon the president the importance of an explanation. At length, after a considerable pause, Mr. Ruggles observed, that it was "against his conscience." "*Conscience!*" exclaimed Mr. M'Kean, as he rose from his seat, "*conscience!*" and he rung changes on the word so long and so loud, that at length the president, in a moment of irritation, gave Mr. M'Kean, in the presence of the whole congress, a challenge to fight him, which was instantly accepted. The president, however, had no more courage to fight than to sign the proceedings of congress; and the next morning he was seen wending his way through the streets of New-York, towards the province of Massachusetts, the legislature of which, not long after, ordered him to be reprimanded.

The only other member of the congress of 1765, who refused to sign the petitions, was Mr. Robert Ogden, at that time speaker of the house of assembly of New-Jersey. This gentleman, Mr. M'Kean strongly solicited in private to adopt a bold and manly course, by affixing his signature to the proceedings of the congress. Arguments, however, were in vain; yet he was reluctant that his constituents in New-Jersey should become acquainted with his refusal. It was, however, communicated to them. The people of New-Jersey, justly indignant at his conduct, burnt his effigy in several towns, and on the meeting of the general assembly, he was removed from the office of speaker. As Mr. M'Kean, in passing through New-Jersey, had without hesitation, when asked, communicated the course which Mr. Ogden had taken, the latter gentleman, it is said, threatened him with a challenge, which, however, ended much as had the precipitate challenge of the president from Massachusetts.

We must necessarily pass over several years of the life of Mr. M'Kean, during which he was engaged in various public employments. A short time before the meeting of the congress of 1774, Mr. M'Kean took up his permanent residence in the city of Philadelphia. The people of the lower counties on the Delaware were anxious that he should represent them in that body, and he was accordingly elected as their delegate. On the 3d of September, he took his seat in that august assemblage. From this time, until the 1st of February, 1783, he continued annually to be elected a member of the great national council, a period of eight years and a half. This was the only instance, it is said, in which any gentleman was continued a member of congress, from 1774, to the signing of the preliminaries of peace in 1783. It is also worthy of notice, that at the same time he represented the state of Delaware in congress, he was president of it in 1781, and from July, 1777, was the chief justice of Pennsylvania. Such an instance of the same gentleman being claimed as a citizen of two states, and holding high official stations in both at the same time, is believed to be without a parallel in the history of our country.

As a member of congress, Mr. M'Kean was distinguished for his comprehensive views of the subjects which occupied the deliberation of that body, and for the firmness and decision which marked his conduct on all questions of great national importance. On the 12th of June, 1776, he was appointed, in connexion with several others, a committee to prepare and digest the form of a confederation between the colonies. This committee reported a draught the same day; but it was not finally agreed to until the 15th of November, 1777, nor was it signed by a majority of the representatives of the respective colonies, until the 9th of July, 177. Even at this late date, New-Jersey, Delaware, and Maryland, had not authorized their delegates to ratify and sign the instrument. But, in the November following, New-Jersey acceded to the confederation, and on the 22d of February, 1779, Mr. M'Kean signed it in behalf of Delaware. Maryland ratified the act of union in March, 1781.

On the great question of a declaration of independence, Mr. M'Kean was, from the first, decidedly in favour of the measure. He subscribed his name to the original intrument deposited in the office of the secretary of state, but it was omitted in the copy published in the journals of congress. This omission it is now impossible satisfactorily to explain The following letter on the subject, addressed by Mr. M'Kean to Mr. Dallas of Pennsylvania, on the 26th of September, 1796, will, it is believed, be thought a valuable document:

"Sir,

"Your favour of the 19th instant, respecting the Declaration of Independence, should not have remained so long unanswered, if the duties of my office of chief justice had not engrossed my whole attention, while the court was sitting.

"For several years past, I have been taught to think less unfavourably of scepticism than formerly. So many things have been misrepresented, misstated, and erroneously printed, (with seeming authenticity,) under my own eye, as in my opinion to render those who doubt of every thing, not altogether inexcusable: The publication of the Declaration of Independence, on the 4th of July, 1776, as printed in the second volume of the Journals of Congress, page 241, and also in the acts of most public bodies since, so far as respects the names of the delegates or deputies, who made that Declaration, has led to the above reflection. By the printed publications referred to, it would appear, as if the fifty-five gentlemen, whose names are there printed, and none other, were on that day personally present in congress, and assenting to the declaration; whereas, the truth is otherwise. The following men were not members of congress on the

4th of July, 1776; namely, Matthew Thornton, Benjamin Rush, George Clymer, James Smith, George Taylor, and George Ross. The five last named were not chosen delegates until the 20th day of the month; the first, not until the 12th day of September following, nor did he take his seat in congress, until the 4th of November, which was four months after. The journals of Congress, (vol. ii. page 277 and 442.) as well as those of the assembly of the state of Pennsylvania, (p. 53) and of the general assembly of New-Hampshire, establish these facts. Although the six gentleman named had been very active in the American cause, and some of them, to my own knowledge, warmly in favour of independence, previous to the day on which it was declared, yet I personally know that none of them were in congress on that day.

"Modesty should not rob any man of his just honour, when by that honour, his modesty cannot be offended. My name is not in the printed journals of congress, as a party to the Declaration of Independence, and this, like an error in the first concoction, has vitiated most of the subsequent publications, and yet the fact is, that I was then a member of congress for the state of Delaware, was personally present in congress, and voted in favour of independence on the 4th of July, 1776, and signed the declaration after it had been engrossed on parchment, where my name, in my own hand writing, still appears. Henry Misner, of the state of New-York, was also in congress, and voted for independence. I do not know how the misstatement in the printed journal has happened. The manuscript *public* journal has no names annexed to the Declaration of Independence, nor has the *secret* journal; but it appears by the latter, that on the 19th day of July, 1776, the congress directed that it should be engrossed on parchment, and signed by *every member*, and that it was so produced on the 2d of August, and *signed.* This is interlined in the *secret* journal, in the hand of Charles Thompson, the secretary. The present secretary of state of the United States, and myself, have lately inspected the journals, and seen this. The journal was first printed by

Mr. John Dunlap, in 1778, and probably copies, with the names then signed to it, were printed in August, 1776, and that Mr. Dunlap printed the names from one of *them*.

"I have now, sir, given you a true, though brief, history of this affair; and, as you are engaged in publishing a new edition of the Laws of Pennsylvania, I am obliged to you for affording the favourable opportunity of conveying to you this information, authorizing you to make any use of it you please.

"I am," &c.

In the life of Mr. Rodney, we have had occasion to remark that Mr. M'Kean and Mr. Read voted in opposition to each other, when the question of independence was put in committee of the whole, on the 1st of July. Delaware was thus divided. As it was improbable, in the estimation of Mr. M'Kean, that the views of Mr. Read would undergo a favourable change before the final question should be taken, he became exceedingly anxious that Mr. Rodney, who he knew was in favour of the declaration, should be present. At his private expense he dispatched an express into Delaware to acquaint Mr. Rodney with the delicate posture of affairs, and to urge him to hasten his return to Philadelphia. Fortunately, by an exertion which patriotism only could have prompted him to make, that gentleman arrived in Philadelphia, just as the members were entering the door of the state house, at the final discussion of the subject. Without even an opportunity of consulting Mr. M'Kean, on the momentous question before them, he entered the hall with his spurs on his boots. Scarcely had he taken his seat, before the report of the chairman of the committee of the whole was read, soon after which the great question was put. Mr. M'Kean and Mr. Rodney voted in favour on the part of Delaware, and thus contributed to that unanimity among the colonies, on this great subject, without which a declaration had been worse than in vain.

At the time congress passed the declaration of independence, the situation of Washington and his army, in New-Jersey was exceedingly precarious. On the 5th of July, it was agreed by several public committees in Philadelphia, to dispatch all the associated militia of the state to the assistance of Washington, where they were to continue, until ten thousand men could be raised to relieve them. Mr. M'Kean was at this time colonel of a regiment of associated militia. A few days following the declaration of independence, he was on his way to Perth Amboy, in New-Jersey, at the head of his battalion. In a letter, dated at head quarters, Perth Amboy, July 26th, 1776, he describes the narrow escape which he had in executing an order of the commander-in-chief, which required him to march his battalion into the town. Having put his troops in motion, under Lieutenant Colonel Dean, he mounted his horse, and proceeded to wait upon the general for more particular orders. At this time, the enemy's batteries were playing along the road which it was necessary for him to take. Amidst balls, which were flying in every direction around him, he proceeded to the general's head quarters. An order had just been issued to prevent the battalion from proceeding into the town. It became necessary, therefore, for him to follow them, in order to stop them. As he turned to execute the order, a horse at a short distance from him was shot through the neck by a cannon ball, and such was the incessant discharge from the enemy's batteries along the road, over which he passed, that it appeared impossible that he should escape. A merciful providence, however, protected him on his return. He executed his order, and safely marched his troops to the camp.

The associate militia being at length discharged, Mr. M'Kean returned to Philadelphia, and was present in his seat in congress on the second of August, when the engrossed copy of the declaration of independence was signed by the members. A few days after this, receiving intelligence of his having been elected a member of the convention in Delaware, assembled for the purpose of forming a constitution for that state, he departed for Dover, which place he reached in a single day. Although excessively fatigued, on his arrival, at the request of a committee of gentlemen of the convention, he retired to his room in the public inn, where he was employed the whole night in preparing a constitution for the future government of the state. This he did without the least assistance, and even without the aid of a book. At ten o'clock the next morning it was presented to the convention, by whom it was unanimously adopted.

In the year 1777, Mr. M'Kean was appointed president of the state of Delaware, and on the twenty-eighth of July of the same year, he received from the supreme executive council the commission of chief justice of Pennsylvania The duties of this latter station he continued to discharge for twenty-two years. At the time of his accepting the commission, he was speaker of the house of assembly, president of Delaware, as already noticed, and member of congress

The duties of so many offices pressed with too much weight upon Mr. M'Kean, and he found himself compelled to offer his resignation, in 1780, to the people of Delaware, as their delegate to congress. They were, however, unwilling to dispense with his services, and he continued still to represent the state in the national council. In July of the following year, on the resignation of Samuel Huntington, he was elected president of congress, a station which he found it necessary in the following October to relinquish, as the duties of it interfered with the exercise of his office of chief justice of Pennsylvania. On accepting his resignation, it was resolved. "that the thanks of congress be given to the honourable Thomas M'Kean, late president of congress, in testimony of their approbation of his conduct in the chair, and in the execution of public business."

We must here devote a paragraph to speak of Mr. M'Kean, in the exercise of his judicial functions. As a judge, he had few equals, in this, or any other country. At this time the law of the state of Pennsylvania was in a great measure unsettled. It devolved upon him to reduce it to a system. His decisions were remarkably accurate, and often profound. He was distinguished for great perspicuity of language, for an easy and perfectly intelligible explication of even intricate and difficult cases. In his manners, while presiding, to a proper affability, he united great dignity. In short, few men while living have acquired a higher reputation than did chief justice M'Kean, and few have enjoyed, after death, a greater share of judicial fame.

In the year 1788, an attempt was made to impeach the conduct of Mr. M'Kean, as chief justice. The ground of accusation arose from the following circumstance. Eleazer Oswald, in a column of a paper of which he was editor, attempted to prejudice the minds of the people, in a cause then in court, in which he was defendant; at the same time casting highly improper reflections upon the judges. In consideration of this contempt of court, the judges inflicted a fine upon Oswald of ten pounds, and directed him to be imprisoned *for the space of one month*, that is, *from the fifteenth day of July to the fifteenth day of August.* At the expiration of twenty eight days, a legal month, Oswald claimed his discharge. The sheriff, upon this, consulted Mr. M'Kean, who not knowing that the sentence was entered upon the record "*for the space of one month*," without the *explanatory* clause, directed the sheriff to detain the prisoner until the morning of the fifteenth of August. Finding his mistake, however, he directed Oswald to be discharged; but as he had been detained beyond the time specified in the sentence, he presented a memorial to the general assembly, complaining of the chief justice, and demanding his impeachment. After a discussion of the subject by the assembly for several days, and a long examination of witnesses, it was at length resolved : " that this house, having, in a committee of the whole, gone into a full examination of the charges exhibited by Eleazer Oswald, of arbitrary and oppressive proceedings in the justices of the supreme court, against the said Eleazer Oswald, are of the opinion, that the charges are unsupported by the testimony adduced, and, consequently, that there is no just cause for impeaching the said justices " .

Of the convention of Pennsylvania, which was assembled on the twentieth of November, 1787, to ratify the constitution of the United States, Mr. M'Kean was delegated a member from the city of Philadelphia. In the convention, Mr

M'Kean and Mr. Wilson, of the latter of whom we have spoken in a former biographical sketch, took the lead. On the twenty-sixth of this month, the former submitted the following motion: "That this convention do assent to, and ratify the constitution agreed to on the seventeenth of September last, by the convention of the United States of America, held at Philadelphia." On a subsequent day, he entered at length into the merits of the constitution, which he demonstrated in the most masterly manner, and triumphantly answered the various objections which had been urged against it. In the conclusion of this eloquent speech, he used the following language: "The law, sir, has been my study from my infancy, and my only profession. I have gone through the circle of office, in the legislative, executive, and judicial, departments of government. and from all my study, observation, and experience, I must declare, that from a full examination and due consideration of this system, it appears to me the *best the world has yet seen.*

"I congratulate you on the fair prospect of its being adopted, and am happy in the expectation of seeing accomplished, what has been long my ardent wish—that you will hereafter have a *salutary permanency in magistracy, and stability in the laws.*"

In the following year, the legislature of Pennsylvania took measures for calling a convention, to consider in what respects their state constitution required alteration and amendment. This convention commenced its session on the 24th of November, 1789; Mr. M'Kean appeared and took his seat as a delegate from the city of Philadelphia. When the convention resolved itself into a committee of the whole, on the subject of altering or amending the constitution, he was appointed chairman. During the whole of the deliberations, he presided with great dignity and ability, for which he received the unanimous thanks of the convention. In 1779, Mr. M'Kean was elected to the chief magistracy of the state of Pennsylvania. His competitor at this time, was the able and distinguished James Ross. Mr. M'Kean belonged to the politics of Mr. J. Ferson, to whose elevation to the presidency of the

United States, his election is supposed to have powerfully contributed. The administration of Mr. M'Kean was marked with ability, and with ultimate benefit to the state; yet the numerous removals from office of his political opponents, produced great excitement in the state, and, perhaps, upon the whole, betrayed, on his part, an unjustifiable degree of political asperity.

During the years 1807 and 1808, through the influence of a number of the citizens of the city and county of Philadelphia, an inquiry was instituted by the legislature into the official conduct of Governor M'Kean. The committee appointed for this purpose reported to the legislature:

"I. That the governor did, premeditatedly, wantonly, unjustly, and contrary to the true intent and meaning of the constitution, render void the late election, (in 1806,) of a sheriff in the city and county of Philadelphia.

"II. That he usurped a judicial authority, in issuing a warrant for the arrest and imprisonment of Joseph Cabrera; and interfered in favour of a convict for forgery, in defiance of the law, and contrary to the wholesome regulations of the prison in Philadelphia, and the safety of the citizens.

"III. That, contrary to the true intent and meaning of the constitution, and in violation of it, did he appoint Dr. George Buchanan lazaretto physician of the port of Philadelphia.

"IV. That, under a precedent, acknowledged to have been derived from the king of Great Britain, and contrary to the express letter of the constitution, did he suffer his name to be stamped upon blank patents, warrants on the treasury, and other official papers, and that, too, out of his presence.

"V. That, contrary to law, did he supersede Dr. James Reynolds as a member of the board of health.

"VI. That, contrary to the obligations of duty, and the injunctions of the constitution, did he offer and authorize overtures to be made to discontinue two actions of the commonwealth against William Duane and his surety, for an alleged forfeiture of two recognizances of one thousand dollars each, on condition that William Duane would discontinue civil actions against his son Joseph B. M'Kean, and others, for damages for a murderous assault, committed by Joseph M'Kean, and others, on William Duane."

This report the committee followed by affixing the following resolution:

"Resolved, That Thomas M'Kean, governor of this commonwealth, be impeached of high crimes and misdemeanours."

On the twenty-seventh of January, the house proceeded to the consideration of the above resolution, and on the same day indefinitely postponed the further consideration of the subject.

Although this attempt to impeach the governor was thus unsuccessful, the following day he presented to the house a reply to the charges which had been exhibited against him by the committee of inquiry. After being read, a motion was made to insert it at large on the journal, which, at length, was carried in the affirmative.

In the course of this reply, which contained, in the view of temperate men, a triumphant vindication of his character, Mr. M'Kean observed as follows. "That I may have erred in judgment; that I may have been mistaken in my general views of public policy; and that I may have been deceived by the objects of executive confidence, or benevolence—I am not so vain nor so credulous as to deny; though, in the present instance, I am still without the proof and without the belief; but the firm and fearless position which I take, invites the strictest scrutiny, upon a fair exposition of our constitution and laws, into the sincerity and truth of the general answer given to my accusers—*that no act of my public life was ever done from a corrupt motive, nor without a deliberate opinion that the act was lawful and proper in itself.*"

At the close of the year 1808, Mr. M'Kean, having occupied the chair of state during the constitutional period of nine years, retired from the cares of a long life to the enjoyment of a peaceful retirement, rendered doubly grateful by the consci... of ... and ho...able fame. In the enj... ... until the twenty-fourth of June, 1817, when he was gathered to the generation of his fathers, at the uncommon age of eighty-three years, two months, and sixteen days. He lies interred in the burial ground of the First Presbyterian Church, in Market-street, Philadelphia.

THE
MARYLAND DELEGATION.

Samuel Chase,
William Paca,
Thomas Stone,
Charles Carroll.

SAMUEL CHASE.

Samuel Chase was the son of the Rev. Thomas Chase, a clergyman of distinction, in the protestant episcopal church who, after his emigration to America, married the daughter of a respectable farmer, and settled, for a time, in Somerset county, in Maryland, where this son was born, on the 17th of April, 1741.

In 1743, Mr. Chase removed to Baltimore, having been appointed to the charge of St. Paul's church, in that place Even in Baltimore, at this period, there was no school of a high order. The instruction of his son, therefore, devolved upon Mr. Chase, than whom few, fortunately, were better qualified for such a charge. His own attainments in classical learning were much superior to those who had been educated in America. Under the instruction of one so well qualified to teach, the son soon outstripped most of his compeers, and at the early age of eighteen was sent to Annapolis, to commence the study of law. After a sedulous attention to his preparatory studies for two years, he was admitted to practise in the mayor's court, and two years from this latter date, was licensed for the chancery, and some of the county courts. Finding the number of practitioners at Annapolis small, he settled in that place as a lawyer, where he was soon after connected in marriage with an amiable and intelligent lady, by whom he had two sons and two daughters, all o whom survived their parents.

The incidents in the life of Mr. Chase, for several years, were but few. Devoted to his professional duties, he not only acquired a respectable share of business, but became highly distinguished for his legal attainments.

The political career of Mr. Chase commenced about the time of the congress of 1774, in which body he acted as a delegate from Maryland. This station he continued to occupy for several years. In the spring of 1776, he was appointed by congress, in conjunction with Dr. Franklin and Mr. Carroll, to a trust of a most important nature. This was a mission to Canada, the object of which was, to induce the inhabitants of that country to withdraw their connexion from Great Britain, and to join the American confederacy. The undertaking was attended with great difficulties; but as Mr. Chase, though young, was distinguished for his abilities, and characterized for a most ardent patriotism, he was appointed one of the commissioners. Mr. Carroll, and his brother, afterwards the archbishop of Baltimore, were added to the commission, under an apprehension that they might exercise a salutary influence with the catholics in Canada. Although the objects of the expedition were not attained, the fidelity of the commissioners was never, for a moment, questioned.

On his return to Philadelphia, Mr. Chase found that a proposition had been made in congress to issue a declaration of independence. The situation of the Maryland delegation, in respect to such a measure, was peculiarly trying. They had been expressly prohibited, by the convention which appointed them, from voting in favour of a declaration of independence; and, as they had accepted their appointments under this restriction, they did not feel at liberty to give such a measure their active and open support.

It was not compatible with the independent and patriotic

spirit of Mr. Chase, quietly to endure such a situation. He left congress, and proceeded to Maryland. He traversed the province, and, assisted by his colleagues and friends, assembled county meetings, and persuaded the inhabitants to send addresses to the convention, then sitting at Annapolis, in favour of independence. Such an expression of cordiality to a measure, the convention could not resist, and at length gave an unanimous vote in its favour. With this vote, Mr. Chase hastened to Philadelphia, where he arrived in time to take his seat on Monday morning, having rode, on the two previous days, one hundred and fifty miles. On the day of his arrival, the resolution to issue a declaration of independence came before the house, and he had the pleasure of uniting with a majority in favour of it.

This success was a sufficient reward for all the labour which he had sustained, in accomplishing an object so desirable. A pure patriotism only, however, could have sustained the fathers of the revolution, under all the toils and fatigue which they endured. They were fitted for high and mighty enterprises. Common dangers, and common sufferings, they regarded not. The object presented to their view, was connected with the liberty not only of themselves, but with the millions of their future posterity. With this object before them, therefore, they heeded not danger, nor were they subdued, or even disheartened, by the most unexpected reverses.

Our limits permit us not to enter into a minute detail of the congressional services rendered by Mr. Chase, during several years which followed the declaration of independence. In the number, variety, and importance of those services, he was probably surpassed by few. He possessed, beyond most others, an ardour of mind, which sometimes, in debate, carried him almost beyond the bounds of propriety. There were some others from time to time in congress of a similar stamp. They were important members; they served to animate that body by the warmth which they manifested in debate, and to rouse the more supine or timid to action, as the necessity of the times required.

In 1783, Mr. Chase being accidentally in Baltimore, was invited to attend the meeting of a club of young men, who assembled at stated times, for the purpose of debating Among the speakers of the evening, there was one who, from his force of argument, and gracefulness of delivery, attracted his attention. At the close of the debate, Mr. Chase entered into conversation with him, and advised him to think of the profession of law. The young man was at the time a clerk in an apothecary's shop. Finding him destitute of the means necessary for an undertaking so expensive, Mr. Chase kindly offered him the benefit of his library, his instruction, and his table. That young man was *William Pinkney*. He accepted the invitation of his generous benefactor, who afterwards had the pleasure of seeing him one of the most distinguished lawyers ever at the American bar. It may be proper to add in this place, that he was afterwards attorney general of the United States, and a minister in successive years at the courts of St. James, at Naples, and St. Petersburg. In the same year, Mr. Chase visited England, on behalf of the state of Maryland, for the purpose of reclaiming a large amount of property, which, while a colony, she had entrusted to the bank of England. In the prosecution of this business, he continued in England about a year, in which time he had the pleasure of becoming acquainted with many of the distinguished men of that country, among whom were Pitt, and Fox, and Burke. Although unsuccessful in accomplishing the object of his mission, while he continued in England, he put the claim in so favourable a train, that at a subsequent period, the state recovered about six hundred and fifty thousand dollars. While in England, he was married to his second wife, the daughter of Dr. Samuel Giles, of Kentbury, with whom, in 1784, he returned to America.

In the year 1786, at the pressing invitation of his friend, Colonel Howard, he removed from Annapolis to Baltimore. By this gentleman, he was generously presented with a square of ten lots of land, upon a spot in which he erected a house, in which he lived until his death. On his removal from Annapolis, the corporation of that city tendered to him the expressions of their respect, in the following address: "Sir, the mayor, aldermen, and common councilmen of the city of Annapolis, impressed with a due sense of the services rendered to this corporation by you, in the capacity of recorder thereof, do take this occasion to assure you of their entire approbation of your conduct in the performance of the duties of that trust, and to acknowledge your ready exertion, at all times, to promote the interest and welfare of this city. They sincerely regret the occasion of this address, as your removal from the city of Annapolis will deprive this body of a faithful and able officer, and the city of a valuable citizen. You have our warmest wishes for your happiness and welfare."

To this address, Mr. Chase returned the following answer: "The address of the mayor, aldermen, and common councilmen of this city, presented me this day, affords me just pleasure, as I flatter myself they speak the genuine sentiments of the citizens. As recorder of the city, duty and inclination urged me to enforce due obedience to the by-laws, and assist in the framing of ordinances for the regulating the police of the city. In the discharge of this duty, I ever received the ready assistance of my brethren on the bench, and of the other members of the corporation, and but a small portion of merit is due to me. My abilities have been much overrated by the corporation; I only wish they had been equal to my inclination to serve them.

"As one of the delegates of Annapolis, my public powers were exerted on all occasions to promote the interest and welfare of the city, and supported by my colleagues, my endeavours were in some instances crowned with success. I feel myself amply rewarded by the approbation of the body over whom you have the honour to preside. There can be nothing more agreeable to a public character, than to receive the public approbation of his conduct, from those who speak the collected and unbiassed sense of his constituents; and it is the only reward a free and virtuous people can bestow, and the only one an honest representative can expect.

"Be pleased to present the corporation my warmest

wishes for their prosperity, and I sincerely hope that the city of Annapolis may be forever distinguished for the harmony and friendship, the benevolence and patriotism of its citizens."

In the year 1788, Mr. Chase was appointed the presiding judge of a court of criminal jurisdiction, for the county and town of Baltimore, at that time organized. This situation, however, did not prevent him from the practice of his profession, in which he continued until the year 1791, when he accepted the appointment of chief justice of the general court of Maryland. In a previous year, Mr. Chase had served in the convention of Maryland, assembled to ratify the federal constitution on the part of Maryland. With this instrument he was not entirely pleased, considering it not sufficiently democratical. He is said to have belonged to the federal party in the country, and so to have continued to the end of his life; but not to have entertained that partiality for England which has been ascribed to that party. With this peculiarity of views and feelings, Mr. Chase was not, as might be expected, without his enemies.

In the year 1794, an event occurred in the city of Baltimore, which gave an opportunity to Judge Chase of exhibiting the firmness of his character, in respect to maintaining the dignity of the bench and the supremacy of the law. The event to which we allude was the tarring and feathering of two men, in the public streets, on an occasion of some popular excitement. The circumstances of the case were investigated by Judge Chase, in the issue of which investigation, he caused two respectable and popular men to be arrested as ring-leaders.

On being arraigned before the court, they refused to give bail. Upon this the judge informed them that they must go to jail. Accordingly, he directed the sheriff to take one of the prisoners to jail. This the sheriff informed the judge he could not do, as he apprehended resistance. "Summon the posse comitatus then," exclaimed the judge. "Sir," said the sheriff, "no one will serve." "Summon me then," said Judge

Chase, in a tone of lofty indignation, "I will be the posse comitatus, and I will take him to jail."

A member of the bar now begged leave to interpose, and requested the judge to waive the commitment. "No, God forbid," replied the judge, "I will do my duty, whatever be the consequences to myself or my family." He now directed the parties to meet him the next day, and to give him the required security. He was told that the next day would be the sabbath "No better day," said Judge Chase, "can be named, on which to execute the laws of the country. I will meet you here, and from this seat of justice I will go to the house of God."

The parties in question, however, neglected to give the required security on the sabbath, on account of which neglect, the judge despatched an express to the governor and council, calling upon them for assistance in the execution of the laws. On Monday the required security was given; but when the grand jury met, instead of finding a bill against the accused, they delivered a presentment against Judge Chase himself, in which they reflected with severity upon his censure of the sheriff, and charged him with having violated the bill of rights, by holding at the same time two incompatible offices, viz. the office of chief justice of the criminal court, and that of the general court of the state. To this presentment Judge Chase replied with becoming moderation, and yet with firmness. In conclusion, he informed the jury that they had touched upon topics beyond their province; he advised them to confine themselves to the line of their duty, assuring them that whatever opinions they might form, or whatever resentments they might indulge, he should ever respect them as the grand inquest of the state of Maryland.

In the year 1796, he was appointed by Washington an associate judge of the supreme court of the United States, a station which he continued to occupy for fifteen years, and in which he generally appeared with great dignity and ability. It was the ill fortune of Judge Chase, however, to have his latter days on the bench embittered by an impeachment by the house of representatives, on which he was tried before the senate of the United States, where he narrowly escaped condemnation. This impeachment was made in 1804, and was recommended by a committee of inquiry, raised, it is said, on the motion of John Randolph, of Virginia, to which he was incited through political animosity. The articles of impeachment originally reported were six in number, to which two others were afterwards added. On these articles Judge Chase was put upon his trial, which began on the second of January, and was finally ended on the fifth of March, 1805.

The articles of impeachment were founded on certain conduct of the judge, on different occasions, at Philadelphia, Richmond, and other places, in which he was said to have transcended his judicial powers. The minute history of this affair, our limits forbid us to detail. It is sufficient to say, that much exertion was made by his political opponents to produce a conviction, but without effect. On five of the charges a majority of the senate acquitted him. On the others, a majority was against him: but as a vote of two thirds is necessary to conviction, he was acquitted of the whole.

This was a severe trial to a man of the independent spirit of Judge Chase. Its disagreeableness was not a little increased by a severe attack of the gout, during the progress of the impeachment. After his acquittal, he continued to exercise his judicial functions, unmolested by his enemies, and with his usual ability.

In the year 1811, his health began to fail him, and though his disease was slow in its progress, he well understood, that it was of a nature to bring him to the grave. His death occurred on the nineteenth of June. In his dying hour, he appeared calm and resigned. He spoke of his domestic affairs with great propriety, and to his weeping family recommended composure and fortitude. He was a firm believer in Christianity, and but a short time before his death, having partaken of the sacrament, he declared himself to be in peace with all mankind. In his will, he directed that no mourning should be worn for him, and requested that only his name, with the dates of his birth and death, should be inscribed on his tomb.

From the foregoing sketch, it is easy to perceive that Judge Chase was no ordinary man. He possessed an intellect of great power, and a courage which was at all times undaunted. It was his unhappiness to have feelings which were too irascible and vehement for his personal comfort, and which betrayed him at times, into a course of conduct, that sober judgment would have pronounced at least impolitic. Yet few men were more sincere, or more firmly patriotic. He ardently loved his friends, and by them, was ardently loved in turn. He loved his country. In the days of her deepest depression, he stood firm to her interests, and will occupy a distinguished place among those who have " graced the rolls of fame."

WILLIAM PACA.

William Paca was born on the 31st of October, 1740. He was the second son of John Paca, a gentleman of large estate, who resided in the county of Harford, in the state of Maryland. His father, sensible of the importance of a good education, placed his son, at a proper age, in the college at Philadelphia, at that time under the care of the learned and eloquent Dr. William Smith. On commencing bachelor of arts, in 1759, he entered the office of Stephen Bradley, a distinguished lawyer of Annapolis, for the purpose of pursuing the profession of law.

Mr. Paca was a diligent student, and early gave promise of eminence in his profession. He was licensed to practice in 1761, and was admitted to the bar at the provincial court in 1764. He established himself at Annapolis, where he had for his competitors, John Price, and Samuel Chase, with the latter of whom he became intimately acquainted, and with whom he acted an important part during the revolutionary struggle.

The political career of Mr. Paca commenced in 1771, at

which time he was appointed to represent the county in the popular branch of the legislature. At this time, and for several years after, much contention existed between the government of Maryland, which was proprietary, and the people. The government consisted of three branches: a house of burgesses, the members of which were selected by the people. The second branch was called the upper house, the members of which were elected and removed, at the pleasure of the proprietor. The governor formed the third branch, without whose assent no act of assembly was valid. And, in addition to this, the proprietor himself, who generally resided in England, claimed the privilege of dissenting from such laws as he pleased, although they had received the sanction of the above branches of the legislature. Hence, there was often no small collision between the lower house, or those who represented the people, and the upper house and governor, who were considered as under the influence of the proprietor.

In this provincial assembly, Mr. Paca represented the people, whose interests he strongly felt, and faithfully guarded. The interests of the proprietor and of the people were often thought to be at variance. An avaricious and oppressive spirit marked the proceedings of the proprietor and his partisans. It was important, therefore, for the people, to have men to represent them in the house of burgesses, who understood their rights, and were sufficiently bold to assert and maintain them. Such a man was Mr. Paca. He was learned as to a knowledge of law, and of the principles of the proprietary government; and at all times, when necessary, sufficiently courageous to resist the aggressions of avarice, and the usurpations of tyranny.

The following anecdote will illustrate the bold and independent spirit of Mr. Paca. In 1771, an act expired in Maryland, the object of which was to regulate the staple of tobacco, and the fees of certain officers. This act the house of burgesses refused to continue, without a reduction of the officers' fees. As neither branch of the assembly would recede from the ground it had taken, the fee bill fell. In this state of things, the governor issued his proclamation directing the officers to proceed according to the old law.

The commotion excited throughout the province was great, and at some places, particularly at Annapolis, even tumultuous. At this latter place, a multitude of citizens collected to express their abhorrence of the conduct of the governor. At the head of this multitude were Mr. Paca and Mr. Chase. A procession was formed, and with these two gentlemen for leaders, they proceeded to a gallows which had been previously erected, upon which they hung the governor's proclamation, in due form, with a halter. At length it was taken down, inclosed in a coffin prepared for the purpose, and consigned to a grave dug beneath the gallows. During the whole ceremony, minute guns were fired from a schooner owned by Mr. Paca, which was stationed at no great distance. In conclusion, the citizens marched back to the city, where they devoted the remainder of the day to festivity.

The controversy to which we have now alluded had long existed, and continued to exist, quite down to the era of the revolutionary struggle. When that struggle commenced, about the year 1774, there were men, therefore, in Maryland, who were well prepared to enter into it, with energy and decision. They had been trained in the school of controversy. They had studied every chapter relating to American rights; and possessing a boldness and a courage commensurate with their knowledge, they were prepared to act a decided part.

Of the illustrious congress of 1774, Mr. Paca was a member, in conjunction with Samuel Chase, and several others. They were instructed by the Maryland convention, from which they received their appointment: "To effect one general plan of conduct, operating on the commercial connexion of the colonies with the mother country, for the relief of Boston, and the preservation of American liberty." As a member of this congress, Mr. Paca so well pleased his constituents, that he was re-appointed to the same station, until the year 1778, at the close of which he retired.

Mr. Paca was an open advocate for a declaration of independence, as were several of his colleagues. For the accomplishment of such an object, they laboured with unwearied zeal. A majority of the people of Maryland, however, were not prepared for such a measure. They still felt a strong affection for the king, and the mother country, towards whom they expressed by their convention, early in the year 1776, many professions of loyalty and regard.

At the same time, they strictly enjoined their representatives in congress, not to consent to any propositions for publishing a declaration of independence, and accompanied these restrictions with a resolution, that Maryland would not be bound by any vote of congress, which should sanction such a measure.

In the life of Mr. Chase, we have related the manner in which a change was effected among the people in relation to this subject, particularly through the instrumentality of Mr. Chase. On the 28th of June, the convention of Maryland recalled their instructions to their delegates, whom they left free to vote in favour of a declaration of independence. In consequence, their vote was given in its favour, shortly after which the convention expressed their approbation of the measure, and in support of it pledged their lives and fortunes and sacred honour.

Early in the year 1778, Mr. Paca was appointed chief justice of the supreme court of his state, an office which he continued to exercise with great ability, until 1780, when he was advanced by congress to the still more important office of chief judge of the court of appeals, in prize and admiralty cases. In this new station, he acquitted himself with great honour. He entered with ability into the subject of international law, and had the happiness to learn that his decisions were highly approved, both at home and abroad.

In 1782, he was elected to the chief magistracy of his native state. Here, again, he was distinguished for great correctness and integrity, for dignity and simplicity. He entered with zeal into the interests of literature and religion, both of which he promoted by his private donat' ... , and his executive patronage. These subjects he officially recommended to the general assembly in the following language. "It is far from our intention," said he, "to embarrass your deliberations with a variety of objects; but we cannot pass over matters of so high concernment as religion and learning. The sufferings of the ministers of the gospel of all denominations, during the war, have been very considerable; and the perseverance and firmness of those, who discharged their sacred functions under many discouraging circumstances, claim our acknowledgments and thanks. The bill of rights and form of government recognize the principle of public support for the ministers of the gospel, and ascertain the mode. Anxiously solicitous for the blessings of government, and the welfare and happiness of our citizens, and thoroughly convinced of the powerful influence of religion, when diffused by its respectable teachers, we beg leave most seriously and warmly to recommend, among the first objects of your attention, on the return of peace. the making such provision as the constitution, in this case, authorizes and approves."

The recommendation of Governor Paca was kindly received by the assembly, which passed several acts in aid of the several denominations of christians, which were at that time numerous in Maryland. The interest which he manifested in favour of religion, met the warm approbation of the various sects; and from the episcopalians, in particular, it elicited, through their convention, a formal expression of thanks.

After holding the office of chief magistrate for one year, Mr. Paca retired to private life, until 1786, when he again accepted the executive chair for a single year.

In 1789, on the organization of the federal government, he received from President Washington the appointment of judge of the district court of the United States for Maryland. This office he held until the year 1799, when he was summoned to another world, in the sixtieth year of his age.

Mr. Paca was twice married. The first time to a daughter of Samuel Chew. in the year 1761, while he was pursuing the study of law. The second time in 1777, to a daughter of a respectable gentleman of Philadelphia, by the name of

Harrison. By the former lady he had five children, one of whom only survives. By the latter he had a son, who died shortly after his mother, whose decease occurred in 1780.

Few men in America, as may be gathered from the preceding sketch, were ever more estimable in their character than Governor Paca. He possessed a mind of superior order, which was greatly improved by his intercourse with mankind, and his extensive acquaintance with books.

In his address he was unusually graceful, and in his social powers was excelled by few. His attention to the young was not the least excellent trait in his character. He sought their company, and took a deep interest in their moral and intellectual improvement. Even after he became governor of the state, he was in the habit of attending a club at Annapolis, composed of young men and gentlemen of science. In this school, many were trained, who afterwards became highly distinguished both as statesmen and lawyers. It was here that that celebrated orator, William Pinkney, first attracted the attention of Judge Chase, an account of whose particularly kind conduct towards him, we have given in the life of that gentleman. We shall only add to this notice of Mr. Paca, that as he lived a life of distinguished usefulness, so he died regretted by all who knew how to estimate moral worth, intellectual elevation, and political integrity.

THOMAS STONE.

THOMAS STONE was the son of David Stone, of Pointon Manor, Charles county, Maryland. His father was a descendant of William Stone, who was governor of Maryland during the protectorate of Oliver Cromwell. The boyhood of Thomas Stone was distinguished by an unusual fondness for learning. At the age of fifteen, having acquired a respectable knowledge of the English language, he obtained the reluctant consent of his father to enter the school of a Mr. Blaizedel, a Scotchman, for the purpose of pursuing the Greek and Latin languages. This school was at the distance of ten miles from his father's residence; yet, such was the zeal of young Stone, that he was in the habit of rising sufficiently early in the morning, to traverse this distance on horseback, and enter the school at the usual time of its commencement.

On leaving the school of Mr. Blaizedel, the subject of our memoir was anxious to prosecute the study of law. But, although his father was a gentleman of fortune, his son was under the necessity of borrowing money to enable him to carry his laudable design into effect. He placed himself under the care of Thomas Johnson, a respectable lawyer of Annapolis. Having finished his preparatory studies, he entered upon the practice of his profession in Fredericktown, Maryland, where having resided two years, he removed to Charles county, in the same state.

During his residence in the former of these places, his business had enabled him to discharge the obligations under which he had laid himself for his education. At the age of twenty-eight, he married the daughter of Dr. Gustavus Brown, with whom he received the sum of one thousand pounds sterling. With this money, he purchased a farm, near the village of Port Tobacco, upon which he continued to reside during the revolutionary struggle.

The business of Mr. Stone, during a considerable part of that period, was not lucrative; and as the soil of the farm upon which he lived was poor, he found it difficult to obtain more than a competent livelihood. The expenses of his family were increased by the charge of four brothers, who were yet of tender years. The situation of many of our fathers, during those trying times, was similar to that of Mr. Stone. They had small patrimonies; business was in a great measure suspended; and, added to this, their time and talents were imperiously demanded by their suffering country. Yet, amidst all these difficulties and trials a pure patriotism continued to burn within their breast, and enabled them more cheerfully to make any and every sacrifice to which they were called by the cause of freedom. Nor should it be forgotten, that in these sacrifices the families of our fathers joyfully participated. They received without a murmur " the spoiling of their goods," being elevated by the reflection, that this was necessary for the achievement of that independence to which they considered themselves and their posterity as entitled.

Although Mr. Stone was a gentleman of acknowledged talents, and of inflexible and incorruptible integrity, it does not appear that he was brought forward into public life until some time in the year 1774. He was not a member of the illustrious congress of that year, but receiving an appointment as a delegate in December, he took his seat in that body in the following May; and, for several years afterwards, was annually re-elected to the same dignified station.

In our biographical sketches of the other gentlemen who belonged about this time to the Maryland delegation, we have had frequent occasion to notice the loyalty and affection which prevailed in that province, for several years, towards the king and the parent country; and hence the reluctance of her citizens to sanction the declaration of independence. When, therefore, towards the close of the year 1775, such a measure began seriously to be discussed in the country, the people of Maryland became alarmed; and, apprehensive lest their delegation in congress, which was composed generally of young men, should be disposed to favour the measure, the convention of that province attempted to restrain them by strict and specific instructions:

" We instruct you," said they, " that you do not, without the previous knowledge and approbation of the convention of this province, assent to any proposition to declare these colonies independent of the crown of Great Britain, nor to any proposition for making or entering into an alliance with any foreign power; nor to any union or confederation of these colonies, which may necessarily lead to a separation from the mother country, unless in your judgments, or in the judgments of any four of you, or a majority of the whole of you, if all shall be then attending in congress, it shall be thought absolutely necessary for the preservation of the liberties of the united colonies; and should a majority of the colonies in congress, against such your judgment, resolve to declare these colonies independent of the crown of Great Britain, or to make or enter into alliance with any foreign power, or into any union or confederation of these colonies, which may necessarily lead to a separation from the mother country, then we instruct you immediately to call the convention of this province, and repair thereto with such proposition and resolve, and lay the same before the said convention for their consideration; and this convention will not hold this province bound by such majority in congress, until the representative body of the province in convention assent thereto."

The cautious policy observable in these instructions, arose, not so much from timidity on the part of the people of Maryland, as from a sincere attachment to the royal government, and an equally sincere affection to the parent country. Soon after, however, the aspect of things in this province began to change. The affections of the people became gradually weaned from Great Britain. It was apparent that a reunion with that country, on constitutional principles, though infinitely desirable, was not to be expected. By the fifteenth of May, 1776, these sentiments had become so strong, that a resolution passed the convention, declaring the authority of the crown at an end, and the necessity that each colony should form a constitution of government for itself.

In the latter part of June, the work of regeneration was accomplished. The people of Maryland generally expressed themselves, in county meetings, decidedly in favour of a declaration of independence. This expression of public sentiment proved irresistible, and the convention proceeded to resolve: "That the instructions given to their deputies be recalled, and the restrictions therein contained, removed; and that the deputies of said colony, or any three or more of them, be authorized and empowered to concur with the other united colonies, or a majority of them, in declaring the united colonies free and independent states; in forming such further compact and confederation between them; in making foreign alliances; and in adopting such other measures as shall be adjudged necessary for securing the liberties of America; and that said colony will hold itself bound by the resolutions of the majority of the united colonies in the premises, provided the sole and exclusive right of regulating the internal government and police of that colony be reserved to the people thereof."

Being thus relieved from the trammels which had before bound them, Mr. Stone and his colleagues joyfully recorded their names in favour of a measure, which was connected with the imperishable glory of their country.

Soon after the declaration of independence, congress appointed a committee to prepare articles of confederation. To act on this committee, Mr. Stone was selected from the Maryland delegation. The duty devolving upon them was exceedingly arduous. Their report of the plan of a confederation was before the house for a long period, and was the subject of debate thirty-nine times. Nor was it at length agreed to, till the fifteenth day of November, 1777. Although the people of Maryland had consented to a declaration of independence, after their first fervour had subsided, their former jealousy returned; and the Maryland convention proceeded to limit the powers of their delegates, as to the formation of the confederation. At the same time, not obscurely hinting in their resolution, that it might be still possible, and certainly desirable, to accommodate the unhappy differences with Great Britain.

The above resolution was expressed in the following terms: "That the delegates, or any *three* or more of them, be authorized and empowered to concur with the other United States, or a majority of them, in forming a confederation, and in making foreign alliances, provided that such confederation, when formed, be not binding upon this state, without the assent of the general assembly; and the said delegates, or any three or more of them, are also authorized and empowered to concur in any measures, which may be resolved on by congress for carrying on the war with Great

Britain, and securing the liberties of the United States; re serving always to this state, the sole and exclusive right of regulating the internal police thereof. And the said delegates, or any three or more of them, are hereby authorized and empowered, notwithstanding any measure heretofore taken, to concur with the congress, or a majority of them, in accommodating our unhappy difference with Great Britain, on such terms as the congress, or a majority of them, shall think proper."

After seeing the confederation finally agreed upon in congress, Mr. Stone declined a re-appointment to that body, but became a member of the Maryland legislature, where he powerfully contributed to meliorate the feelings of many, who were strongly opposed to the above plan of confederation. He had the pleasure, however, with other friends of that measure, to see it at length approved by the general assembly and the people generally.

Under this confederation, in 1783, he was again elected to a seat in congress. In the session of 1784 he acted for some time as president pro tempore. On the breaking up of congress this year, he finally retired from that body, and again engaged actively in the duties of his profession. His practice now became lucrative in Annapolis, whither he had removed his residence; and in professional reputation he rose to great distinction As an advocate, he excelled in strength of argument. He was often employed in cases of great difficulty; and by his brethren of the bar, it was thought eminently desirable, at such times, to have him for their colleague.

In 1787, Mr. Stone was called to experience an affliction which caused a deep and abiding melancholy to settle upon his spirits. This was the death of Mrs. Stone, to whom he was justly and most tenderly attached. During a long state of weakness and decline, induced by injudicious treatment on the occasion of her having the small pox by inoculation, Mr. Stone watched over her with the most unwearied devotion. At length, however, she sank to the grave. From this time, the health of Mr. Stone evidently declined. In the autumn of the same year his physicians advised him to make a sea voyage; and in obedience to that advice, he repaired to Alexandria, to embark for England. Before the vessel was ready to sail, however, he suddenly expired, on the fifth of October, 1787, in the forty-fifth year of his age.

Mr. Stone was a professor of religion, and distinguished for a sincere and fervent piety. To strangers, he had the appearance of austerity; but among his intimate friends, he was affable, cheerful, and familiar. In his disposition he was uncommonly amiable, and well disposed. In person, he was tall, but well proportioned.

Mr. Stone left one son and two daughters. The son died in 1793, while pursuing the study of law. One of the daughters, it is said, still lives, and is respectably married in the state of Virginia.

CHARLES CARROLL.

CHARLES CARROLL was a descendant of Daniel Carroll, an Irish gentleman, who emigrated from England to America about the year 1689. He settled in the province of Maryland, where, a few years after, he received the appointment of judge, and register of the land office, and became agent for Lord Baltimore.

Charles Carroll, the father of the subject of the present sketch, was born in 1702. His son, Charles Carroll, surnamed of Carrollton, was born September 8, 1737, O.S. at Annapolis, in the province of Maryland.

At the age of eight years, he was sent to France for the purpose of obtaining an education. He was placed at a college of English jesuits, at St. Omer's, where he remained for six years. Afterwards he staid some time at Rheims, whence he was removed to the college of Lewis le Grand. On leaving college, he entered upon the study of the civil law, at Bourges: from which place he returned to Paris, where he remained till 1757, in which year he removed to London, and commenced the study of law. He returned to America in 1764, an accomplished scholar, and an accomplished man Although he had lived abroad, and might naturally be supposed to have imbibed a predilection for the monarchical institutions of Europe, he entered with great spirit into the controversy between the colonies and Great Britain, which, about the time of his arrival, was beginning to assume a most serious aspect.

A few years following the repeal of the stamp act, the violent excitement occasioned by that measure, in a degree subsided throughout all the colonies. In this calmer state of things the people of Maryland participated. But about the year 1771, great commotion was excited in that province, in consequence of the arbitrary conduct of Governor Eden and his council, touching the fees of the civil officers of the colonial government These fees, as was noticed in the life of Mr. Paca, had become, in the estimation of the popular branch of the assembly, from the manner in which they were charged, exceedingly exorbitant. To correct the abuses growing out of the indefinite character of the law, a new law was framed; and, after being passed by the lower house, was sent to the upper house for their concurrence. This, however, was refused; and the assembly was prorogued, without coming to any agreement on the subject. Shortly after, Governor Eden issued his proclamation, the ostensible object of which was to prevent oppressions and extortions on the part of the officers, in exacting unreasonable and excessive fees. The proclamation was in reality, however, highly exceptionable in the view of the people, as it affected to settle the point, which was the prerogative only of the people. The fees in question were considered in the light of a tax, the power to lay which the people justly claimed to themselves.

The controversy which grew out of this arbitrary exercise of power on the part of Governor Eden, became exceedingly spirited. It involved the great principles of the revolution. Several writers of distinguished character arrayed themselves on different sides of the question. Among these writers, no one was more conspicuous than Mr. Carroll. The natural consequence of his firmness in defence of the rights of the people was, that great confidence was reposed in him on their part, and he was looked up to as one who was eminently qualified to lead in the great struggle which was approaching between the colonies and the parent country.

From what has been observed respecting Mr. Carroll, it may justly be inferred that his mind was made up at an early day, as to the course duty required him to take in respect to this coming storm. An anecdote is related of him, which will illustrate his influence with the people of Maryland. By a resolution of the delegates of Maryland, on the 22d day of June, 1774, the importation of tea was prohibited. Sometime after, however, a vessel arrived at Annapolis, having a quantity of this article on board. This becoming known, the people assembled in great multitudes, to take effectual measures to prevent its being landed. At length the excitement became so high, that the personal safety of the captain of the vessel became endangered. In this state of things, the friends of the captain made application to Mr. Carroll, to interpose his influence with the people in his behalf. The public indignation was too great to be easily allayed. This Mr. Carroll perceived, and advised the captain and his friends, as the only probable means of safety to himself, to set fire to the vessel, and burn it to the water's edge. This alternative was indeed severe; but, as it was obviously a measure of necessity, the vessel was drawn out, her sails were set, her colours unfurled, in which attitude the fire was applied to her, and, in the presence of an immense concourse of people, she was consumed. This atonement was deemed satisfactory, and the captain was no farther molested.

In the early part of 1776, Mr. Carroll, whose distinguished exertions in Maryland had become extensively known, was appointed by congress, in connexion with Dr. Franklin and Samuel Chase, on a commission to proceed to Canada, to persuade the people of that province to relinquish their allegiance to the crown of England, and unite with the Americans in their struggle for independence.

In the discharge of their duties, the commissioners met with unexpected difficulties. The defeat and death of Montgomery, together with the compulsion which the American troops found it necessary to exercise, in obtaining the means of support in that province, conspired to diminish the ardour of the Canadians in favour of a union with the colonies, and even, at length, to render them hostile to the measure. To conciliate their affections, and to bring to a favourable result the object of their mission, the commissioners employed their utmost ingenuity and influence. They issued their proclamations, in which they assured the people of the disposition of congress to remedy the temporary evils, which the inhabitants suffered in consequence of the presence of the American troops, so soon as it should be in their power to provide specie, and clothing, and provisions. A strong tide, however, was now setting against the American colonies, the strength of which was much increased by the roman catholic priests, who, as a body, had always been opposed to any connexion with the united colonies. Despairing of accomplishing the wishes of congress, the commissioners at length abandoned the object, and returned to Philadelphia.

The great subject of independence was, at this time, undergoing a discussion in the hall of congress. It has been already noticed, that the Maryland delegation, in that body, had been instructed by their convention to refuse their assent to a declaration of independence. On returning to Maryland, Mr. Carroll resumed his seat in the convention, and, with the advocates of a declaration of independence, urged the withdrawal of the above instructions, and the granting of power to their delegates to unite in such a declaration. The friends of the measure had at length the happiness, on the 28th of June, of procuring a new set of instructions, which secured the vote of the important province of Maryland in favour of the independence of America.

On the same day on which the great question was decided in congress, in favour of a declaration of independence, Mr. Carroll was elected a delegate to that body from Maryland,

and accordingly took his seat on the eighteenth of the same month.

Although not a member of congress at the time the question of a declaration of independence was settled, Mr. Carroll had the honour of greatly contributing to a measure so auspicious to the interests of his country, by assisting in procuring the withdrawal of the prohibiting instructions, and the adoption of a new set, by which the Maryland delegates found themselves authorized to vote for independence. He had the honour, also, of affixing his signature to the declaration on the second of August, at which time the members generally signed an engrossed copy, which had been prepared for that purpose. From the printed journals of congress, it would appear, that the declaration was signed on the fourth of July, the same day on which the final question was taken. This is an error. The declaration, as first published, had only the name of Hancock affixed to it; and it was only on the nineteenth of July, that a resolution was adopted, directing the declaration to be engrossed on parchment, with a view to a general signature on the part of the members.

The truth of this statement may be inferred from the following letter, addressed by Mr. Secretary Adams to Mr. Carroll, on the twenty-fourth of June, 1824:

"Sir,

"In pursuance of a joint resolution of the two houses of congress, a copy of which is hereto annexed, and by direction of the president of the United States, I have the honour of transmitting to you two *fac simile* copies of the original declaration of independence, engrossed on parchment, conformably to a secret resolution of congress of nineteenth July, 1776, to be signed by every member of congress, and accordingly signed on the second day of August of the same year. Of this document, unparalleled in the annals of mankind, the original, deposited in this department, exhibits your name as one of the subscribers. The rolls herewith transmitted, are copies as exact as the art of engraving can present, of the instrument itself, as well as of the signers to it.

'While performing the duty thus assigned me, permit me to felicitate you, and the country, which is reaping the reward of your labours, as well that your hand was affixed to this record of glory, as that, after the lapse of near half a century, you survive to receive this tribute of reverence and gratitude, from your children, the present fathers of the land.

"With every sentiment of veneration, I have the honour," &c.

A signature to the declaration, was an important step for every individual member of congress. It exposed the signers of it to the confiscation of their estates, and the loss of life, should the British arms prove victorious. Few men had more at stake in respect to property than Mr. Carroll, he being considered the richest individual in the colonies. But wealth was of secondary value in his estimation, in comparison with the rights and liberties of his country. When asked whether he would annex his name, he replied, "most willingly," and seizing a pen, instantly subscribed " to this record of glory " "There go a few millions," said some one who watched the pen as it traced the name of "Charles Carroll, of Carrollton," on the parchment. Millions would indeed have gone, for his fortune was princely, had not success crowned the American arms, in the long fought contest.

Mr. Carroll was continued a member of congress until 1778, at which time he resigned his seat in that body, and devoted himself more particularly to the interests of his native state. He had served in her convention in 1776, in the latter part of which year he had assisted in drafting her constitution. Soon after, the new constitution went into operation, and Mr. Carroll was chosen a member of the senate of Maryland. In 1781 he was re-elected to the same station, and in 1788, on the adoption of the federal constitution, was chosen to the senate of the United States.

In 1791 Mr. Carroll relinquished his seat in the national senate, and was again called to the senate of his native state. This office he continued to hold until 1804, at which time the democratic party was successful in electing their candidate, to the exclusion of this long tried and faithful patriot. At this time, Mr. Carroll took leave of public life, and sought in retirement the quiet enjoyment of his family circle.

Since the date of his retirement from public office, few incidents have occurred in the life of this worthy man, which demand particular notice. Like a peaceful stream, his days have glided along, and have continued to be lengthened out, while the generation of illustrious men, with whom he acted on the memorable fourth of July, 1776, have all descended to the tomb.

At the age of nearly ninety-two years, he alone survives. " He seems an aged oak, standing alone on the plain, which time has spared a little longer, after all its contemporaries have been levelled with the dust. Sole survivor of an assembly of as great men as the world has witnessed, in a transaction, one of the most important that history records; what thoughts, what reflections, must at times fill his soul! If he dwell on the past, how touching its recollections; if he survey the present, how happy, how joyous, how full of the fruition of hope, which his ardent patriotism indulged, if he glance at the future, how must the prospect of his country's advancement almost bewilder his weakened conceptions. Fortunate, distinguished patriot! Interesting relic of the past!"

To few men has it been permitted to number so many years—to none, to have filled them up more honourably and usefully, than Charles Carroll. Happy in the recollection of the past—conscious of a life well spent, and possessing

<blockquote>
A peace above all earthly dignities—
A still and quiet conscience,
</blockquote>

He may well hope to pass the remaining hours of the evening of his life in tranquillity; and may be assured, that when called to follow his illustrious predecessors to the grave, liberty, and intelligence, and patriotism, and affection, will weep at his departure, while they will rejoice that his honour is placed where no accident can reach it, and no stain can tarnish it.

THE

VIRGINIA DELEGATION.

George Wythe,
Richard Henry Lee,
Thomas Jefferson,
Benjamin Harrison,
Thomas Nelson, Jun.
Francis Lightfoot Lee,
Carter Braxton.

GEORGE WYTHE.

George Wythe was a native of the county of Elizabeth city, Virginia, where he was born in the year 1726. His father was a respectable farmer, in easy circumstances, and bestowed upon his son a competent patrimony. At a proper age he was placed at school; but the knowledge which he here obtained was extremely limited and superficial, being confined to the English language, and the elementary rules of arithmetic. Fortunately for young Wythe, his mother was a woman of extensive knowledge for those times, and undertook to supply the defect of his scholastic education. By her assistance, the powers of his mind, which were originally strong and active, rapidly unfolded. He became accurately versed in the Latin and Greek languages, and made honourable attainments in several of the solid sciences, and in polite literature.

Before he became of age, he had the misfortune to lose his excellent mother, whose death was, not long after, followed by that of his father. Being deprived, at this unguarded period of life, of the counsel and example of these natural guardians, he became devoted, for several years, to amusement and dissipation, to which he was strongly enticed by the fortune that had been left him. During this period, his literary pursuits were almost entirely neglected; and there was the greatest reason to fear he would not escape that vortex into which so many young men remedilessly sink. At the age of thirty, the principles which had been instilled into his mind by his virtuous parents, asserted their proper influence over him. He abandoned his youthful follies, applied himself with indefatigable industry to study, and from this date, during a life which was protracted to the uncommon age of eighty years, he maintained a rigid and inflexible integrity of character.

Devoting himself to the profession of law, he pursued his preparatory studies under the direction of Mr. John Lewis. The courts in Virginia, where he was called to practice, were filled by gentlemen of distinguished ability in their profession. With these he soon held an equal rank, and eventually, by his superior learning, greater industry, and more powerful eloquence, occupied the chief place at the bar.

The estimation in which he was held by his fellow-citizens, was early manifested in an appointment from his native county to a seat in the house of burgesses. This station he held for several years, even to the dawn of the revolution. In this assembly were found, from time to time, men of distinguished genius and of great attainments. Among these, George Wythe was conspicuous. In 1764, he assisted in preparing a petition to the king, a memorial to the house of lords, and a remonstrance to the house of commons, on the subject of the stamp act, which was then occupying the deliberations of parliament. The remonstrance to the house of commons was the production of his pen. The tone and language of this paper were both in spirit and style of too independent a character for the times, especially in the estimation of the more timid in the house of burgesses, who required, before it received their sanction, that its asperities should be softened.

We have had frequent occasion, in the course of these biographical sketches, to allude to the friendly feelings of the Americans, at this time, to the parent country. Few, if any, were to be found whose views or wishes extended to a separation from Great Britain. Hence, the language which was used by the colonies, in setting forth their rights, was generally supplicatory in its style. Their remonstrances were mild and conciliatory. These, however, it was at length found, were in vain, and a loftier tone was adopted.

The passage of the celebrated stamp act, in January, 1765, diffused a spirit of discontent and opposition throughout all the American colonies, and was the signal for the commencement of those stronger measures which led on to the great revolutionary struggle.

In measures of this kind, it is well known that Virginia took the lead. About this time, Patrick Henry, a young man, became a member of the house of burgesses. Although a young man, he was possessed of a most powerful eloquence, and of an intrepidity of character which eminently fitted him to take the lead in the work of opposition.

Towards the close of the session, in May, 1765, Mr. Henry presented to the house the following resolutions:

"Resolved, That the first adventurers and settlers of this, his majesty's colony and dominion, brought with them, and transmitted to their posterity, and all other his majesty's subjects, since inhabiting in this, his majesty's said colony, all the privileges, franchises, and immunities, that have at any time been held, enjoyed, and possessed by the people of Great Britain.

"That by two royal charters granted by King James the First, the colonists aforesaid are declared entitled to all the privileges and immunities of denizens and natural born subjects, to all intents and purposes, as if they had been abiding and born within the realm of England.

"That the taxation of the people by themselves, or by persons chosen by themselves to represent them, who can only know what taxes the people are able to bear, and the easiest mode of raising them, is the distinguishing characteristic of British freedom, and without which the ancient constitution cannot subsist.

"That his majesty's liege people of this most ancient colony have, uninterruptedly, enjoyed the right of being thus governed by their own assembly in the article of their taxes and internal police; and that the same hath never been forfeited, or any other way given up, but hath been constantly recognized by the king and people of Great Britain.

"Resolved, therefore, that the general assembly of this colony have the sole right and power to lay taxes and impositions upon the inhabitants of this colony: and that any attempt to vest such power in any person or persons whatsoever, other than the general assembly aforesaid, has a manifest tendency to destroy British as well as American freedom."

The language of these resolutions, so much stronger than the house had been accustomed to hear, at once caused no inconsiderable alarm among many of its members. A powerful opposition arose to their passage, and in this opposition were to be found some of the warmest friends of American independence. Among these was Mr. Wythe; not that he, and many others, did not admit the justice of the sentiments contained in the resolutions; but they remonstrated on the ground of their tending to involve the colony, at a time when it was unprepared, in open hostility with Great Britain. The eloquence of Henry, however, silenced, if it did not convince the opposition, and produced the adoption of the resolutions without any material alteration. As the fifth resolution was carried by a majority of only a single vote, the house, on the following day, in the absence of Henry, rescinded that resolution, and directed it to be erased from the journals.

The above resolutions spread rapidly through the American colonies, and in every quarter of the country found men, who were ready to justify both their spirit and language. They served to rouse the energies of the American people, and were among the measures which powerfully urged on the revolutionary contest. The bold and decided measure thus adopted in the colony of Virginia, loudly called upon the patriots of other states to follow her in measures of a similar character. This they were not backward in doing. After the temporary revival of the affection of the colonies, consequent upon the repeal of the stamp act, had ceased, their opposition became a principle, and in its operation was strong and lasting. In the history of the opposition of America to Great Britain, the colony of Virginia did themselves immortal honour. In this honour, as an individual, Mr. Wythe largely participates. For many years, during the approach of the great conflict, he held a seat in the house of burgesses; and by his learning, his boldness, his patriotic firmness, powerfully contributed to the ultimate liberty and independence of his country.

In 1775, he was appointed a delegate from his native state to the continental congress in Philadelphia; and in the following year, assisted in bringing forward and publishing to the world the immortal declaration of independence. During this latter year, Mr. Wythe was appointed, in connexion with Thomas Jefferson, Edward Pendleton, and several others, to revise the laws of the state of Virginia, and to accommodate them to the great change which had been effected in her transition from a colony to an independent state. In this important work, only the three gentlemen mentioned were actually engaged. The original commission included also the names of George Mason and Thomas Ludwell Lee; the former of whom deceased before the committee entered upon the duties assigned them: and the latter tendered his resignation, leaving the arduous task to be accomplished by the gentlemen already named.

"The report of this committee was at length made, and showed such an intimate knowledge of the great principles of legislation, as reflected the highest honour upon those who formed it. The people of Virginia are indebted to it for the best parts of their present code of laws. Among the changes then made in the monarchical system of jurisprudence, which had been previously in force, the most important were effected by the act abolishing the right of primogeniture, and directing the real estate of persons dying intestate, to be equally divided among their children, or other nearest relations; by the act for regulating conveyances, which converted all estates in tail into fees simple, thus destroying one of the supports of the proud and overbearing distinctions of particular families; and finally by the act for the establishment of religious freedom. Had all the proposed bills been adopted by the legislature, other changes of great importance would have taken place. A wise and universal system of education would have been established, giving to the children of the poorest citizen the opportunity of attaining science, and thus of rising to honour and extensive usefulness. The proportion between crimes and punishments would have been better adjusted, and malefactors would have been made to promote the interests of the commonwealth by their labour. But the public spirit of the assembly could not keep pace with the liberal views of Wythe."

In the year 1777, Mr. Wythe was elected speaker of the house of delegates, and during the same year was appointed judge of the high court of chancery of Virginia. On the new organization of the court of equity, in a subsequent year, he was appointed sole chancellor, a station which he filled, with great ability, for more than twenty years.

During the revolution, Mr. Wythe suffered greatly in respect to his property. His devotion to public services left him little opportunity to attend to his private affairs. The greater part of his slaves he lost by the dishonesty of his superintendant, who placed them in the hands of the British. By economy and judicious management, however, Mr. Wythe was enabled, with the residue of his estate, and with his salary as chancellor, to discharge his debts, and to preserve his independence.

Of the convention of 1787, appointed to revise the federal constitution, Mr. Wythe was a delegate from Virginia, having for his colleagues Washington, Henry, Randolph, Blair, Madison, and Mason. "During the debates, he acted for the most part as chairman. Being convinced that the confede-

3 B

ration was defective in the energy necessary to preserve the union and liberty of America, this venerable patriot, then beginning to bow under the weight of years, rose in the convention, and exerted his voice, almost too feeble to be heard, in contending for a system, on the acceptance of which he conceived the happiness of his country to depend. He was ever attached to the constitution, on account of the principles of freedom and justice which it contained; and in every change of affairs he was steady in supporting the rights of man. His political opinions were always firmly republican. Though in 1798 and 1799, he was opposed to the measures which were adopted in the administration of President Adams, and reprobated the alien and sedition laws, and the raising of the army, yet he never yielded a moment to the rancour of party spirit, nor permitted the difference of opinion to interfere with his private friendships. He presided twice successively in the college of electors in Virginia, and twice voted for a president whose political principles coincided with his own.

"After a short, but very excruciating sickness, he died, June 8, 1806, in the eighty-first year of his age. It was supposed that he was poisoned; but the person suspected was acquitted by a jury of his countrymen. By his last will and testament, he bequeathed his valuable library and philosophical apparatus to his friend, Mr. Jefferson, and distributed the remainder of his little property among the grandchildren of his sister, and the slaves whom he had set free. He thus wished to liberate the blacks, not only from slavery, but from the temptations to vice. He even condescended to impart to them instruction; and he personally taught the Greek language to a little negro boy, who died a few days before his preceptor.

"Chancellor Wythe was indeed an extraordinary man. With all his great qualities, he possessed a soul replete with benevolence, and his private life is full of anecdotes, which prove, that it is seldom that a kinder and warmer heart throbbed in the breast of a human being. He was of a social and affectionate disposition. From the time when he was emanci pated from the follies of youth, he sustained an unspotted reputation. His integrity was never even suspected.

"While he practised at the bar, when offers of an extraordinary, but well merited compensation, were made to him by clients, whose causes he had gained, he would say, that the labourer was indeed worthy of his hire; but the lawful fee was all he had a right to demand; and as to presents, he did not want, and would not accept them from any man. This grandeur of mind, he uniformly preserved to the end of his life. His manner of living was plain and abstemious. He found the means of suppressing the desires of wealth by limiting the number of his wants. An ardent desire to promote the happiness of his fellow men, by supporting the cause of justice, and maintaining and establishing their rights, appears to have been his ruling passion.

"As a judge, he was remarkable for his rigid impartiality, and sincere attachment to the principles of equity; for his vast and various learning, and for his strict and unwearied attention to business. Superior to popular prejudices, and every corrupting influence, nothing could induce him to swerve from truth and right. In his decisions, he seemed to be a pure intelligence, untouched by human passions, and settling the disputes of men, according to the dictates of eternal and immutable justice. Other judges have surpassed him in genius, and a certain facility in despatching causes; but while the vigour of his faculties remained unimpaired, he was seldom surpassed in learning, industry, and judgment.

"From a man, entrusted with such high concerns, and whose time was occupied by so many difficult and perplexing avocations, it could scarcely have been expected, that he should have employed a part of it in the toilsome and generally unpleasant task of the education of youth. Yet, even to this, he was prompted by his genuine patriotism and philanthropy, which induced him for many years to take great delight in educating such young persons as showed an inclination for improvement. Harassed as he was with business, and enveloped with papers belonging to intricate suits in chancery, he yet found time to keep a private school for the instruction of a few scholars, always with very little compensation, and often demanding none. Several living ornaments of their country received their greatest lights from his sublime example and instruction. Such was the upright and venerable Wythe."

RICHARD HENRY LEE.

RICHARD HENRY LEE, a descendant from an ancient and distinguished family in Virginia, was born in Westmoreland county, of that province, on the twentieth of January, 1732. As the schools of the country for many years furnished but few advantages for an education, those who were able to meet the expense, were accustomed to send their sons abroad for instruction. At a proper age, young Lee was sent to a flourishing school, then existing at Wakesfield, in the county of Yorkshire, England. The talents which he possessed, industriously employed under the guidance of respectable tutors, rendered his literary acquisitions easy and rapid; and in a few years he returned to his native country, with a mind well stored with scientific and classical knowledge.

For several years following his return to America, he continued his studies with persevering industry, greatly adding to the stock of knowledge which he had gained abroad, by which he was still more eminently fitted for the conspicuous part he was destined to act in the approaching revolutionary struggle of his country.

About the year 1757, Mr. Lee was called to a seat in the house of burgesses. For several years, however, he made but an indifferent figure, either as an orator or the leader of a party, owing, it is said, to a natural diffidence, which prevented him from displaying those powers with which he was gifted, or exercising that influence to which he was entitled. This impediment, however, was gradually removed, when he rapidly rose into notice, and became conspicuous as a poli

Richard Henry Lee

tical leader in his country, and highly distinguished for a natural, easy, and at the same time impressive eloquence.

In the year 1765, Patrick Henry, proposed the celebrated resolutions against the stamp act, noticed in the preceding sketch of the life of Mr. Wythe. During the debate on these resolutions, Mr. Lee arrived at the seat of government, soon after which he entered with great spirit into the debate, and powerfully assisted in carrying these resolutions through the house, in opposition to the timidity of some, and the mistaken judgment of others.

The above strong and spirited resolutions served, as has already been noticed in a former page, to rouse the energies of the Americans, and to concentrate that feeling, which was spending itself without obtaining any important object. Not long after the above resolutions were carried, Mr. Lee presented to his fellow citizens the plan of an association, the object of which was an effectual resistance to the arbitrary power of the mother country, which was manifesting itself in various odious forms; and especially in that detestable measure, the stamp act. The third article of the constitution of this association will show the patriotic and determined spirit which prevailed in the county of Westmoreland, the people of which generally united in the association. "As the stamp act does absolutely direct the property of people to be taken from them, without their consent, expressed by their representatives, and as in many cases it deprives the British American subject of his right to be tried by jury, we do determine, at every hazard, and paying no regard to death, to exert every faculty to prevent the execution of the stamp act, in every instance, within the colony."

The influence of this association, and of other associations of a similar kind, rendered the execution of the stamp act difficult, and even impossible. It was a measure to which the Americans would not submit; and the ministry of Great Britain were reluctantly forced to repeal it. To Mr. Lee, as well as to his countrymen, the removal of the stamp act was an occasion of no small joy; but the clause accompanying the repealing act which declared *the power of parliament to bind the colonies in all cases whatever,* was a dark cloud, which in a measure obscured the brightness of the prospect, and foreboded an approaching storm.

In the year 1773, Mr. Lee brought forward in the Virginia house of burgesses his celebrated plan for the formation of a committee of correspondence, whose object was to disseminate information, and to kindle the flame of liberty, throughout the continent; or, in other language, "to watch the conduct of the British parliament, to spread more widely correct information on topics connected with the interests of the colonies, and to form a closer union of the men of influence in each." The honour of having first established corresponding societies is claimed both by Massachusetts and Virginia; the former placing the merit to the account of her distinguished patriot, Samuel Adams; and the latter assigning it to Richard Henry Lee. It is probable, however, that each of these distinguished men are entitled to equal honour, in respect to originating a plan which contributed, more than most others, to a unity of sentiment and harmony of action among the different leaders in the respective colonies. Without concert between them, each of these individuals seems to have introduced the plan, about the same period, to the legislatures of their respective colonies. It is certain, however, that in respect to Mr. Lee, the plan of these corresponding societies was not the result of a few days reflection only. It had occupied his thoughts for several years; had been there forming and maturing, and, at length, was proposed and adopted, to the infinite advantage of the cause of liberty in the country.

Of the distinguished congress which met at Philadelphia in 1774, Mr. Lee was a delegate from Virginia, with Washington nd Henry. In the deliberations of this celebrated body, . Lee acted a conspicuous part, and served on several comittees; and to his pen is attributed the memorial, which the continental congress authorized, to the people of British America. In the following year, Mr. Lee received the unanimous suffrage of the district in which he resided to the assembly of Virginia, by which he was deputed to represent the colony in the second congress, which was to meet on the tenth of

May of that year. At the same time, he received an expression of the thanks of the assembly, "for his cheerful undertaking, and faithful discharge of the trust reposed in him, during the session of the last congress."

On the meeting of this second congress, it was apparent that all hope of peace and reconciliation with the mother country was at an end. Indeed, hostilities had actually commenced; the busy note of preparation was heard in all the land. Washington was summoned by the unanimous voice of congress to the command of the American armies; and his commission and instructions it fell to Mr. Lee to furnish, as the chairman of a committee appointed for that purpose. During the same session, also, he was placed on committees which were appointed to the important duties of preparing munitions of war, encouraging the manufacture of saltpetre and arms, and for devising a plan for the more rapid communication of intelligence throughout the colonies.

The period had now arrived, when the thoughts of the American people were turned, in solemn earnest, to the great subject of American independence. Most of the colonies were already prepared to hail with joy a measure which should declare to the world their determination to be accounted a free and independent people. Most of the provincial assemblies had published resolutions in favour of such a declaration, and had even instructed their delegates to urge upon congress the importance and necessity of this decisive step.

Mr. Lee was selected to move the resolution in congress on this great subject. This he did on the seventh of June, 1776, in the following words: "That these united colonies are, and of right ought to be, free and independent states; that they are absolved from all allegiance to the British crown; and that all political connexion between them and the state of Great Britain is, and ought to be, totally dissolved."

The motion, thus introduced by Mr. Lee, he followed by one of the most luminous and eloquent speeches ever delivered, either by himself or any other gentleman, on the floor of congress. "Why then, sir," (said he, in conclusion,) "why do we longer delay? Why still deliberate? Let this happy day give birth to an American republic. Let her arise, not to devastate and to conquer, but to re-establish the reign of peace and of law. The eyes of Europe are fixed upon us, she demands of us a living example of freedom, that may exhibit a contrast in the felicity of the citizen to the ever increasing tyranny which desolates her polluted shores. She invites us to prepare an asylum, where the unhappy may find solace, and the persecuted repose! She entreats us to cultivate a propitious soil, where that generous plant which first sprung and grew in England, but is now withered by the poisonous blasts of Scottish tyranny, may revive and flourish, sheltering under its salubrious and interminable shade, all the unfortunate of the human race. If we are not this day wanting in our duty, the names of the American legislators of 1776 will be placed by posterity at the side of Theseus, Lycurgus, and Romulus, of the three Williams of Nassau, and of all those whose memory has been, and ever will be, dear to virtuous men and good citizens."

The debate on the above motion of Mr. Lee was protracted until the tenth of June, on which day congress resolved: " that the consideration of the resolution respecting independence be postponed till the first Monday in July next; and, in the mean while, that no time be lost, in case the congress agree thereto, that a committee be appointed to prepare a declaration to the effect of the said resolution."

On the day on which this resolution was taken, Mr. Lee was unexpectedly summoned to attend upon his family in Virginia, some of the members of which were at that time dangerously ill. As the mover of the original resolution for independence, it would, according to parliamentary usage, have devolved upon Mr. Lee to have been appointed chairman of the committee selected to prepare a declaration, and, as chairman, to have furnished that important document. In the absence of Mr. Lee, however, Mr. Jefferson was elected to that honour, by whom it was drawn up with singular energy of style and argument.

In the following month, Mr. Lee resumed his seat in congress, in which body he continued till June, 1777, during which period he continued the same round of active exertions for the welfare of his country. It was his fortune, however, as well as the fortune of others, to have enemies, who charged him with disaffection to his country, and attachment to Great Britain. The ground upon which this charge was made, was, that contrary to his former practice, previously to the war, he received the rents of his tenants in the produce of their farms, instead of colonial money, which had now become greatly depreciated. This accusation, though altogether unjust, and unwarrantable, at length gained so much credit, that the name of Mr. Lee was omitted by the assembly, in their list of delegates to congress. This gave him an opportunity, and furnished him with a motive, to demand of the assembly an inquiry into the nature of the allegations against him. The inquiry resulted in an entire acquittal, and in an expression of thanks to Mr. Lee, which was conveyed, on the part of the house, by their speaker, Mr. Wythe, in the following language:—" It is with peculiar pleasure, sir, that I obey this command of the house, because it gives me an opportunity, while I am performing an act of duty to them, to perform an act of justice to yourself. Serving with you in congress, and attentively observing your conduct there, I thought that you manifested, in the American cause, a zeal truly patriotic; and as far as I could judge, exerted the abilities for which you are confessedly distinguished, to promote the good and prosperity of your own country in particular, and of the United States in general. That the tribute of praise deserved, may reward those who do well, and encourage others to follow your example, the house have come to this resolution: that the thanks of this house be given by the speaker to Richard Henry Lee, for the faithful services he has rendered his country, in discharge of his duty, as one of the delegates from this state in general congress."

At a subsequent period, Mr. Lee was again elected a delegate to congress; but during the session of 1778 and 1779, in consequence of ill health, he was obliged frequently to absent himself from the arduous duties which devolved upon him, and which he could no longer sustain. From this time, until 1784, Mr. Lee declined accepting a seat in congress, from a belief that he might be more useful to his native state, by holding a seat in her assembly. In this latter year, however, the people of Virginia again honoured him, by appointing him one of her representatives to congress, of which body he was unanimously elected president. In this exalted station he presided with great ability; and on the expiration of his time of service, he received the thanks of congress for his able and faithful discharge of the duties of president, while acting in that station."

To the adoption of the federal constitution without amendment, although not a member of the convention which discussed its merits, he was strongly opposed. The tendency of the constitution, he apprehended, was to consolidation. To guard against this, it was his wish that the respective states should impart to the federal head only so much power as was necessary for mutual safety and happiness. Under the new constitution, Mr. Lee was appointed the first senator from Virginia; in the exercise of which office, he offered several amendments to the constitution, from the adoption of which he hoped to lessen the danger to the country, which he had apprehended.

About the year 1792, Mr. Lee, enfeebled by his long attention to public duties, and by the infirmities of age, retired to the enjoyment of his family and friends. Not long after, he had the pleasure of receiving from the senate and house of delegates of Virginia, the following unanimous vote of thanks: "Resolved, unanimously, that the speaker be desired to convey to Richard Henry Lee, the respects of the senate; that they sincerely sympathise with him in those infirmities, which have deprived their country of his valuable services, and that they ardently wish he may, in his retirement, with uninterrupted happiness, close the evening of a life, in which he hath so conspicuously shone forth as a statesman and a patriot, that while mindful of his many exertions to promote the public interests, they are particularly thankful for his conduct as a member of the legislature of the United States."

The life of Mr. Lee was continued until the nineteenth of June, 1794, when he breathed his last, at the age of sixty-three years.

Few men, in any age or in any country, have shone with greater brilliancy, or have left a more desirable name, than Richard Henry Lee. Both in public and private life, he had few equals. In his public career, he was distinguished for no common ardour and disinterestedness. As an orator, he exercised an uncommon sway over the minds of men. His manners were perfectly graceful, and his language universally chaste. "Although somewhat monotonous, his speeches," says a writer, " were always pleasing, yet he did not ravish your senses, nor carry away your judgment by storm. His was the mediate class of eloquence, described by Rollin in his belles lettres. He was like a beautiful river, meandering through a flowery mead, but which never overflowed its banks. It was Henry who was the mountain torrent, that swept away every thing before it; it was he alone, who thundered and lightened; he alone attained that sublime species of eloquence, also mentioned by Rollin."

In private life, Mr. Lee was justly the delight of all who knew him. He had a numerous family of children, the offspring of two marriages, who were eminently devoted to their father, who in his turn delighted to administer to their innocent enjoyments, and to witness the expansion of their intellectual powers.

We conclude this hasty sketch, with the following account of Mr. Lee, from the flowing pen of the author of the life of Patrick Henry.—" Mr. Lee," says he, " had studied the classics in the true spirit of criticism. His taste had that delicate touch, which seized with intuitive certainty every beauty of an author, and his genius that native affinity, which combined them without an effort. Into every walk of literature and science, he had carried his mind of exquisite selection, and brought it back to the business of life, crowned with every light of learning, and decked with every wreath that all the muses and all the graces could entwine. Nor did these light decorations constitute the whole value of its freight. He possessed a rich store of political knowledge, with an activity of observation, and a certainty of judgment, which turned that knowledge to the very best account. He was not a lawyer by profession, but he understood thoroughly the constitution both of the mother country and of her colonies, and the elements, also, of the civil and municipal law. Thus, while his eloquence was free from those stiff and technical restraints, which the habit of forensic speaking are so apt to generate, he had all the legal learning which is necessary to a statesman. He reasoned well, and declaimed freely and splendidly. The note of his voice was deep and melodious. It was the canorous voice of Cicero. He had lost the use of one of his hands, which he kept constantly covered with a black silk bandage, neatly fitted to the palm of his hand, but leaving his thumb free; yet, notwithstanding this disadvantage, his gesture was so graceful and highly finished, that it was said he had acquired it by practising before a mirror. Such was his promptitude, that he required no preparation for debate. He was ready for any subject, as soon as it was announced, and his speech was so copious, so rich, so mellifluous, set off with such bewitching cadence of voice, and such captivating grace of action, that while you listened to him, you desired to hear nothing superior; and, indeed, thought him perfect. He had quick sensibility and a fervid imagination."

THOMAS JEFFERSON.

THOMAS JEFFERSON was born on the second day of April, O. S. 1743, at a place called Shadwell, in the county of Albermarle, and state of Virginia, a short distance from Monticello. His family were among the earliest emigrants from England. They sustained an honourable standing in the territory in which they resided, and lived in circumstances of

Th: Jefferson

considerable affluence. His father, Peter Jefferson, was much known in the province, as a gentleman of considerable scientific attainments, and more than ordinary firmness and integrity. It was probably in consequence of these qualifications, that he was selected as one of the commissioners appointed to the delicate and responsible task of determining the division line between Virginia and North Carolina. On the decease of the father, the son inherited from him an extensive and valuable estate.

Of the early incidents in the life of Thomas Jefferson, but little is known. He was entered, while yet a youth, a student in the college of William and Mary, in Williamsburg; but the precise standing which he occupied among his literary associates, is probably now lost. He doubtless, however, left the college with no inconsiderable reputation. He appears to have been imbued with an early love of letters and science, and to have cherished a strong disposition to the physical sciences especially; and to ancient classical literature, he is understood to have had a warm attachment, and never to have lost sight of them, in the midst of the busiest occupations.

On leaving college, he applied himself to the study of the law under the tuition of George Wythe, of whose high judicial character we have had occasion to speak in a preceding memoir. In the office of this distinguished man, he acquired that unrivalled neatness, system, and method in business, which through all his future life, and in every office that he filled, gave him so much power and despatch. Under the direction of his distinguished preceptor, he became intimately acquainted with the whole round of the civil and common law. From the same distinguished example he caught that untiring spirit of investigation, which never left a subject till he had searched it to the very foundation. In short, Mr. Wythe performed for him, as one of his eulogists remarks, what Jeremiah Gridley did for his great rival, Mr. Adams; he placed on his head the crown of legal preparation, and well did it become him.

For his able legal preceptor, Mr. Jefferson always entertained the greatest respect and friendship. Indeed, the attachment of preceptor and pupil was mutual, and for a long series of years continued to acquire strength and stability. At the close of his life, in 1806, it was found that Mr. Wythe had bequeathed his library and philosophical apparatus to his pupil, as a testimony of the estimation in which he was held by his early preceptor and aged friend

Mr. Jefferson was called to the bar in the year 1766. With the advantages which he had enjoyed with respect to legal preparation, it might naturally be expected that he would appear with distinguished credit in the practice of his profession. The standing which he occupied at the bar, may be gathered from the following account, the production of the biographer of Patrick Henry. " It has been thought that Mr. Jefferson made no figure at the bar; but the case was far otherwise. There are still extant, in his own fair and neat hand, in the manner of his master, a number of arguments, which were delivered by him at the bar, upon some of the most intricate questions of the law; which, if they shall ever see the light, will vindicate his claim to the first honours of the profession. It is true, he was not distinguished in popular debate; why he was not so, has often been matter of surprise to those who have seen his eloquence on paper, and heard it in conversation. He had all the attributes of the mind, and the heart, and the soul, which are essential to eloquence of the highest order. The only defect was a physical one. he wanted volume and compass of voice, for a large deliberative assembly; and his voice, from the excess of his sensibility, instead of rising with his feelings and conceptions, sunk under their pressure, and became guttural and inarticulate. The consciousness of this infirmity, repressed any attempt in a large body, in which he knew he must fail. But his voice was all sufficient for the purposes of judicial debate; and there is no reason to doubt that, if the service of his country had not called him away so soon from his profession, his fame as a lawyer would now have stood upon the same distinguished ground, which he confessedly occupied as a statesman, an author, and a

The year previous to Mr. Jefferson's admission to the bar, Mr. Henry introduced into the Virginia house of burgesses, then sitting at Williamsburg, his celebrated resolutions against the stamp act. Mr. Jefferson was, at this time, present at the debate. "He was then," he says, "but a student, and stood in the door of communication, between the house and the lobby, where he heard the whole of this magnificent debate. The opposition to the last resolution was most vehement; the debate upon it, to use his own strong language, 'most bloody;' but," he adds, "torrents of sublime eloquence from Henry, backed by the solid reasoning of Johnson, prevailed; and the resolution was carried by a single vote. I well remember," he continues, "the cry of 'treason,' by the speaker, echoed from every part of the house, against Mr. Henry: I well remember his pause, and the admirable address with which he recovered himself, and baffled the charge thus vociferated."

He here alludes to that memorable exclamation of Mr. Henry, now become almost too familiar for quotation: "Cæsar had his Brutus, Charles the First his Cromwell, and George the Third ('treason!' cried the speaker; 'treason! treason!' echoed the house;) may profit by their example. If this be treason, make the most of it."

The talents of Mr. Jefferson, which were early well known, permitted him not long to remain in a private station, or to pursue the ordinary routine of his profession. A career of more extensive usefulness, and objects of greater importance, were now presented to him. His country demanded his services; and at the early age of twenty-five, that is, in the year 1769, he entered the house of burgesses in Virginia, and then first inscribed his name as a champion of his country's rights.

At a former period, the attachment of the American colonies to England was like that of an affectionate child towards a venerable parent. In Virginia, this attachment was unusually strong. Various circumstances combined to render it so. Many of the families of that province were allied to distinguished families in England, and the sons of the former sought their education in the universities of the mother country. It was not singular, therefore, that a strong affection should exist, on the part of this colony, for the people in England, nor that the people of the colonies generally should have come to the severance of these ties with peculiar reluctance. Resistance, however, was at length forced upon them, by the rash course pursued by the British ministry. The rights of the colonies were invaded, their choicest privileges were taken away, and loudly were the patriots of America called upon, by the sufferings of the country, to awake to a strong and effectual resistance. At this time, Mr. Jefferson commenced his political career, and has himself given us, in few words, an outline of the reasons which powerfully impelled him to enter the lists, with other American patriots, against the parent country.

" The colonies," says he, " were taxed internally and externally; their essential interests sacrificed to individuals in Great Britain, their legislatures suspended; charters annulled; trials by jurors taken away; their persons subjected to transportation across the Atlantic, and to trial by foreign judicatories; their supplications for redress thought beneath answer, themselves published as cowards in the councils of their mother country, and courts of Europe; armed troops sent amongst them, to enforce submission to these violences; and actual hostilities commenced against them. No alternative was presented, but resistance or unconditional submission. Between these there could be no hesitation. They closed in the appeal to arms."

In the year 1773, Mr. Jefferson became a member of the first committee of correspondence, established by the provincial assemblies. We have already noticed the claim which Virginia and Massachusetts have respectively urged, to the honour of having first suggested this important measure in the revolution. Both, probably, in respect to this, are entitled to equal credit; but to whomsoever the honour belongs, that honour is, indeed, great, since this measure, more than any other, contributed to that union of action and sentiment, which characterized the proceedings of the several colonies, and which was the foundation of their final triumph over an ancient and powerful kingdom.

In 1774, Mr. Jefferson published a "Summary View of the Rights of British America," a valuable production among those intended to show the dangers which threatened the liberties of the country, and to encourage the people in their defence. This pamphlet was addressed to the king, whom, in language respectful but bold, it reminded that America was settled by British freemen, whose rights had been violated; upon whom the hand of tyranny was thus heavily lying, and from the sufferings which they were experiencing, they must be, and they would be, free.

The bold and independent language of this pamphlet gave great umbrage to Lord Dunmore, the royal governor of the province. Mr. Jefferson, on avowing himself the author of the pamphlet, was threatened with a prosecution for high treason by the governor; a threat, which he probably would have carried into effect, could he have hoped that the vindictive measure would succeed.

In the following year, 1775, Mr. Jefferson was selected by the Virginia legislature to answer Lord North's famous "Conciliatory proposition," called, in the language of the day, his "Olive branch;" but it was an olive branch that concealed a serpent; or, as the former President Adams observed, "it was an asp, in a basket of flowers." The task assigned him, was performed by Mr. Jefferson in a manner the most happy and satisfactory. The reply was cool and calm and close—marked with uncommon energy and keen sagacity. The document may be found in most of the histories of that period, and is manifestly one of the most nervous and manly productions of that day. It concluded with the following strong and independent language:

"These, my lord, are our sentiments, on this important subject, which we offer only as an individual part of the whole empire. Final determination we leave to the general congress, now sitting, before whom we shall lay the papers your lordship has communicated to us. For ourselves, we have exh... ... every mode of application, which our inven tion could suggest, as proper and promising. We have decently remonstrated with parliament—they have added new injuries to the old ; we have wearied our king with supplications—he has not deigned to answer us ; we have appealed to the native honour and justice of the British nation—their efforts in our favour have hitherto been ineffectual. What then remains to be done? That we commit our injuries to the even handed justice of that Being, who doth no wrong, earnestly beseeching Him to illuminate the councils, and prosper the endeavours of those to whom America hath confided her hopes ; that through their wise directions, we may again see reunited the blessings of liberty, prosperity, and harmony with Great Britain."

In the month of June, 1775, Mr. Jefferson appeared and took his seat in the continental congress, as a delegate from Virginia. In this enlightened assembly, he soon became conspicuous among the most distinguished for their abilities and patriotism. He was appointed on various important committees, towards the discharge of whose duties he contributed his full share. The cause of liberty lay near his heart, nor did he hesitate to incur all necessary hazard in maintaining and defending it.

Antecedently to the year 1776, a dissolution of the union with Great Britain had not been contemplated, either by congress, or the nation. During the spring of that year, however, the question of independence became one of deep and solemn reflection, among the American people. It was perceived by many in all parts of the land, that the hope of reconciliation with the parent country was at an end. It was, indeed, an unequal contest, in which the colonies were engaged. It was a measure of unexampled boldness, which they were contemplating—a step which, should it not receive the smiles of a propitious Providence, would evidently involve them and their posterity in calamities, the full measure and duration of which no political prophet could foretel. But, then, it was a measure rendered necessary, by the oppression which they were suffering. The "shadows, clouds, and darkness," which rested on the future, did not deter them.

The language which they adopted, and the feelings which they indulged, were the language and feelings of the patriotic Hawley, who said, "We must put to sea—Providence will bring us into port."

It was fortunate for the cause of America, and for the cause of freedom, that there was a class of men at that day, who were adequate to the high and mighty enterprise of sundering the ties which bound the colonies. For this they were doubtless specially raised up by the God of heaven; for this they were prepared by the lofty energies of their minds, and by that boldness and intrepidity of character, which, perhaps, never so signally marked another generation of men.

The measure thus determined upon was, at length, brought forward in the continental congress. We have already noticed in several preceding sketches, the debate on this subject, and the important part which various individuals took in urging it forward. It belongs to this place to notice, particularly, the important services which Mr. Jefferson rendered in relation to it. A resolution had been presented by Richard Henry Lee to declare America free and independent. The debate upon this resolution was continued from the seventh to the tenth of June, when the further consideration of it was postponed until the first of July, and at the same time a committee of five was appointed to prepare provisionally a draught of a declaration of independence. At the head of this committee was placed Thomas Jefferson. He was at this time but thirty-two years of age, and was probably the youngest member of the committee, and one of the youngest men in the house, for he had only served part of the former session.

Mr. Jefferson being chairman of this committee, the important duty of preparing the draught of the document was assigned to him. It was a task of no ordinary magnitude, and demanded the exercise of no common judgment and foresight. By the act itself, a nation was to stand or fall. Nay, in its effects, it was to exercise a powerful influence upon other nations on the globe, and might extend forward to the end of time.

To frame a document, which should precisely meet the exigencies of the case—which should set forth the causes of complaint, according to truth—which should abide the scrutiny of enemies at home and abroad—which should stand the test of time, especially of a day which would come, when the high wrought excitement, then existing, would have subsided—*this* was no ordinary task. Indeed, there were few minds, even at that day, which would have felt adequate to the undertaking.

From his study, Mr. Jefferson at length presented to his colleagues the original draught. A few changes only in the document were suggested by two of them, Dr. Franklin and Mr. Adams. The whole merit of the paper was Mr. Jefferson's. On being reported to congress, it underwent a few other slight alterations; none of which, however, altered the tone, the frame, the arrangement, or the general character of the instrument.

"It has sometimes been said," observes an eloquent writer, "as if it were a derogation from the merits of this paper, that it contains nothing new; that it only states grounds of proceeding, and presses topics of argument, which had often been stated and pressed before. But it was not the object of the declaration to produce any thing new. It was not to *invent* reasons for independence, but to state those which governed the congress. For great and sufficient reasons it was proposed to declare independence; and the proper business of the paper to be drawn, was, to set forth those causes, and justify the authors of the measure, in any event of fortune, to the country and to posterity. The cause of American independence, moreover, was now to be presented to the world in such a manner, if it might so be, as to engage its sympathy, to command its respect, to attract its admiration; and in an assembly of most able and distinguished men, Thomas Jefferson had the high honour of being the selected advocate of this cause. To say that he performed his great work well, would be doing him injustice. To say that he did excellently well, admirably well, would be inadequate and belittling praise. Let us rather say, that he so discharged the duty assigned him, that all Americans may well rejoice that the work of drawing the little deed of their *liberties* devolved on his hands."

In 1778, Mr. Jefferson was appointed by congress, in conjunction with Dr. Franklin and Silas Deane, a commissioner to France, for the purpose of forming a treaty of alliance and commerce with that nation. In consequence, however, of ill health, and impressed with the conviction that he could be of greater service to his country, and especially to his state, by continuing at home, he declined accepting the office, and Arthur Lee was appointed in his place.

Between 1777 and 1779, Mr. Jefferson was employed, conjointly with George Wythe and Edmund Pendleton, on a commission for revising the laws of Virginia. This was an arduous service, requiring no less than one hundred and twenty-six bills, which were drawn by these gentlemen, and which for simplicity and perspicuity have seldom been excelled. In respect to Mr Jefferson, it should be noticed, that, besides the laborious share which he took in revising the laws of the state, to him belongs the honour of having first proposed the important laws in the Virginia code, forbidding the importation of slaves; converting estates tail into fees simple; annulling the rights of primogeniture; establishing schools for general education, and confirming the rights of freedom in religious opinion, with several others.

In 1779, Patrick Henry, who was the first republican governor, under the renovated constitution, and the successor of the earl of Dunmore, having served his appointed term, retired from that office, upon which Mr. Jefferson was chosen to succeed him. To this office he was re-elected the following year, and continued in office until June, 1781.

The administration of Mr. Jefferson, as governor of Virginia, during the above term, was arduous and difficult. The revolutionary struggle was progressing, and the southern states were particularly the theatre of hostile operations. At three several times, during his magistracy, the state of Virginia was invaded by the enemy; the first time in the spring of 1780, by the ferocious General Tarlton, whose military movements were characterized by unusual barbarity, and who was followed in his invasion, by the main army, under Lord Cornwallis.

While the eyes of all were directed to these military movements in the south, the state experienced a still more unexpected and disastrous attack, from a body of troops, under the guidance of the infamous Arnold, whom treachery had rendered more daring and more vindictive.

In respect to preparations for hostilities within her own limits, the state of Virginia was sadly deficient; nor had the habits and pursuits of Mr. Jefferson been of a kind which fitted him for military enterprise. Aware, however, of the necessity of energy and exertion, in this season of danger and general distress, he applied his mind, with alacrity and ardour, to meet the exigencies of the case. Scarcely had Arnold left the coast, when Cornwallis entered the state, on its southern border. At this time, the condition of Virginia was extremely distressing; she was wholly unprepared: her troops were fighting in remote parts of the country; she had few military stores; and, to add to her distress, her finances were exhausted. On the approach of Arnold in January, the general assembly had hastily adjourned. to meet again at Charlottesville, on the twenty-fourth of May.

In the mean time, a most anxious part devolved upon the governor. He had few resources, and was obliged to depend, in a great measure, upon his personal influence to obtain the munitions of war, and to raise and set in motion troops from different parts of the state. The various expedients which he adopted were indicative of much sagacity, and were attended by success highly important to the common cause.

On the twenty-fourth of May, the legislature was to meet at Charlottesville. They were not formed for business, however, until the twenty-eighth. A few days following which, the term for which Mr. Jefferson had been elected expired, when he again found himself a private citizen.

On leaving the chair of state, Mr. Jefferson retired to Monticello, when intelligence was received two days after, that a body of troops under command of General Tarlton were rapidly hastening to Charlottesville, for the purpose of surprising and capturing the members of the assembly. They had only time, after the alarm was given, to adjourn to meet at Staunton, and to disperse, before the enemy entered the village. Another party had directed their course to Monticello to capture the ex-governor. Fortunately, an express hastened from Charlottesville, to convey intelligence to Mr. Jefferson of their approach. Scarcely had the family time to make arrangements, indispensable for their departure, and to effect their escape, before the enemy were seen ascending the hill, leading to the mansion-house. Mr. Jefferson himself, mounting his horse, narrowly escaped, by taking a course through the woods. This flight of Mr. Jefferson, eminently proper, and upon which his safety depended, has unwarrantably excited in times gone by the ridicule and censure of his enemies.

Agreeably to their appointment, the legislature assembled at Staunton on the seventh, soon after which, at the instigation of Mr. George Nicholas, an inquiry was moved into the conduct of Mr. Jefferson in respect to remissness in the discharge of his duty, at the time of Arnold's invasion. The ensuing session of the legislature was fixed upon for the investigation of the charges. At the arrival of the appointed time, Mr. Nicholas had become convinced that the charges were without foundation, and this impression having generally obtained, no one appeared to bring forward the investigation. Upon this, Mr. Jefferson, who had been returned a member of the assembly, rose in his place, and entered into a justification of his conduct. His statement was calm, lucid, and convincing. On concluding it, the house unanimously adopted the following resolution:

"Resolved, That the sincere thanks of the general assembly be given to our former governor, Thomas Jefferson, for his impartial, upright, and attentive administration, whilst in office. The assembly wish, in the strongest manner, to declare the high opinion they entertain of Mr. Jefferson's ability, rectitude, and integrity, as chief magistrate of this commonwealth; and mean, by thus publicly avowing their opinion, to obviate and to remove all unmerited censure."

To this it may be added, that Mr. Nicholas, some time after, did Mr. Jefferson the justice to acknowledge, in a public manner, the erroneous views which he had entertained, and to express his regret that more correct information had not been obtained, before the accusation had been brought forward.

In the year 1781, Mr. Jefferson composed his "Notes on Virginia," a work which grew out of a number of questions, proposed to him by M. De Marbois, the secretary of the French legation in the United States. It embraced a general view of the geography of Virginia, its natural productions, statistics, government, history, and laws. In 1787, Mr. Jefferson published the work, under his own signature. It attracted much attention in Europe, as well as in America; dispelled many misconceptions respecting this continent, and gave its author a place among men distinguished for science. It is still admired, and will long be admired, for the happy simplicity of its style, and for the extent and variety of its information.

In 1782, Mr. Jefferson received the appointment of minister plenipotentiary, to join commissioners already in Europe, to settle the conditions of peace between the United States and Great Britain. Before his embarkation, however, intelligence was received, that the preliminaries of peace had been signed. The necessity of his mission being removed, congress dispensed with his leaving America.

In November, 1783, he again took his seat in the continental congress; but in May following was appointed minister plenipotentiary to act abroad in the negotiations of commercial treaties, in conjunction with Dr. Franklin and Mr. Adams. In the month of July, Mr. Jefferson sailed for France, and joined the other commissioners at Paris, in August.

Although ample powers had been imparted to the commissioners, they were not as successful in forming commercial treaties as had been expected. It was of great importance to the United States to effect a treaty of this kind with Great Britain, and for this purpose Mr. Jefferson and Mr. Adams proceeded to London. In this important object they failed, owing, probably, to the hostile feelings which the ministry indulged towards America, and to the wounded pride which still rankled in their breasts; and, moreover, to a selfish policy which they had adopted in respect to their navigation system, by which they intended to increase their own navigation at the expense of other nations, and especially of the United States. The only treaties which the commissioners were at this time able to negotiate, were with Morocco and Prussia.

In 1785, Mr. Jefferson was appointed to succeed Doctor Franklin as minister plenipotentiary to the court of Versailles. The duties of this station he continued to perform until October, 1789, when he obtained leave to retire, just on the eve of that tremendous revolution which has so much agitated the world in our times.

The discharge of Mr. Jefferson's diplomatic duties while abroad, "was marked by great ability, diligence, and patriotism; and while he resided at Paris, in one of the most interesting periods, his character for intelligence, his love of knowledge, and of the society of learned men, distinguished him in the highest circles of the French capital. No court in Europe had, at that time, in Paris, a representative commanding or enjoying higher regard, for political knowledge, or for general attainment, than the minister of this then infant republic."

During his residence in France, Mr. Jefferson found leisure to visit both Holland and Italy. In both countries he was received with the respect and attention due to his official station, as the minister of a rising republic, and as a man of learning and science.

In the year 1789, he returned to his native country. His talents and experience recommended him to President Washington for the first office in his gift. He was accordingly placed at the head of the department of state, and immediately entered on the arduous duties of that important station.

Soon after Mr. Jefferson entered on the duties of this office, congress directed him to prepare and report a plan for establishing a uniform system of currency, weights, and measures. This was followed, at a subsequent day, by reports on the subject of tonnage duties payable by France, and on the subject of the cod and whale fisheries. Each of these reports displayed the usual accuracy, information, and intelligence of the writer.

Towards the close of the year 1791, the relation of the United States to several countries abroad became embarrassing, and gave occasion to Mr. Jefferson to exercise those talents of a diplomatic character, with which he was pre-eminently endowed. "His correspondence with the ministers of other powers residing here, and his instructions to our own diplomatic agents abroad, are among our ablest state papers. A thorough knowledge of the laws and usages of nations, perfect acquaintance with the immediate subject before him, great felicity, and still greater facility, in writing, show themselves in whatever effort his official situation called on him to make. It is believed, by competent judges, that the diplomatic intercourse of the government of the United States, from the first meeting of the continental congress in 1774 to the present time, taken together, would not suffer, in respect to the talent with which it has been conducted, by comparison with any thing which other and older states can produce; and to the attainment of this respectability and distinction, Mr. Jefferson has contributed his full part."

On the sixteenth of December, 1793, Mr. Jefferson communicated his last official report to congress, on the nature and extent of the privileges and restrictions on the commerce of the United States in foreign countries, and the measures which he deemed important to be adopted by the United States, for the improvement of their commerce and navigation.

This report, which has ever been considered as one of primary importance, gave rise to a long and interesting discussion in the national legislature. In regard to the measures recommended in the report, a wide difference prevailed in congress, among the two great parties, into which that body had become obviously and permanently divided. Indeed, it may be said to have been this report, which finally separated the statesmen of the country into two great political parties, which have existed almost to the present time,

On the thirty-first of December, 1793, Mr. Jefferson tendered his resignation as secretary of state, and again retired to private life. The interval which elapsed between his resignation of the above office, and his being summoned again to the councils of the nation, he employed in a manner most delightful to himself, viz. in the education of his family, the management of his estate, and the pursuit of philosophical studies, to the latter of which, though long neglected, in his devotion to higher duties, he returned with renewed ardour.

The attachment of a large proportion of his fellow-citizens, which Mr. Jefferson carried with him into his seclusion, did not allow him long to enjoy the pleasures of a private life, to which he appears to have been sincerely devoted. General Washington had for some time determined upon a relinquishment of the presidential chair, and in his farewell address, in the month of September, 1796, announced that intention. This distinguished man, having thus withdrawn himself, the two political parties brought forward their respective candidates, Mr. Adams and Mr. Jefferson. On counting the votes in February, 1797, in the presence of both houses of congress, it was found that Mr. Adams was elected president, he having the highest number of votes, and Mr. Jefferson vice president, upon which respective offices they entered on the following fourth of March.

In the life of Mr. Adams, we had occasion to allude to the unsettled state of the country, and the general dissatisfaction with his administration, which prevailed. During this period, however, Mr. Jefferson resided chiefly at Monticello, pursuing the peaceful and noiseless occupations of private life. The time, at length, approached for a new election of president. Mr. Jefferson was again proposed by the republican party as a candidate for that office. The candidate of the federal party was Mr. Burr.

On the eleventh of February, 1801, the votes were counted in the presence of both houses of congress, and the result declared by the vice president to be, for Thomas Jefferson seventy-three; for Aaron Burr seventy-three; John Adams sixty-five

The vice president then, in pursuance of the duty enjoined upon him, declared that Thomas Jefferson and Aaron Burr, having an equal number of votes, it remained for the house of representatives to determine the choice. Upon this, the two houses separated, " and the house of representatives returned to their chamber, where seats had been previously prepared for the members of the senate. A call of the members of the house, arranged according to states, was then made; upon which it appeared that every member was present, except General Sumpter, who was unwell, and unable to attend. Mr. Nicholson, of Maryland, was also unwell, but attended, and had a bed prepared for him in one of the committee rooms, to which place the ballot box was carried to him, by the tellers, appointed on the part of the state.

"The first ballot was eight states for Mr. Jefferson, six for Mr. Burr, and two divided; which result continued to be the same after balloting thirty-five times."

Thus stood affairs, after a long and even distressing contest, when a member of the house, (General Smith,) communicated to the house the following extract of a letter from Mr. Burr: " It is highly improbable that I shall have an equal number of votes with Mr. Jefferson: but if such should be the result, every man who knows me, ought to know, that I would utterly disclaim all competition. Be assured that the federal party can entertain no wish for such an exchange.

" As to my friends, they would dishonour my views, and insult my feelings, by a suspicion that I would submit to be instrumental in counteracting the wishes and expectations of the United States; and I now constitute you my proxy to declare these sentiments, if the occasion shall require."

This avowal of the wishes of Mr. Burr, induced two federal members to withdraw; in consequence of which, on the thirty-sixth balloting, Mr. Jefferson was elected president. Colonel Burr, by the provision of the constitution, became, of course, vice president.

On the fourth of March, 1801, Mr. Jefferson, agreeable to the constitution, took the oath of office, in the presence of both houses of congress, on which occasion he delivered his inaugural address.

In this address, after expressing his diffidence in his powers satisfactorily to discharge the duties of the high and responsible office assigned him, he proceeded to state the principles by which his administration would be governed. These were, " Equal and exact justice to all men, of whatever state or persuasion, religious or political: peace, commerce, and honest friendship with all nations, entangling alliances with none : the support of the state governments in all their rights, as the most competent administration for our domestic concerns, and the surest bulwarks against anti-republican tendencies : the preservation of the general government in its whole constitutional vigour, as the sheet anchor of our peace at home, and safety abroad : a jealous care of the right of election by the people, a mild and safe corrective of abuses which are lopped by the sword of revolution, where peaceable remedies are unprovided: absolute acquiescence in the decisions of the majority, the vital principle of republics, from which is no appeal but to force, the vital principle and immediate parent of despotisms : a well disciplined militia, our best reliance in peace, and for the first moments of war, till regulars may relieve them : the supremacy of the civil over the military authority: economy in the public expense, that labour may be lightly burthened : the honest payment of our debts, and sacred preservation of the public faith : encouragement of agriculture, and of commerce as its hand-maid : the diffusion of information, and a rraignment of all abuses at the bar of public reason. freedom of religion: freedom of the press : and freedom of person, under the protection of the habeas corpus : and trial by juries impartially selected.—These principles," added Mr. Jefferson, " should be the creed of our political faith; and should we wander from them in moments of error or of alarm, let us hasten to retrace our steps, and to regain the road which alone leads to peace, liberty, and safety."

To enter into a minute detail of the administration of Mr Jefferson would neither comport with the duties of a biographer, nor with the limits which must necessarily be prescribed to the present sketch. At a future day, more distant by far than the present, when the remembrance of political asperities shall have passed away, can exact justice be done to Mr. Jefferson and his administration. That he was a distinguished man, distinguished as a statesman, none can deny. But as the measures of his administration were called in question, in respect to their policy, and as the day of excitement has scarcely passed by, it is deemed more judicious to leave the subject to the research and deliberation of the future historian, than, in this place, to attempt to settle questions, about which there was, while he lived, and still may exist, an honest difference of opinion.

On the meeting of congress in December, 1801, Mr. Jefferson, varying from the practice of the former presidents, communicated *a message* to congress, instead of delivering a speech in person. The change in this respect thus introduced was obviously so popular and acceptable, that it has been adopted on every subsequent similar occasion.

The principal acts which characterized the first term of Mr. Jefferson's career, were, a removal from responsible and lucrative offices of a great portion of those whose political opinions were opposed to his own; the abolition of the internal taxes; a reorganization of the judiciary; an extension of the laws relative to naturalization; the purchase of Louisiana, and the establishment of commercial and friendly relations with various western tribes of indians.

On the occurrence of a new presidential election, in 1805, the administration of Mr. Jefferson had been so acceptable, that he was re-elected by a majority, not of eight votes, as in the former instance, but by one hundred and forty-eight. Inspired with new zeal by this additional proof of confidence which his fellow-citizens had given him, he took occasion, in his second inaugural address, to assert his determination to abide by those principles upon which he had administered the government, and the approbation of which, on the part of the people, he read in their re-election of him to the same exalted station. In continuing his inaugural address, he took occasion to observe: "I do not fear that any motives of interest may lead me astray; I am sensible of no passion which could seduce me knowingly from the path of justice; but the weaknesses of human nature, and the limits of my own understanding, will produce errors of judgment sometimes injurious to your interests; I shall need, therefore, all the indulgence I have heretofore experienced: the want of it will certainly not lessen with increasing years. I shall need, too, the favour of that Being in whose hands we are, who led our forefathers, as Israel of old, from their native land, and planted them in a country flowing with all the necessaries and comforts of life; who has covered our infancy with his providence, and our riper years with his wisdom and power."

On the second election of Mr. Jefferson to the presidency, the vice presidency was transferred from Mr. Burr to George Clinton, of New-York. A merited odium had settled upon Mr. Burr in consequence of his unprincipled duel with General Hamilton, in which the latter gentleman had fallen a victim to murderous revenge. From this time, Mr. Burr sunk, as it was thought, into final obscurity; but his future conduct showed, that, while unobserved by his fellow citizens, he had been achieving a project, which, but for the sagacity and effective measures of Mr. Jefferson, might have led even to a dissolution of the union.

In the autumn of 1806, the movements of Mr. Burr first attracted the notice of government. He had purchased and was building boats on the Ohio, and engaging men to descend that river. His declared purpose was to form a settlement on the banks of the Washita, in Louisiana; but the character of the man, the nature of his preparations, and the incautious disclosures of his associates, led to the suspicion that his true object was either to gain possession of New-Orleans, and to erect into a separate government the country watered by the Mississippi and its branches, or to invade, from the territories of the United States, the rich Spanish province of Mexico.

From the first moment of suspicion, he was closely watched by the agents of the government. At Natchez, while on his way to New Orleans, he was cited to appear before the supreme court of the Mississippi Territory. But he had so enveloped his projects in secrecy, that sufficient evidence to convict him could not be produced, and he was discharged. Hearing, however, that several persons, suspected of being his accomplices, had been arrested at New-Orleans and elsewhere, he fled in disguise from Natchez, was apprehended on the Tombigbee, and conveyed a prisoner to Richmond. Two indictments were found against him, one charging him with treason against the United States, the other with preparing and commencing an expedition against the dominions of Spain.

In August, 1807, he was tried upon those indictments before John Marshall, the chief justice of the United States. Full evidence of his guilt not being exhibited, he was acquitted by the jury. The people, however, believed him guilty, and by their desertion and contempt he was reduced to a condition of the most abject wretchedness. The ease with which his plans were defeated, demonstrated the strength of the government; and his fate will ever be an impressive warning to those who, in a free country, listen to the suggestions of criminal ambition.

While these domestic troubles were, in a measure, agitating the country, questions of still greater importance were engaging the attention of the government in respect to our foreign relations. War was at this time waging between England and France. America, taking advantage of the belligerent state of these kingdoms, was advantageously employing herself, as a neutral power, in carrying from port to port the productions of France and her dependent kingdoms, and also to the ports of those kingdoms the manufactures of England.

Great Britain, at this time, and indeed from the peace of 1783, had claimed a right to search for and seize her seamen, even on board of neutral vessels while traversing the ocean. In the exercise of this pretended right, many unlawful seizures were made, against which Washington, Adams, and Jefferson, had successively remonstrated in vain. Added to this, the Americans were not tolin t'. carrying ther't, their vessels being seized by British cruisers while transporting to the continent the products of the French colonies, and condemned by the English courts as lawful prizes. In May, 1806, were issued the British orders in council, by which several European ports, under the control of France, were declared to be in a state of blockade, although not invested with a British fleet, and American vessels, in attempting to enter those ports, were captured and condemned.

As a measure retaliatory to the above orders in council, the French emperor issued a decree at Berlin, in 1806, declaring the British islands in a state of blockade. In consequence of these measures of the two belligerents, the commerce of the United States severely suffered, and their merchants were oud in their demands on the government for redress and protection.

In June, 1807, an act was committed which raised the indignation of the whole American people, and concentrated upon the British government the whole weight of popular indignation. This was an attack upon the frigate Chesapeake, just as she was leaving her port, for a distant service, by order of a British admiral, in consequence of which three of her men were killed, and four taken away. This outrage occasioned an immediate proclamation on the part of Mr. Jefferson, requiring all British armed vessels immediately to depart from the waters of the United States, and forbidding all such to enter. Instructions were forwarded to the American minister at the court of Great Britain, to demand satisfaction for the insult, and security against future aggression. Congress was summoned to meet, and to decide upon the further measures which should be adopted.

In the mean time, the British government promptly disavowed the act of the officer, by whom the above outrage had been committed, and offered reparation for the injuries done, which some time after was carried into effect.

From this time, the conduct of the belligerents was such, in respect to each other, as to bear oppressively upon the American nation, leaving the government of the latter no other alternative, but abject submission, or decided retaliation. In respect to the latter course, two measures only could be adopted, a declaration of war, or a suspension of the commerce of the United States. The latter alternative was adopted, and on the twenty-second of December, 1807, an act passed both houses of congress, laying a general embargo.

In respect to the policy of the embargo, the most prominent feature in the administration of Mr. Jefferson, different opinions prevailed among the American people. By the administration, it was acknowledged to be only an experiment, which, while it showed the spirit of the nation, and operated with no inconsiderable severity upon the interests of the belligerents, left the way open to negociations, or, if necessary to actual war.

Before the result of that system of measures which had been recommended by Mr. Jefferson was fully known, the period arrived when a new election to the presidency was to take place. As Mr. Jefferson had reached the age of sixty-five years, forty of which had almost uninterruptedly been devoted to the arduous duties of public life, he was desirous, at the close of his then presidential term, of ending his political career.

Having formed this determination, he alluded to it in a message to congress, in the following language: " Availing myself of this, the last occasion which will occur of addressing the two houses of the legislature at their meeting, I cannot omit the expression of my sincere gratitude for the repeated proofs of confidence manifested to me by themselves, and their predecessors, since my call to the administration, and the many indulgences experienced at their hands. The same grateful acknowledgments are due to my fellow-citizens generally, whose support has been my great encouragement, under all embarrassments. In the transactions of their business, I cannot have escaped error. It is incident to our imperfect nature. But I may say with truth, my errors have been of the understanding, not of intention; and that the advancement of their rights and interests has been the constant motive of every measure. On these considerations, I solicit their indulgence. Looking forward with anxiety to their future destinies, I trust, that in their steady character, unhaken by difficulties, in their love of liberty, obedience to law, and support of public authorities, I see a sure guarantee of the permanence of our republic; and retiring from the charge of their affairs, I carry with me the consolation of a firm persuasion, that heaven has in store for our beloved country, long ages to come of prosperity and happiness."

From the time of his retirement from public life, in 1807, Mr. Jefferson resided at Monticello, and lived as became a wise man. "Surrounded by affectionate friends, his ardour in the pursuit of knowledge undiminished, with uncommon health, and unbroken spirits, he was able to enjoy largely the rational pleasures of life, and to partake in that public prosperity, which he had so much contributed to produce. His kindness and hospitality, the charm of his conversation, the ease of his manners, the extent of his acquirements, and especially the full store of revolutionary incidents which he possessed, and which he knew when and how to dispense, rendered his abode, in a high degree, attractive to his admiring countrymen, while his high public and scientific character drew towards him every intelligent and educated traveller from abroad."

Although Mr. Jefferson had withdrawn from public life, he was still anxious to promote the objects of science, taste, and literature; and especially solicitous to see established a university in his native state. To this object he devoted several years of incessant and anxious attention, and by the enlightened liberality of the legislature of Virginia, and the co-operation of other able and zealous friends, he lived to see it accomplished. Of this institution, of which he was the father, he was elected the rector, and, during the declining years of his life, devoted himself, with unceasing ardour, to its permanent prosperity.

It has often been the lot of those who have devoted themselves to the public service, to suffer in the decline of life from the hand of poverty. This was the lot of Mr. Jefferson. His patrimony was originally large, but was unavoidably neglected, in his attendance upon the duties of the high official stations which he had filled. Partial efforts were made in his native state, and in other parts of the country, to relieve his embarrassments: but the precise extent of the measures adopted, in reference to this subject, we have not the means of ascertaining.

At length, the day on which this illustrious man was to terminate his long and useful career, approached. That day, by the appointment of heaven, was to be the fourth of July, 1826 He saw its approach with undisturbed serenity. He had no wish to live beyond that day. It was a day which, fifty years before, he had helped to make immortal. His wishes were answered; and at ten minutes before one o'clock, on that day—memorable, also, for the departure of his compatriot, Adams—Mr. Jefferson himself expired at Monticello. At this time he had reached the age of eighty-three years, two months, and twenty-one days. In stature, he was six feet and two inches high. His person was erect and well formed, though spare. The colour of his eyes was light, but they beamed with intelligence.

We shall not attempt minutely to delineate the character of Mr. Jefferson; this must be left to others, who may possess greater facilities of doing him justice. It may be observed, however, that in his manners he was simple and unaffected; at the same time possessing no inconsiderable share of dignity. In disposition he was uncommonly liberal and benevolent. In seasons of danger and perplexity, he exhibited no ordinary fortitude and strength of mind. His opinions were slowly formed, but yielded with great reluctance. Over his passions he possessed an uncommon control.

In his domestic habits, he was quite simple. He rose early, and through the whole day was unusually diligent in his application, either to business or study. He was ardently devoted to literature and science, with almost every branch of which he was well acquainted. Of his peculiar opinions on religious subjects, we are designedly silent. In respect to these, the best and wisest of his countrymen have entertained very different sentiments At a future day, it will be easier to decide in respect to their true character and tendency.

It remains to notice only one circumstance more. "In a private memorandum found among some other obituary papers and relics of Mr. Jefferson, is a suggestion, in case a monument over him should ever be thought of, that a granite obelisk, of small dimensions, should be erected, with the following inscription:

"HERE WAS BURIED
THOMAS JEFFERSON,
Author of the Declaration of Independence,
Of the Statutes of Virginia, for Religious Freedom,
And Father of the University of Virginia."

BENJAMIN HARRISON.

BENJAMIN HARRISON was the descendant of a family long distinguished in the history of Virginia. Both his father and grandfather bore the name of Benjamin, and lived at Berkeley, where they owned, and where the family still owns, a seat, beautifully situated on the banks of the James River, in full view of City Point, the seaport of Petersburg and Richmond

The father of Mr. Harrison married the eldest daughter of Mr. Carter, the king's surveyor general, by whom he had six sons and four daughters. Two of the latter, with himself, were, at the same time, during the occurrence of a thunder storm, killed by lightning in the mansion house at Berkeley.

The subject of the present memoir was the eldest son of the preceding, but the date of his birth has not been satisfactorily ascertained. He was a student in the college of William and Mary at the time of his father's death; but, in consequence of a misunderstanding with an officer of the college, he left it before the regular period of graduation, and returned home.

The management of his father's estate now devolved upon him; and though young to be entrusted with a charge so important, and involving responsibilities so weighty, he displayed an unusual share of prudence and judgment.

His ancestors having long been distinguished as political leaders in the province, he was summoned at an early date, even before he had attained to the age required by law, to sustain the reputation which they had acquired. He commenced his political career as a member of the legislature, about the year 1764, a station which he may be said to have held through life, since he was always elected to a seat, whenever his other political employments admitted of his occupying it. As a member of the provincial assembly, Mr Harrison soon became conspicuous. To strong good sense he united great firmness and decision of character. Besides, his fortune being ample, and his connexions by marriage highly respectable, he was naturally marked out as a political leader, in whom general confidence might well be reposed.

The royal government, aware of his influence and respectability, was, at an early day, anxious to enlist him in its favour, and accordingly proposed to create him a member of the executive council in Virginia, a station corresponding to the privy council in England, and one which few would have had the firmness to have declined.

Mr. Harrison, however, though a young man, was not to be seduced from the path of duty by the rank and influence conferred by office. Even at this time, the measures of the British ministry, although not as oppressive as at a later day, were such as neither he nor the patriotic burgesses of Virginia could approve. In opposition to the royal cause, he identified himself with the people, whose rights and liberties he pursued with an ardour which characterized most of the patriots of the revolution.

Passing over the following ten years of Mr. Harrison's life, in which few incidents either of a private or political nature are recorded of him, we arrive at the year 1774, the era of the memorable congress which laid the foundation of American liberty, of which body Mr. Harrison was a member.

From this period until the close of 1777, during nearly every session of congress, Mr. Harrison represented his native state in that distinguished assembly. Our limits forbid us entering into a minute detail of the important services which he rendered his country during his career in the national legislature. As a member of the board of war, and as chairman of that board, an office which he retained until he left congress, he particularly distinguished himself. According to the testimony of a gentleman who was contemporary with him in congress, he was characterized for great firmness, good sense, and a peculiar sagacity in difficult and critical situations. In seasons of uncommon trial and anxiety, he was always steady, cheerful, and undaunted.

Mr. Harrison was also often called to preside as chairman of the committee of the whole house, in which station he was extremely popular. He occupied the chair during the deliberations of congress on the despatches of Washington, the settlement of commercial restrictions, the state of the colonies, the regulation of trade, and during the pendency of the momentous question of our national independence. By his correctness and impartiality, during the warm and animated debates which were had on questions growing out of these important subjects, he gained the general confidence and approbation of the house.

An interesting anecdote is related of him, on the occasion of the members affixing their signatures to the declaration of independence. While signing the instrument, he noticed Mr. Gerry of Massachusetts standing beside him. Mr. Harrison himself was quite corpulent; Mr. Gerry was slender and spare. As the former raised his hand, having inscribed his name on the roll, he turned to Mr. Gerry, and facetiously observed, that when the time of hanging should come, *he* should have the advantage over him. "It will be over with me," said he, "in a minute, but you will be kicking in the air half an hour after I am gone."

Toward the close of the year 1777, Mr. Harrison resigned

his seat in congress, and returned to Virginia. He was soon after elected a member of the house of burgesses, of which body he was immediately chosen speaker, a station which he held until the year 1782.

In this latter year, Mr. Harrison was elected to the office of chief magistrate of Virginia, and became one of the most popular governors of his native state. To this office he was twice re-elected. In 1785, having become ineligible by the provisions of the constitution, he returned to private life, carrying with him the universal esteem and approbation of his fellow citizens.

In 1788, when the new constitution of the United States was submitted to Virginia, he was returned a member of her convention. Of the first committee chosen by that body, that of privileges and elections, he was appointed chairman. Owing, however, to his advanced years, and to infirmities which were now coming in upon him, he took no very active part in the debates of the convention. He was a friend, however, to the constitution, provided certain amendments could be made to it, and opposed its ratification until these should be incorporated with it. When the question was taken in the convention as to its unconditional ratification, the majority in the affirmative was but ten. A minority so respectable in point of number and character was not to be slighted. Hence, the convention appointed a committee to prepare and report such amendments as they should deem necessary. Of this committee Mr. Harrison was a member, and, in connexion with his colleagues, introduced such a series of amendments as were thought advisable, and which, after passing the convention, formed the basis of the alterations which were subsequently made.

In 1790, Mr. Harrison was again proposed as a candidate to the executive chair. Finding, however, that if run it must be in opposition to Mr. Beverley Randolph, who was at that time governor, a gentleman distinguished for his great amiableness of character, and a particular and intimate friend of Governor Harrison, the latter declined the designed honour, in consequence of which, Mr. Randolph was elected, but by only a majority of two or three votes.

In the spring of 1791, Mr. Harrison was attacked by a severe fit of the gout, of which however he partially recovered. In the month of April, he was elected a member of the legislature. On the evening of the day after, however, a recurence of his disease took place, which on the following day terminated his life.

In his person, Mr. Harrison was above the ordinary height; he possessed a vigorous constitution, and in his manners was remarkably dignified. Owing to the free manner in which he lived, he, at length, became quite corpulent; his features were less handsome, and the vigour of his constitution was much impaired.

Those who recollect him represent his talents as rather useful than brilliant. He seldom entered into public discussions, nor was he fond of writing; yet when occasion required, he appeared with respectability in both.

Mr. Harrison became connected by marriage with Elizabeth Bassett, daughter of Colonel William Bassett, of the county of New Kent, a niece to the sister of Mrs. Washington. He had many children, seven of whom only attained to any number of years. Several of his sons became men of considerable distinction, but no one has occupied so conspicuous a place in society as his third son, William Henry Harrison. While young, this gentleman distinguished himself in a battle with the Indians at the rapids of Miami; since which time, he has filled the office of governor of Indiana Territory served as a high military officer on the north-western frontier, been sent as a delegate from the state of Ohio in congress, and more recently been appointed to the important office of minister plenipotentiary to Mexico.

THOMAS NELSON, Jun.

Thomas Nelson was born at York on the twenty-sixth of December, 1738. He was the eldest son of William Nelson, a merchant of highly respectable character, who was descended from an English family, which settled at York, in the province of Virginia. By his prudence and industry, the latter acquired a large fortune. After the meridian of life, he held several offices of high distinction; and at his death, which occurred a few years before the revolution, left a character, not only sullied by no stain, but justly venerated for the many virtues which adorned it.

At the age of fourteen, Thomas Nelson was sent to England, for the purpose of acquiring an education. He was for some time placed at a private school, in a village in the neighbourhood of London; whence he was removed to the university of Cambridge, where he enjoyed the instruction of that distinguished man, Doctor Beilby Porteus, afterwards bishop of London. Under the guidance of this excellent man and accomplished scholar, young Nelson became deeply imbued with a taste for literary pursuits.

About the close of 1761, he returned to his native country, and in the following year became connected by marriage with a daughter of Philip Grymes, Esq. of Brandon, with whom he settled at York. The ample fortune given him by his father, at the time of his marriage, enabled him to maintain a style of no common elegance and hospitality.

At what period Mr. Nelson commenced his political career, we have not been able to ascertain. He was, however, a member of the house of burgesses in 1774, and during the same year was appointed to the first general convention, which met at Williamsburg on the first of August. The next year, 1775, he was a second time returned a member to the general convention of the province, during the session of which, he introduced a resolution for organizing a military force in the province, a step which obviously placed the colony of Virginia in the attitude of opposition to the mother country. This plan was at first startling to some of the warmest friends of liberty; but in the issue, it proved a measure of high importance to the colonies.

In July, 1775, the third convention of Virginia delegates assembled at Richmond, and in the following month Mr. Nelson was appointed a delegate to represent the colony in the continental congress, which was to assemble at Philadelphia. Agreeably to this appointment, he took his seat in that body on the thirteenth of September.

From this time, until May, 1777, Mr. Nelson continued to represent the colony of Virginia in the national council, where he was frequently appointed on important committees, and was highly distinguished for his sound judgment and liberal sentiments. In the month of May, of the year mentioned above, while attending in his place in congress, he was suddenly attacked with a disease of the head, probably of a paralytic nature, which, for a time, greatly impaired his mental faculties, particularly his memory.

He now returned to Virginia, soon after which he resigned his seat in congress. His health gradually returning, his services were again demanded by the public, and by the governor and council he was appointed brigadier general and commander in chief of the forces of the commonwealth. In this office he rendered the most important services to his country in general, and to the colony of Virginia in particular. His ample fortune enabled him, in cases of emergency, to advance money to carry forward the military operations of the day, nor did the generosity of his nature allow him to withhold his hand whenever occasion demanded advancements.

In 1779, the health of Mr. Nelson being, as it was thought, confirmed, he was induced again to accept a seat in congress. The arduous duties, however, to which he was called, connected with the long confinement which those duties required, induced a recurrence of his former complaint, which compelled him again to return home.

Happily for his country, his health was again restored, and he entered with great animation into several military expeditions against the British, who, at that time, were making the southern states the chief theatre of war. In 1781, Mr. Jefferson, who had for three years filled the executive chair, left it, upon which General Nelson was called to succeed him. This was a gloomy period in the annals of Virginia. In repeated instances the state was invaded, and the path of the enemy marked by wanton and excessive barbarity. The legislature were several times interrupted in their deliberations, and repeatedly obliged to adjourn to a different and more retired place. Immediately following the accession of Mr. Nelson to the executive chair, they were driven, as was noticed in the life of Mr. Jefferson, by Tarlton, from Charlottesville to Staunton.

At this time they passed a law, "by which the governor, with the advice of the council, was empowered to procure, by impress or otherwise, under such regulations as they should devise, provisions of every kind, all sorts of clothing, accoutrements and furniture proper for the use of the army, negroes as pioneers, horses both for draught and cavalry, wagons, boats, and other vessels, with their crews, and all other things which might be necessary for supplying the militia, or other troops, employed in the public service."

According to this law, Mr. Nelson could not constitutionally act, except with the advice of his council. Owing to the capture of two of the council by Tarlton, and to the resignation of two others, that body was reduced to four members, the least number which agreeably to the constitution could act. Even this number, in the distracted state of the country, it was difficult and nearly impossible to keep together.

Thus circumstanced, Governor Nelson determined, at the risk of public censure, to take those measures which the safety of the state and the good of the country demanded. These measures were taken; and though departing from the strict line of duty as defined by the laws of the commonwealth, it was owing to his prompt and independent course that the army was kept together until the battle of Yorktown gave the finishing stroke to the war.

Soon after the occurrence of that memorable and glorious

event, Governor Nelson had the pleasure of receiving a just expression of thanks from General Washington, who, in his general orders of the 20th of October, 1781, thus spoke of him: "The general would be guilty of the highest ingratitude, a crime of which he hopes he shall never be accused, if he forgot to return his sincere acknowledgments to his excellency Governor Nelson, for the succours which he received from him, and the militia under his command, to whose activity, emulation, and bravery, the highest praises are due. The magnitude of the acquisition will be ample compensation for the difficulties and dangers which they met with so much firmness and patriotism."

At the expiration of a month, following the surrender of Lord Cornwallis, Governor Nelson finding his health impaired by the arduous duties to which he had been called, tendered his resignation as chief magistrate of Virginia.

The many services which he had rendered, the great self-denial which he had practised, the uncommon liberality which he had manifested, entitled him to the gratitude of the people, and to the unmolested enjoyment of the few years which remained to him. But scarcely had his resignation been accepted, when an accusation was laid before the legislature by his enemies, charging him with having transcended his powers in acting without the consent of his council.

Soon after the presentment of this accusation, Governor Nelson addressed a letter to the legislature, requesting an investigation of his official conduct. In compliance with this request, a committee was appointed for that purpose, who, at length, having reported, the legislature, on the 31st of December, 1781, passed the following act:

"An act to indemnify THOMAS NELSON, Junior, Esquire, late governor of this commonwealth, and to legalise certain acts of his administration. Whereas, upon examination it appears that previous to, and during the seige of York, Thomas Nelson, Esquire, late governor of this commonwealth, was compelled by the peculiar circumstances of the state and army, to perform many acts of government without the advice of the council of state, for the purpose of procuring subsistence and other necessaries for the allied army under the command of his excellency General Washington: be it enacted, that all such acts of government, evidently productive of general good, and warranted by necessity, be judged and held of the same validity, and the like proceedings be had on them, as if they had been executed by and with the advice of the council, and with all the formalities prescribed by law. And be it further enacted, that the said Thomas Nelson, Jun. Esq. be, and hereby is, in the fullest manner, indemnified and exonerated from all penalties and dangers which might have accrued to him from the same."

Having thus been honourably acquitted of charges from which his noble and patriotic conduct ought to have saved him, he now retired wholly from public life. His death occurred on the 4th of January, 1789, just after he had completed his fiftieth year. Few patriots of the revolution have descended to the grave more justly honoured and beloved. Few possessed a more ample fortune; few contributed more liberally to support the cause of liberty. It was the patriotism, the firmness, the generosity, the magnanimous sacrifices of such men, that conducted the colonies through a gloomy contest of seven years continuance, and gave them a rank among the independent nations of the earth.

We shall conclude this notice of this illustrious man, by presenting to our readers the tribute, which was happily and affectionately paid to his memory by Colonel Innes:

"The illustrious General Thomas Nelson is no more! He paid the last great debt to nature, on Sunday, the fourth of the present month, at his estate in Hanover. He who undertakes barely to recite the exalted virtues which adorned the life of this great and good man, will unavoidably pronounce a panegyric on human nature. As a man, a citizen, a legislator, and a patriot, he exhibited a conduct untarnished and undebased by sordid or selfish interest, and strongly marked with the genuine characteristics of true religion, sound benevolence, and liberal policy. Entertaining the most ardent love for civil and religious liberty, he was among the first of that glorious band of patriots whose exertions dashed and defeated the machinations of British tyranny, and gave United America freedom and independent empire. At a most important crisis, during the late struggle for American liberty, when this state appeared to be designated as the theatre of action for the contending armies, he was selected by the unanimous suffrage of the legislature to command the virtuous yeomanry of his country; in this honourable employment he remained until the end of the war; as a soldier, he was indefatigably active and coolly intrepid, resolute and undejected in misfortunes, he towered above distress, and struggled with the manifold difficulties to which his situation exposed him, with constancy and courage. In the memorable year 1781, when the whole force of the southern British army was directed to the immediate subjugation of this state, he was called to the helm of government; this was a juncture which indeed 'tried men's souls.' He did not avail himself of this opportunity to retire in the rear of danger; but on the contrary, took the field at the head of his countrymen; and at the hazard of his life, his fame, and individual fortune, by his decision and magnanimity, he saved not only his country, but all America, from disgrace, if not from total ruin. Of this truly patriotic and heroic conduct, the renowned commander in chief, with all the gallant officers of the combined armies employed at the siege of York, will bear ample testimony; this part of his conduct even contemporary jealousy, envy, and malignity were forced to approve, and this, more impartial posterity, if it can believe, will almost adore. If, after contemplating the splendid and heroic parts of his character, we shall inquire for the milder virtues of humanity, and seek for the man, we shall find the refined, beneficent, and social qualities of private life, through all its forms and combinations, so happily modified and united in him, that in the words of the darling poet of nature, it may be said,

> 'His life was gentle, and the elements
> So mixed in him, that nature might stand up
> And say to all the world this was a man.'"

FRANCIS LIGHTFOOT LEE.

Francis Lightfoot Lee, the fourth son of Thomas Lee, was born on the fourteenth day of October, 1734. His father for several years held the office of president of the king's council of the provincial government of Virginia. He had several sons, all of whom were highly distinguished for their talents, and for the services which they rendered their country. Philip Ludwell, a member of the king's council, Thomas Ludwell, a member of the Virginia assembly; Richard Henry, as the champion of American freedom, William, as a sheriff and alderman of London, and afterwards a commissioner of the continental congress at the courts of Berlin and Vienna; and Arthur as a scholar, a politician, and diplomatist.

Francis Lightfoot, the subject of the present memoir, was perhaps not less distinguished, although he had not the advantages, which were enjoyed by the elder sons, of an education at the English universities. His advantages, however, were not of a moderate character. He was placed under the care of a domestic tutor of the name of Craig, a gentleman distinguished for his love of letters, and for his ability to impart useful knowledge to those of whom he had the care. Under such a man, the powers of Francis Lightfoot rapidly unfolded. He acquired an early fondness for reading and mental investigation, and became well acquainted with the various branches of science and literature.

The fortune bequeathed him by his father rendered the study of a profession unnecessary. He, therefore, devoted himself for several years to reading, and to the enjoyment of his friends. He was a man, however, in whom dwelt the spirit of the patriot, and who could not well be neglected, nor could he well neglect his country, when the political troubles of the colonies began.

In 1765, he was returned a member of the house of burgesses from the county of Loudon, where his estate was situated. In this situation, he proved himself to be a gentleman of strong good sense and discriminating judgment; and to this office he was annually re-elected until 1772; when having become connected by marriage with a daughter of Colonel John Tayloe, of the county of Richmond, he removed to that county, the citizens of which soon after elected him a member of the house of burgesses.

In 1775, Mr. Lee was chosen a member of the continental congress, by the Virginia convention. This was an eventful period in the annals of America. It was the year in which was shed the first blood in the revolutionary struggle. It was emphatically the year of "clouds and darkness," in which indeed the hope of better days was indulged, but in which, notwithstanding this hope, "men's souls were tried."

Mr. Lee continued a member of congress until the spring of 1779. During his attendance upon this body, he seldom took part in the public discussions, but few surpassed him in his warmth of patriotism, and in his zeal to urge forward those measures which contributed to the success of the American arms, and the independence of the country. To his brother, Richard Henry Lee, the high honour was allotted of bringing forward the momentous question of independence, and to him, and his associates in that distinguished assembly, the not inferior honour was granted of aiding and supporting and finishing this important work.

As already noticed, Mr. Lee retired from congress in the year 1779. It was his wish to be exempted from public care, and in the pleasures of home to seek those enjoyments which were consentaneous to his health and happiness.

This seclusion, however, he was not permitted long to enjoy. The internal condition of Virginia, at this time, was one of much agitation and perplexity. His fellow citizens, justly appreciating the value of such a man, summoned him by their suffrages to represent them in the legislature of Virginia. Although reluctantly, he obeyed the summons, and took his seat in that body. He was fond of ease, and of the pleasures of domestic life; still he was conscious of his obligations, and most faithfully discharged them. While a member of the continental congress, he had been characterized for integrity, sound judgment, and love of country. In his present office, he was distinguished for the same virtues.

He could not content himself, however, long in this situation. He became wearied with the duties of public life; and, at length, relinquished them for the pleasures of retirement.

In this latter course of life, he not only enjoyed himself highly, but contributed greatly to the happiness of many around him. The benevolence of his disposition, and the urbanity of his manners, recommended him both to the old and the young, to the gay and the grave. The poor shared in his benevolence and advice. In his intercourse with his particular friends, he was uncommonly pleasing and instructive.

Mr. Lee, having no children to require his care and attention, devoted much of his time to the pleasures of reading, farming, and the company of his friends. His death was occasioned by a pleurisy, which disease about the same time, also, attacked his beloved wife, and terminated the life of both, within a few days of each other. It is said, that he had embraced the religion of the gospel, and that under its supporting hope and consolation, he made his exit in peace from the world.

CARTER BRAXTON.

CARTER BRAXTON was the son of George Braxton, a wealthy planter of Newington, in the county of King and Queen, in Virginia, where he was born on the tenth of September, 1736. His mother was the daughter of Robert Carter, who was for some time a member, and the president of the king's council.

Carter Braxton was liberally educated, at the college of William and Mary. About the time that he left college, it is supposed that he fell in love, although this is not well ascertained. On this event, he became possessed of a considerable fortune, consisting chiefly of land and slaves. His estate was much increased, by his marriage, at the early age of nineteen years, with the daughter of Mr. Christopher Robinson, a wealthy planter of the county of Middlesex.

He had the misfortune to lose his wife within a few years of his marriage, soon after which he embarked for England, for the purpose of improving his mind and manners. He returned to America in 1760; and, in the following year, was married to the eldest daughter of Richard Corbin, of Lanneville, by whom he had sixteen children. The life of Mrs. Braxton was continued until the year 1814. Of her numerous children, one only, a daughter, it is believed, is still living.

The ample fortune of Mr. Braxton rendering the study of a profession unnecessary, he became a gentleman planter. He lived in considerable splendour, according to the fashion of the landed aristocracy at that day. Yet, it is said, that his fortune was not impaired by it.

Upon his return from a voyage to England, he was called to a seat in the house of burgesses; and in 1765, particularly distinguished himself at the time that Patrick Henry brought forward his celebrated resolutions on the stamp act.

From this date, until 1776, the political career of Mr Braxton corresponded, in general, with that of the other delegates from Virginia, of whom we have given a more particular and circumstantial account. It will be unnecessary therefore, to observe in this place more than that Mr. Braxton was, during this period, for the most part, a member of the house of burgesses, and a member of the first convention which ever met in Virginia. Nor is it necessary to speak particularly of the patriotic zeal and firmness which characterized him, in all the duties which he was called upon to discharge.

On the twenty-second of October, 1775, the distinguished Peyton Randolph died at Philadelphia, while presiding over congress. In the following month, the convention of Virginia proceeded to appoint his successor, upon which Mr. Braxton seat, and was present on the occasion which gave birth to the declaration of independence.

In June. 1776, the convention of Virginia reduced the number of their delegates in congress to five, any three of whom, it was directed, should be sufficient. In consequence of this resolution, Mr. Harrison and Mr. Braxton were omitted.

In the month of October, 1776, the first general assembly under the republican constitution, assembled at Williamsburg. Of this assembly Mr. Braxton was a member, and soon after taking his seat, he had the pleasure of receiving, in connexion with Thomas Jefferson, an expression of the public thanks in the following language:

"*Saturday, October* 12*th*, 1776.

"Resolved. *unanimously*, that the thanks of this house are justly due to Thomas Jefferson and Carter Braxton, Esquires, for the diligence, ability, and integrity, with which they executed the important trust reposed in them, as two of the delegates for this county in the general congress."

Of the above first session of the legislature of Virginia, Mr Braxton was an active member. This session, as might be supposed, was interesting and important, from the circumstance that being the first, it was called upon to accommodate the government to the great change which the people had undergone in their political condition. From this time, he continued to be a delegate in the house for several years, where he proved himself to be faithful to his constituents, and a zealous advocate for civil and religious liberty.

In 1786, he received an appointment as a member of the council of state of the commonwealth, which office he continued to execute until the thirtieth of March, 1791. After an interval of a few years, during which he occupied a seat in the house of delegates, he was again elected into the executive council, where he continued until October, 1797, on the tenth of which month he was removed to another world, by means of an attack of paralysis.

Mr. Braxton was a gentleman of cultivated mind, and respectable talents. Although not distinguished by the impressive eloquence of Henry and Lee, his oratory was easy and flowing. In his manners, he was peculiarly agreeable, and the language of his conversation and eloquence was smooth and flowing.

The latter days of Mr. Braxton were embittered by several unfortunate commercial speculations, which involved him in pecuniary embarrassments, from which he found it impossible to extricate himself. Several vexatious law-suits, in which he became engaged, contributed still farther to diminish his property, and unfortunately led him unintentionally to injure several of his friends, who were his sureties. The morning of his days was indeed bright; but, like many a morning which appears in the natural world without clouds, his was followed, towards the close of the day, by clouds and darkness, under which he sunk, imparting an impressive lesson of the passing nature of the form and fashion of the present world

THE NORTH CAROLINA DELEGATION.

WILLIAM HOOPER,
JOSEPH HEWES,
JOHN PENN.

WILLIAM HOOPER.

WILLIAM HOOPER was a native of Boston, province of Massachusetts Bay, where he was born on the seventeenth of June, 1742.

His father's name was also William Hooper. He was born in Scotland, in the year 1702, and soon after leaving the university of Edinburgh emigrated to America. He settled in Boston, where he became connected in marriage with the daughter of Mr. John Dennie, a respectable merchant. Not long after his emigration, he was elected pastor of Trinity Church, in Boston, in which office, such were his fidelity and affectionate intercourse with the people of his charge, that long after his death he was remembered by them with peculiar veneration and regard.

William Hooper, a biographical notice of whom we are now to give, was the eldest of five children. At an early age he exhibited indications of considerable talent. Until he was seven years old, he was instructed by his father; but, at length, became a member of a free grammar school in Boston, which at that time was under the care of Mr. John Lovell, a teacher of distinguished eminence. At the age of fifteen, he entered Harvard university, where he acquired the reputation of a good classical scholar; and, at length, in 1760, commenced bachelor of arts, with distinguished honour.

Mr. Hooper had destined his son for the ministerial office. But his inclination turning towards the law, he obtained his father's consent to pursue the studies of that profession, in the office of the celebrated James Otis. On being qualified for the bar, he left the province of Massachusetts, with the design of pursuing the practice of his profession in North Carolina. After spending a year or two in that province, his father became exceedingly desirous that he should return home. The health of his son had greatly suffered, in consequence of an excessive application to the duties of his profession. In addition to this, the free manner of living, generally adopted by the wealthier inhabitants of the south, and in which he had probably participated, had not a little contributed to the injury of his health.

Notwithstanding the wishes of his father, in regard to his favourite son, the latter, at length, in the fall of 1767, fixed his residence permanently in North Carolina, and became connected by marriage with Miss Ann Clark, of Wilmington, in that province.

Mr. Hooper now devoted himself with great zeal to his professional duties. He early enjoyed the confidence of his fellow citizens, and was highly respected by his brethren at the bar, among whom he occupied an enviable rank.

In the year 1773, he was appointed to represent the town of Wilmington, in which he resided, in the general assembly. In the following year he was elected to a seat in the same body, soon after taking which, he was called upon to assist in opposing a most tyrannical act of the British government, in respect to the laws regulating the courts of justice in the province.

The former laws in relation to these courts being about to expire, others became necessary. Accordingly, a bill was brought forward, the provisions of which were designed to regulate the courts as formerly. But the advocates of the British government took occasion to introduce a clause into the bill, which was intended to exempt from attachment all species of property in North Carolina, which belonged to non-residents. This bill having passed the senate, and been approved of by the governor, was sent to the house of representatives, where it met with a most spirited opposition. In this opposition Mr. Hooper took the lead. In strong and animated language, he set forth the injustice of this part of the bill, and remonstrated against its passage by the house. In consequence of the measures which were pursued by the respective houses composing the general assembly, the province was left for more than a year without a single court of law. Personally to Mr. Hooper, the issue of this business was highly injurious, since he was thus deprived of the practice of his profession, upon which he depended for his support. Conscious, however, of having discharged his duty, he bowed in submission to the pecuniary sacrifices to which he was thus called, preferring honourable poverty to the greatest pecuniary acquisitions, if the latter must be made at the expense of principle.

On the twenty-fifth of August, 1774, Mr. Hooper was elected a delegate to the general congress, to be held at Philadelphia. Soon after taking his seat in this body, he was placed upon several important committees, and when occasion required, took a share in the animated discussions, which were had on the various important subjects which came before them. On one occasion, and the first on which he addressed the house, it is said, that he so entirely rivetted the attention of the members by his bold and animated language, that many expressed their wonder that such eloquence should flow forth from a member from North Carolina.

In the following year, Mr. Hooper was again appointed a delegate to serve in the second general congress, during whose session he was selected as the chairman of a committee appointed to report an address to the inhabitants of Jamaica. The draught was the production of his pen. It was characterized for great boldness, and was eminently adapted to produce a strong impression upon the people for whom it was designed. In conclusion of the address, Mr. Hooper used the following bold and animated language:

"That our petitions have been treated with disdain, is now become the smallest part of our complaint: ministerial insolence is lost in ministerial barbarity. It has, by an exertion peculiarly ingenious, procured those very measures, which it laid us under the hard necessity of pursuing, to be stigmatized in parliament as rebellious; it has employed additional fleets and armies for the infamous purpose of compelling us to abandon them; it has plunged us in all the horrors and calamities of a civil war: it has caused the treasure and blood of Britons (formerly shed and expended for far other ends) to be spilt and wasted in the execrable design of spreading slavery over British America: it will not, however, accomplish its aim; in the worst of contingencies, a choice will still be left, which it never can prevent us from making."

In January, 1776, Mr. Hooper was appointed, with Dr. Franklin and Mr. Livingston, a committee to report to congress a proper method of honouring the memory of General Montgomery, who had then recently fallen beneath the walls of Quebec. This committee, in their report, recommended the erection of a monument, which, while it expressed the respect and affection of the colonies, might record, for the benefit of future ages, the patriotic zeal and fidelity, enterprise and perseverance of the hero, whose memory the monument was designed to celebrate. In compliance with the recommendation of this committee, a monument was afterwards erected by congress in the city of New-York.

In the spring, 1776, the private business of Mr. Hooper so greatly required his attention in North Carolina, that he did not attend upon the sitting of congress. He returned, however, in season to share in the honour of passing and publishing to the world the immortal declaration of independence.

On the twentieth of December, 1776, he was elected a delegate to congress for the third time. The embarrassed situation of his private affairs, however, rendered his longer absence from Carolina inconsistent with his interests. Accord ingly, in February, 1777, he relinquished his seat in congress, and not long after tendered to the general assembly his resignation of the important trust.

But, although he found it necessary to retire from this particular sphere of action, he was nevertheless usefully employed in Carolina. He was an ardent friend to his country, zealously attached to her rights, and ready to make every required personal sacrifice for her good. Nor like many other patriots of the day, did he allow himself to indulge in despondency. While to others the prospect appeared dubious, he would always point to some brighter spots on the canvass, and upon these he delighted to dwell.

In 1786, Mr. Hooper was appointed by congress one of the judges of a federal court, which was formed for the purpose of settling a controversy which existed between the states of New-York and Massachusetts, in regard to certain lands, the jurisdiction of which each pretended to claim. The point at issue was of great importance, not only as it related to a considerable extent of territory, but in respect of the people of these two states, among whom great excitement prevailed on the subject. Fortunately, the respective parties themselves appointed commissioners to settle the dispute, which was, at length, amicably done, and the above federal court were saved a most difficult and delicate duty.

In the following year, the constitutional infirmities of Mr. Hooper increasing, his health became considerably impaired. He now gradually relaxed from public and professional exertions, and in a short time sought repose in retirement, which he greatly coveted. In the month of October, 1790, at the early age of forty-eight years, he was called to exchange worlds. He left a widow, two sons, and a daughter, the last of whom only, it is believed, still lives.

In his person, Mr. Hooper was of middle stature, well formed, but of delicate and slender appearance. He carried a pleasing and intelligent countenance. In his manners he was polite and engaging, although towards those with whom he was not particularly acquainted, he was somewhat reserved. He was distinguished for his powers of conversa tion; in point of literary merit he had but few rivals in the neighbourhood in which he dwelt.

As a lawyer, he was distinguished for his professional knowledge, and indefatigable zeal in respect to business with which he was entrusted. Towards his brethren he ever maintained a high and honourable course of conduct, and particularly towards the younger members of the bar. As a politician, he was characterized for judgment, ardour, and constancy. In times of the greatest political difficulty and danger, he was calm, but resolute. He never desponded; but trusting to the justice of his country's cause, he had an unshaken confidence that heaven would protect and deliver her.

JOSEPH HEWES.

Joseph Hewes was born near Kingston, in New-Jersey, in the year 1730. His parents were Aaron and Providence Hewes, who were members of the society of friends, and who originally belonged to the colony of Connecticut. They were induced, however, to remove from New-England, on account of the prejudices which existed among the descendants of the puritans against those who adopted the quaker dress, or professed the quaker faith.

At the period of their removal, many parts of New-England were suffering from the frequent hostilities of the indians, who, roving through the forests in their vicinity, often made sudden incursions upon the inhabitants of those colonies, and generally marked their route with the most shocking barbarities. The murderous spirit of the indians was also, at this time, much inflamed by an act of the government of Massachusetts, which had increased the premium on indian scalps and indian prisoners to a hundred pounds for each. By way of retaliation, the indians often made their sanguinary incursions into the territory of Massachusetts, and not unfrequently extended their journies among the inoffensive farmers of Connecticut. Hence, many of the latter, desirous of a more quiet and secure life, were induced to seek a permanent residence in the remoter parts of the country.

Among those who thus fled from the annoyance of prejudice, and from the deeper wrath of a savage foe, were the parents of Joseph Hewes. But even in their flight they narrowly escaped the death which they wished to avoid. On passing the Housatonic River, a party of the indians came so nearly upon them, that Mrs. Hewes was wounded in the neck by a ball shot from the gun of a savage.

In New-Jersey, however, where they at length arrived, they found a peaceful and secure home. Here, some time after their settlement, their son Joseph Hewes was born. Of the incidents of his younger days we know but little. At a proper age he became a member of Princeton College, from which, having graduated in due course, he was placed in the counting-house of a gentleman at Philadelphia, to be educated as a merchant.

On leaving the counting-house of his employer, he entered into the mercantile business for himself, and soon became an active and thrifty merchant.

At the age of thirty he removed to North Carolina, and settled in the village of Edenton. The same prosperity which had attended him at Philadelphia, followed him to a more southern province, and in a few years he acquired a handsome fortune.

Mr. Hewes, both before and after his removal to North Carolina, sustained the reputation of a man of probity and honour. He acquired the confidence and esteem of the people among whom he lived, and was soon called to represent them in the colonial legislature of the province. This distinction was conferred upon him for several successive years with increasing usefulness to his constituents, and increasing credit to himself.

At length, in the year 1774, a congress, well known in the

annals of the American colonies, assembled in Philadelphia. In that body were three delegates from North Carolina, of whom Mr. Hewes was one.

The instructions and powers given to the delegates of this congress by the people of the several colonies, were considerably diversified. No public body, at that time, contemplated a separation from the mother country, and with no powers to this effect were any of the delegates to the congress of 1774 invested. Their object respected the means most proper to restore harmony between themselves and Great Britain, to obtain redress of grievances which the colonies suffered, and to secure to them the peaceful enjoyment of their unalienable rights, as British subjects.

No delegates to this congress carried with them credentials of a bolder stamp, than those from North Carolina. They were invested with such powers as might "make any acts done by them, or consent given in behalf of this province, obligatory in honour upon any inhabitant thereof, who is not an alien to his country's good, and an apostate to the liberties of America."

On the meeting of this congress, two important committees were appointed; the one, to "state the rights of the colonies in general, the several instances in which these rights are violated or infringed, and the means most proper to be pursued for obtaining a restoration of them;" the other, to "examine and report the several statutes which affect the trade and manufactures of the colonies." Of the former of these committees, Mr. Hewes was appointed a member, and assisted in preparing their celebrated report.

This report contained a temperate, but clear declaration of the rights of the English colonies in North America, which were expressed in the following language:

"1. That they are entitled to life, liberty, and property; and they have never ceded to any sovereign power whatever a right to dispose of either, without their consent.

"2. That our ancestors, who first settled these colonies, were, at the time of their emigration from the mother country, entitled to all the rights, liberties, and immunities of free and natural born subjects, within the realm of England.

"3. That by such emigration they by no means forfeited, surrendered, or lost, any of those rights; but that they were, and their descendants now are, entitled to the exercise and enjoyment of all such of them as their local and other circumstances enable them to exercise and enjoy.

"4. That the foundation of English liberty, and of free government, is a right in the people to participate in their legislative council; and as the English colonists are not represented, and, from their local and other circumstances, cannot properly be represented in the British parliament, they are entitled to a free and exclusive power of legislation in their several provincial legislatures, where their right of representation can alone be pursued in all cases of taxation and internal polity, subject only to the negative of their sovereign, in such manner as has been heretofore used and accustomed, but if from the necessity of the case, and a regard to the mutual interests of both countries, we cheerfully consent to the operation of such acts of the British parliament as are bona fide restrained to the regulation of our external commerce, for the purpose of securing the commercial advantages of the whole empire to the mother country, and the commercial benefit of its respective members; excluding every idea of taxation, internal or external, for raising a revenue on the subjects in America, without their consent.

"5. That the respective colonies are entitled to the common law of England, and, more especially, to the great and inestimable privilege of being tried by their peers of the vicinage, according to the course of that law.

"6. That they are entitled to the benefit of such of the English statutes as existed at the time of their colonization, and which they have, by experience, respectively found applicable to their several local and other circumstances.

"7. That these his majesty's colonies are likewise entitled to all the immunities and privileges granted and confirmed to them by royal charters, or secured by their several codes of provincial laws.

"8. That they have a right peaceably to assemble, consider of their grievances, and petition the king; and that all prosecutions, prohibitory proclamations, and commitments for the same, are illegal.

"9. That the keeping a standing army in these colonies in times of peace, without consent of the legislature of that colony in which such army is kept, is against the law.

"10. It is indispensably necessary to good government, and rendered essential by the English constitution, that the constituent branches of the legislature be independent of each other; and therefore the exercise of legislative power in several colonies by a council appointed during pleasure by the crown, is unconstitutional, dangerous, and destructive to the freedom of American legislation.

"All and each of which the aforesaid deputies, in behalf of themselves and their constituents, do claim, demand, and insist on, as their indisputable rights and liberties, which cannot be legally taken from them, altered, or abridged, by any power whatever, without their consent, by their representatives in their several provincial legislatures."

To the above declaration of rights was added an enumeration of the wrongs already sustained by the colonies; after stating which, the report concluded as follows:

"To these grievous acts and measures, Americans cannot submit; but in hopes their fellow subjects in Great Britain will, on a revision of them, restore us to that state in which both countries found happiness and prosperity, we have, for the present, only resolved to pursue the following peaceable measures: 1. To enter into a non-importation, non-consumption, and non-exportation agreement, or association. 2. To prepare an address to the people of Great Britain, and a memorial to the inhabitants of British America. And, 3. to prepare a loyal address to his majesty, agreeably to resolutions already entered into."

Few measures adopted by any session of congress during the revolutionary struggle, were more remarkable than that of the congress of 1774, which recommended the system of non-importation. It was a measure dictated by the highest patriotism, and proceeded upon the acknowledged fact, that the same exalted patriotism which existed among them, existed, also, among the American people. The efficiency of the measure, it was obvious, must lie in the union of the people to support it. They must adopt and persevere in a system of privation. A willingness to do this generally prevailed throughout the colonies; and to the government of Great Britain was presented the spectacle of thirteen colonies adopting a measure, novel, perhaps, in the history of the world, and supporting it at the sacrifice of a great portion of those comforts which they had been accustomed to enjoy.

Although a merchant, and one who had been engaged in commercial transactions with England for the space of twenty years, Mr. Hewes cheerfully assisted in forming a plan of the non-importation association, and most readily became a member of it.

The manner in which Mr. Hewes had acquitted himself during the session of this congress, was so acceptable to the people of North Carolina, that he was again appointed to the same high office, and in the month of May, 1775, again appeared at Philadelphia, and continued in congress until the adjournment of that body, on the last day of July. During the recess of congress, between July and September, he made a visit to his friends in New-Jersey, and in the latter month again resumed his place. From this date until the twenty-ninth of October, 1779, Mr. Hewes continued to represent the state of North Carolina, with the exception of something more than a year, during which he devoted himself to his private affairs, and to the interests of his state at home.

The last time that he appeared in congress was on the twenty-ninth of October, of the year last mentioned, after which, an indisposition under which he had laboured for some time confined him to his chamber, and at length, on the tenth of November, terminated his life, in the fiftieth year of his age. His funeral was attended on the following day by congress, by the general assembly of Pennsylvania, the president and his family, ex........ ..., the minister plenipotentiary of France, and a numerous assemblage of citizens. In testimony of their respect for his memory, congress resolved to wear a crape around the left arm, and to continue in mourning for the space of one month.

Although the events in the life of Mr. Hewes, which we have been able to collect, are few, they perhaps sufficiently speak his worth, as a man of integrity, firmness, and ardent patriotism. To this may be added, that in personal appearance he was prepossessing, and characterized in respect to his disposition for great benevolence, and in respect to his manners for great amenity. He left a large fortune, but no children to inherit it.

JOHN PENN.

John Penn, was a native of the county of Caroline, in the province of Virginia, where he was born on the seventeenth day of May, 1741. He was the only child of his parents, Moses and Catharine Penn.

The early education of young Penn was greatly neglected by his parents, who appear in no degree to have appreciated the value of knowledge. Hence, on his reaching the age of eighteen, he had only enjoyed the advantages conferred by a common school, and these for the space of but two or three years.

The death of Mr. Penn occurred in the year 1759, on which event his son became his own guardian, and the sole manager of the fortune left him, which, though not large, was competent. It was fortunate that his principles, at this early age, were in a good degree established; otherwise he might, at this unguarded period of life, left as he was without paternal counsel and direction, have become the dupe of the unprincipled, or giving loose to licentious passions, have ruined himself by folly and dissipation.

Although the cultivation of his mind had been neglected in

the manner we have stated, he possessed intellectual powers of no ordinary strength; and, as he now enjoyed a competent fortune, and possessed a disposition to cultivate those powers, it is not surprising that his progress should have been rapid.

Fortunately he lived in the vicinity of Edmund Pendleton, a gentleman of rare endowments, highly distinguished for his legal attainments, and well known as one of the most accomplished statesmen of Virginia. Mr. Pendleton being a relative, young Penn sought access to his library, which was one of the best in the province. The privilege which was thus freely and liberally granted him, was by no means neglected. By means of reading, the powers of his mind soon began to unfold themselves, and he, at length, determined to devote himself to the study of law.

Such a project, on the part of a young man whose early education had been so greatly neglected, and whose only guide through the labyrinth that lay before him, was to be his own good sense, was indicative of powers of no ordinary character. Our country has furnished examples of a similar kind; and to the obscure and neglected, they present the most powerful motives to exertion and perseverance. The author of our being has prescribed no narrow limits to human genius, nor conferred upon any one class of persons the exclusive privilege of becoming intellectually great.

At the age of twenty-one, Mr. Penn reaped in part the reward of his toil and indefatigable industry, in being licensed as a practitioner of law. The habits of study and application which he had now formed, were of great advantage to him in pursuing the business of his profession. He rose with great rapidity into notice, and soon equalled the most distinguished at the bar. As an advocate, in particular, there were few who surpassed him.

In 1774, Mr. Penn moved to the province of North Carolina, where he soon occupied as distinguished a place at the bar, as he had done in Virginia; although by his removal to another province it was necessary to understand and apply a new code of laws. With these he made himself acquainted with ease and celerity

In 1775, he was elected a member of the continental congress, in which body he took his seat on the twelfth of October. He was successively re-elected to congress, in the years 1777, 1778, and 1779, in which body he was distinguished for his promptitude and fidelity. He was seldom absent from his seat, and hesitated not, either from want of firmness or patriotism, to urge forward those measures, which were calculated to redress the wrongs, and establish and perpetuate the rights of his country.

After the return of peace, Mr. Penn retired to the enjoyment of private life. The incidents in the remaining portion of his history were, therefore, probably few; and differed in nothing from those which usually belong to individuals of respectability, in the shades of peaceful retreat. His death occurred in the month of September, 1788, at the age of forty-six years. He had three children, two of whom died unmarried.

THE
SOUTH CAROLINA DELEGATION.

Edward Rutledge,
Thomas Heyward,
Thomas Lynch, Jun.
Arthur Middleton.

EDWARD RUTLEDGE.

Edward Rutledge, the first of the South Carolina delegation, who affixed his name to the Declaration of Independence, was born in the city of Charleston, November, 1749. He was the youngest son of Doctor John Rutledge, who emigrated from Ireland to South Carolina, about the year 1755. His mother was Sarah Hert, a lady of respectable family, and large fortune. At the age of twenty-seven, she became a widow with seven children. Her eldest son was John Rutledge, distinguished for his patriotic zeal during the revolution. Her youngest son was the subject of the present memoir.

Of the early years of Edward Rutledge we have little to record. He was placed under the care of David Smith, of New-Jersey, by whom he was instructed in the learned languages; but he appears not to have made as rapid attainments as some others, although, as a scholar, he was respectable. Before he had devoted as much time to academic studies, as would have been desirable, he commenced the study of law with his elder brother, who, at that time, was becoming the most eminent advocate at the Charleston bar. Although at this time he was still young, he was capable of appreciating the advantages which he enjoyed, and was strongly impelled to exertion, by the brilliant and successful example which his brother held constantly before him.

In 1769, at the age of twenty years, he sailed for England, to complete his legal education. He became a student at the Temple. He derived great advantage from an attendance upon the English courts, and houses of parliament. In the latter place, he had an opportunity of listening to the eloquence of some of the most distinguished orators who lived at that day.

In 1773, he returned to his native country, and entered upon the duties of his profession. He was at this time distinguished for his quickness of apprehension, fluency of speech, and graceful delivery. Hence he early excited the admiration of those who heard him, and gave promise of that future eminence to which he was destined to arrive.

The general esteem in which he was held, was evinced in 1774, by his appointment to the distinguished congress which assembled at Philadelphia in that year. He was at this time but twenty-five years of age. It was a high honour for so young a man to be called to serve in the national council, with men of exalted powers and pre-eminent experience. It furnished unquestionable proof of the estimation in which he was held, and strong presumptive evidence that this estimation of his talents and moral worth was not unjust. As the proceedings of the congress of 1774 were conducted with closed doors, and an injunction of secrecy laid upon its members, it is impossible, at this day, to ascertain the precise share of influence which the individual members exerted, on all the measures which they advocated. Mr. Rutledge was, however, with the other delegates of South Carolina, formally thanked by the provincial congress, for the spirited and independent course he had pursued, and was again elected to the important station which he held.

In the congress of 1776, he took an active part in the discussions which preceded the declaration of independence. He is said to have proposed some alterations in the original draught of that celebrated instrument: but the precise nature of them it is now impossible to ascertain. The merit of the instrument doubtless wholly belongs to Mr. Jefferson. Some alterations, indeed, were made in it; but they were chiefly verbal, while the spirit and texture remained untouched.

At a subsequent date, Mr. Rutledge was appointed, with Dr. Franklin and John Adams, as commissioners to wait upon Lord Howe, who had requested congress to appoint such a committee to enter with him into negotiations for peace. In a former page we had occasion to allude to the appointment of these commissioners, and to state that the conference was productive of no beneficial results.

On the breaking up of the conference, Lord Howe despatched his own barge to convey the commissioners from Long Island to New-York. A little before reaching the shore, Doctor Franklin, putting his hand in his pocket, began chinking some gold and silver coin. This, when about leaving the boat, he offered to the sailors, who had rowed it. The British officer, however, who commanded the boat, prohibited the sailors accepting it. After the departure of the boat, one of the commissioners inquired why he had offered money to the sailors. "Why," said the doctor, in reply, "the British think we have no hard money in the colonies, and I thought I would show them to the contrary. I risked nothing," added he, "for I knew that the sailors would not be permitted to accept it."

Mr. Rutledge was again appointed to congress, in the year 1779; but in consequence of ill health he was unable to reach the seat of government, and returned home. In 1780, during the investment of Charleston by the British, Mr. Rutledge was taken prisoner by the enemy, and sent to St. Augustine as a prisoner, where he was detained nearly a year before he was exchanged. Soon after his exchange was effected, he landed at Philadelphia, near which he resided, until a short time before the city of Charleston was evacuated by the British, when he returned to the place of his nativity, and to the enjoyment of the society of his friends and relations.

From this period, for the space of seventeen years, Mr. Rutledge was successfully engaged in the practice of his profession, and from time to time in important services which he rendered to the state, as a member of her legislature.

In 1798, he relinquished his station at the bar, and was elected the chief magistrate of South Carolina. His constitution, however, became much impaired in consequence of severe and repeated attacks of the gout, to which he was subject. He continued, however, to perform his official duties until within a short time before his death. This event is supposed to have been somewhat hastened, by a necessary attendance upon the sitting of the legislature at Columbia, and an unfortunate exposure to rain and cold during his return from the latter place to Charleston. On reaching home, he was confined by a severe illness, which terminated his life on the 23d day of January, 1800.

The death of Mr. Rutledge was felt to be a severe loss, both by the people of Charleston and by the state at large. Few men were more deservedly respected; no one could be more generally beloved. Military and other funeral honours were paid to him on the occasion of his being carried to his long home; and the universal regret expressed at his departure, showed full well how sincerely he was lamented.

Both in his public and private character, Mr. Rutledge was adorned with many virtues. In his disposition, he was uncommonly benevolent; he entered with great feeling into the sufferings of his fellow men, and felt it not only his duty, but his pleasure, to administer to their necessities. His deeds of kindness were many, were widely extended, and are still remembered with affection and gratitude.

As an orator, he was deservedly eminent. He had faults, indeed, both in point of manner and style, being too studied in respect to the former, and too metaphorical, and sometimes inaccurate, in respect to the latter. He also, it is said, addressed himself rather to the passions than to the understanding: yet, with these faults there were few speakers who commanded greater attention, or were more successful. He was less impetuous, and perhaps less commanding, than his brother John Rutledge; but he possessed more of the style of Cicero. There was a suavity in his manner, a conciliatory attraction in his arguments, which had frequently the effect of subduing the prejudices of the unfriendly, and which seldom failed to increase the ardour and inflexibility of steady friends. The eloquence of John Rutledge, like that of Patrick Henry of Virginia, was as a mountain torrent; that of Edward Rutledge, that of a smooth stream gliding along the plain; the former hurried you forward with a resistless impetuosity; the latter conducted you with fascinations, that made every progressive step appear enchanting.

In his person, Mr. Rutledge was above the middle size, and of a florid, but fair complexion. His countenance expressed great animation; and, on account of his intelligent and benevolent aspect, was universally admired.

On his return from Europe, Mr. Rutledge married the daughter of Henry Middleton, by whom he left a son, Major Henry M. Rutledge, of Tennessee; and a daughter, who, it is believed, now resides at Charleston. Upon the death of his first wife, he married the widow of Nicholas Eveleigh, comptroller of the treasury of the United States, in the time of Washington's administration. This lady is supposed to be still living.

THOMAS HEYWARD.

Thomas Heyward was born in St. Luke's parish, in the province of South Carolina, in the year 1746. His father, Colonel Daniel Heyward, was a planter of great wealth, which he had chiefly acquired by his industry.

Unlike many gentlemen of fortune, Mr. Heyward did not appear to idolize his possessions: at least, convinced of the importance of intellectual cultivation, he determined to bestow upon his son all the advantages which a thorough education might impart. Accordingly, the best school in the province was selected for young Heyward, who, by his diligence, became well acquainted with the Latin language, and with such other branches as were at that time taught in the most respectable provincial seminaries.

Having finished his scholastic studies, he entered the law office of a Mr. Parsons, a gentleman who at that time was distinguished for his professional learning and practical skill. On accomplishing the usual term of study, young Mr. Heyward, according to the fashion adopted by families of fortune, was sent to England to complete his legal preparation. He was entered as a student in one of the Inns of Court. Although he had in expectancy a large fortune, he devoted himself with great ardour to the study of law, emulating the diligence of those who expected to derive their subsistence from the practice of the profession.

On completing his studies in England, he commenced the tour of Europe, which occupied him several years. This was an advantage which he enjoyed beyond most of the youth of the colonies: nor did he neglect to improve the superiour means which were thus allowed him of gaining a knowledge of the different countries of Europe. He enjoyed a rare opportunity of contrasting the industry and simplicity of his countrymen, with the indolence, and luxury, and licentiousness, the pride and haughtiness, so prevalent on the old continent.

At length, satisfied with the observations which he had made of men and manners abroad, he returned, with pleasure, to his native country; and impressed with the obligations of application to some honest calling, he devoted himself, with great zeal for a man of fortune, to the labours of the law.

In 1775, Mr. Heyward was elected to supply a vacancy in congress, occasioned by the recall of the distinguished John Rutledge, whose presence was required at home to assist in defending the state against a threatened invasion. This honour, owing to his peculiar modesty, he at first declined. He wa , l.. .. ..

of his appointment, and arrived in Philadelphia in season to attend upon the discussion of the great question of American independence.

In the year 1778, Mr. Heyward was appointed a judge of the criminal courts of the new government. A sense of duty alone prompted him to accept of this arduous and responsible station. Soon after his elevation to the bench, he was called to the painful duty of presiding at the trial and condemnation of several persons charged with a treasonable correspondence with the British army, which, at that time, was in the vicinity of Charleston. The condemnation of these persons was followed by their execution, which took place within view of the enemy, and which served to render the judge most obnoxious to the British.

In the spring of 1780, the city of Charleston was besieged by General Clinton, and was taken possession of by him, on the 12th of May. Judge Heyward, at this time, had command of a battalion. On the reduction of the place, he became a prisoner of war. As he had been one of the leaders of the revolution, he, with several others who had acted a similarly distinguished part, were transported to St. Augustine, while the other prisoners were confined on board some prison ships in the harbour of Charleston. During his absence, he suffered greatly in respect to his property; his plantation being much injured by a party of marauders, and all his slaves seized and carried away. Some of his slaves were afterwards reclaimed; but one hundred and thirty were finally lost, being transported, as was supposed, for the benefit of the sugar planters on the island of Jamaica.

Judge Heyward, and his fellow prisoners at St. Augustine, at length had leave to return to Philadelphia. On his passage thither, he narrowly escaped a watery grave. By some accident he fell overboard; but, fortunately, kept himself from sinking by holding to the rudder of the ship, until assistance could be rendered to him.

On returning to Carolina, he resumed his judicial duties; in the exercise of which he continued till 1798. During this interval, he acted as a member of a convention for forming the state constitution, in 1790. In the following year, he retired from all public labours and cares, except those which were attached to his commission as judge.

Mr. Heyward was twice married, in 1773, to a Miss Matthews, a lady of affectionate disposition, and great personal charms. Sometime after her death, he was again connected in marriage with a Miss Savage. By both of these wives he had children, the history of whom, however, we have not ascertained. Judge Heyward died in March, 1809, in the sixty-fourth year of his age.

Although we have been able to collect but few incidents in the life of Thomas Heyward, our readers may be assured that he was among the most estimable of the men who lived in his time, and one of the most firm, honest, intelligent, and fearless, who embarked in the revolution. He was characterized for sound judgment, and an ardent disposition. Possessing such a character, he naturally acquired, and was justly entitled to, the confidence and esteem of his fellow-citizens.

It was happy for America, happy for the cause of freedom, that the God of heaven raised up such a generation of men at a time when the civil and religious liberties of the country demanded their wisdom, fortitude, and patriotism; and at a time, too, when, without their existence, and without their exalted virtues, the world had never seen so brilliant an exhibition of political liberty, order, and peace, as is presented in the government of republican America.

THOMAS LYNCH.

Thomas Lynch was the son of a gentleman of the same name, and was born on the fifth of August, 1749, at Prince George's Parish, in the province of South Carolina. The family was an ancient one, and is said to have originally emigrated from Austria to England, where they settled in the county of Kent; sometime after which, a branch passed over to Ireland, and thence some of the descendants removed to South Carolina. The name of the family is said to have been derived from a field of *pulse* called *lince*, upon which the inhabitants of a certain town in Austria lived, for some time, during a siege which was laid to it; and from which circumstance they changed the name of the town to *Lince* or *Lintz*, which name was adopted by the principal family of the place.

The precise period when Jonack Lynch, the great grandfather of Thomas Lynch, the subject of the present memoir, emigrated from Ireland to America is uncertain, but, probably, at an early period after the settlement of the colony. At his death, he left his son Thomas a slender patrimony, which, however, by his industry, and especially by the purchase of a large tract of land, which he devoted to the cultivation of rice, was increased to a princely fortune. This fortune, at his death, was left to a son by the name of Thomas, father of the subject of the present sketch.

At an early age, young Thomas Lynch was sent to a flourishing school, at that time maintained at Georgetown, South Carolina. Before he had reached his thirteenth year, his father removed him from this school and sent him to England, to enjoy those higher advantages, which that country presented to the youth of America. Having passed some time in the collegiate institution of Eaton, he was entered a member of the university of Cambridge, the degrees of which institution he received in due course. On leaving the university, he sustained a high reputation, both in respect to his classical attainments, and for the virtues which adorned his character.

This intelligence, communicated by some friend to his father, was so highly flattering, that he was induced to continue his son abroad for some years longer, and wrote to him, expressing his wish that he should enter his name at the temple, with a view to the profession of law. This he accordingly did, devoting himself with his characteristic zeal to the philosophy of jurisprudence, and to the principles of the British constitution.

About the year 1772, after an absence of eight or nine years, young Mr. Lynch returned to South Carolina. He returned an eminently accomplished man; in his manners graceful and insinuating, and with a mind enriched with abundant stores of knowledge, justly the pride of his father, and an ornament to the society in which he was destined to move.

Although he was eminently qualified to enter upon the profession of law, he succeeded in persuading his father to allow him to relinquish the pursuit of a profession which his fortune rendered it unnecessary for him to pursue. Such a preliminary course was unnecessary to entitle him to the confidence and esteem of his fellow-citizens. These he at once enjoyed.

In 1775, on the raising of the first South Carolina regiment of provincial regulars, he was appointed to the command of a company. Having received his commission, he soon enlisted his quota of men, in some of the neighbouring counties, and at the head of them took up his march for Charleston. Unfortunately, during the march he was attacked by a violent bilious fever, which greatly injured his constitution, and from the effects of which he never afterwards entirely recovered.

On his recovery, he joined his regiment, but was at this time unable, from the feeble state of his health, to perform the duties of his station according to his wishes. Added to this affliction, the unwelcome intelligence was received of the dangerous illness of his father, who was at that time attending in his place upon congress in Philadelphia. He immediately made the necessary arrangements to hasten to a dying father, if possible to administer to him the support and consolation which an affectionate son only could impart. To his surprise, his application for a furlough for this purpose was denied by the commanding officer, Col. Gadsden. This disappointment, however, and the controversy which grew out of the above refusal, were terminated by his election to congress, as the successor of his father. He now lost no time in hastening to Philadelphia, where he found his father still living, and so far recovered that the hope was indulged that he might yet be able to reach Carolina.

The health of the younger Mr. Lynch, soon after joining congress, began also to decline with the most alarming rapidity. He continued, however, his attendance upon that body, until the declaration of independence had been voted, and his signature affixed to that important instrument. He then set out for Carolina in company with his father, who had hitherto been detained by feeble health in Philadelphia; but the father lived only to reach Annapolis, when a second paralytic attack terminated his valuable life.

After this afflicting event, the son proceeded to Carolina; but such was his own enfeebled state of health, that he had little reason to anticipate the long continuance of life. A change of climate, in the view of his physicians and friends, presented the only hope of his ultimate recovery. A voyage to Europe was at that time eminently hazardous, on account of exposure to capture. A vessel, however, was found proceeding to St. Eustatia, on board of which, accompanied by his amiable and affectionate wife, he embarked, designing to proceed by a circuitous route to the south of France.

From the time of their sailing, nothing more is known of their fate. Various rumours were from time to time in circulation concerning the vessel in which they sailed; but their friends, after months of cruel suspense, were obliged to adopt the painful conclusion, that this worthy pair found a watery grave during some tempest, which must have foundered the ship in which they sailed.

Although the life of Mr. Lynch was thus terminated, at an early age, he had lived sufficiently long to render eminent services to his country, and to establish his character as a man of exalted views and exalted moral worth. Few men possessed a more absolute control over the passions of the heart, and few evinced in a greater degree the virtues which adorn the human mind. In all the relations of life, whether as a husband, a friend, a patriot, or the master of the slave, he appeared conscious of his obligations, and found his pleasure in discharging them.

That a man of so much excellence, of such ability and integrity, such firmness and patriotism, so useful to his country, so tender and assiduous in all the obligations of life, should have been thus cut off, in the midst of his course, and in a manner so painful to his friends, is one of those awful dispensations of Him whose way is in the great deep, and whose judgments are past finding out.

ARTHUR MIDDLETON.

Arthur Middleton was the son of Henry Middleton, and was born in the year 1743, at the seat of his father, at Middleton place, near the banks of the Ashley.

At the early age of twelve years, he was sent to the celebrated school of Hackney, in the neighbourhood of London; whence, after spending two years, he was removed to the school of Westminster. The advantages which he here enjoyed resulted in a thorough acquaintance with the Greek and Roman classics, especially in a knowledge of the former, in which he is said to have greatly excelled. The taste which he acquired for classical literature he preserved through life, and from the indulgence of it derived an exalted pleasure, lost to minds of a heavier mould.

At the age of eighteen or nineteen, young Middleton became a member of one of the colleges of the university of Cambridge. Having for his companions young men frequently of dissipated habits, he was often powerfully tempted to enter into their youthful follies; but fortunately he escaped the contagion of their pernicious examples, and devoted that leisure to the improvement of his mind, which the less reflecting devoted to amusements and vicious indulgence. In his twenty-second year, he was graduated bachelor of arts, and left the university with the reputation of an accomplished scholar, and a moral man.

By means of his father's liberality, he was now enabled to travel. After visiting several parts of England, he proceeded to the continent, where he spent two years, chiefly in the southern parts of Europe. At Rome, he passed several months in viewing the various objects of taste afforded by that ancient and splendid spot. He here greatly improved his taste for music and painting; and even became well versed in the principles of sculpture and architecture.

Soon after his return to South Carolina, he was connected in marriage with the daughter of Walter Izzard, Esq. Having still a fondness for travelling, he, soon after his marriage, again embarked on a visit to Europe, accompanied by his wife. In this tour he visited many places in England, whence proceeding to the continent, they passed through several of the principal cities of France and Spain. In 1773, Mr. Middleton once more returned to America, and now settled down on the delightful banks of the Ashley.

The father of Mr. Middleton was, at this time, a man of great wealth, and both by himself and family the approaching controversy between Great Britain and her American colonies might have been viewed with great concern, had not the patriotism with which they were imbued much preferred the welfare of their country, to their private interests. A rupture with the mother country would necessarily put to hazard the wealth which had long been enjoyed by the family, and might abridge that influence, and diminish those comforts, which that wealth naturally gave them. But what were these in comparison with the rights and liberties of a country, destined to embrace millions within its bosom? Between the alternatives presented, there was no room to hesitate. Both father and son, in the spirit which had long characterized the family, stood forth in the defence of the rights of America, and "left not a hook to hang a doubt on," that they were patriots of the noblest stamp.

In the spring of 1775, Mr. Arthur Middleton was chosen on a secret committee, who were invested with authority to place the colony in a state of defence. In the exercise of the trust with which they were charged, they immediately took possession of the public magazine of arms and ammunition, and removed its contents to a place of safety.

In the following June, the provincial congress of South Carolina proceeded to appoint a council of safety, consisting of thirteen persons. This council, of which Mr. Middleton was a member, took measures to organize a military force, the officers of which received commissions at their hands, and under their signatures. Among the members of this committee, no one exhibited more activity, or manifested a greater degree of resolution and firmness, than did Arthur Middleton.

In February, 1776, the provincial legislature of South Carolina appointed a committee to prepare and report a constitution, which "should most effectually secure peace and good order in the colony, during the continuance of the dispute with Great Britain." This duty was assigned to Mr Middleton and ten others.

Having discharged the duty to the satisfaction of the assembly, Mr. Middleton was soon after elected by that body a representative of South Carolina in the congress of the United States, assembled at Philadelphia. Here he had an opportunity of inscribing his name on the great charter of American liberties. At the close of the year 1777, Mr. Middleton relinquished his seat in congress, and returned to South Carolina, leaving behind him, in the estimation of those who had been associated with him in the important measures of congress, during the time he had been with them, the character of a man of the purest patriotism, of sound judgment, and unwavering resolution.

In the spring of 1778, the assembly of South Carolina proceeded to the formation of a new constitution, differing, in many important points, from that of 1776. On presenting it to the governor, John Rutledge, for his approbation, that gentleman refused to assent to it. But, as he would not embarrass the assembly in any measures which they might deem it expedient to adopt, he resigned the executive chair, upon which the assembly proceeded by a secret ballot again to fill it. On counting the votes, it was found that Mr. Middleton was elected to the office by a considerable majority. But, entertaining similar views in respect to the constitution, expressed by the distinguished gentleman who had vacated the chair of state, he frankly avowed to the assembly, that he could not conscientiously accept the appointment, under the constitution which they had adopted. The candour with which he had avowed his sentiments, and the sterling integrity of the man, exhibited in refusing an honour from conscientious scruples, instead of diminishing their respect for him, contributed to raise him still higher in the confidence of his fellow-citizens. The assembly proceeded to another choice, and elected Mr. Rawlins Lowndes to fill the vacancy, who gave his sanction to the new constitution.

During the year 1779, the southern states became the principal theatre of the war. Many of the plantations were wantonly plundered, and the families and property of the principal inhabitants were exposed to the insults and ravages of the invaders. During these scenes of depredation, Middleton place did not escape. Although the buildings were spared, they were rifled of every thing valuable. Such articles as could not easily be transported were either wantonly destroyed, or greatly injured. Among those which were injured, was a valuable collection of paintings belonging to Mr. Middleton. Fortunately, at the time the marauders visited Middleton place, the family had made their escape a day's journey to the north of Charleston.

On the investment of the latter place, in the following year, Mr. Middleton was present, and actively engaged in the defence of the city. With several others, on the surrender of this place, he was taken prisoner, and was sent by sea to St. Augustine, in East Florida, where he was kept in confinement for nearly a year. At length, in July, 1781, he was exchanged, and proceeded in a cartel to Philadelphia. On his arrival at the latter place, Governor Rutledge, in the exercise of authority conferred upon him by the general assembly of South Carolina, appointed him a representative in congress. To this office he was again elected in 1782; but in the month of November of that year, he returned to South Carolina on a visit to his family, from whom he had been separated during a long and anxious period.

On the signing the preliminaries of peace, Mr. Middleton declined accepting a seat in congress, preferring the pleasures of retirement with his family, to any honour which could be conferred upon him. He occasionally, however, accepted of a seat in the state legislature, in which he was greatly instrumental in promoting the tranquillity and happiness of his fellow-citizens.

The life of Mr. Middleton was terminated on the 1st of January, 1787. His death was occasioned by an intermittent fever, which he took in the preceding month of November, by an injudicious exposure to the unsettled weather of the autumnal season.

In his person, Mr. Middleton was of ordinary size, symmetrically proportioned, with fine features, and countenance expressive of firmness and decision.

THE GEORGIA DELEGATION.

Button Gwinnett,
Lyman Hall,
George Walton

BUTTON GWINNETT.

Button Gwinnett was a native of England, where he was born about the year 1732. His parents were respectable in life, and gave their son as good an education as their moderate circumstances would allow. On coming of age, Mr. Gwinnett became a merchant in the city of Bristol.

Some time after his marriage in England, he removed to America, and selecting Charleston, South Carolina, as a place of settlement, he continued there for about two years; at the expiration of which, having sold his stock in trade, he purchased a large tract of land in Georgia, where he devoted himself extensively to agricultural pursuits.

Mr. Gwinnett had from his earliest emigration to America taken a deep interest in the welfare of the colonies; but, from the commencement of the controversy with Great Britain, he had few anticipations that the cause of the colonies could succeed. A successful resistance to so mighty a power as that of the United Kingdoms, to him appeared extremely doubtful; and such continued to be his apprehensions, until about the year 1775, when his views experienced no inconsiderable change.

This change in his sentiments, touching the final issue of the controversy, produced a corresponding change in his conduct. He now came forth as the open advocate of strong and decided measures, in favour of obtaining a redress, if possible, of American grievances, and of establishing the rights of the colonies on a firm and enduring basis. In the early part of the year 1776, he was elected by the general assembly, held in Savannah, a representative of the province of Georgia, in congress. Agreeably to his appointment he repaired to Philadelphia, and in the following month of May, for the first time, took his seat in the national council. In October, he was re-elected for the year ensuing to the same responsible station.

In the month of February, 1777, a convention of citizens from Georgia was held in Savannah to frame a constitution for the future government of the state. Of this convention Mr. Gwinnett was a member, and is said to have furnished the outlines of that constitution, which was subsequently adopted.

Shortly after the above convention, occurred the death of Mr. Bullock, the president of the provincial council. To this office Mr. Gwinnett was immediately elevated. Unfortunately, while he represented the colony in congress, he was a competitor with Colonel Lackland M'Intosh, for the office of brigadier general of the continental brigade, about to be levied in Georgia, to which office the latter was appointed. The success of his rival, Mr. Gwinnett bore with little fortitude. His ambition was disappointed, and being naturally hasty in his temper, and in his conclusions, he seems, from this time, to have regarded Colonel M'Intosh as a personal enemy.

On becoming president of the executive council, Mr. Gwinnett adopted several expedients by which to mortify his adversary. Among these, one was the assumption of great power over the continental army in Georgia, in consequence of which General M'Intosh was treated with much disrespect by a part of his officers and soldiers. To humble his adversary still further, Mr. Gwinnett, in an expedition which he had projected against East Florida, designed to command the continental troops and the militia of Georgia himself, to the exclusion of General M'Intosh from the command even of his own brigade.

Just at this period, it became necessary to convene the legislature for the purpose of organizing the new government. In consequence of the station which Mr. Gwinnett held as president of the council, he was prevented from proceeding at the head of the expedition destined against East Florida. The troops, therefore, were by *his* orders placed under the command of a subordinate officer of M'Intosh's brigade. The expedition entirely failed, and probably contributed to the failure of Mr. Gwinnett's election to the office of governor, in May, 1777.

This failure blasted the hopes of Mr. Gwinnett, and brought his political career to a close. In the disappointment and mortification of his adversary, General M'Intosh foolishly exulted. The animosity between these two distinguished men, from this time, continued to gather strength, until Mr. Gwinnett, unmindful of the high offices which he had held, of his obligations to society, and of his paramount obligations to the author of his being, presented a challenge to General M'Intosh. They fought at the distance of only twelve feet. Both were severely wounded. The wound of Mr. Gwinnett proved mortal; and on the 27th of May, 1777, in the forty-fifth year of his age, he expired.

Thus fell one of the patriots of the revolution; and though entitled to the gratitude of his country, for the services which he rendered her, her citizens will ever lament that he fell a victim to a false ambition, and to a false sense of honour. No circumstances could justify an action so criminal, none can ever palliate one so dishonourable.

In his person, Mr. Gwinnett was tall, and of noble and commanding appearance. In his temper, he was irritable;

yet in his language he was mild, and in his manners polite and graceful. Happy had it been for him, had his ambition been tempered with more prudence; and probably happy for his country, had his political career not been terminated in the prime of life.

LYMAN HALL.

Lyman Hall was a native of Connecticut, where he was born about the year 1731. After receiving a collegiate education, and having acquired a competent knowledge of the theory and practice of medicine, he removed, in 1752, to South Carolina. He was induced, however, during the same year, to remove to Georgia, where he established himself at Sunbury, in the district of Medway. In this place he continued attending to the duties of his profession, until the commencement of the revolutionary contest.

On the arrival of this important crisis in the history of the colonies, the patriotism of Doctor Hall became greatly excited to the interests and dangers of his country. He perceived that the approaching storm must necessarily be severe; but with the kindred spirits of the north, he was determined to meet it with patriotic firmness and resolution. Having accepted of a situation in the parish of St. John, which was a frontier settlement, both his person and property were exposed to great danger, from his proximity to the Creek indians and to the royal province of Florida.

The parish of St. John, at an early period of the contest, entered with great spirit into the general opposition of the country against Great Britain, while a majority of the inhabitants of Georgia entertained different sentiments. So widely different were the views and feelings of the people of this parish from those of the inhabitants of the province generally that an almost entire separation took place between them.

In July, 1774, the friends of liberty held a general meeting at Savannah, where Doctor Hall appeared as a representative of the parish of St. John. The measures, however, adopted at that time, fell far short of the wishes both of this patriot and his constituents. In January, 1775, another meeting was held at Savannah, at which it was agreed to petition the king for a redress of grievances, and for relief from the arbitrary acts of the British ministry.

The parish of St. John, dissatisfied with the temporizing policy of the Savannah convention, in the following month made application to the committee of correspondence in Charleston, South Carolina, to form an alliance with them, by which their trade and commerce should be conducted on the principles of the non-importation association. The patriotic views and feelings of this independent people were highly applauded by the committee, but they found themselves under the necessity, by the rules of the continental association, of declining the alliance.

Upon receiving this denial, the inhabitants of St John agreed to pursue such independent measures as the patriotic principles which they had adopted should appear to justify. Accordingly, they resolved not to purchase slaves imported into Savannah, nor to hold any commercial intercourse with that city, nor with surrounding parishes, unless for the necessaries of life, and these to be purchased by direction of a committee. Having taken this independent stand, they next proceeded to choose a representative to congress, and on counting the votes, it was found that Doctor Hall was unanimously elected.

In the following May, Doctor Hall appeared in the hall of congress, and by that body was unanimously admitted to a seat. But, as he represented not the colony of Georgia, but only a parish of the colony, it was at the same time resolved to reserve the question as to his right to vote for the further deliberation of the congress.

The above question at length coming before the house, on the occasion of congress taking the opinions of its members by colonies, Doctor Hall expressed his willingness to give his vote only in those cases in which the sentiments of congress were not taken by colonies.

Fortunately for the cause of liberty, or the 15th of July, 1775, the convention of Georgia acceded to the general confederacy, and proceeded to the appointment of five delegates to congress, three of whom attended at the adjourned meeting of that body, September 13, 1775.

Among the delegates thus appointed, Dr. Hall was one. To this station he was annually re-elected until 1780, at the close of which year he finally retired from the national legislature.

At length Georgia fell temporarily into the power of the British. On this event, Doctor Hall removed his family to the north, and suffered the confiscation of all his property by the British government established in the state. In 1782, he returned to Georgia, and in the following year was elected to the chief magistracy of the state.

After enjoying this office for a time, he retired from the cares of public life, and about the sixtieth year of his age, died at his residence in the county of Burke, whither he had removed.

Doctor Hall in his person, was tall and well proportioned. In his manners he was easy, and in his deportment dignified and courteous. He was by nature characterised for a warm and enthusiastic disposition, which, however, was under the guidance of a sound discretion. His mind was active and discriminating. Ardent in his own feelings, he possessed the power of exciting others to action; and though in congress he acted not so conspicuous a part as many others, yet his example and his exertions, especially in connexion with those of the inhabitants of the circumscribed parish of St. John, powerfully contributed to the final accession of the whole colony of Georgia to the confederacy; thus presenting in array against the mother country the whole number of her American colonies.

GEORGE WALTON.

George Walton, the last of the Georgia delegation, who signed the declaration of independence, and with an account of whom we shall conclude these biographical notices, was born in the county of Frederick, Virginia, about the year 1740. He was early apprenticed to a carpenter, who being a man of selfish and contracted views, not only kept him closely at labour during the day, but refused him the privilege of a candle, by which to read at night.

Young Walton possessed a mind by nature strong in its powers, and though uncultivated, not having enjoyed even the advantages of a good scholastic education, he was ardently bent on the acquisition of knowledge; so bent, that during the day, at his leisure moments, he would collect light wood, which served him at night instead of a candle. His application was close and indefatigable; his acquisitions rapid and valuable.

At the expiration of his apprenticeship, he removed to the province of Georgia, and entered the office of a Mr. Young, with whom he pursued the preparatory studies of the profession of law, and in 1774, he entered upon its duties.

At this time the British government was in the exercise of full power in Georgia. Both the governor and his council were firm supporters of the British ministry. It was at this period that George Walton, and other kindred spirits, assembled a meeting of the friends of liberty, at the *liberty pole*, at Tondee's tavern in Savannah, to take into consideration the means of preserving the constitutional rights and liberties of the people of Georgia, which were endangered by the then recent acts of the British parliament.

At this meeting, Mr. Walton took a distinguished part. Others, also, entered with great warmth and animation into the debate. It was, at length, determined, to invite the different parishes of the province, to come into a general union and co-operation with the other provinces of America to secure their constitutional rights and liberties.

In opposition to this plan, the royal governor and his council immediately and strongly enlisted themselves, and so far succeeded by their influence, as to induce another meeting, which was held in January, 1775, to content itself with preparing a petition to be presented to the king. Of the committee appointed for this purpose Mr. Walton was a member. The petition, however, shared the fate of its numerous predecessors.

In February, 1775, the committee of safety met at Savannah. But notwithstanding that several of the members advocated strong and decisive measures, a majority were for pursuing, for the present, a temporising policy. Accordingly, the committee adjourned without concerting any plan for the appointment of delegates to the continental congress. This induced the people of the parish of St. John, as noticed in the preceding memoir, to separate, in a degree, from the provincial government, and to appoint Mr. Hall a delegate to represent them in the national legislature.

In the month of July, 1775, the convention of Georgia acceded to the general confederacy, and five delegates, Lyman Hall, Archibald Bullock, John Houston, John J. Zubly, and Noble W. Jones, were elected to represent the state in congress.

In the month of February, 1776, Mr. Walton was elected to the same honourable station, and in the following month of October, was re-elected. From this time, until October, 1781, he continued to represent the state of Georgia at the seat of government, where he displayed much zeal and intelligence, in the discharge of the various duties which were assigned him. He was particularly useful on a committee, of which Robert Morris and George Clymer were his associates, appointed to transact important continental business in Philadelphia, during the time that congress was obliged to retire from that city.

In December, 1778, Mr. Walton received a colonel's commission in the militia, and was present at the surrender of Savannah to the British arms. During the obstinate defence of that place, Colonel Walton was wounded in the thigh, in consequence of which he fell from his horse, and was made a prisoner by the British troops. A brigadier-general was demanded in exchange for him; but in September, 1779, he was exchanged for a captain of the navy.

In the following month, Colonel Walton was appointed governor of the state; and in the succeeding January, was elected a member of congress for two years.

The subsequent life of Mr. Walton was filled up in the discharge of the most respectable offices within the gift of the state. In what manner he was appreciated by the people of Georgia, may be learnt from the fact that he was at six different times elected a representative to congress; twice appointed governor of the state; once a senator of the United States; and at four different periods a judge of the superior courts, which last office he held for fifteen years, and until the time of his death.

It may be gathered from the preceding pages, respecting Mr. Walton, that he was no ordinary man. He rose into distinction by the force of his native powers. In his temperament he was ardent, and by means of his enthusiasm in the great cause of liberty, rose to higher eminence, and secured a greater share of public favour and confidence, than he would otherwise have done.

Mr. Walton was not without his faults and weaknesses. He was accused of a degree of pedantry, and sometimes indulged his satirical powers beyond the strict rules of propriety. He was perhaps, also, too contemptuous of public opinion, especially when that opinion varied from his own.

The death of Mr. Walton occurred on the second day of February, 1804. During the latter years of his life, he suffered intensely from frequent and long continued attacks of the gout, which probably tended to undermine his constitution, and to hasten the event of his dissolution. He had attained however to a good age, and closed his life, happy in having contributed his full share towards the measure of his country's glory.

SKETCH

OF THE

LIFE OF WASHINGTON.

GEORGE WASHINGTON, the third son of Augustine Washington, was born Feb 22, 1732, near the banks of the Potomac, in the county of Westmoreland, Virginia. When but ten years old, he was deprived of his father, in consequence of which the care of his improvement devolved exclusively upon his remaining parent, who admirably fulfilled her duty towards him; but, from the limited extent of her fortune, his education was confined to the strictly useful branches of knowledge. In 1743, his elder brother married a connexion of lord Fairfax, the proprietor of the northern neck of Virginia; in consequence of which George was introduced to the acquaintance of that nobleman, who gave him, when in his eighteenth year, an appointment as surveyor in the western part of the territory mentioned. In 1751, his military bent induced him to accept the station of one of the adjutant-generals of Virginia, with the rank of major. Soon afterwards, he was sent, by governor Dinwiddie, on a perilous mission, in consequence of the French troops having taken possession of a tract of country claimed by Virginia, and commenced the erection of a line of posts, to be extended from the lakes to that river. After great toil and danger, he reached the station of the French commander, to whom he delivered the governor's letter; and, having received an answer from him, he returned. As no disposition was indicated to comply with the requisition which had been made, a regiment was raised to maintain the rights of the British crown, and Mr. Washington was appointed its lieutenant-colonel. On the death of the colonel, Mr. Fry, he succeeded to the command, and greatly distinguished himself by his defence of fort Necessity against a very superior French force. He was obliged, at length, to capitulate, but on highly favorable terms, and the legislature of Virginia passed a vote of thanks to him for his conduct on the occasion. In the course of the winter of 1754, orders were received from England for settling the rank of the officers of his majesty's forces; and, those who were commissioned by the king being directed to take rank of the provincial officers, colonel Washington resigned his commission in disgust. He then retired to a country-seat, which he had acquired by the death of his brother, who, having served in the expedition against Carthagena, had named it *Mount Vernon*, in honor of the admiral who commanded the fleet in that enterprise. He did not, however, remain long in private life. In the spring of 1755, he was invited, by general Braddock, to enter his family as a volunteer aid-de-camp, in his expedition to the Ohio. The history of this disastrous expedition, and the admirable conduct of Washington, are too well known to need repetition: had his counsels been followed, the result, in all probability, would have been different. In the battle with the Indians, he had two horses killed under him, and four balls passed through his coat; but, to the astonishment of all, he escaped unhurt, while every other officer on horseback was either killed or wounded. His reputation was now established, and he was immediately appointed to the command of a regiment, consisting of sixteen companies, raised by the legislature of Virginia, for the defence of the province, after the intelligence of the defeat of Braddock, and the retreat of Dunbar. had been received. He was also designated, in his commission, as the commander-in-chief of all the forces raised and to be raised in the colony; and, as a still further proof of the public confidence, he was intrusted with the unusual privilege of selecting his field-officers.

During the years 1755 — 1758, he was engaged in protecting the frontier from the incursions of the French and Indians —a duty from which he was at length relieved by the capture of fort Duquesne. After this expulsion of the French from the Ohio, the hostile operations of the Indians ceased, and Virginia was relieved from the dangers with which she had been threatened; and, as the health of colonel Washington had been much impaired by his arduous labors, and his domestic affairs required his attention, he resigned his commission, having established an exactness of discipline in his regiment, which reflected the greatest credit on his military character. He soon afterwards married Mrs. Custis, a young lady to whom he had been long attached, and who, besides a large fortune, possessed great personal attractions and accomplishments of mind. Previously to his resignation, he had taken his seat in the general assembly, of which he had been elected a member by the county of Frederick. For several years after his marriage, the attention of colonel Washington was principally directed to the management of his estate. He continued a most respectable member of the legislature of the province, and took an early and decided part against the claims of supremacy asserted by the British parliament.

As hostilities approached, he was chosen by the independent companies formed through the northern parts of Virginia to command them, and was also elected a member of the first congress which met at Philadelphia. Here he was placed on all those committees whose duty it was to make arrangements for defence. When it became necessary to appoint a commander-in-chief, his military character, the solidity of his judgment, the steady firmness of his temper, the dignity of his person and deportment, the confidence inspired by his patriotism and rectitude, and the independence of his fortune, combined to designate him, in the opinion of all, for that important station, and, accordingly, on the fourteenth of June, 1775, he was unanimously chosen "general and commander-in-chief of the armies of the United Colonies, and all the forces now raised or to be raised by them." After expressing his high sense of the honor conferred upon him, his firm determination to exert every power he possessed in the service of his country, and her "glorious cause," and his diffidence of his abilities and experience, and declining all compensation for his services, at the same time avowing an intention to keep an exact account of his expenses, which he should rely on congress to discharge, he proceeded, as soon as the necessary arrangements could be made, to the head-quarters of the American army, then at Cambridge, in the neighborhood of Boston. On arriving there, he bent the whole force of his mind to overcome the great difficulties with which he was obliged to struggle, in consequence of the want of ammunition, clothing and magazines, the deficiency of arms and discipline, and the evils of short enlistments.

The history of this campaign before Boston is a history of successive exertions to surmount almost insuperable obstacles, by one who was solicitous, in the extreme, to perform some great and useful achievement, in order to prove himself worthy of his high station. In one of his letters to congress, at this period, he says, "I cannot help acknowledging that I have many disagreeable sensations on account of my situation; for to have the eyes of the whole continent fixed upon me, with anxious expectation of hearing of some great event, and to be restrained in every military operation, for want of the necessary means to carry it on, is not very pleasing, especially as the means used to conceal my weakness from the enemy, conceal it also from our friends and add to their wonder." This was written in February, after a council of war had expressed an opinion, chiefly on account of the want of ammunition for the artillery, against the execution of a bold plan which he had formed of crossing the ice, and attacking general Howe, in Boston. He then took possession of the heights of Dorchester, in the persuasion that a general action would ensue, as the position enabled him to annoy the ships in the harbor and the soldiers in the town.

The British general, in consequence, was reduced to the alternative of either dislodging the Americans or evacuating the place, and endeavored to accomplish the former; but the troops which were embarked for the purpose were scattered by a furious storm, and disabled from immediately prosecuting the enterprise. Before they could be again in readiness for the attack, the American works were made so strong that an attempt upon them was thought unadvisable; and the evacuation could no longer be delayed. It took place on the seventeenth of March, and gave great joy to the United Colonies. Congress passed a vote of thanks to the general and his army, "for their wise and spirited conduct in the seige and acquisition of Boston," and directed a medal of gold to be struck in commemoration of the event.

As soon as the British fleet had put to sea, the American army proceeded, by divisions, to New York, where it arrived on the fourteenth of April. Every effort was made by Washington to fortify the city, before the appearance of the enemy. In the beginning of July, the British troops were landed on Staten island, and some efforts were made by lord Howe, who commanded the fleet, to open negotiations for the restoration of peace; but they failed, in consequence of the refusal of the American commander to receive any communication not addressed to him in such a way as to acknowledge his public character. The English commander had directed his letters to "George Washington, esquire," and then to "George Washington, &c., &c., &c.," but declining an unequivocal recognition of his station. The disastrous affair of Long island soon afterwards occurred, on the twenty-seventh of August, in which Washington was obliged to behold the carnage of his troops without being able to assist them. It constrained him to withdraw his forces entirely from the island, which he accomplished on the night of the twenty-eighth, with such secrecy, that all the troops and military stores, with the greater part of the provisions, and all the artillery, except such heavy pieces as could not be drawn through the roads, rendered almost impassable by rains, were carried over in safety. From the commencement of the action, on the morning of the twenty-seventh, until the American forces had passed the East river, on the morning of the twenty-ninth, his exertions and fatigues were unremitted. Throughout that time, he was almost constantly on horseback, and never closed his eyes. The manner in which this operation was performed, greatly enhanced his military reputation, and it may justly be ranked among those skilful manœuvres which distinguish a master in the art of war. No ordinary talents, certainly, are requisite to withdraw, without loss, a defeated, dispirited and undisciplined army from the view of an experienced and able enemy, and to transport them in safety across a large river, while watched by a numerous and vigilant fleet.

In consequence of the operations of the British general, it soon became indispensable to evacuate New York. This was done on the fifteenth of September, with an inconsiderable loss of men. The strongest point of the position which Washington then took, was at Kingsbridge, but it was soon afterwards deemed necessary to withdraw altogether from York island, and the army moved towards the White Plains. General Howe followed, and the battle of the White Plains ensued, in which a portion of the American forces, occupying a hill on the right of the army, under the command of general MacDougal, were driven from their station after an animated engagement. Washington then changed his position for another, and Howe, considering this too strong to be attempted with prudence, retired down the North river, for the purpose of investing fort Washington, on York island. It was taken, and its garrison made prisoners of war; on which the American general retreated into New Jersey.

His situation now was gloomy in the extreme. All his efforts to raise the militia had been ineffectual; and no confidence could be entertained of receiving reinforcements from any quarter. But that unyielding firmness, which constituted one of the most valuable and prominent traits of his character, enabled him to bear up against every difficulty. "Undismayed," says Marshall, "by the dangers which surrounded him, he did not, for an instant, relax his exertions, nor omit any thing which could obstruct the progress of the enemy, or improve his own condition. He did not appear to despair of the public safety, but struggled against adverse fortune, with the hope of yet vanquishing the difficulties which surrounded him, and constantly showed himself to his harassed and enfeebled army, with a serene, unembarrassed countenance, betraying no fears in himself, and invigorating and inspiring with confidence the bosoms of others. To this unconquerable firmness, to this perfect self-possession, under the most desperate circumstances, is America, in a great degree, indebted for her independence."

In his retreat through New Jersey, Washington was followed by the British army, flushed with victory, highly disciplined, and perfectly equipped, whilst his own troops were dispirited, destitute, and daily decreasing by the expiration of their terms of service. In December, the British general made an attempt to get possession of a number of boats for the transportation of his forces over the Delaware; but, having failed, he went into quarters. Washington, having, about the same time, been joined by some effective reinforcements, meditated a blow on the enemy while distributed in their cantonments, which might retrieve, in a measure, the disastrous posture of American affairs, relieve Philadelphia from immediate danger, and rouse the drooping spirits of his countrymen. He accordingly formed the plan of attacking all the British posts on the Delaware at the same instant; but only that part of it succeeded which was conducted by him in person. It is unnecessary to give the particulars of the successes at Trenton and Princeton· Besides the immediate advantages accruing from them in saving Philadelphia, and recovering New Jersey, the moral effects which they produced in re-animating the spirit of the people, were incalculable. Confidence in the commander-in-chief became universal. Immediately afterwards, congress declared, that, in the then state of things, the very existence of civil liberty depended on the right execution of military powers, to a vigorous direction of which, distant, numerous and deliberative bodies were unequal, and authorized general Washington to raise sixteen additional regiments, conferring upon him, at the same time,* for six months, dictatorial power, for the conduct of the war.

In the beginning of 1777, Washington caused all his soldiers to be inoculated, as the small-pox had proved more fatal in his camp than the sword of the enemy. During this winter, while the two armies were in their respective quarters, he used every exertion to raise a powerful force for the ensuing campaign; but his efforts were not attended with corresponding success. Not allowing himself to be dispirited, he endeavored to make the most of the means in his hands, which, however, so far from enabling him to carry into effect the offensive operations he had meditated, were unequal even to defensive war.

In July, general Howe embarked his forces; and, it having been ascertained that the destination of the fleet was against Philadelphia, Washington moved southward to the Delaware. On the twenty-fifth of August, the British disembarked at the ferry of Elk river, and, on the tenth of September, the battle of Brandywine was fought, in which the Americans were defeated. It opened the way to Philadelphia for the enemy; and, on the twenty-sixth, they entered the city, though not before Washington had made an effort to engage them again on the sixteenth, which was frustrated by a violent rain, that rendered the fire-arms of the Americans unfit for use, and obliged them to retreat, without any thing more than a skirmish between the advanced parties. "From the twenty-fifth of August," says Marshall, "when the British army landed at the head of Elk, until the twenty-sixth of September, when it entered Philadelphia, the campaign had been active, and the duties of the American general uncommonly arduous. The best English writers bestow high encomiums on sir William Howe for his military skill and masterly movements during this period. At Brandywine, especially, Washington is supposed to have been 'out-generalled, more out-generalled than in any action of the war.' If all the operations of this trying period be examined, and the means in possession of both be considered, the American chief will appear in no respect inferior to his adversary. With an army decidedly inferior, not only in numbers, but in every military requisite, except courage, in an open country, he employed his enemy near thirty days in advancing about sixty miles. In this time, he fought one general action, and, though defeated, was able to re-assemble the same undisciplined, unclothed, and almost unfed, army, and, the fifth day afterwards, again to offer battle. When the armies were separated by a storm, which involved him in the most distressing circumstances, he extricated himself from them and still maintained a respectable and imposing countenance. The only advantage which he is supposed to have given was at the battle of Brandywine; and that was produced by the contrariety and uncertainty of the intelligence received. In a new army, where military talent has not been well tried, the general is peculiarly exposed to the chance of employing not the best instruments. In a country, too, which is covered with wood, precise information of the numbers composing different columns is to be gained with difficulty."

After the occupation of Philadelphia, the British general having divided his force, so as to give Washington a fair opportunity to engage him with advantage, he determined to avail himself of it by surprising the camp which had been formed at Germantown, and attacking both wings, in front and rear, at the same time. He made all his arrangements with his wonted caution and address; and, on the fourth of October, the enterprise was carried into effect, and, for a time, seemed certain of a successful issue, but the darkness of the morning, produced by a fog of uncommon density, introducing confusion into the American troops, Washington was compelled to relinquish his hopes, and to direct his attention to secure the retreat of his men. This he did without loss. Decided approbation was expressed by congress, both of the plan of this enterprise, and of the courage with which it was executed; and their thanks were voted to the general and the army.

Having taken all possible measures to cut off the enemy from supplies, Washington took post at White Marsh, where an attempt to surprise him was made by general Howe; but it was disconcerted, intelligence having reached him of the intended stroke. He then distributed his soldiers in winter quarters at Valley Forge, where their sufferings were excessive in consequence of the intense severity of the season, and their want of most of the necessaries for comfort, and even for existence. Every effort was made by him to improve their condition, and augment their numbers; and for these ends, he exercised, though with caution, the dictatorial powers entrusted to him by congress.

His incessant labors and unyielding patriotism could not, however, save him from the imputations which want of success, even though occasioned by insuperable obstacles, always engenders; and a combination was formed to deprive him of his command, and substitute in his place the victor of Saratoga, general Gates. But to weaken his hold upon the confidence and affection of the great body of the people and the army, was found impossible; and even the troops who had conquered under Gates received the idea of the change with indignation. The machinations of his enemies were frustrated without any efforts on his part, and only did injury to themselves. They made no undue impression on his steady mind, nor did they change one of his measures. His sensibilities were for his country, and not for himself.

In June, 1778, the British evacuated Philadelphia, which was rendered a dangerous position for them by the part it was now evident that France was about to take in the war, and the naval force which had been prepared by that power before she declared herself They retreated upon New York, through Jersey, followed by Washington, who, in opposition to the opinion of a council of general officers, and taking his measures on his own responsibility, brought them to an action on the 24th of the month, at Monmouth, which, though not a decided victory, was yet favorable to the American arms, and productive of great satisfaction to congress and the country He passed the night in his cloak, in the midst of his soldiers, intending to renew the engagement on the following morning; but, before the return of the day, the enemy had marched off in silence, and effected their retreat to New York. Marshall has given an extract from a letter of Lafayette to him respecting this battle, in which he says, " Never was general Washington greater in war than in this action: his presence stopped the retreat; his dispositions fixed the victory. His fine appearance on horseback, his calm courage, roused by the animation produced by the vexation of the morning *(lé dépit de la matinée,)* gave him the air best calculated to excite enthusiasm."

In the year 1779, congress had formed the plan of an invasion of Canada, which was deemed altogether inexpedient by Washington; and, in consequence, he requested a personal interview. This was acceded to; and, on his arrival in Philadelphia, a committee was appointed to confer with him on that particular subject, and on the general state of the army and the country. The result of their conferences was, that the expedition against Canada was abandoned; and every arrangement recommended by the commander-in-chief received the attention to which all his opinions were entitled. From this period to the siege of

Yorktown, no incident calling for particular mention occurred in Washington's career. He remained in the neighborhood of New York, watching the enemy, and taking every measure for the welfare of the country, without being able to perform any striking exploit. He had to contend with difficulties the mastering of which required higher qualities than are necessary to gain a brilliant victory. His soldiers could scarcely be kept from perishing with cold and hunger, or from dispersing and living on plunder. They were daily leaving the service; some regiments mutinied; others revolted and marched home; and he could obtain no compliance with his urgent requisitions for recruits. Nothing could be looser and more precarious than the thread by which the army was kept together; and in any other hands than his, it must inevitably have been broken. But, in spite of every obstacle and disaster, he prevented the enemy from accomplishing any thing material, and adopted such preparatory steps as might enable him to turn to advantage any fortunate incident which might occur.

In 1781, he planned, in conjunction with count de Rochambeau, a grand enterprise against New York; but circumstances concurred to induce an alteration in his views, and to direct them to operations in the south. He continued, however, arrangements for the attempt on the city, in order to deceive sir Henry Clinton as to his real intentions, which he did with considerable address. In August, he commenced his movement; and, having taken measures for the transportation of his army down the Chesapeake, he proceeded to Virginia with De Rochambeau and the chevalier de Chatelleux. On the 14th of September, he reached Williamsburg, and had an immediate interview with count de Grasse, the admiral of the French fleet, which was lying in the bay at the time, for the purpose of adjusting a plan of co-operation with regard to the investment of the British in Yorktown, to which they had retired. The siege commenced on the 28th of September; and, on the 19th of October, after severe fighting, lord Cornwallis was reduced to the necessity of surrendering the posts of Yorktown and Gloucester Point, with their garrisons, and the ships in the harbor, with their seamen, to the land and naval forces of America and France.

The capture of Cornwallis was generally considered as the finishing stroke of the war; but it produced no disposition in the American commander-in-chief to relax in those exertions which might yet be necessary to secure the great object of the contest. He hastened to Philadelphia to confer with congress respecting the military establishment of the succeeding year. He addressed a circular to all the state sovereignties, pressing the importance of supplies. He promised and made all possible exertions towards expelling the British from New York and Charleston. He felt alarm; and proclaimed increased danger, lest the debates in the British parliament concerning peace should beget supineness in America. During the winter-quarters, when the military situation of affairs in general would have allowed of his absence from camp, he remained there in order to watch and allay the discontents of the American troops, who supposed themselves ill-treated by congress and the states. After the treaty of peace was signed, those discontents, which he knew at least to be plausible, gave him much trouble and disquietude. He added to his reputation by the manner in which he noticed and counteracted the famous Newburgh letters, and suppressed the mutiny of the Philadelphia line. While, however, he vindicated discipline, and enforced subordination to the civil authorities, he deeply sympathized with the suffering troops, and used every lawful means of procuring redress for their grievances.

On the 25th of November, 1783, peace and independence being achieved, the British forces evacuated New York, and Washington made his public entry into that city, attended by a splendid volunteer retinue. On the 4th of December, he took his solemn farewell of the principal officers of the American army, assembled in a hotel at New York. On the 19th of that month, at Annapolis, where congress was then in session, he resigned, in form, to that body, the commission which he had so long and gloriously borne, and returned to private life, which he so much loved. After peace was proclaimed, congress unanimously passed a resolution for the erection of an equestrian statue of their general, at the place which should be established for the seat of government. Te legislature of Virginia also decreed to him "a statue of the finest marble and best workmanship," with an appropriate inscription. It was placed in the capitol of Virginia.

Washington took great interest in the navigation of the Virginia rivers he exerted himself to procure joint legislative acts of Virginia and Maryland for the improvement of the Potomac. He negotiated with the latter on the part of the former state; and the legislature of Maryland, anxious to bear some testimony to his worth, unanimously passed a bill authorizing the treasurer to subscribe, "for the benefit of general Washington," the same number of shares in each of the navigation companies to be formed, as were to be taken for the state. Washington was embarrassed by this generous and honorable proceeding In a fine letter of acknowledgment, he declined the large donation for himself, but asked it for some objects of a public nature. The shares were then reserved for the use of a seminary of learning established in the vicinity of James and Potomac rivers

In 1787, the legislature of Virginia unanimously elected him one of their delegates to the convention to be held at Philadelphia for the revisal of the federal system He finally consented to serve, making a painful sacrifice of his plans and expectations of uninterrupted retirement, in order to assist in "averting the contemptible figure which the American communities were about to make in the annals of mankind, with their separate, independent, jealous state sovereignties." The convention, when assembled at Philadelphia, unanimously chose him for their president; and no member of that august body more decidedly approved the constitution which they gave to the country. All America, as soon as it was adopted, looked to him as the first president under it, with an eye of affectionate confidence and desire which could not be resisted. His reluctance to quit his retreat was extreme The expression of his feelings on this head, in his private letters, is a striking mixture of genuine diffidence, personal disappointment and elevated patriotism. Neither the animosity of parties, nor the preponderance of the enemies of the new system in some of the states, could deprive him of a single vote for the station of president. From Mount Vernon to New York, when congress was in session, the journey of Washington had the character of a triumph. He delivered his inaugural address on the 30th of April, 1789, and, throughout his administration, acted up to the principles and promises therein contained. As before in his military capacity, so now in his civil, he declined receiving any thing beyond his actual expenditures, in his official character. We need not repeat the names of the eminent men whom he associated with him, in the arduous business of putting the government into successful operation. The machinery of the system was to be contrived, adapted, set in motion, and gave rise continually to the most important questions to be decided, and a conflict of strong prejudices, keen jealousies, partial interests, and untried theories. Washington was chosen as the man of the nation, the guardian of the universal weal : in no instance did he act or appear otherwise. His incessant application to business impaired his robust constitution. Successive attacks of a severe disease compelled him, in 1790, to retire, for a short time, to Mount Vernon. On all points of consequence connected with domestic or foreign affairs, he consulted his able cabinet with much deference, collected their opinions anxiously, and decided only after mature deliberation.

The occurrence and progress of the French revolution occasioned that complete division of parties, and those bitter animosities, which engendered the most perplexity and chagrin for Washington, and emboldened or exasperated men to impeach, in the end, even his spirit of impartiality and love of freedom In the outset, he felt a lively interest in the success of that revolution he did not hesitate to avow his sympathies and wishes, but when the reign of terror and the order of Jacobins were established, he experienced repugnance and horror, in common with so many other true friends of liberty and humanity throughout the civilized world. In his circular of 1783, he had said, "There is a natural and necessary progression from the extreme of anarchy to the extreme of tyranny; and arbitrary power is most easily established on the ruins of liberty abused to licentiousness," and in 1793, he perceived that this maxim was to be verified in the case of France. The result justified the caution with which he avoided an alliance with that power; but, independent of the fatal character of French affairs, he knew that peace was indispensable for the United States, in the infancy of their national existence and union. The proclamation of neutrality, and his resolute enforcement of it; Jay's treaty with Great Britain; and the general firmness of Washington's opinions and proceedings, sustained by the unequalled favor and authority of his name with the people, saved our young republic from being hurried into a dreadful vortex. The vigor and lenity of Washington's government were exemplified in the manner in which the insurrection in the western parts of Pennsylvania, in 1794, were suppressed not a drop of blood was shed.

At the expiration of eight years, having served two terms, Washington retired from the presidency, though, had he consented to retain the station, there can be no doubt he would have been unanimously re-elected His valedictory address to the nation is too well known for comment. His last speech to congress was delivered on the 7th of December, 1796. He returned to Mount Vernon to enjoy the pleasures of retirement; but he was not left to perfect repose. No sooner had war with France become probable (1798,) than all eyes were directed to him as the person to lead the American army. President Adams nominated him to the chief command of all the land forces, and the senate unanimously confirmed the appointment. He accepted it, asking only not to be called into the field until his presence should be required, and refusing to receive any emoluments annexed to it before he was in a situation to incur expense. The occasion for his services, which was anticipated, did not happen. His devotedness to the cause of his country was not the less appreciated.

His public toils were now finished; but the period allowed him for the enjoyment of a private life was short. On Friday, the 13th of December, 1799, exposure to rain produced an inflammatory affection of his throat. He expired in the night of Saturday, having been early aware of the certainty of his fate. He manifested an equanimity, in his last moments, suitable to the whole tenor of his life. Funeral honors were paid to him in every part of his country, with the most sincere and impressive manifestations of sorrow. His character is thus drawn by chief justice Marshall

"General Washington was rather above the common size; his frame was robust, and his constitution vigorous, capable of enduring great fatigue, and requiring a considerable degree of exercise for the preservation of his health His exterior created in the beholder the idea of strength united with manly gracefulness. His manners were rather reserved than free, though they partook nothing of that dryness and sternness which accompany reserve when carried to an extreme; and, on all proper occasions, he could relax sufficiently to show how highly he was gratified by the charms of conversation and the pleasures of society. His person and whole deportment exhibited an unaffected and indescribable dignity, unmingled with haughtiness, of which all who approached him were sensible; and the attachment of those who possessed his friendship, and enjoyed his intimacy, was ardent, but always respectful. His temper was humane, benevolent and conciliatory, but there was a quickness in his sensibility to any thing apparently offensive, which experience had taught him to watch and to correct. In the management of his private affairs, he exhibited an exact, yet liberal economy. His funds were not prodigally wasted on capricious and ill-examined schemes, nor refused to beneficial though costly improvements. They remained, therefore, competent to that expensive establishment which his reputation, added to a hospitable temper, had in some measure imposed upon him, and to those donations which real distress has a right to claim from opulence. He made no pretensions to that vivacity which fascinates, or to that wit which dazzles and frequently imposes on the understanding. More solid than brilliant, judgment rather than genius constituted the most prominent feature of his character. As a military man, he was brave, enterprising and cautious. That malignity which has sought to strip him of all the higher qualities of a general, has conceded to him personal courage, and a firmness of resolution which neither dangers nor difficulties could shake. But candor will allow him other great and valuable endowments. If his military course does not abound with splendid achievements, it exhibits a series of judicious measures, adapted to circumstances, which probably saved his country. Placed, without having studied the theory, or been taught in the school of experience the practice of war, at the head of an undisciplined, ill-organized multitude, which was unused to the restraints and unacquainted with the ordinary duties of a camp, without the aid of officers possessing those lights which the commander-in-chief was yet to acquire, it would have been a miracle, indeed, had his conduct been absolutely faultless. But, possessing an energetic and distinguishing mind, on which the lessons of experience were never lost, his errors, if he committed any, were quickly repaired; and those measures which the state of things rendered most advisable were seldom, if ever, neglected. Inferior to his adversary in the numbers, in the equipment, and in the discipline of his troops, it is evidence of real merit, that no great and decisive advantages were ever obtained over him, and the opportunity to strike an important blow never passed away unused. He has been termed the American Fabius; but those who compare his actions with his means, will perceive at least as much of Marcellus as of Fabius in his character."

It was a habit adopted by general Washington, at an early stage of his life, to preserve copies of all his important letters, as well those of a private as those of a public nature The transcripts of his revolutionary papers occupy forty-four large folio volumes. Each class of subjects is brought together in a strict chronological order, and a copious index is added to every volume. After the revolution had terminated, and he was settled on his farm, though relieved from public duties, his correspondence continued to be very extensive with eminent persons in this country and in Europe; and from that time till his acceptance of the presidency, his copied letters fill six folio volumes; and, even during the period of his presidency, his habits of industry enabled him to find leisure for preparing seven volumes of recorded letters, besides many others of which press copies were taken, and which are not preserved in books. There are fourteen other volumes, in which are recorded the transactions of the president with congress and the heads of departments, and which consist of letters that passed between him and the secretaries, on special subjects; also opinions, reports and intelligence from the secretaries. Among other records is a private journal kept by him, in which his official acts and intercourse with the departments are daily noted down. His letters remained numerous and important to the end of his life. This great collection shows, in a striking light, the industrious, methodical and careful habits of Washington.

CPSIA information can be obtained
at www.ICGtesting.com
Printed in the USA
LVHW081619111122
732928LV00006B/339